500
Delicious delights

500

Delicious delights

Macaroons, Cake pops, Cupcakes, Traybakes, Brownies, Whoopie pies & more

LOVE FOOD™

This edition published by Parragon Books Ltd in 2014
LOVE FOOD is an imprint of Parragon Books Ltd

Parragon Books Ltd
Chartist House
15–17 Trim Street
Bath BA1 1HA, UK
www.parragon.com/lovefood

ISBN: 978-1-4723-5129-6

Printed in China

Project Managed by Andrea O'Connor
Cover and Internal Design by Beth Kalynka
Cover Photography by Ian Garlick
New Internal Photography by Mike Cooper
New Internal Home Economy by Sumi Glass
New Recipes by Rachel Carter
Introduction text by Anne Sheasby

Notes for the Reader
This book uses both metric and imperial measurements. Follow the same units of measurement
throughout; do not mix metric and imperial. All spoon measurements are level: teaspoons are
assumed to be 5 ml, and tablespoons are assumed to be 15 ml. Unless otherwise stated, milk is
assumed to be full fat and eggs and individual vegetables are medium.

Garnishes, decorations and serving suggestions are all optional and not necessarily included in the
recipe ingredients or method. The times given are an approximate guide only. Preparation times
differ according to the techniques used by different people and the cooking times may also vary
from those given. Optional ingredients, variations or serving suggestions have not been included
in the time calculations.

The publisher would like to thank iStock for the use of images on the chapter openers.

Contents

Introduction

Prepare yourself for an amazing journey through a vast and glorious wonderland of 500 delicious sweet delights. Satisfy your sugar cravings and enjoy creating, sharing and chomping your way through some truly scrumptious sweet bakes and desserts.

This book covers an extensive range of sweet sensations, starting with a creative collection of large cakes, traybakes and bars, followed by a mouth-watering selection of cupcakes, muffins and melt-in-the-mouth cookies and biscuits.

Next up are some hard-to-resist pastries, tarts and fancies of every description, featuring delectable doughnuts and extravagant éclairs, plus moreish macaroons and fabulous fritters.

A further section offers a quirky selection of fantastic sweet treats and desserts that are just that little bit different, such as sweets and chocolates, fun cake pops, jellies and luscious lollies, as well as silky smooth ice cream and sorbets. Or, try your hand at creating some new bakes on the block, including popular push pops or desserts made in a jar.

The grand finale chapter showcases extra special sweet delights that are perfect for occasions or themed celebrations, featuring amazing large and small cakes, decadent cupcakes and cookies, impressive whoopie pies and sumptuous desserts.

Equipment

Kitchen scales

A good-quality set of scales is essential for accurately measuring ingredients for recipes and they hold the key to successful baking. Digital scales are the most accurate but spring or balance scales are just as good if used correctly.

Measuring spoons

These are useful for accurately measuring small quantities of ingredients, such as raising agents, ground spices and extracts.

Mixing bowls and measuring jugs

Two or three different-sized mixing bowls are useful. Heatproof glass bowls are durable and practical, and melamine or ceramic bowls come in assorted bright and breezy colours. A heatproof glass jug makes measuring liquids easy.

Spoons

Wooden spoons are essential for creaming, mixing and stirring, so it's good to have a few in varying sizes. Heat-resistant and durable nylon, silicone or melamine spoons can be used instead of wooden spoons. A large metal spoon is ideal for folding in or combining ingredients.

Baking sheets/trays and tins

Metal baking sheets and trays, both standard and non-stick, are invaluable for baking biscuits, cookies and other sweet treats. Silicone baking sheets are another option.

Baking tins come in a wide range of shapes and sizes, including sandwich tins, deep or shallow round and square cake tins, loaf tins, brownie/traybake tins, cupcake and muffin tins, loose-based tart tins, plus individual or mini tins.

Electric hand-held mixers and electric stand mixers

An electric mixer makes light work of mixing or whisking mixtures such as cake batters. Hand-held ones are easy to use, or a freestanding stand mixer can be used for many tasks.

Cupcake and muffin cases

Widely available in supermarkets, kitchenware shops and online in numerous cheerful colours and patterns, and several sizes. Paper cases are usually greaseproof. Reusable silicone cupcake and muffin cases are obtainable in a range of colours and sizes and are good reusable alternatives.

Piping bags and nozzles

Piping bags and a small selection of piping nozzles are essential for adding that special finishing flourish to cakes and desserts.

Strong nylon or fabric bags are washable and re-usable, while disposable polythene or paper bags save work.

A few stainless steel or plastic piping nozzles are your key to perfect piping. They should include a plain writing nozzle, large plain nozzle and a small and large star nozzle.

Specialist Equipment

Creative cake pops

Cake pops create perfect party treats and gifts for all ages. Cake pop moulds/tins and cake pop sticks are readily available from kitchenware shops and online.

Popular push pops

Get creative with this latest craze! Push pops have been recreated as fun desserts or sweet treats. Each dessert is assembled in layers of various edible delights inside an individual reusable plastic container with a 'push-up' function at the base. Lidded push pop holders are available online and in some good kitchenware shops.

Jars (for recipes baked in a jar)

Wide-mouthed preserving jars can be used to create chic desserts, including hot baked and layered chilled desserts. Standard 225-ml/8-fl oz jars are an ideal size for these impressive individual puds, which look fab and taste great too.

Cookie cutters

Cookie cutters, made of metal or tough plastic in a range of bright colours, are readily available from kitchenware shops and online. They come in various sizes and shapes, including plain or fluted/crinkle round cutters, as well as an assortment of novelty shapes.

Specialist tins and moulds

Specialist cake tins and moulds are available from kitchenware shops and online. Shapes are wide-ranging and include tins for creating novelty shapes, madeleines, large and mini bundt cakes, doughnuts and many more.

Ice-cream makers

Available from kitchenware shops, other retailers and online, these vary in price and capacity, but are a worthwhile investment if your family enjoy delicious home-made ice cream. They allow you to recreate your favourite flavours of scrumptious ice cream or Italian gelato, as well as fabulous frozen yogurt or zingy sorbet.

Ingredients

Flour

There are numerous types of flour, wheat flour being the most widely used. White flour is the most refined type, as well as the most versatile. Self-raising flour has added baking powder. Wholemeal or whole wheat flours are milled from the entire wheat grain. They impart a nutty flavour and have a slightly coarse texture.

Sugar

Caster sugar

Ideal for many cakes, bakes and desserts as the fine grains dissolve easily. Unrefined golden caster sugar has a light golden colour with a delicate caramel flavour.

Granulated sugar

This has coarser grains than caster sugar, so is perfect for sprinkling over cakes and cookies as a decoration.

Light and dark soft brown or muscovado sugars

These have more depth of flavour than white sugars and add both richness and colour to your bakes and desserts.

Icing sugar

This has a fine powdery texture and dissolves instantly in water. It is perfect for icings and frostings, as well as confectionery, plus for dusting over finished cakes as a decoration.

Butter

Butter, both salted and unsalted, is ideal for making cakes, pastries and other sweet delights. Butter gives a richer, creamier flavour and a more melt-in-the-mouth texture than other fats.

Eggs

Ideally, choose free-range or organic eggs where you can as these tend to be more flavourful and the chickens will have had a better upbringing to higher welfare standards. It is best to use fresh eggs at room temperature, so take them out of the refrigerator 30–60 minutes before you want to use them.

Leavening agents

Both baking powder and bicarbonate of soda are used as raising agents in cake, bread and batter recipes.

Chocolate

We all love chocolate but it can vary considerably in quality and flavour. Plain or dark chocolate is the prime choice for cooking as it has an intense flavour and good melting properties. Choose bars that contain between 50% and 70% cocoa solids. Milk and white chocolates are also used in some recipes, but they are not as flavourful and are less suited to melting.

Cocoa powder

Unsweetened cocoa powder is a fine, reddy-brown powder that has a bitter but intense chocolate flavour. It is widely used as a flavouring in cakes, confectionery and desserts.

Extracts and essences

Used sparingly, extracts and essences, such as vanilla and almond extracts, can be used to impart a wonderful flavour to many sweet recipes.

Specialist Ingredients

Gold leaf

Edible gold leaf is available as sheets, dust, flakes and petals. Perfect for adding an impressive flourish to desserts, cakes and confectionery, and it is easily obtainable online.

Popping candy

Popping candy, from good kitchenware shops and online, adds a surprising mouth-popping, tongue-tingling sensation and decorative touch to sweet recipes.

Funfetti sprinkles

Funfetti, otherwise known as hundreds and thousands, is readily available in a range of vibrant colours, shapes and sizes. These bright sugar sprinkles are perfect for cheering up many a cupcake or dessert.

Food colourings

Concentrated food colourings are available in a rainbow of vibrant colours in either paste, liquid or gel form. They give a good deep colour and are just the job for colouring cakes, batters, icings and frostings. Choose 100% natural food colourings, if you can.

Cooking Techniques

Creaming butter and sugar

Butter or margarine and sugar are beaten together thoroughly to form a light, pale and fluffy mixture. The butter or margarine should be a soft, spreadable consistency before you start. Use a wooden spoon or an electric hand-held mixer on a low speed.

Adding eggs

With many recipes, whole eggs should be beaten before gradually adding them to creamed and other mixtures. Beat well after each addition to make sure all the egg has been incorporated before adding the next spoonful.

Adding flour and folding in

Always sift the flour with any raising agents or ground spices before adding to a mixture so that they are evenly distributed. When folding in flour or dry ingredients, use a large metal spoon to gently work them through the mixture, retaining as much air in the mixture as possible.

Whisking

To make whisked sponge batters or egg white-based dishes, including meringues or macaroons, large amounts of air need to be incorporated and trapped in the mixture. Use an electric hand-held mixer for speed, or use a large balloon whisk and plenty of elbow grease!

Rubbing fat into flour

This technique is used for pastries, scones, teabreads and some cakes. The fat (usually butter) needs to be chilled and diced or coarsely grated before rubbing into the flour.

Melting chocolate

Chocolate can be melted on the hob or in the microwave. To melt chocolate on the hob, break the chocolate into pieces and place in a large heatproof bowl. Set the bowl over a pan of simmering water, making sure the bowl does not touch the water underneath, and leave until the chocolate has melted, stirring occasionally. Remove the bowl from the pan and stir the chocolate until smooth.

To melt chocolate in the microwave, break the pieces into a bowl and microwave for 1-2 minutes at a time on a medium setting until almost completely melted. Remove from the microwave and leave to stand for 2 minutes, then stir until smooth. Watch it closely as it can burn if heated too high.

Greasing and lining tins

Follow the recipe instructions for preparing tins before use. Grease tins with melted or softened butter or a flavourless vegetable oil.

Specialist Cooking Techniques

Blind-baking pastry cases

Sometimes the pastry for a recipe needs to be blind-baked, which means the pastry case is baked partially or completely before the filling is added. Preheat the oven and roll and line your tin with pastry as directed. Prick the pastry base all over with a fork, then line it with a large piece of greaseproof paper and fill with baking beans (or use dried beans). Bake as directed until the case looks set, then carefully remove the paper and beans and return the pastry case to the oven for a few more minutes to firm up and lightly colour the base (or for longer if the pastry case needs to be fully baked).

Deep-frying doughnuts

Heat some vegetable oil in a large, deep pan or in an electric deep-fat fryer to a temperature of 180–190°C/350–375°F, or until a cube of bread browns in 30 seconds. Once the oil is hot enough, carefully slide the doughnuts into the hot oil in batches and cook them as directed until golden brown all over. Remove the doughnuts from the oil with a slotted spoon, then drain and cool on kitchen paper before decorating.

Decoration Techniques

Adding colouring to a mixture/icing

When adding food colouring to a mixture, such as cake batter or icing, always add it gradually using a cocktail stick, mixing it in thoroughly after each addition until you achieve the desired depth of colour.

Piping icing/frosting

Piping icing and frosting is easy to master and gives an impressive finish. Different-shaped nozzles will produce varied end results. Depending on the type of icing/frosting you are piping, choose a suitable piping bag fitted with the nozzle of your choice, then spoon the icing/frosting into the bag. Gently press the icing/frosting down into the bag to remove any pockets of air, then twist the bag tightly at the top to prevent the contents escaping.

Decorating with chocolate

Chocolate is perfect for making simple or elaborate decorations to embellish cakes and desserts. Even simple chocolate curls or shavings add a decadent finish.

To make piped chocolate shapes for decoration, spoon melted chocolate into a paper piping bag and snip off the very end tip of the bag. Pipe simple shapes, such as flowers, swirls or motifs, onto a tray lined with non-stick baking paper. Don't make them too intricate or they will be too fragile. Leave in a cool place until set, then carefully peel the paper away from the chocolate.

Dazzling Decorations

Fabulous feather icing

To feather-ice, spoon glacé icing over the top of the cake, cupcake or cookie to cover completely. Spoon contrasting coloured glacé icing into a piping bag fitted with a fine nozzle and quickly pipe parallel lines across the top. Use a cocktail stick to draw lightly across the piped lines in alternate directions to create a feathered effect.

Ready-to-roll fondant icing

Ready-to-roll fondant icing (also known as sugar paste) is a soft and pliable icing. You'll find packs of white or ivory ready-to-roll fondant icing in most supermarkets, and ready-coloured versions are available from specialist suppliers or online.

Use a food colouring paste to colour this type of icing, as liquid will make it sticky. Smear a little food colouring (from the end of a cocktail stick or skewer) onto the icing, then knead it in until you have an even colour.

Sugar decorations

A simple and easy way to add a touch of colourful and funky fun to iced cakes, bakes and desserts is to jazz them up with one of the many decorating items on offer. These include readily obtainable products, like sugar sprinkles (from sugar strands, funfetti and shimmer pearls, to flower shapes and mini stars and hearts), sugar flowers and shapes, rose petals or violets, dragées, and mini sweets and chocolates.

More specialist decorating items are readily available online or from specialist suppliers, include sanding or glimmering sugar, tiny pots of edible glitter, and lustre spray or edible silk or lustre food dust, all of which add elegance and style and are obtainable in an array of colours.

Troubleshooting Tips
& Savvy Solutions for Success

Tips

Always follow either metric or imperial measurements for a recipe – not a mixture of both.

When using a set of measuring spoons, always use a level spoonful, unless stated otherwise in the recipe.

Always preheat the oven before you start (check the recipe to see at what stage you need to do this). Preheat the oven to the required temperature for 10–15 minutes before use, so that it has time to reach the correct temperature.

Low-fat spreads are not usually suitable for baking as they contain a high proportion of water, so use butter where possible.

Don't over-mix when folding in as this can knock air out of the mixture and result in heavy, close-textured cakes or flat meringues.

When preparing choux pastry, always sift the flour and salt together onto a sheet of greaseproof paper, then add it all at once to the combined melted water and butter mixture. Once the flour has been added and the mixture beaten, let it cool slightly before gradually beating in the eggs.

Pastry too tough or crumbly
Be careful when adding the liquid to a dough as too much will result in tough pastry and too little will produce a crumbly pastry that is hard to handle. Add just enough liquid to bind the dough, adding it gradually and sprinkling it evenly over the surface. Over-worked pastry can also be tough, so work quickly and lightly.

Pastry shrinking during baking
Keep everything cool when making pastry. It is important to 'rest' the pastry before baking to minimize shrinkage. For shortcrust pastry, wrap it in clingfilm and leave to rest for at least 30 minutes in the refrigerator before rolling it out. Once you have lined your tin with pastry, rest it again in the refrigerator for 20–30 minutes before baking.

Curdling cake batter
Curdling is the term used when the water from the eggs separates out from the fat globules in a cake mixture, and is usually caused by the eggs being too cold. To help prevent curdling, use eggs at room temperature and add them gradually. If the creamed mixture does start to curdle, stir in a tablespoon or two of the measured flour to help bind the mixture back together, before adding more egg.

How to tell if a cake is cooked
An easy way to check the doneness of baked large and small cakes is to insert a fine skewer or cocktail stick into the centre of the cake. If it comes out clean (with no signs of uncooked mixture on it), then the cake is ready. If it's sticky and there is any uncooked mixture or wetness on the skewer, then the cake should be returned to the oven for a few more minutes to finish baking.

Perfectly baked sponge cakes (such as Victoria sandwich cake) should feel spongy and spring back when lightly pressed with a fingertip.

Cake Dilemmas and Solutions

Over-peaked, domed or cracked in centre
- Too much raising agent used in the cake mixture
- Oven temperature was too hot
- Size of the tin used was too small

Dip in centre/sunk in middle
- Oven door was opened too soon (before the cake was set)
- Cake was not cooked for long enough

Dense and heavy texture when making cake mixture
- Insufficient creaming
- Eggs were added too quickly and the mixture curdled
- Too heavy-handed when folding in

Burnt bottom or top
- Oven was too hot
- Cake was over-baked or left in the oven for too long

Cake failed to rise
- No raising agent was included in the mixture

Cake rose unevenly
- Cake mixture was not sufficiently mixed
- There was an uneven temperature inside the oven

Large cakes & traybakes

Angel food cake

Ingredients

oil, for greasing

8 large egg whites

1 tsp cream of tartar

1 tsp almond extract

250 g/9 oz caster sugar

115 g/4 oz plain flour,
plus extra for dusting

Decoration

250 g/9 oz summer berries

1 tbsp lemon juice

2 tbsp icing sugar

1. Preheat the oven to 160°C/325°F/Gas Mark 3. Grease and lightly flour a 24-cm/9½-inch ring tin.

2. In a clean, grease-free bowl, whisk the egg whites until they hold soft peaks. Add the cream of tartar and whisk again until the whites are stiff but not dry. Whisk in the almond extract, then add the caster sugar, a tablespoon at a time, whisking hard between each addition. Sift in the flour and fold in lightly and evenly using a large metal spoon.

3. Spoon the mixture into the prepared cake tin. Bake in the preheated oven for 40–45 minutes, or until golden brown. Run the tip of a knife around the edge of the cake to loosen from the tin. Leave to cool in the tin for 10 minutes, then turn out onto a wire rack to cool. To decorate, place the berries, lemon juice and icing sugar in a saucepan and heat until the sugar has dissolved. Spoon over the cake.

Millionaire's shortbread

Ingredients

75 g/2¾ oz margarine, plus extra for greasing

60 g/2¼ oz soft light brown sugar

140 g/5 oz plain flour

40 g/1½ oz rolled oats

100 g/3½ oz plain chocolate, broken into pieces

25 g/1 oz white chocolate, broken into pieces (optional)

Filling

25 g/1 oz butter

2 tbsp soft light brown sugar

225 ml/8 fl oz condensed milk

1. Preheat the oven to 180°C/350°F/Gas Mark 4. Beat together the margarine and sugar in a bowl until light and fluffy. Beat in the flour and the rolled oats. Use your fingertips to bring the mixture together, if necessary.

2. Press the mixture into the base of a greased 20-cm/8-inch square, shallow cake tin. Bake in the preheated oven for 25 minutes, or until just golden and firm. Leave to cool in the tin.

3. Place the ingredients for the filling in a saucepan and heat gently, stirring until the sugar has dissolved. Bring slowly to the boil over a very low heat, then boil very gently for 3–4 minutes, stirring constantly, until thickened.

4. Pour the caramel filling over the oat layer in the tin and leave to set.

5. Put the plain chocolate in a heatproof bowl set over a saucepan of gently simmering water and heat until melted. Spread over the caramel. If using the white chocolate, melt in the same way and pipe lines of white chocolate over the plain chocolate. Using a cocktail stick, feather the white chocolate into the plain chocolate. Leave to set, then cut into squares to serve.

#3

Serves
10

Hummingbird cake

Ingredients

250 g/9 oz plain flour

250 g/9 oz caster sugar

1 tsp ground cinnamon

1 tsp bicarbonate of soda

3 eggs, beaten

200 ml/7 fl oz sunflower oil, plus extra
for greasing

100 g/3½ oz pecan nuts, roughly chopped,
plus extra to decorate

3 ripe bananas, mashed

85 g/3 oz canned crushed pineapple
(drained weight), plus 4 tbsp juice from
the can

Filling & frosting

175 g/6 oz full-fat soft cheese

55 g/2 oz butter

1 tsp vanilla extract

400 g/14 oz icing sugar

1. Preheat the oven to 180°C/350°F/Gas Mark 4. Lightly grease 3 x 23-cm/9-inch sandwich cake tins and line the bases with baking paper.

2. Sift together the flour, sugar, cinnamon and bicarbonate of soda into a large bowl. Add the eggs, oil, nuts, bananas, pineapple and pineapple juice, and stir with a wooden spoon until evenly mixed.

3. Divide the mixture between the prepared tins and smooth level. Bake in the preheated oven for 25–30 minutes, or until golden brown and firm to the touch.

4. Remove the cakes from the oven and leave to cool in the tins for 10 minutes, then turn out onto wire racks to cool completely.

5. To make the filling and frosting, beat together the soft cheese, butter and vanilla extract in a bowl until smooth. Sift in the icing sugar and mix until smooth.

6. Sandwich the cakes together with half of the mixture, spread the remaining frosting over the top, then sprinkle with pecan nuts and serve.

#4

Serves
10

Classic chocolate cake

Ingredients

55 g/2 oz cocoa powder

7 tbsp boiling water

200 g/7 oz butter, softened, plus extra
for greasing

125 g/4½ oz caster sugar

70 g/2½ oz soft light brown sugar

4 eggs, beaten

1 tsp vanilla extract

200 g/7 oz self-raising flour

Frosting

200 g/7 oz plain chocolate, broken

115 g/4 oz butter

100 ml/3½ fl oz double cream

1. Preheat the oven to 180°C/350°F/Gas Mark 4. Grease 2 x 20-cm/8-inch sandwich tins and line with baking paper.

2. Blend the cocoa powder and water to a smooth paste and set aside. Put the butter, caster sugar and brown sugar into a large bowl and beat together until pale and creamy. Gradually beat in the eggs, then stir in the cocoa paste and vanilla extract. Sift in the flour and fold in gently. Divide the mixture between the prepared tins. Bake in the preheated oven for 25–30 minutes, or until risen and just springy to the touch. Leave to cool in the tins for 5 minutes, then turn out onto wire racks to cool completely.

3. To make the frosting, put the chocolate and butter into a heatproof bowl set over a saucepan of simmering water, making sure the bowl doesn't touch the water, and heat until melted. Remove from the heat and stir in the cream. Leave to cool for 20 minutes. Chill in the refrigerator for 40–50 minutes, stirring occasionally, until thick. Sandwich the sponges together with one third of the frosting, then spread the remainder over the top and sides of the cake.

Apricot flapjacks

Makes
10

Ingredients

175 g/6 oz margarine,
plus extra for greasing

85 g/3 oz demerara sugar

55 g/2 oz clear honey

140 g/5 oz ready-to-eat dried apricots,
chopped

2 tsp sesame seeds

225 g/8 oz rolled oats

1. Preheat the oven to 180°C/350°F/Gas Mark 4. Grease a
26 x 17-cm/10½ x 6½-inch shallow baking tin.

2. Put the margarine, sugar and honey into a small saucepan
over a low heat and heat until the ingredients have melted – do not boil. When the ingredients
are well combined, stir in the apricots, sesame seeds and oats.

3. Spoon the mixture into the prepared tin and smooth the surface with the back of a spoon.
Bake in the preheated oven for 20–25 minutes, or until golden brown. Remove from the oven,
cut into 10 bars and leave to cool completely before removing from the tin.

#6

Coffee & walnut cake

Serves
10

Ingredients

175 g/6 oz butter, softened, plus extra
for greasing

175 g/6 oz light muscovado sugar

3 large eggs, beaten

175 g/6 oz self-raising flour

1½ tsp baking powder

115 g/4 oz walnut pieces

3 tbsp strong black coffee (cafetiere or
instant made up with hot water to taste)

walnut halves, to decorate

Frosting

115 g/4 oz butter, softened

200 g/7 oz icing sugar

1 tbsp strong black coffee

½ tsp vanilla extract

1. Preheat the oven to 180°C/350°F/Gas Mark 4. Grease 2 x
20-cm/8-inch sandwich tins and line with baking paper.

2. Beat the butter and muscovado sugar together until pale
and creamy. Gradually add the eggs, beating well after each addition.

3. Sift together the flour and baking powder into the mixture, then fold in lightly and evenly with
a metal spoon. Fold in the walnut pieces and the coffee. Divide the mixture between the prepared
tins and smooth the surfaces. Bake in the preheated oven for 20–25 minutes, or until golden brown
and springy to the touch. Turn out onto wire racks to cool completely.

4. To make the frosting, beat together the butter, icing sugar, coffee and vanilla extract, mixing
until smooth and creamy.

5. Use about half the mixture to sandwich the cakes together, then spread the remaining frosting
on top and swirl with a palette knife. Decorate with walnut halves.

New York cheesecake

Ingredients

100 g/3½ oz butter, plus extra for greasing

150 g/5½ oz digestive biscuits, finely crushed

1 tbsp granulated sugar

900 g/2 lb cream cheese

250 g/9 oz caster sugar

2 tbsp plain flour

1 tsp vanilla extract

finely grated zest of 1 orange

finely grated zest of 1 lemon

3 eggs

2 egg yolks

300 ml/10 fl oz double cream

1. Preheat the oven to 180°C/350°F/Gas Mark 4. Melt the butter in a small saucepan. Remove from the heat and stir in the biscuits and granulated sugar. Press the biscuit mixture tightly into the base of a 23-cm/9-inch round springform cake tin. Bake in the preheated oven for 10 minutes, then remove from the oven and transfer to a wire rack to cool.

2. Increase the oven temperature to 200°C/400°F/Gas Mark 6. Use an electric hand-held mixer to beat the cheese until creamy, then gradually add the caster sugar and flour and beat until smooth. Increase the speed and beat in the vanilla extract, orange zest and lemon zest, then beat in the eggs and egg yolks one at a time. Finally, beat in the cream. Scrape any mixture from the sides of the bowl and beaters into the mixture. It should be light and fluffy – beat on a faster setting if you need to.

3. Grease the sides of the cake tin and pour in the filling. Smooth the top, transfer to the oven and bake for 15 minutes, then reduce the temperature to 110°C/225°F/Gas Mark ¼ and bake for a further 30 minutes. Turn off the oven and leave the cheesecake inside for 2 hours to cool and set. Chill in the refrigerator overnight before serving.

4. Slide a knife around the edge of the cheesecake then unclip and remove from the tin to serve.

Chocolate fudge cake

Ingredients

oil, for greasing

150 g/5½ oz plain chocolate, broken into pieces

3 tbsp milk

175 g/6 oz plain flour

1 tbsp baking powder

225 g/8 oz butter, softened

175 g/6 oz dark muscovado sugar

3 eggs, beaten

2 tsp vanilla extract

175 g/6 oz icing sugar

chocolate curls or grated chocolate, to decorate

1. Preheat the oven to 180°C/350°F/Gas Mark 4. Grease a 23-cm/9-inch round cake tin and line with baking paper. Place 55 g/2 oz of the chocolate and 2 tablespoons of the milk in a small saucepan and gently heat, without boiling, until melted. Remove from the heat.

2. Sift together the flour and baking powder into a large bowl and add 175 g/6 oz of the butter, the muscovado sugar, eggs and 1 teaspoon of the vanilla extract. Beat until smooth, then stir in the melted chocolate mixture, mixing evenly. Spoon the mixture into the prepared tin and smooth level. Bake in the preheated oven for 50–60 minutes, until firm to the touch and just beginning to shrink away from the sides of the tin. Leave to cool in the tin for 10 minutes, then turn out onto a wire rack to cool completely. Carefully slice the cake horizontally into two layers.

3. Melt the remaining chocolate and butter in a small saucepan over a low heat. Remove from the heat and beat in the icing sugar, vanilla extract and milk until smooth. Sandwich the cake layers together with half the mixture, then swirl the remainder on top. Sprinkle with chocolate curls.

Serves
10

Victoria sponge cake

Ingredients

175 g/6 oz self-raising flour

1 tsp baking powder

175 g/6 oz butter, softened,
plus extra for greasing

175 g/6 oz golden caster sugar

3 eggs

3 tbsp raspberry jam

300 ml/10 fl oz double cream, whipped

16 fresh strawberries, halved

icing sugar, for dusting

1. Preheat the oven to 180°C/350°F/Gas Mark 4. Grease 2 x 20-cm/8-inch sandwich tins and line with baking paper.

2. Sift together the flour and baking powder into a bowl and add the butter, sugar and eggs. Mix together, then beat well until smooth.

3. Divide the mixture evenly between the prepared tins and smooth the surfaces. Bake in the preheated oven for 25–30 minutes, or until well risen and golden brown, and the cakes feel springy when lightly pressed.

4. Leave to cool in the tins for 5 minutes, then turn out and peel off the baking paper. Transfer to wire racks to cool completely. Sandwich the cakes together with the raspberry jam, whipped cream and strawberry halves. Dust with icing sugar.

Peach cobbler

Ingredients

6 peaches, peeled and sliced
175 g/6 oz caster sugar
½ tbsp lemon juice
1½ tsp cornflour
½ tsp almond extract or vanilla extract
185 g/6½ oz plain flour
1½ tsp baking powder
½ tsp salt
85 g/3 oz butter, diced
1 egg
6 tbsp milk
ice cream, to serve

1. Preheat the oven to 220°C/425°F/Gas Mark 7. Place the peaches in a 23-cm/9-inch square baking dish. Add 4 tablespoons of the sugar, the lemon juice, cornflour and almond extract and toss together. Bake in the preheated oven for 20 minutes.

2. Meanwhile, sift the flour, all but 2 tablespoons of the remaining sugar, the baking powder and the salt into a bowl. Rub in the butter with your fingertips until the mixture resembles breadcrumbs. Mix the egg and 5 tablespoons of the milk in a jug, then mix into the dry ingredients with a fork until a soft, sticky dough forms. If the dough seems too dry, stir in the extra tablespoon of milk.

3. Reduce the oven temperature to 200°C/400°F/Gas Mark 6. Remove the peaches from the oven. Drop spoonfuls of the dough over the surface, without smoothing. Sprinkle with the remaining sugar, return to the oven and bake for a further 15 minutes, or until the topping is golden brown and firm – it will spread as it cooks. Serve hot or at room temperature, with ice cream.

Frosted carrot cake

Ingredients

175 ml/6 fl oz sunflower oil,
plus extra for greasing
175 g/6 oz light muscovado sugar
3 eggs, beaten
175 g/6 oz grated carrots
85 g/3 oz sultanas
55 g/2 oz walnut pieces
grated rind of 1 orange
175 g/6 oz self-raising flour
1 tsp bicarbonate of soda
1 tsp ground cinnamon
½ tsp grated nutmeg
200 g/7 oz full-fat soft cheese
100 g/3½ oz icing sugar
2 tsp orange juice
strips of orange zest, to decorate

1. Preheat the oven to 180°C/350°F/Gas Mark 4. Grease a 23-cm/9-inch square cake tin and line the base with baking paper.

2. In a large bowl beat together the oil, muscovado sugar and eggs. Stir in the grated carrots, sultanas, walnuts and orange rind.

3. Sift together the flour, bicarbonate of soda, cinnamon and nutmeg, then stir evenly into the carrot mixture.

4. Spoon the mixture into the prepared cake tin and bake in the preheated oven for 40–45 minutes, until well risen and firm to the touch.

5. Remove the cake from the oven and place the tin on a wire rack for 5 minutes. Turn out onto the wire rack to cool completely.

6. Beat together the soft cheese, icing sugar and orange juice in a bowl. Spread over the top of the cake, swirling with a palette knife. Decorate with orange zest and cut into squares to serve.

19

#12 Marshmallow bars

Makes 10

Ingredients

85 g/3 oz dairy toffees
55 g/2 oz butter
2 tbsp golden syrup
140 g/5 oz mini pink and white marshmallows
115 g/4 oz crispy rice cereal
2 tbsp sugar-coated chocolate drops

1. Line a 28 x 18-cm/11 x 7-inch shallow cake tin with baking paper.

2. Put the toffees, butter, golden syrup and 115 g/4 oz of the marshmallows into a large heatproof bowl set over a saucepan of simmering water. Heat until melted, stirring occasionally.

3. Remove the bowl from the heat. Stir in the rice cereal until thoroughly mixed. Quickly spoon the mixture into the prepared tin and smooth the surface.

4. Scatter over the remaining marshmallows and the chocolate drops, gently pressing down. Chill in the refrigerator for about 2 hours, or until firm. Use a sharp knife to cut into 10 bars.

#13 Pumpkin spice cake

Serves 10

Ingredients

175 ml/6 fl oz sunflower oil, plus extra for greasing
175 g/6 oz soft light brown sugar
3 eggs, beaten
250 g/9 oz canned pumpkin purée
85 g/3 oz raisins
grated rind of 1 orange
70 g/2½ oz walnut pieces
225 g/8 oz self-raising flour
1 tsp bicarbonate of soda
2 tsp mixed spice
250 g/9 oz mascarpone cheese
85 g/3 oz icing sugar
3 tbsp maple syrup

1. Preheat the oven to 180°C/350°F/Gas Mark 4. Grease a 23-cm/9-inch square cake tin and line with baking paper.

2. In a large bowl beat together the oil, brown sugar and eggs. Stir in the pumpkin purée, raisins, orange rind and 55 g/2 oz of the walnut pieces.

3. Sift together the flour, bicarbonate of soda and mixed spice, and fold into the pumpkin mixture. Spoon the mixture into the prepared tin and bake in the preheated oven for 35–40 minutes, or until golden brown and firm to the touch. Leave to cool in the tin for 5 minutes, then turn out onto a wire rack to cool completely.

4. Put the mascarpone cheese, icing sugar and maple syrup into a bowl and beat together until smooth. Spread over the top of the cake, swirling with a palette knife. Finely chop the remaining walnut pieces and scatter over the top of the cake.

20

Pear & chocolate squares

Makes 16

Ingredients

140 g/5 oz wholemeal plain flour

140 g/5 oz self-raising flour

175 g/6 oz butter, diced, plus extra for greasing

100 g/3½ oz ground almonds

85 g/3 oz caster sugar

450 g/1 lb firm ripe pears, peeled, cored and roughly chopped

2 large eggs, separated

25 g/1 oz cocoa powder

2 tsp baking powder

175 g/6 oz soft dark brown sugar

5 tbsp milk

1. Preheat the oven to 180°C/350°F/Gas Mark 4. Grease and line the base of an 18-cm/7-inch deep square cake tin. Sift the wholemeal flour and self-raising flour into a bowl. Add the butter and rub in with your fingertips until the mixture resembles fine breadcrumbs.

2. Transfer 25 g/1 oz of the mixture to a separate bowl and set aside. Add the ground almonds, caster sugar, pears and 1 egg white to the remaining mixture. Mix well.

3. Sift together the cocoa powder and baking powder. Stir into the reserved 25 g/1 oz butter mixture with the brown sugar. Add the remaining egg white, the egg yolks and milk. Mix well.

4. Spread half the chocolate mixture over the base of the prepared tin. Spread the pear mixture over the top. Cover with the remaining chocolate mixture and smooth the surface. Bake in the preheated oven for 1 hour 10 minutes–1 hour 20 minutes, or until risen and the centre is firm to the touch. Leave to cool in the tin, then turn out and cut into 16 squares.

Rich fruit cake

Serves 10

Ingredients

350 g/12 oz sultanas

225 g/8 oz raisins

115 g/4 oz ready-to-eat dried apricots, chopped

85 g/3 oz stoned dates, chopped

4 tbsp dark rum or brandy (optional)

finely grated rind and juice of 1 orange

225 g/8 oz butter, softened, plus extra for greasing

225 g/8 oz light muscovado sugar

4 eggs, beaten

70 g/2½ oz chopped mixed peel

85 g/3 oz glacé cherries, quartered

40 g/1½ oz blanched almonds, chopped

200 g/7 oz plain flour

1 tsp ground mixed spice

1. Place the sultanas, raisins, apricots and dates in a large bowl and stir in the rum, if using, orange rind and orange juice. Cover and leave to soak for several hours or overnight. Preheat the oven to 150°C/300°F/Gas Mark 2. Grease a 20-cm/8-inch round cake tin and line with baking paper.

2. Beat the butter and sugar together until pale and creamy. Gradually beat in the eggs, beating well after each addition. Stir in the soaked fruits, mixed peel, glacé cherries and blanched almonds. Sift together the flour and mixed spice, then fold lightly and evenly into the mixture. Spoon the mixture into the prepared cake tin and smooth the surface, making a slight depression in the centre with the back of the spoon.

3. Bake in the preheated oven for 2¼–2¾ hours, or until the cake is beginning to shrink away from the sides of the tin and a skewer inserted in the centre comes out clean. Leave to cool completely in the tin. Turn out the cake, remove the paper, then wrap in greaseproof paper and foil and store for at least 2 months before use.

Classic cherry cake

Serves
10

Ingredients

oil, for greasing

250 g/9 oz glacé cherries, quartered

85 g/3 oz ground almonds

200 g/7 oz plain flour

1 tsp baking powder

200 g/7 oz butter

200 g/7 oz caster sugar

3 large eggs

finely grated rind and juice of 1 lemon

6 sugar cubes, crushed

1. Preheat the oven to 180°C/350°F/Gas Mark 4. Grease a 20-cm/8-inch round cake tin and line with baking paper.

2. Stir together the cherries, ground almonds and 1 tablespoon of the flour. Sift the remaining flour into a separate bowl with the baking powder. Cream together the butter and caster sugar until light and fluffy. Gradually add the eggs, beating well with each addition to mix evenly.

3. Add the flour mixture and fold lightly and evenly into the creamed mixture with a metal spoon. Add the cherry mixture and fold in evenly. Finally, fold in the lemon rind and juice. Spoon the mixture into the prepared cake tin and sprinkle with the crushed sugar cubes. Bake in the preheated oven for 1–1¼ hours, or until risen, golden brown and the cake is just beginning to shrink away from the sides of the tin. Leave to cool in the tin for 15 minutes, then turn out onto a wire rack to finish cooling.

Plum traybake

Serves
9

Ingredients

200 g/7 oz plain flour

2 tbsp granulated sugar

1 egg, beaten

100 ml/3½ fl oz milk

25 g/1 oz butter, plus extra for greasing

10 g/¼ oz fresh yeast

600 g/1 lb 5 oz plums, halved and stoned

50 g/1¾ oz cinnamon sugar

50 g/1¾ oz chopped hazelnuts, for sprinkling (optional)

whipped cream or ice cream, to serve (optional)

1. Sift the flour into a bowl, then add the sugar. Make a well in the centre, add the egg and mix to combine, pulling in the flour mixture from the side of the bowl.

2. Put the milk and butter into a small saucepan and heat over a low heat until the butter is melted. Remove from the heat and leave to cool to lukewarm. Crumble the yeast into the mixture, stir to dissolve and leave to stand for 5 minutes. Pour the yeast mixture into the flour mixture and knead well.

3. Cover the bowl and leave to rise for at least 30 minutes until the dough has doubled in size.

4. Preheat the oven to 180°C/350°F/Gas Mark 4 and grease a 23-cm/9-inch square cake tin. Make 1–2 cuts in each plum half.

5. Rub a little butter on your hands, then knock back the dough and press it into the prepared tin. Firmly press the plum halves, cut-side up, into the dough. Sprinkle over the cinnamon sugar and leave to stand for 15 minutes. Sprinkle the chopped hazelnuts over the plums, if using.

6. Bake in the preheated oven for about 30 minutes, then remove from the oven and leave to cool slightly. Serve lukewarm with whipped cream, if using.

#18 Lemon drizzle cake

Serves
12

Ingredients

2 eggs

175 g/6 oz caster sugar

150 g/5½ oz soft margarine,
plus extra for greasing

finely grated rind of 1 lemon

175 g/6 oz self-raising flour

125 ml/4 fl oz milk

140 g/5 oz icing sugar, plus extra
for dusting

50 ml/1¾ fl oz fresh lemon juice

1. Preheat the oven to 180°C/350°F/Gas Mark 4. Grease an
18-cm/7-inch square cake tin and line with baking paper.

2. Place the eggs, caster sugar and margarine in a mixing
bowl and beat hard until smooth and fluffy. Stir in the lemon rind, then sift in the flour lightly
and fold in lightly and evenly. Stir in the milk, mixing evenly, then spoon into the prepared tin,
smoothing level. Bake in the preheated oven for 45–50 minutes, or until golden brown and firm to
the touch. Remove from the oven and stand the tin on a wire rack.

3. Place the icing sugar and lemon juice in a small saucepan and heat gently, stirring until the
sugar dissolves. Do not boil.

4. Prick the warm cake all over with a skewer, and spoon the hot syrup evenly over the top, allowing
it to be absorbed.

5. Leave to cool completely in the tin, then turn out the cake, cut into 12 pieces and dust with a little
icing sugar before serving.

#19 Rose gateau

Serves
10

Ingredients

oil or melted butter, for greasing

175 g/6 oz plain flour

1 tbsp baking powder

175 g/6 oz butter, softened

175 g/6 oz caster sugar

3 eggs, beaten

2 tsp rosewater

2 tbsp milk

150 ml/5 fl oz whipping cream

200 g/7 oz icing sugar, sifted

Decoration

fresh rose petals, washed and patted dry

½ egg white

caster sugar, for sprinkling

1. Preheat the oven to 180°C/350°F/Gas Mark 4. Grease
2 x 23-cm/9-inch sandwich cake tins and line the bases with
baking paper.

2. Sift together the flour and baking powder into a large bowl. Add the butter, caster sugar, eggs
and 1 teaspoon of the rosewater. Beat until smooth, then stir in the milk. Divide the mixture
between the prepared tins and smooth. Bake in the preheated oven for 25–30 minutes, until risen,
firm and golden brown. Leave to cool in the tins for 2–3 minutes, then turn out onto wire racks to
cool completely.

3. Whip the cream with ½ teaspoon of the rosewater until just thick enough to hold its shape. Use
to sandwich the cakes together. Mix the icing sugar with the remaining rosewater and a little water
to a thick pouring consistency. Spoon over the cake and drizzle down the sides. Leave to set.

4. Brush the rose petals with the egg white, sprinkle with caster sugar and arrange on top of the
cake to decorate.

Blackberry semifreddo yogurt cake

Ingredients

300 g/10½ oz blackberries

2 tbsp icing sugar

1 kg/2 lb 4 oz Greek-style yogurt

50 g/1¾ oz meringue shells, lightly crushed

fresh mint leaves, torn, to decorate

1. Line a 20-cm/8-inch round cake tin with clingfilm.

2. Reserve a few blackberries for decoration. Place the remaining blackberries and the icing sugar in a food processor and process until a smooth coulis forms. Transfer about one third of the coulis to a serving jug, passing it through a sieve if you prefer it to be seedless.

3. Add the yogurt to the food processor and process until blended. Tip the mixture into a mixing bowl and gently fold in the meringue pieces.

4. Tip into the prepared tin and place in the freezer for 2 hours, or until the mixture is just beginning to solidify but can still hold its shape.

5. When ready to serve, invert the cake onto a serving plate. Drizzle over the coulis and scatter with the reserved blackberries and mint leaves.

6. If you want to make this in advance, cover with clingfilm and freeze until solid. Transfer it to the refrigerator about 1 hour before serving. The coulis can also be frozen. Thaw at room temperature for 1 hour before serving.

Gingerbread

Serves
12–16

Ingredients

450 g/1 lb plain flour
1 tbsp baking powder
1 tsp bicarbonate of soda
1 tbsp ground ginger
175 g/6 oz butter
175 g/6 oz soft light brown sugar
175 g/6 oz black treacle
175 g/6 oz golden syrup
1 egg, beaten
300 ml/10 fl oz milk

1. Line a 23-cm/9-inch square cake tin, 5 cm/2 inches deep, with baking paper. Preheat the oven to 160°C/325°F/Gas Mark 3.

2. Sift together the flour, baking powder, bicarbonate of soda and ginger into a large mixing bowl. Place the butter, sugar, treacle and golden syrup in a saucepan and heat over a low heat until the butter has melted and the sugar dissolved. Leave to cool a little. Mix the egg with the milk and add to the cooled mixture. Add the liquid ingredients to the flour mixture and beat well using a wooden spoon until the mixture is smooth and glossy.

3. Pour the mixture into the prepared tin and bake in the centre of the preheated oven for 1½ hours until well risen and just firm to the touch. Remove from the oven and leave to cool in the tin. Remove from the tin with the lining paper. Wrap with foil and place in an airtight container for up to 1 week to allow the flavours to mature. Cut into wedges to serve.

22 Coffee Bundt cake

Serves
14

Ingredients

400 g/14 oz plain flour, plus extra for dusting
1 tbsp baking powder
1 tsp bicarbonate of soda
3 tbsp espresso coffee powder
275 g/9¾ oz lightly salted butter, softened, plus extra for greasing
125 g/4½ oz light muscovado sugar
225 ml/8 fl oz maple syrup
3 eggs, beaten
225 ml/8 fl oz buttermilk
225 ml/8 fl oz double cream

Decoration

4 tbsp maple syrup
200 g/7 oz icing sugar
15 g/½ oz butter, melted
20 chocolate-coated coffee beans

1. Preheat the oven to 180°C/350°F/Gas Mark 4. Grease and lightly flour a 3-litre/5¼-pint Bundt tin.

2. Sift together the flour, baking powder, bicarbonate of soda and coffee powder into a bowl. In a separate bowl, beat together the butter and muscovado sugar until pale and creamy. Gradually whisk in the maple syrup. Slowly beat in the eggs, adding 3 tablespoons of the flour mixture to prevent curdling.

3. Mix together the buttermilk and cream, and add half to the butter mixture. Sprinkle in half of the flour mixture and gently fold together. Add the remaining buttermilk and flour mixtures and gently mix together until just combined.

4. Spoon the mixture into the prepared tin and smooth the surface. Bake in the preheated oven for about 50 minutes, or until well risen and a skewer inserted into the centre comes out clean. Leave in the tin for 10 minutes, then loosen with a knife and turn out onto a wire rack to cool completely.

5. To decorate, beat the maple syrup in a bowl with 150 g/5½ oz of the icing sugar and the butter, until smooth and thickly coating the back of a wooden spoon. Transfer the cake to a serving plate and spoon the icing around the top of the cake so it starts to run down the sides.

6. Beat the remaining icing sugar in a small bowl with 1½–2 teaspoons of water to make a smooth paste. Using a teaspoon, drizzle the icing over the cake and scatter the coffee beans over the top.

23 Boston cream pie

Serves
10

Ingredients

4 large eggs, beaten

115 g/4 oz caster sugar

115 g/4 oz plain flour

70 g/2½ oz butter, plus extra
for greasing

115 g/4 oz plain chocolate, grated

1 tbsp golden syrup

150 ml/5 fl oz double cream

Filling

2 eggs

55 g/2 oz caster sugar

1 tsp vanilla extract

2 tbsp plain flour

2 tbsp cornflour

300 ml/10 fl oz milk

150 ml/5 fl oz double cream,
softly whipped

1. Preheat the oven to 180°C/350°F/Gas Mark 4. Grease 2 x 23-cm/9-inch sandwich tins and line with baking paper. Place the eggs and sugar in a heatproof bowl set over a saucepan of simmering water. Beat with an electric hand-held mixer until the mixture is thick and pale and leaves a trail when the whisk is lifted. Sift in the flour and fold in gently. Melt two thirds of the butter in a pan over a low heat, leave to cool, then pour over the mixture in a thin stream and fold in until just incorporated. Divide the mixture between the prepared tins and bake in the preheated oven for 20–25 minutes, or until light golden and springy to the touch. Leave to cool in the tins for 5 minutes, then turn out onto wire racks to cool completely.

2. To make the filling, whisk together the eggs, sugar and vanilla extract. Blend the flour and cornflour to a paste with 4 tablespoons of the milk, then whisk into the egg mixture. Heat the remaining milk until almost boiling and pour onto the egg mixture, stirring constantly. Return to the pan and cook over a low heat, whisking constantly, until smooth and thick. Pour into a bowl and cover with dampened greaseproof paper. Leave until cold, then fold in the whipped cream. Use to sandwich the sponges together.

3. Place the chocolate, golden syrup and remaining butter in a heatproof bowl. Heat the cream until almost boiling, then pour over the chocolate. Leave for 1 minute, then stir until smooth. Spread the chocolate mixture over the top of the cake to glaze.

 24 Red velvet cake

Serves
10

Ingredients

265 g/9½ oz butter,
plus extra for greasing

4 tbsp water

55 g/2 oz cocoa powder

3 eggs, beaten

250 ml/9 fl oz buttermilk

1 tbsp vanilla extract

2 tbsp edible red food colouring

280 g/10 oz plain flour

55 g/2 oz cornflour

1½ tsp baking powder

325 g/11½ oz caster sugar

250 g/9 oz cream cheese

1. Preheat the oven to 190°C/375°F/Gas Mark 5. Grease 2 x 23-cm/9-inch sandwich tins and line with baking paper.

2. Place 225 g/8 oz of the butter, the water and cocoa powder in a small saucepan and heat gently, without boiling, stirring until melted and smooth. Remove from the heat and leave to cool slightly.

3. Beat together the eggs, buttermilk, 2 teaspoons of the vanilla extract and the food colouring in a bowl. Beat in the butter mixture. Sift together the flour, cornflour and baking powder, then stir into the mixture with all but 3 tablespoons of the caster sugar. Divide the mixture between the prepared tins and bake in the preheated oven for 25–30 minutes, or until risen and firm to the touch. Leave to cool in the tins for 3–4 minutes, then turn out onto wire racks to cool completely.

4. Beat together the cream cheese with the remaining butter, sugar and vanilla extract until smooth. Use about half the mixture to sandwich the cakes together, then spread the remainder over the top.

27

Iced Madeira cake

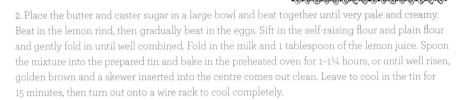

Ingredients

175 g/6 oz butter, softened, plus extra for greasing

175 g/6 oz caster sugar

finely grated rind of 1 lemon

3 eggs, lightly beaten

140 g/5 oz self-raising flour

115 g/4 oz plain flour

2 tbsp milk

4 tbsp lemon juice

175 g/6 oz icing sugar

2 tsp lemon curd, warmed

1. Preheat the oven to 160°C/325°F/Gas Mark 3. Grease a 900-g/2-lb loaf tin and line with baking paper.

2. Place the butter and caster sugar in a large bowl and beat together until very pale and creamy. Beat in the lemon rind, then gradually beat in the eggs. Sift in the self-raising flour and plain flour and gently fold in until well combined. Fold in the milk and 1 tablespoon of the lemon juice. Spoon the mixture into the prepared tin and bake in the preheated oven for 1–1¼ hours, or until well risen, golden brown and a skewer inserted into the centre comes out clean. Leave to cool in the tin for 15 minutes, then turn out onto a wire rack to cool completely.

3. Sift the icing sugar into a bowl. Add the remaining lemon juice and stir to make a smooth, thick icing. Gently spread it over the top of the cake. Drizzle over the lemon curd and drag a skewer through the icing to create a swirled effect.

Tres leches cream cake

Ingredients

butter, for greasing

4 eggs

170 g/5¾ oz granulated sugar

125 g/4½ oz plain flour

1 tsp baking powder

¼ tsp salt

5 tbsp milk

1 tsp vanilla extract or 1 vanilla pod, scraped

2 egg whites

350 ml/12 fl oz evaporated milk

350 ml/12 fl oz sweetened condensed milk

4 tbsp whipping cream

chopped glacé cherries, to decorate

Topping

600 ml/1 pint whipping cream

3 tbsp caster sugar

1. Preheat the oven to 180°C/350°F/Gas Mark 4. Grease a 23-cm/9-inch square cake tin. Put the eggs and sugar into a large bowl and whisk together until doubled in volume. Slowly add the flour, baking powder and salt, mixing well with a wooden spoon. Stir in the milk and the vanilla extract. Whisk the egg whites until they hold stiff peaks, then gently fold into the mixture.

2. Pour the mixture into the prepared tin, smoothing the surface. Bake in the preheated oven for 30 minutes. Remove the cake from the oven, prick all over with a fork, then transfer to a wire rack to cool.

3. Meanwhile, thoroughly mix together the evaporated milk, condensed milk and cream in another bowl.

4. Gradually pour the mixture over the top of the cooled cake, pausing after each addition to allow it to be absorbed, until the cake is completely saturated. Leave to stand for 30 minutes.

5. To make the topping, whip the cream with the sugar until it holds stiff peaks. Just before serving, spread the cream evenly over the cake, cut into 12 pieces and decorate each piece with chopped glacé cherries.

27 Espresso slab cake

Serves 10

Ingredients

3 tbsp cocoa powder

1 tbsp espresso coffee powder

4 tbsp boiling water

200 g/7 oz self-raising flour

1 tsp baking powder

175 g/6 oz butter, softened, plus extra for greasing

175 g/6 oz caster sugar

3 eggs

1 tsp vanilla extract

1 tbsp milk

Frosting

200 g/7 oz mascarpone cheese

40 g/1½ oz caster sugar

1 tbsp espresso coffee, cooled

4 tbsp double cream

85 g/3 oz plain chocolate, melted

1. Preheat the oven to 180°C/350°F/Gas Mark 4. Grease an 18 x 28-cm/7 x 11-inch traybake tin and line the base with baking paper.

2. Put the cocoa powder, coffee powder and boiling water in a heatproof bowl and mix to a smooth paste. Leave to cool for 10 minutes.

3. Sift together the flour and baking powder into another bowl and add the butter, sugar, eggs, vanilla extract, milk, and cocoa mixture. Beat with an electric hand-held mixer for 2–3 minutes, until smooth and creamy.

4. Spoon the cake mixture into the prepared tin and smooth the surface with a palette knife. Bake in the preheated oven for 30–35 minutes, or until risen and just firm to the touch. Leave the cake to cool in the tin for 10 minutes, then turn out onto a wire rack to cool completely.

5. To make the frosting, put the mascarpone cheese, sugar, coffee and cream in a bowl and beat together until smooth. Spread over the top of the cake. Spoon the melted chocolate into a paper piping bag, snip off the end and pipe thin zig-zag lines across the frosting. Leave to set.

28 Chocolate marbled loaf

Serves 8

Ingredients

55 g/2 oz plain chocolate

3 tbsp milk

70 g/2½ oz butter, plus extra for greasing

85 g/3 oz caster sugar

1 egg, beaten

3 tbsp soured cream

115 g/4 oz self-raising flour, plus extra for dusting

½ tsp baking powder

½ tsp vanilla extract

1. Preheat the oven to 160°C/325°F/Gas Mark 3. Grease a 450-g/1-lb loaf tin and line the base with baking paper. Dust the tin with flour, shaking out the excess.

2. Break up the chocolate and place in a small heatproof bowl with the milk, set over a saucepan of gently simmering water and heat until just melted. Remove from the heat.

3. Cream together the butter and sugar until light and fluffy. Beat in the egg and soured cream. Sift the flour and baking powder over the mixture, then fold in lightly and evenly using a metal spoon. Spoon half the mixture into a separate bowl and stir in the chocolate mixture. Add the vanilla extract to the plain mixture.

4. Spoon the chocolate and vanilla mixtures alternately into the prepared tin, swirling lightly with a knife or skewer for a marbled effect. Bake in the preheated oven for 40–45 minutes, or until well-risen and firm to the touch. Leave to cool in the tin for 10 minutes, then turn out onto a wire rack to cool completely.

Blueberry cheesecake bars

Ingredients

200 g/7 oz digestive biscuits, crushed

70 g/2½ oz butter, melted

175 g/6 oz blueberries

450 g/1 lb full-fat soft cheese

½ tsp vanilla extract

150 g/5½ oz caster sugar

3 eggs, beaten

150 ml/5 fl oz soured cream

1 tbsp cornflour

1. Preheat the oven to 150°C/300°F/Gas Mark 2. Grease a 28 x 18-cm/11 x 7-inch traybake tin and line with baking paper. Put the crushed biscuits into a bowl and stir in the melted butter. Press into the base of the prepared tin, levelling smooth with the back of a spoon. Chill in the refrigerator.

2. Purée half the blueberries in a blender or food processor and set aside. Put the cheese, vanilla extract and sugar into a large bowl and beat with a wooden spoon until smooth. Gradually beat in the eggs, then fold in the soured cream and cornflour.

3. Scatter the remaining blueberries over the biscuit base, then spoon over the cheesecake mixture and gently level the surface with a spatula. Drop small spoonfuls of the blueberry purée over the mixture, then cut through it with the tip of a knife to create a rippled effect.

4. Bake in the preheated oven for 50–55 minutes, or until just set. Turn off the oven and leave the cheesecake inside until cold, then transfer to the refrigerator and chill for 2–3 hours. To serve, carefully remove from the tin and cut into bars.

Apple crumb cake

Ingredients

500 g/2 lb cooking apples

175 g/6 oz butter, softened, plus extra for greasing

175 g/6 oz caster sugar

3 large eggs, beaten

2 tbsp milk

225 g/8 oz self-raising flour

1 tsp ground cinnamon

½ tsp grated nutmeg

clotted cream, to serve

Topping

85 g/3 oz self-raising flour

55 g/2 oz butter, chilled and diced

55 g/2 oz demerara sugar

55 g/2 oz blanched hazelnuts, chopped

1. Preheat the oven to 180°C/350°F/Gas Mark 4. Grease a 23-cm/9-inch round springform cake tin and line with baking paper. Peel, core and chop the apples.

2. Put the butter and caster sugar into a large bowl and beat together until pale and fluffy, then gradually beat in the eggs. Stir in the milk. Sift together the flour and spices and gently fold in until thoroughly incorporated. Spoon half the mixture into the prepared tin and scatter over half the apples. Spoon over the remaining mixture and spread evenly. Top with the remaining apples.

3. To make the topping, sift the flour into a bowl, then add the butter and rub in until the mixture resembles breadcrumbs. Stir in the demerara sugar and nuts, then sprinkle the mixture evenly over the cake.

4. Bake in the preheated oven for 1 hour, then cover loosely with foil to prevent over-browning. Cook for a further 10–20 minutes, or until golden brown and firm to the touch. Leave to cool in the tin for 20 minutes, then unclip the tin and carefully transfer to a wire rack. Serve warm or cold, with clotted cream.

Fudge blondies

Ingredients

125 g/4½ oz butter, softened, plus extra for greasing

200 g/7 oz soft light brown sugar

2 large eggs, beaten

1 tsp vanilla extract

250 g/9 oz plain flour

1 tsp baking powder

125 g/4½ oz soft butter fudge, chopped into small pieces

75 g/2¾ oz macadamia nuts, roughly chopped

icing sugar, for dusting

1. Preheat the oven to 180°C/350°F/Gas Mark 4. Grease a 20-cm/8-inch shallow square cake tin and line with baking paper.

2. Place the butter and brown sugar in a large bowl and whisk together until pale and creamy. Gradually whisk in the eggs and vanilla extract. Sift together the flour and baking powder into the mixture and beat together until well mixed.

3. Add the fudge and chopped nuts and stir together until combined. Spoon the mixture into the prepared tin and smooth the surface.

4. Bake in the preheated oven for 40–45 minutes, or until risen and golden brown. Leave to cool in the tin, then dust with sifted icing sugar and cut into squares.

32 Poppy seed streusel

Serves 12

Ingredients

225 g/8 oz self-raising flour

260 g/9¼ oz caster sugar

3 eggs, lightly beaten

finely grated rind of ½ lemon

100 ml/3½ fl oz sunflower oil

3 tbsp milk

50 g/1¾ oz poppy seeds

115 g/4 oz plain flour

70 g/2½ oz butter, at room temperature, diced, plus extra for greasing

icing sugar, for dusting

1. Preheat the oven to 160°C/325°F/Gas Mark 3. Grease a 23 x 33-cm/9 x 13-inch Swiss roll tin. Sift the self-raising flour into a large bowl. Add 175 g/6 oz of the sugar, the eggs, lemon rind, oil and milk. Beat with an electric hand-held mixer until combined. Stir in the poppy seeds. Spoon the mixture into the prepared tin, gently spreading out to the edges using a spatula.

2. Place the plain flour and butter in a bowl. Use your fingertips to rub the butter into the flour until the mixture resembles fine breadcrumbs. Stir in the remaining sugar. Spoon the streusel over the cake mixture, pressing down gently. Bake in the preheated oven for 45–50 minutes, or until the top is light golden and a skewer inserted into the cake comes out clean. Leave to cool in the tin for 20 minutes then transfer to a wire rack and leave to cool completely. Dust with icing sugar and cut into squares to serve.

#33 Bumblebee cake

Serves 8–10

Ingredients

oil or melted butter, for greasing

235 g/8½ oz plain flour

1 tbsp baking powder

350 g/12 oz butter, softened

175 g/6 oz caster sugar

3 eggs, beaten

1 tsp vanilla extract

finely grated rind of 1 lemon

4 tbsp lemon juice

250 g/9 oz icing sugar, sifted

3 tbsp clear honey

Decoration

250 g/9 oz white ready-to-roll icing

a few drops of yellow and black edible food colouring

1. Preheat the oven to 160°C/325°F/Gas Mark 3. Grease a 1.5-litre/2½-pint ovenproof pudding basin.

2. Sift the flour and baking powder into a bowl and add half of the butter, the caster sugar, eggs and vanilla extract. Beat well until smooth, then stir in the lemon rind and 2 tablespoons of the lemon juice.

3. Spoon the mixture into the prepared basin and smooth level. Bake in the preheated oven for 1¼–1½ hours, or until risen, firm and golden brown. Leave to cool in the basin for 5 minutes, then turn out onto a wire rack to finish cooling.

4. Beat together the remaining butter, the icing sugar, honey and remaining lemon juice until smooth. Slice the cake horizontally into three layers. Use about a quarter of the buttercream mixture to sandwich the layers together.

5. Using a piping bag with a large, plain nozzle, pipe the remaining mixture in lines around the cake to resemble a beehive.

6. To make the decoration, reserve a quarter of the white icing, then colour half the remainder yellow and half black. Shape into small bees, making the wings from the white icing and fixing with a dab of water. Press the bees into the frosting to stick.

32

Fruity cheesecake bars

Ingredients

oil or melted butter, for greasing

70 g/2½ oz digestive biscuits

1 tbsp soft light brown sugar

15 g/½ oz butter, melted

1 tsp water

225 g/8 oz cream cheese

55 g/2 oz clear honey

2 eggs, lightly beaten

1 tsp vanilla extract

1 tsp grated lemon rind

115 g/4 oz fresh mixed berries (blackberries, blueberries, strawberries or raspberries, diced if large)

125 g/4½ oz fresh rhubarb, diced

1. Preheat the oven to 180°C/350°F/Gas Mark 4. Grease a 20-cm/8-inch square baking tin.

2. Pulse the digestive biscuits and brown sugar in a food processor until coarsely ground. Add the melted butter and the water, and process until the mixture is moist. Press the mixture into the prepared tin in an even layer. Bake in the preheated oven for about 10–12 minutes, or until it begins to colour. Remove from the oven (do not switch off the oven) and leave to cool while you prepare the filling.

3. Beat together the cream cheese and honey with an electric hand-held mixer until smooth. Add the eggs, vanilla extract and lemon rind, and beat until fluffy.

4. Spread the cream cheese mixture on top of the cooled base in an even layer. Sprinkle the berries and rhubarb evenly over the top. Bake in the preheated oven for about 30 minutes, or until the filling is almost set. Remove from the oven and leave to cool to room temperature, then chill in the refrigerator for about 2 hours.

5. Slice into 8 bars and serve chilled.

Berry squares

Ingredients

175 g/6 oz butter, softened, plus extra for greasing

175 g/6 oz caster sugar

1 tsp vanilla extract

3 eggs, beaten

175 g/6 oz self-raising flour

55 g/2 oz dried cranberries

175 g/6 oz blueberries

200 g/7 oz mascarpone cheese, or full-fat cream cheese

100 g/3½ oz icing sugar

1. Preheat the oven to 180°C/350°F/Gas Mark 4. Grease a shallow 18 x 28-cm/7 x 11-inch rectangular cake tin and line with paper.

2. Put the butter, sugar and vanilla extract into a bowl and cream together until pale and fluffy. Gradually add the eggs, beating well after each addition.

3. Fold in the flour with a metal spoon, then stir in the cranberries and 100 g/3½ oz of the blueberries. Spoon the mixture into the prepared tin and spread evenly over the base. Bake in the preheated oven for 25–30 minutes, or until risen, firm and golden brown. Leave to cool in the tin for 15 minutes, then turn out and transfer to a wire rack to cool completely.

4. Whisk together the mascarpone cheese and icing sugar until smooth, then spread over the cake with a palette knife. Scatter the remaining blueberries over the cake and cut into 12 squares.

Cherry brownies

Makes
12

Ingredients

175 g/6 oz plain chocolate, broken into pieces

175 g/6 oz butter, plus extra for greasing

225 g/8 oz caster sugar

3 large eggs, beaten

1 tsp vanilla extract

125 g/4½ oz self-raising flour

175 g/6 oz fresh cherries, stoned

85 g/3 oz white chocolate, roughly chopped

1. Preheat the oven to 180°C/350°F/Gas Mark 4. Grease a shallow 24 x 20-cm/9½ x 8-inch cake tin and line with baking paper.

2. Put the plain chocolate and butter into a large, heatproof bowl set over a saucepan of barely simmering water and heat until melted. Remove from the heat and leave to cool for 5 minutes.

3. Whisk the sugar, eggs and vanilla extract into the chocolate mixture. Sift in the flour and fold in gently. Pour the mixture into the prepared tin. Scatter over the cherries and white chocolate. Bake in the preheated oven for 30 minutes. Loosely cover the top of the brownies with foil and bake for a further 15–20 minutes, or until just firm to the touch. Leave to cool in the tin, then cut into 12 pieces.

Rhubarb meringue bars

Makes
15

Ingredients

225 g/8 oz plain flour

150 g/5½ oz butter, at room temperature, diced, plus extra for greasing

130 g/4¾ oz caster sugar

1 large egg, lightly beaten

500 g/1 lb 2 oz young pink rhubarb stalks, trimmed and cut into 2-cm/¾-inch pieces

115 g/4 oz frozen raspberries

icing sugar, for dusting

Topping

3 large egg whites

125 g/4½ oz caster sugar

1. Preheat the oven to 180°C/350°F/Gas Mark 4. Grease a 23 x 33-cm/9 x 13-inch Swiss roll tin and line with baking paper.

2. Sift the flour into a large bowl and add the diced butter. Rub the butter into the flour until it resembles coarse breadcrumbs. Stir in 85 g/3 oz of the sugar and the egg, and mix with a round-bladed knife until beginning to clump together.

3. Turn the crumbly dough into the prepared tin and, using lightly floured hands, press out firmly into an even layer in the base of the tin. Smooth level with the back of a spoon. Bake in the preheated oven for 15 minutes until pale golden.

4. Place the rhubarb in a bowl and stir in the remaining sugar and raspberries. Spread over the baked base and return to the oven for 30 minutes. Remove from the oven and increase the oven temperature to 200°C/400°F/Gas Mark 6.

5. To make the topping, place the egg whites in a bowl and whisk until they hold stiff peaks. Gradually whisk in the sugar, one spoonful at a time, to make a firm, glossy meringue. Spread the meringue over the fruit to the edges of the tin. Return to the oven and bake for a further 5–10 minutes, or until the top of the meringue is golden. Dust with icing sugar, cut into 15 squares and serve warm or cold.

Orange poppy seed cake

Serves
10

Ingredients

oil or melted butter, for greasing
300 g/10½ oz plain flour,
plus extra for dusting
200 g/7 oz butter
200 g/7 oz golden caster sugar
3 large eggs, beaten
finely grated rind of 1 orange
55 g/2 oz poppy seeds
2 tsp baking powder
150 ml/5 fl oz milk
125 ml/4 fl oz orange juice
strips of orange zest, to decorate

Syrup

140 g/5 oz golden caster sugar
150 ml/5 fl oz orange juice

1. Preheat the oven to 160°C/325°F/Gas Mark 3. Grease and lightly flour a 1.7-litre/3-pint ring tin.

2. Cream together the butter and sugar until pale and fluffy, then add the eggs gradually, beating thoroughly after each addition. Stir in the orange rind and poppy seeds. Sift in the flour and baking powder, then fold in evenly. Add the milk and orange juice, stirring to mix evenly.

3. Spoon the mixture into the prepared tin and bake in the preheated oven for 45–50 minutes, or until firm and golden brown. Leave to cool in the tin for 10 minutes, then turn out onto a wire rack to cool completely.

4. To make the syrup, place the sugar and orange juice in a saucepan and heat gently until the sugar melts. Bring to the boil and simmer for about 5 minutes, until reduced and thickened.

5. Spoon the syrup over the cake while it is still warm. Top with the strips of orange zest and serve warm or cold.

39 Salted caramel squares

Makes
16

Ingredients

115 g/4 oz butter, softened,
plus extra for greasing
55 g/2 oz caster sugar
175 g/6 oz plain flour
55 g/2 oz ground almonds

Topping

175 g/6 oz butter
115 g/4 oz caster sugar
3 tbsp golden syrup
400 ml/14 fl oz canned condensed milk
¼ tsp sea salt crystals
85 g/3 oz plain chocolate, melted

1. Preheat the oven to 180°C/350°F/Gas Mark 4. Grease a 20-cm/8-inch shallow square cake tin. Put the butter and sugar into a bowl and beat together until pale and creamy. Sift in the flour and add the ground almonds. Knead to a crumbly dough. Press into the base of the prepared tin and prick the surface all over with a fork. Bake in the preheated oven for 15 minutes, or until pale golden. Leave to cool.

2. To make the topping, put the butter, sugar, golden syrup and condensed milk into a saucepan over a low heat and heat gently until the sugar has dissolved. Increase the heat to medium, bring to the boil, then simmer for 6–8 minutes, stirring constantly, until the mixture is very thick. Stir in half the salt, then quickly pour the caramel over the shortbread base. Sprinkle over the remaining salt.

3. Spoon the chocolate into a paper piping bag and snip off the end. Pipe the chocolate over the caramel and swirl with the tip of a knife. Leave to cool, chill for 2 hours and cut into 16 squares.

White chocolate rocky road

Ingredients

200 g/7 oz white chocolate

70 g/2½ oz butter

100 g/3½ oz shortbread biscuits

15 g/½ oz mini pink and white marshmallows

100 g/3½ oz glacé cherries, halved

1 tbsp freeze-dried raspberries

1. Line a 20-cm/8-inch square cake tin with baking paper.

2. Break the chocolate into small pieces and cut the butter into cubes. Place both in a heatproof bowl set over a saucepan of gently simmering water and heat until melted.

3. Place the biscuits in a polythene bag, seal and gently crush with a rolling pin to make small pieces. Add to the melted chocolate mixture, then stir in the marshmallows and two thirds of the cherries.

4. Spoon the mixture into the tin, spreading evenly. Place the remaining cherries on the surface and scatter over the raspberries.

5. Leave to set in a cool place for about 1 hour.

6. Cut into 20 squares and serve.

Pineapple coconut ring

Serves
12

Ingredients

432 g/15½ oz canned pineapple rings
115 g/4 oz butter, softened, plus extra
for greasing
175 g/6 oz caster sugar
2 eggs and 1 egg yolk, beaten
225 g/8 oz plain flour,
plus extra for dusting
1 tsp baking powder
½ tsp bicarbonate of soda
40 g/1½ oz desiccated coconut
175 g/6 oz cream cheese
175 g/6 oz icing sugar

1. Preheat the oven to 180°C/350°F/Gas Mark 4. Grease and lightly flour a 24-cm/9½-inch ring tin. Drain the pineapple rings, place in a blender or food processor and process briefly until just crushed.

2. Beat together the butter and caster sugar until light and fluffy. Gradually beat in the eggs until combined. Sift together the flour, baking powder and bicarbonate of soda over the egg mixture and fold in. Fold in the crushed pineapple and the coconut. Spoon the mixture into the prepared tin and bake in the preheated oven for 25 minutes, or until a skewer inserted into the centre comes out clean.

3. Leave to cool in the tin for 10 minutes, then turn out onto a wire rack to cool completely. Mix the cream cheese and icing sugar together and spread over the cooled cake.

42

Devil's food cake

Serves
10

Ingredients

140 g/5 oz plain chocolate, broken
100 ml/3½ fl oz milk
2 tbsp cocoa powder
140 g/5 oz butter, softened, plus extra
for greasing
140 g/5 oz light muscovado sugar
3 eggs, separated
4 tbsp soured cream or crème fraîche
200 g/7 oz plain flour
1 tsp bicarbonate of soda

Frosting

140 g/5 oz plain chocolate
40 g/1½ oz cocoa powder
4 tbsp soured cream or crème fraîche
1 tbsp golden syrup
40 g/1½ oz butter
4 tbsp water
200 g/7 oz icing sugar

1. Preheat the oven to 160°C/325°F/Gas Mark 3. Grease and line 2 x 20-cm/8-inch round sandwich tins.

2. Place the chocolate, milk and cocoa powder in a heatproof bowl set over a saucepan of simmering water and heat gently, stirring, until melted and smooth. Remove from the heat.

3. In a large bowl, beat together the butter and muscovado sugar until pale and creamy. Beat in the egg yolks, then beat in the soured cream and the melted chocolate mixture. Sift in the flour and bicarbonate of soda, then fold in evenly. In a separate, clean bowl, whisk the egg whites until they hold stiff peaks. Lightly fold into the mixture. Divide the mixture between the prepared cake tins, smooth the surfaces and bake in the preheated oven for 35–40 minutes, or until risen and firm to the touch. Cool in the tins for 10 minutes, then turn out onto wire racks to cool completely.

4. To make the frosting, place the chocolate, cocoa powder, soured cream, golden syrup, butter and water in a saucepan and heat gently, until melted. Remove from the heat. Sift in the icing sugar, stirring until smooth. Leave to cool, stirring occasionally, until the mixture begins to thicken.

5. Split the cakes in half horizontally with a sharp knife, to make four layers. Sandwich the cakes together with about a third of the frosting. Spread the remainder over the top and sides of the cakes, swirling with a palette knife.

43 Raspberry charlotte

Serves
8–10

Ingredients

800 g/1 lb 12 oz fresh raspberries, plus extra to decorate

9 sheets leaf gelatine

175 g/6 oz caster sugar

3–4 tbsp water, plus extra for soaking

grated rind of ½ lemon

25–30 sponge fingers

400 ml/14 fl oz whipping cream

icing sugar, to decorate

whipped cream, to serve (optional)

1. Purée the raspberries in a food processor, then pass them through a sieve to remove the seeds. Soak the gelatine in a bowl of cold water. Heat the sugar in a small saucepan with the water, stirring until the sugar crystals have dissolved. Remove the sugar syrup from the stove, squeeze the excess water out of the soaked gelatine, add to the syrup and stir to dissolve. Stir in the raspberry purée and lemon rind. Cover and chill in the refrigerator until the mixture begins to set.

2. Place a 26-cm/10½-inch cake ring on a plate. Cover the plate completely inside the ring with tightly packed sponge fingers. Completely line the ring with sponge fingers arranged vertically, leaving no gaps.

3. Whip the cream until it holds stiff peaks, then fold it into the raspberry mixture. Carefully fill the cake ring with the raspberry mixture, making sure that the sponges do not slip out of place, then smooth the top. Leave to set slightly.

4. Carefully remove the cake ring. Decorate with raspberries and dust with icing sugar. Serve chilled, with dollops of whipped cream, if using.

44 Chocolate crumble squares

Makes
12

Ingredients

1½ tbsp custard powder

175 g/6 oz caster sugar

200 ml/7 fl oz milk

175 g/6 oz butter, softened, plus extra for greasing

3 eggs

150 g/5½ oz self-raising flour, sifted

25 g/1 oz cocoa powder, sifted

Topping

50 g/1¾ oz self-raising flour

40 g/1½ oz butter, at room temperature, diced

1½ tbsp caster sugar

icing sugar, for dusting

1. Grease a 28 x 18-cm/11 x 7-inch traybake tin and line the base with baking paper. Blend the custard powder and 1½ tablespoons of the sugar with 2 tablespoons of the milk in a small heatproof bowl until smooth. Heat the remaining milk in a small saucepan until almost boiling, then whisk into the custard mixture. Return to the pan and slowly bring to the boil, stirring constantly, until smooth and thick. Pour into a clean bowl, cover the surface with a sheet of baking paper to prevent a skin forming and leave until cold. Preheat the oven to 180°C/350°F/Gas Mark 4.

2. Place the butter, remaining sugar, eggs, flour and cocoa powder in a large bowl and beat until smooth and creamy. Spoon into the prepared tin and level the surface with a spatula. Drop small dollops of custard over the top, swirling into the chocolate mixture with a knife.

3. To make the topping, place the flour and butter in a bowl and rub together. Stir in the sugar and scatter over the top of the cake. Bake in the preheated oven for 30–35 minutes. Leave to cool in the tin, then dust with icing sugar and cut into 12 squares to serve.

#45 Dorset apple cake

Serves 10

Ingredients

250 g/9 oz apples
225 g/8 oz plain flour
1 tsp baking powder
125 g/4½ oz chilled butter, diced,
plus extra for greasing
125 g/4½ oz caster sugar,
plus extra for sprinkling
finely grated rind of 1 lemon
2 eggs, beaten
whipped cream, to serve (optional)

1. Preheat the oven to 190°C/375°F/Gas Mark 5. Lightly grease a 20-cm/8-inch round springform cake tin. Peel and core the apples, cut one apple into quarters lengthways, then thinly slice the quarters vertically and set aside. Dice the remaining apples and set aside.

2. Sift together the flour and baking powder into a large bowl. Add the butter and rub it in with your fingertips until the mixture resembles breadcrumbs. Add the sugar, diced apple, lemon rind and eggs to the flour mixture and mix to a firm dough. Turn into the prepared tin and prick several times with a fork. Decorate the top of the cake with the apple slices.

3. Bake the cake in the preheated oven for 40 minutes. Remove from the oven and leave to cool for 1–2 minutes. Remove the springform, leaving the cake on the base of the tin, then transfer to a wire rack to cool completely. Sprinkle with caster sugar and serve with whipped cream, if using.

#46 Chocolate macaroon cake

Serves 10

Ingredients

85 g/3 oz plain chocolate,
broken into pieces
175 g/6 oz butter, softened, plus extra
for greasing
175 g/6 oz caster sugar
175 g/6 oz self-raising flour
½ tsp baking powder
3 large eggs, beaten
2 tbsp cocoa powder
14 chocolate macaroons
white chocolate and plain chocolate
curls, to decorate

Icing

175 g/6 oz plain chocolate,
finely chopped
450 ml/15 fl oz double cream

1. Preheat the oven to 180°C/350°F/Gas Mark 4. Grease 2 x 23-cm/9-inch sandwich tins and line with baking paper. Put the chocolate in a heatproof bowl set over a saucepan of gently simmering water and heat until melted. Remove from the heat and cool, stirring occasionally.

2. Place the butter, sugar, flour, baking powder, eggs and cocoa powder in a large bowl and beat with an electric hand-held mixer until smooth and creamy. Fold in the melted chocolate.

3. Spoon the mixture into the prepared tins and level the surfaces. Bake in the preheated oven for 20–25 minutes, or until risen and just firm to the touch. Leave to cool in the tins for 5 minutes, then turn out and leave to cool completely.

4. To make the icing, place the chocolate in a heatproof bowl. Heat 300 ml/10 fl oz of the cream in a saucepan until just boiling, then pour over the chocolate and stir until smooth. Leave to cool for 20–30 minutes, stirring occasionally, until thick enough to spread. Whip the remaining cream until it holds soft peaks.

5. Sandwich the cakes together with one third of the chocolate icing and all the whipped cream. Spread the remaining icing over the top and sides of the cake. Gently press the macaroon shells onto the icing around the side of the cake. Decorate the top with chocolate curls.

Coconut layer cake

Ingredients

6 large eggs, beaten

175 g/6 oz caster sugar

175 g/6 oz plain flour

70 g/2½ oz desiccated coconut

55 g/2 oz butter, melted and cooled, plus extra for greasing

toasted coconut shavings, to decorate

Frosting

250 g/9 oz mascarpone cheese

4 tbsp coconut milk

25 g/1 oz caster sugar

150 ml/5 fl oz double cream

1. Preheat the oven to 180°C/350°F/Gas Mark 4. Grease 3 x 20-cm/8-inch round sandwich tins and line with baking paper.

2. Put the eggs and sugar into a large, heatproof bowl set over a saucepan of simmering water. Beat with an electric hand-held mixer until the mixture is thick and pale, and leaves a trail when the whisk is lifted.

3. Sift in half of the flour and gently fold into the whisked mixture, then sift and fold in the remaining flour, followed by the coconut. Pour the butter over the mixture in a thin stream and fold in until just incorporated.

4. Divide the mixture between the prepared tins and bake in the preheated oven for 20–25 minutes, or until light golden and springy to the touch. Leave to cool in the tins for 5 minutes, then turn out onto a wire rack to cool completely.

5. To make the frosting, put the mascarpone cheese, coconut milk and sugar into a bowl and beat together until smooth. Whip the cream until it holds soft peaks, then fold it into the mixture. Sandwich the cakes together with one third of the frosting and spread the remainder over the top and sides of the cake. Decorate with coconut shavings.

Blueberry slices

Ingredients

250 g/9 oz plain flour, plus extra for dusting

1 tsp baking powder

175 g/6 oz butter, at room temperature, diced, plus extra for greasing

85 g/3 oz caster sugar

1 egg, lightly beaten

Topping

2 eggs

150 ml/5 fl oz whipping cream

55 g/2 oz caster sugar

4 tbsp blueberry jam

200 g/7 oz fresh blueberries

1. Preheat the oven to 180°C/350°F/Gas Mark 4. Grease a 23 x 33-cm/9 x 13-inch Swiss roll tin and line with baking paper. Sift together the flour and baking powder into a large bowl and add the butter. Rub the butter into the flour until it resembles coarse breadcrumbs. Stir in the sugar and egg and mix with a round-bladed knife until beginning to clump together.

2. Gather the dough together and knead lightly on a floured surface. Press the dough into the base of the prepared tin in an even layer, using floured hands. Prick all over with the prongs of a fork. Bake in the preheated oven for 15 minutes. Remove from the oven and leave to cool.

3. To make the topping, place the eggs, cream and sugar in a bowl and whisk together until smooth. Spread the jam over the base then gently spoon over the eggs and cream mixture. Scatter over the blueberries and return to the oven for 25 minutes. Cut into slices and serve warm or cold.

Piñata party cake

Ingredients

450 g/1 lb butter, softened,
plus extra for greasing

450 g/1 lb caster sugar

8 large eggs, beaten

450 g/1 lb self-raising flour

115 g/4 oz plain flour

4 tbsp milk

Frosting

100 g/3½ oz white chocolate, broken

200 g/7 oz butter, softened

400 g/14 oz icing sugar, sifted

Filling & decoration

280 g/10 oz mixed sweets such as jelly
babies, jelly beans and sugar-coated
chocolate drops

2 tbsp pastel-coloured confetti sugar
sprinkles

1. Preheat the oven to 160°C/325°F/Gas Mark 3. Thoroughly grease 2 x 2-litre/3½-pint ovenproof bowls. Put the butter and sugar into a large bowl and beat with an electric hand-held mixer until pale and creamy. Gradually beat in the eggs a little at a time. Sift together the self-raising flour and plain flour, then fold into the creamed mixture with the milk. Divide the mixture evenly between the prepared bowls, making a dip in the centre. Bake in the preheated oven for 50 minutes, then loosely cover each bowl with foil and bake for a further 20–30 minutes, or until firm to the touch and a skewer inserted in the centre of the cakes comes out clean. Leave to cool in the bowls for 10 minutes, then turn out onto a wire rack to cool completely. Wrap the cold cakes in foil and chill in the refrigerator for 4–5 hours or overnight.

2. To make the frosting, put the chocolate in a heatproof bowl set over a saucepan of gently simmering water and heat until melted. Remove from the heat and leave to cool for 15 minutes. Put the butter into a large bowl and gradually beat in the sugar, then beat in the melted chocolate.

3. To assemble, level the top of each cake with a serrated knife. Scoop out the centres of the cakes, leaving a 4-cm/1½-inch border. Place one cake, cut-side up, on a flat plate or board covered with a sheet of baking paper. Spread some of the frosting around the rim of the cake and pile the sweets and half of the sprinkles into the centre. Invert the second cake on top to enclose the sweets and make a globe-shaped cake, pressing down gently to seal. Using a palette knife, spread a thin layer of frosting all over the cake to secure any loose crumbs, then chill in the refrigerator for 1 hour. Spread the remaining frosting in a thick layer over the cake and decorate with the remaining sugar sprinkles. Carefully transfer to a serving plate.

#50 Swiss roll

Serves 8

Ingredients

oil or melted butter, for greasing

150 g/5½ oz plain flour

1½ tsp baking powder

175 g/6 oz butter, softened

175 g/6 oz caster sugar,
plus extra for sprinkling

3 eggs, beaten

1 tsp vanilla extract

2 tbsp milk

115 g/4 oz raspberry jam, warmed

1. Preheat the oven to 180°C/350°F/Gas Mark 4. Grease a 23 x 33-cm/9 x 13-inch Swiss roll tin and line with baking paper, making sure the paper comes 1 cm/½ inch above the rim. Lay a sheet of baking paper on the work surface and sprinkle with caster sugar.

2. Sift together the flour and baking powder into a large bowl and add the butter, sugar, eggs and vanilla extract. Beat well until the mixture is smooth, then beat in the milk. Spoon the mixture into the prepared tin and smooth into the corners with a palette knife. Bake in the preheated oven for 15–20 minutes, or until risen, firm and golden brown.

3. Turn the sponge out onto the sugared baking paper and spread with the jam. Roll up the sponge firmly from one short side to enclose the jam, using the paper to hold it in place.

4. Transfer to a wire rack and leave to cool, then remove the paper and sprinkle with caster sugar. Cut into 8 slices and serve.

#51 Choc cheesecake bars

Makes 12

Ingredients

250 g/9 oz plain flour

2 tsp baking powder

3 tbsp cocoa powder

140 g/5 oz butter, plus extra for greasing

140 g/5 oz caster sugar

1 egg

icing sugar and chopped hazelnuts,
for sprinkling

Filling

250 g/9 oz butter, softened

280 g/10 oz caster sugar

2 tsp vanilla extract

4 eggs, lightly beaten

750 g/1 lb 10 oz cream cheese

100 ml/3½ fl oz whipping cream

1 tbsp cornflour

1. Preheat the oven to 160°C/325°F/Gas Mark 3. Grease a 20 x 30-cm/8 x 12-inch baking tray, at least 5 cm/2 inches deep.

2. To make the base, sift together the flour, baking powder and cocoa powder into a large bowl. Rub in the butter and sugar, then add the egg and mix to a crumbly dough. Spread three quarters of the mixture on the prepared baking tray, pressing firmly into the base and up the sides. Reserve the remaining mixture.

3. To make the filling, beat together the butter, sugar and vanilla extract in a large bowl. Gradually beat in the eggs. Add the cheese, cream and cornflour, and beat until smooth.

4. Spread the cheesecake mixture onto the base and smooth flat with a spatula. Break apart the reserved crumble mixture with your fingertips and sprinkle over the top.

5. Bake in the preheated oven for 1¼ hours. Leave to cool completely, then carefully remove from the baking tray. Dust with icing sugar, sprinkle with chopped hazelnuts and cut into 12 bars.

Chocolate brownies

Makes
25

Ingredients

115 g/4 oz lightly salted butter, cut into pieces, plus extra for greasing

100 g/3½ oz plain chocolate, roughly chopped

2 eggs

175 g/6 oz light muscovado sugar

2 tsp vanilla extract

55 g/2 oz plain flour

25 g/1 oz cocoa powder

40 g/1½ oz pecan nuts or walnuts, roughly chopped

1. Preheat the oven to 200°C/400°F/Gas Mark 6. Grease and line an 18-cm/7-inch shallow, loose-based square cake tin. Put the butter and chocolate in a heatproof bowl set over a saucepan of gently simmering water and heat until melted. Leave to cool slightly.

2. Put the eggs, sugar and vanilla extract in a bowl and beat with an electric hand-held mixer until the mixture begins to turn frothy. Stir in the chocolate mixture until combined. Sift together the flour and cocoa powder into the bowl and scatter in the nuts. Stir gently, then turn into the prepared tin and level the surface.

3. Bake in the preheated oven for 18–20 minutes, or until the crust feels dry but gives a little when gently pressed. (If you're unsure, it's better to slightly under-cook brownies.) Leave to cool in the tin for 10 minutes, then transfer to a wire rack to cool completely. Cut into 25 squares.

53 Mulled sponge loaf

Serves
8

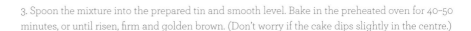

Ingredients

oil or melted butter, for greasing

175 g/6 oz plain flour

1 tbsp baking powder

1 tsp ground mixed spice

175 g/6 oz butter, softened

175 g/6 oz light muscovado sugar

3 eggs, beaten

1 tsp vanilla extract

finely grated rind of 1 orange

2 tbsp orange juice

70 g/2½ oz icing sugar

100 ml/3½ fl oz port or red wine

1 star anise

Decoration

10 fresh cranberries

10 fresh bay leaves

1 egg white

caster sugar, for sprinkling

1. Preheat the oven to 180°C/350°F/Gas Mark 4. Grease a 1.2-litre/2-pint loaf tin and line with baking paper.

2. Sift together the flour, baking powder and mixed spice into a large bowl and add the butter, muscovado sugar, eggs and vanilla extract. Beat well until the mixture is smooth, then stir in the orange rind and juice.

3. Spoon the mixture into the prepared tin and smooth level. Bake in the preheated oven for 40–50 minutes, or until risen, firm and golden brown. (Don't worry if the cake dips slightly in the centre.)

4. Remove the tin from the oven and stand it on a wire rack. Place the icing sugar, port and star anise in a saucepan and gently heat until boiling. Boil rapidly for 2–3 minutes to reduce slightly. Remove and discard the star anise.

5. Spoon the syrup over the cake and leave to soak for 30 minutes. Turn out the cake from the tin, upside down.

6. Brush the cranberries and bay leaves with egg white and sprinkle with caster sugar, then arrange on top of the cake.

Glazed fruit & nut cake

Serves
10

Ingredients

oil or melted butter, for greasing

250 g/9 oz plain flour, plus extra for dusting

1 tbsp baking powder

1 tsp ground mixed spice

175 g/6 oz butter, softened

175 g/6 oz dark muscovado sugar

3 eggs, beaten

1 tsp vanilla extract

2 tbsp milk

300 g/10½ oz mixed dried fruit

85 g/3 oz chopped mixed nuts

Decoration

3 tbsp clear honey, warmed

350 g/12 oz mixed glacé fruits, such as pineapple, cherries and orange

55 g/2 oz whole shelled nuts, such as Brazil nuts, almonds and walnuts

1. Preheat the oven to 160°C/325°F/Gas Mark 3. Grease and lightly flour a 23-cm/9-inch round springform cake tin.

2. Sift together the flour, baking powder and mixed spice into a large bowl and add the butter, sugar, eggs and vanilla extract. Beat well until the mixture is smooth, then stir in the milk, dried fruit and nuts.

3. Spoon the mixture into the prepared tin and smooth level. Bake in the preheated oven for about 1 hour, or until risen, firm and golden brown.

4. Leave to cool in the tin for 30 minutes, then remove the springform and transfer the cake to a wire rack to cool completely.

5. Brush the top of the cake with a little of the warmed honey, then arrange the glacé fruits and whole shelled nuts on top. Brush with the remaining honey and leave to set.

Guava bars

Makes
9

Ingredients

250 g/9 oz plain flour

350 g/12 oz soft light brown sugar

½ tsp bicarbonate of soda

¼ tsp salt

150 g/5½ oz porridge oats

225 g/8 oz butter, softened, plus extra for greasing

150 ml/5 fl oz clear honey

425 g/15 oz ready-made guava paste, sliced

1. Preheat the oven to 200°C/400°F/Gas Mark 6. Lightly grease a 20 x 30-cm/8 x 12-inch traybake tin.

2. Mix together the flour, sugar, bicarbonate of soda, salt and oats. Add the butter and rub in until the mixture resembles breadcrumbs. Add the honey and mix well. Press half the crumble mixture into the prepared tin.

3. Cut the guava paste into thin strips and lay them on top of the crumble. Cover with the remaining crumble mixture and lightly press into place using the back of a fork. Bake in the preheated oven for 30 minutes until golden brown. Remove from the oven and leave to cool in the tray.

4. Cut into strips about the size of a muesli bar and serve.

#56 Choc & ginger flapjacks

Makes 12

Ingredients

215 g/7½ oz butter, plus extra for greasing

115 g/4 oz soft light brown sugar

3 tbsp golden syrup

1 tbsp stem ginger syrup

2 pieces stem ginger, finely chopped

350 g/12 oz rolled oats

175 g/6 oz plain chocolate, broken

1. Preheat the oven to 180°C/350°F/Gas Mark 4. Grease a 28 x 18-cm/11 x 7-inch shallow baking tin.

2. Put 175 g/6 oz of the butter, the sugar, golden syrup and stem ginger syrup into a large saucepan over a low heat and gently heat until melted. Remove from the heat and stir in the ginger and oats.

3. Spoon the mixture into the prepared tin and smooth the surface. Bake in the preheated oven for 15–20 minutes, or until pale golden. Leave to cool in the tin.

4. To make the topping, put the chocolate and the remaining butter into a heatproof bowl set over a saucepan of gently simmering water and heat until melted. Stir until smooth, then spread over the cooled flapjacks. Chill in the refrigerator for 1 hour, or until set. Cut into 12 bars.

#57 Chocolate coffee cake

Serves 10

Ingredients

40 g/1½ oz butter, plus extra for greasing

85 g/3 oz white chocolate, broken

125 g/4½ oz caster sugar

4 large eggs, beaten

2 tbsp very strong black coffee

1 tsp vanilla extract

125 g/4½ oz plain flour

Frosting

175 g/6 oz white chocolate, broken into pieces

85 g/3 oz butter

125 g/4½ oz crème fraîche

125 g/4½ oz icing sugar, sifted

1 tbsp coffee liqueur

1. Preheat the oven to 180°C/350°F/Gas Mark 4. Grease 2 x 20-cm/8-inch sandwich tins and line with baking paper. Place the butter and chocolate in a bowl set over a saucepan of gently simmering water and heat until just melted. Stir to mix, then remove from the heat. Place the sugar, eggs, coffee and vanilla extract in a bowl set over a saucepan of hot water and whisk until it leaves a trail when the whisk is lifted.

2. Remove from the heat, sift in the flour and mix in lightly and evenly. Quickly stir in the butter and chocolate mixture, then divide the mixture between the prepared tins. Bake in the preheated oven for 25–30 minutes, until risen, golden brown and springy to the touch. Leave to cool in the tins for 2 minutes, then turn out onto wire racks to cool completely.

3. To make the frosting, place the chocolate and butter in a bowl set over a saucepan of gently simmering water and heat until melted. Remove from the heat, stir in the crème fraîche, then add the icing sugar and coffee liqueur, and mix. Chill the icing until thick. Use one third of the icing to sandwich the cakes together, then spread the remainder over the cake.

58 Berry meringue cake

Serves
12

Ingredients

3 egg yolks

150 g/5½ oz caster sugar

2 tsp vanilla extract

100 ml/3½ fl oz milk

100 g/3½ oz butter, plus extra
for greasing

280 g/10 oz plain flour, plus extra
for dusting

2 tsp baking powder

Topping

3 egg whites

100 g/3½ oz caster sugar

1 tsp cornflour

200 g/7 oz redcurrants, removed
from stalks

200 g/7 oz blueberries

icing sugar, for dusting

1. Preheat the oven to 180°C/350°F/Gas Mark 4. Grease and lightly flour a 28-cm/11-inch round springform cake tin.

2. Put the egg yolks, sugar and vanilla extract in a bowl and beat with an electric hand-held mixer until fluffy.

3. Bring the milk and butter to the boil in a small saucepan over a medium heat, pour into the egg and sugar mixture and beat together until very thick. Sift together the flour and baking powder into a bowl and gently fold in the milk mixture. Pour into the prepared tin and bake in the preheated oven for about 18 minutes, until pale golden. Remove from the oven and leave to cool. Do not switch off the oven.

4. To make the topping, whisk the egg whites until they hold stiff peaks. Gradually whisk in the sugar, 1 tablespoon at a time until the mixture is firm and glossy. Fold in the cornflour. Pick through the berries, reserving 1 tablespoon of each kind, then gently fold the remaining berries into the meringue. Spread the meringue over the cake.

5. Scatter the reserved berries on top of the meringue. Increase the oven temperature to 220°C/425°F/Gas Mark 7, place the cake on the middle shelf and bake for a further 10–15 minutes. Leave to cool, dust with icing sugar and serve.

59 Orange squares

Makes
12

Ingredients

2 eggs, separated

125 g/4½ oz sugar

grated rind of 1 orange

25 g/1 oz sponge cake crumbs

15 g/½ oz plain flour

85 g/3 oz ground almonds

15 g/½ oz butter, melted,
plus extra for greasing

Glaze

6 tbsp caster sugar

2½ tbsp apricot jam

250 ml/8½ fl oz orange juice

pared zest of 1 large orange

1. Preheat the oven to 190°C/375°F/Gas Mark 5 and grease a 20 x 30-cm/8 x 12-inch baking tray.

2. To make the base, use an electric hand-held mixer to whisk the egg yolks with half of the sugar and the orange rind until fluffy. Beat the egg whites until forming firm peaks, gradually whisking in the remaining sugar as you beat. Fold the whipped egg white into the egg yolk mixture. Add the cake crumbs with the flour, ground almonds and melted butter and mix to combine. Spoon the mixture into the prepared baking tray and smooth it flat. Bake in the preheated oven for about 40–45 minutes. Leave to cool in the tray for 5 minutes and then transfer to a wire rack to cool completely.

3. To make the glaze, put the sugar, apricot jam, orange juice and zest in a saucepan. Boil it down to about two thirds of the original volume, remove the zest and brush over the cake. Cut the cake into 12 squares and serve.

#60 Polenta & blueberry sticky loaf cake

Serves
10

Ingredients

150 g/5½ oz butter, softened
225 g/8 oz caster sugar
3 eggs, beaten
150 g/5½ oz polenta
100 g/3½ oz ground almonds
2 tsp baking powder
150 g/5½ oz blueberries
finely grated zest and juice of 1 lemon

1. Preheat the oven to 180°C/350°F/Gas Mark 4. Line a 900-g/2-lb loaf tin with baking paper.

2. Cream the butter with 175 g/6 oz of the sugar until pale, light and fluffy. Add the eggs, polenta, ground almonds and baking powder, and gently beat to combine. Fold in the blueberries and lemon zest, then pour the mixture into the prepared tin.

3. Bake in the preheated oven for 35–40 minutes until golden and risen, and a skewer inserted in the centre of the cake comes out clean.

4. To make the glaze, put the remaining sugar in a small saucepan with the lemon juice. Bring to the boil and boil for 1–2 minutes, until slightly thickened and syrupy.

5. Remove the cake from the oven and leave in the tin. Pierce the surface all over with a cocktail stick and pour the syrup over the cake. Leave to cool completely before turning out of the tin. Cut into 10 slices to serve.

Sesame, marshmallow & cranberry squares

Ingredients

150 g/5½ oz rolled oats

55 g/2 oz sesame seeds

40 g/1½ oz soft light brown sugar

35 g/1¼ oz mini marshmallows

70 g/2½ oz dried cranberries

8 tbsp clear honey

5 tbsp sunflower oil, plus extra
for greasing

a few drops of vanilla extract

1. Preheat the oven to 160°C/325°F/Gas Mark 3. Lightly grease a 28 x 18-cm/11 x 7-inch baking tin and line the base with baking paper.

2. Put the oats, sesame seeds, sugar, marshmallows and cranberries into a mixing bowl and stir. Make a well in the centre, add the honey, oil and vanilla extract, then stir again.

3. Press the mixture into the prepared tin and level using a metal spoon. Bake in the preheated oven for 20 minutes, or until golden and bubbling.

4. Leave to cool in the tin for 10 minutes, then cut into 20 squares. Leave to cool completely before turning out of the tin.

Coconut slices

Ingredients

125 g/4½ oz butter,
plus extra for greasing

225 g/8 oz golden caster sugar

2 eggs, beaten

finely grated rind of 1 orange

4 tbsp orange juice

150 ml/5 fl oz soured cream

140 g/5 oz self-raising flour

175 g/6 oz desiccated coconut

1 egg white

200 g/7 oz icing sugar

toasted shredded coconut, to decorate

1. Preheat the oven to 180°C/350°F/Gas Mark 4. Grease a 23-cm/9-inch square cake tin and line the base with baking paper.

2. Cream together the butter and caster sugar until pale and fluffy, then gradually beat in the eggs. Stir in the orange rind, 3 tablespoons of the orange juice and the soured cream. Evenly fold in the flour and half of the desiccated coconut using a metal spoon.

3. Spoon the mixture into the prepared tin and level the surface. Bake in the preheated oven for 35–40 minutes, or until risen and firm to the touch. Leave to cool in the tin for 10 minutes, then turn out onto a wire rack and leave to cool completely.

4. Lightly beat the egg white, then stir in the icing sugar and the remaining desiccated coconut, adding enough of the remaining orange juice to mix to a thick paste. Spread over the top of the cake, sprinkle with toasted shredded coconut, then leave to set before slicing.

#63 Cinnamon & walnut cake

Serves
10

Ingredients

250 g/9 oz soft light brown sugar

250 g/9 oz plain flour

2 tsp ground cinnamon, plus extra for dusting

1 tsp bicarbonate of soda

3 eggs, beaten

200 ml/7 fl oz sunflower oil, plus extra for greasing

125 g/4½ oz walnuts, finely chopped

1 large ripe banana (about 175 g/6 oz unpeeled weight), mashed

walnut pieces, to decorate

Frosting

175 g/6 oz cream cheese

225 g/8 oz butter, softened

1 tsp ground cinnamon

225 g/8 oz icing sugar, sifted

1. Preheat the oven to 180°C/350°F/Gas Mark 4. Grease 3 x 20-cm/8-inch sandwich tins and line with baking paper.

2. Put the sugar into a large bowl and sift in the flour, cinnamon and bicarbonate of soda. Add the eggs, oil, walnuts and banana and beat with a wooden spoon until thoroughly mixed.

3. Divide the mixture between the prepared tins and gently smooth the surfaces. Bake in the preheated oven for 20–25 minutes, or until golden brown and firm to the touch. Leave to cool in the tins for 10 minutes, then turn out onto wire racks to cool completely.

4. To make the frosting, put the cheese, butter and cinnamon into a bowl and beat together until smooth and creamy. Stir in the icing sugar and mix until smooth.

5. Sandwich the three cakes together with one third of the frosting and spread the remainder over the top and sides of the cake. Decorate with the walnut pieces and a dusting of cinnamon.

#64 Chocolate babka loaf

Makes
9

Ingredients

6 egg yolks

175 g/6 oz butter, melted, plus extra for greasing

200 g/7 oz caster sugar

½ tsp salt

275 ml/9 fl oz milk

5 tsp easy-blend dried yeast

475 g/1 lb 1 oz plain flour, plus extra for dusting

225 g/8 oz plain chocolate, roughly chopped

1 tbsp cocoa powder

½ tsp ground cinnamon

100 g/3½ oz walnuts, roughly chopped

icing sugar, for dusting

1. Whisk the egg yolks in a bowl, then gradually add the butter. Add half of the sugar and salt, and stir to combine. Heat the milk in a small saucepan until lukewarm. Add the yeast and stir. Sift the flour into a large bowl, then pour in the egg mixture and milk, stirring constantly. Mix until a smooth, elastic dough forms. Transfer to a bowl, cover with clingfilm and chill in the refrigerator for 1½ hours. Put the chocolate, cocoa powder and cinnamon into a food processor and process until fine crumbs form. Combine the chocolate mixture with the remaining sugar.

2. Grease a 25-cm/10-inch loaf tin and line a baking tray with baking paper. Turn out the dough onto a lightly floured work surface, then roll out to a 25-cm/10-inch square. Place on the prepared tray. Spread the chocolate mixture on the dough, top with the walnuts, then fold over the two opposite sides of the square to meet in the middle, and press down. Place in the prepared tin, with the joins at the base, cover with a damp tea towel and leave to rise for 1 hour. Meanwhile, preheat the oven to 180°C/350°F/Gas Mark 4. Bake the loaf in the middle of the preheated oven for 40–45 minutes, until golden brown. Leave to cool in the tin for 10 minutes, then turn out onto a wire rack and leave to cool completely. Dust with icing sugar and serve.

Crisp chocolate bites

Makes 12

Ingredients

115 g/4 oz butter, plus extra
for greasing

3 tbsp golden syrup

150 g/5½ oz white chocolate, broken
into small pieces

125 g/4½ oz toasted rice cereal

125 g/4½ oz plain chocolate,
broken into small pieces

1. Grease and line the base of a 20-cm/8-inch square
cake tin.

2. Put half of the butter, 1 tablespoon of the golden syrup
and the white chocolate in a bowl set over a saucepan of gently simmering water and heat until
melted. Remove from the heat and stir in 50 g/1¾ oz of the rice cereal until well combined. Press
into the prepared tin and smooth the surface.

3. Put the remaining butter, golden syrup and plain chocolate in a bowl set over a saucepan of
gently simmering water and heat until melted. Remove from the heat and stir in the remaining rice
cereal. Pour over the hardened white chocolate layer, leave to cool, then chill until hardened.

Rich chocolate rum torte

Serves 8

Ingredients

oil or melted butter, for greasing

70 g/2½ oz plain chocolate, broken
into pieces

2 tbsp milk

175 g/6 oz plain flour

1 tbsp baking powder

175 g/6 oz butter, softened

175 g/6 oz dark muscovado sugar

3 eggs, beaten

1 tsp vanilla extract

chocolate curls or grated chocolate,
to decorate

Frosting

225 g/8 oz plain chocolate, broken
into pieces

225 ml/8 fl oz double cream

2 tbsp dark rum

1. Preheat the oven to 180°C/350°F/Gas Mark 4. Grease and
line 3 x 18-cm/7-inch sandwich cake tins.

2. Place the chocolate and milk in a small saucepan and
heat gently, without boiling, until melted. Stir and remove from the heat.

3. Sift together the flour and baking powder into a large bowl and add the butter, sugar, eggs and
vanilla extract. Beat well until smooth, then stir in the chocolate mixture.

4. Divide the mixture between the prepared tins and smooth level. Bake in the preheated oven for
20–25 minutes, until risen and firm to the touch. Leave to cool in the tins for 5 minutes, then turn
out onto wire racks to finish cooling.

5. To make the frosting, melt the chocolate with the cream and rum in a small saucepan over a low
heat. Remove from the heat and leave to cool, stirring occasionally, until the frosting reaches a
spreadable consistency.

6. Sandwich the cakes together with one third of the chocolate frosting, then spread the remainder
over the top and sides of the cake, swirling with a palette knife. Sprinkle with chocolate curls and
leave to set.

#67 Morello cherry cake

Ingredients

250 g/9 oz self-raising flour, plus extra for dusting

90 g/3¼ oz caster sugar

large pinch of cinnamon

125 g/4½ oz cold butter, cut into small dice, plus extra for greasing

1 egg, lightly beaten

Filling & topping

750 g/1 lb 10 oz medium-fat soft cheese or quark

2 tbsp lemon juice

55 g/2 oz cornflour

3 eggs, lightly beaten

125 g/4½ oz caster sugar

2 tsp vanilla extract

350 g/12 oz (drained weight) Morello cherries from a jar

icing sugar, for dusting

1. Grease a 28-cm/11-inch round springform cake tin and line with baking paper.

2. To make the cake, sift together the flour, sugar and cinnamon in a bowl. Add the diced butter and rub into the flour mixture with your fingers until it resembles coarse breadcrumbs. Add the beaten egg and knead the mixture to a smooth dough. Wrap in clingfilm and leave to rest in the refrigerator for 30 minutes. Preheat the oven to 160°C/325°F/Gas Mark 3.

3. Roll the dough out on a floured surface, put it in the base of the prepared tin, press up the sides and prick several times with a fork. Bake in the preheated oven for about 20 minutes, or until lightly browned, remove and leave in the tin to cool. Leave the oven switched on.

4. To make the filling, mix together the cheese, lemon juice and cornflour in a bowl until smooth and creamy. Beat the eggs, caster sugar and vanilla extract until light and fluffy and stir into the cheese mixture.

5. Spoon the filling into the cake base. Arrange the drained cherries over the filling and continue baking for a further 50 minutes, until set and golden. Leave to cool. Remove the baking paper and dust with icing sugar before serving.

#68 Icebox chocolate cake

Ingredients

225 g/8 oz plain chocolate, broken into pieces

225 g/8 oz butter, plus extra for greasing

3 tbsp black coffee

55 g/2 oz soft light brown sugar

a few drops of vanilla extract

225 g/8 oz digestive biscuits, crushed

85 g/3 oz raisins

85 g/3 oz walnuts, chopped

1. Grease and line a 450-g/1-lb loaf tin. Place the chocolate, butter, coffee, sugar and vanilla extract in a saucepan over a low heat and stir until the chocolate and butter have melted, the sugar has dissolved and the mixture is well combined.

2. Stir in the crushed biscuits, raisins and walnuts, and stir well.

3. Spoon the mixture into the prepared tin. Leave to set for 1–2 hours in the refrigerator, then turn out and cut into thin slices to serve.

Frosted fruits cake

Ingredients

280 g/10 oz butter, softened,
plus extra for greasing

280 g/10 oz caster sugar

5 eggs, beaten

1 tbsp vanilla extract

280 g/10 oz self-raising flour

3 tbsp milk

5 tbsp raspberry or strawberry jam

150 ml/5 fl oz double cream

350–400 g/12–14 oz summer fruits, such as
strawberries, raspberries and blueberries

icing sugar, for sprinkling

Frosting

200 g/7 oz cream cheese

100 g/3½ oz butter, softened

1 tsp lemon juice

100 g/3½ oz icing sugar

pink food colouring

1. Preheat the oven to 180°C/350°F/Gas Mark 4. Grease 2 x 20-cm/8-inch sandwich tins and line with baking paper. Put the butter and caster sugar into a bowl and beat together until pale and creamy. Gradually beat in the eggs, then stir in the vanilla extract. Sift in the flour and fold in gently. Stir in the milk. Divide the mixture between the prepared tins. Bake in the preheated oven for 35–40 minutes, or until springy to the touch. Turn out onto wire racks to cool.

2. Place one of the cakes on a flat serving plate and spread with the jam. Whip the cream until it just holds its shape. Spread the cream over the jam, almost to the edges of the cake. Position the second cake on top, pressing down gently until the cream is level with the edges of the cake.

3. To make the frosting, beat together the cream cheese and butter. Add the lemon juice and icing sugar and beat until light and creamy. Beat a dash of pink food colouring into the frosting to colour it a very pale shade of pink. Using a palette knife, spread a very thin layer over the top and sides of the cake to seal in the crumbs. The cake will still show through at this stage but will be covered by the second layer of frosting. Chill in the refrigerator for 15 minutes.

4. Use the palette knife to spread a thicker layer of frosting around the sides of the cake. Spread the remainder over the top. Once evenly covered, use the edge of the palette knife to swirl the frosting as smoothly or as roughly as you like. Arrange the fruit on top of the cake. Put a little icing sugar in a small, fine sieve and gently tap it over the fruit to lightly frost.

Chocolate pecan blondies

Makes
12

Ingredients

250 g/9 oz white chocolate, broken into pieces

40 g/1½ oz butter, plus extra for greasing

175 g/6 oz plain chocolate

2 large eggs, beaten

85 g/3 oz caster sugar

115 g/4 oz self-raising flour

100 g/3½ oz pecan nuts, roughly chopped

1. Preheat the oven to 180°C/350°F/Gas Mark 4. Grease a 20-cm/8-inch shallow square baking tin and line with baking paper.

2. Place 85 g/3 oz of the white chocolate in a heatproof bowl and add the butter. Set the bowl over a saucepan of gently simmering water and heat, stirring occasionally, until melted and smooth. Meanwhile, roughly chop the remaining white chocolate and the plain chocolate.

3. Beat the eggs and sugar together in a large bowl, then stir in the melted chocolate mixture. Sift the flour over the top. Add the chopped chocolate and pecan nuts, and mix well.

4. Spoon the mixture into the prepared tin and smooth the surface. Bake in the preheated oven for 35–40 minutes, or until golden brown and just firm to the touch in the centre. Leave in the tin to cool completely, then turn out and cut into 12 pieces.

71 Glazed gingerbread

Serves
12

Ingredients

250 g/9 oz plain flour

1 tsp bicarbonate of soda

1½ tsp ground ginger

1 tsp ground mixed spice

115 g/4 oz butter, plus extra for greasing

115 g/4 oz light muscovado sugar

150 g/5½ oz golden syrup

85 g/3 oz black treacle

2 large eggs, beaten

2 tbsp milk

Icing

115 g/4 oz icing sugar

1 tbsp stem ginger syrup

1–2 tbsp water

1 piece stem ginger, finely chopped

1. Preheat the oven to 160°C/325°F/Gas Mark 3. Grease an 18-cm/7-inch square cake tin and line with baking paper.

2. Sift together the flour, bicarbonate of soda, ginger and mixed spice into a large bowl. Put the butter, sugar, golden syrup and treacle in a saucepan and heat gently, stirring constantly, until the butter has melted. Leave to cool for 5 minutes.

3. Stir the melted mixture into the flour mixture and mix well. Add the eggs and milk, and beat until thoroughly incorporated.

4. Spoon the mixture into the prepared tin and bake in the preheated oven for 1–1¼ hours, or until well risen and firm to the touch. Leave to cool in the tin for 15 minutes, then turn out onto a wire rack to cool completely.

5. To make the icing, sift the icing sugar into a bowl. Stir in the stem ginger syrup and enough of the water to make a smooth icing that just coats the back of a wooden spoon. Spoon the icing over the top of the cake, allowing it to run down the sides. Scatter over the stem ginger and leave to set.

Cherry & almond cake

Serves
8

Ingredients

300 g/10½ oz glacé cherries

175 g/6 oz butter, softened, plus extra
for greasing

175 g/6 oz golden caster sugar

3 eggs

40 g/1½ oz ground almonds

280 g/10 oz plain flour

1½ tsp baking powder

70 g/2½ oz flaked almonds

1. Preheat the oven to 160°C/325°F/Gas Mark 3. Grease an
18-cm/7-inch square cake tin and line with baking paper.

2. Cut the cherries in half, then put them in a sieve and rinse to remove all the syrup. Pat dry with
kitchen paper and set aside.

3. Put the butter, sugar, eggs and ground almonds in a bowl. Sift in the flour and baking powder.
Beat thoroughly until smooth, then stir in the cherries. Spoon the mixture into the prepared tin
and smooth the top. Sprinkle the flaked almonds over the cake. Bake in the preheated oven for
1½ –1¾ hours, until well risen and a skewer inserted into the centre of the cake comes out clean.

4. Leave to cool in the tin for 10 minutes, then turn out onto a wire rack to cool completely.

73 Date & walnut cake

Serves
8

Ingredients

100 g/3½ oz dried dates,
stoned and chopped

½ tsp bicarbonate of soda

finely grated rind of ½ lemon

100 ml/3½ fl oz hot black tea

40 g/1½ oz butter,
plus extra for greasing

70 g/2½ oz light muscovado sugar

1 small egg

125 g/4½ oz self-raising flour

25 g/1 oz walnuts, chopped

walnut halves, to decorate

1. Preheat the oven to 180°C/350°F/Gas Mark 4. Grease a
450-g/1-lb loaf tin and line with baking paper.

2. Put the dates, bicarbonate of soda and lemon rind into a
bowl and add the hot tea. Leave to soak for 10 minutes until soft.

3. Cream together the butter and muscovado sugar until light and fluffy, then whisk in the egg. Stir
in the date mixture.

4. Fold in the flour using a large metal spoon, then fold in the walnuts. Spoon the mixture into the
prepared tin and smooth the surface. Top with the walnut halves.

5. Bake in the preheated oven for 35–40 minutes, or until risen, firm and golden brown. Leave to
cool in the tin for 10 minutes, then turn out onto a wire rack to cool completely.

74 Coconut jam squares

Makes
9

Ingredients

150 g/5½ oz butter, softened,
plus extra for greasing
70 g/2½ oz caster sugar
1 large egg yolk
200 g/7 oz plain flour
6 tbsp seedless raspberry jam
cocoa powder, for dusting (optional)

Topping

2 large egg whites
115 g/4 oz caster sugar
40 g/1½ oz desiccated coconut

1. Preheat the oven to 180°C/350°F/Gas Mark 4. Grease a 23-cm/9-inch shallow square cake tin.

2. Beat together the butter and sugar in a large bowl until fluffy. Beat in the egg yolk, then sift in the flour and mix to a soft dough. Knead lightly, then press into the base of the prepared tin. Prick all over with a fork and bake in the preheated oven for 20–25 minutes, or until pale golden. Do not switch off the oven.

3. Meanwhile, to make the topping, put the egg whites into a large bowl and whisk until they hold stiff peaks. Gradually whisk in the sugar to make a firm, glossy meringue. Fold in two thirds of the coconut. Spread the jam over the cooked base in the tin, then spoon the meringue over the jam. Sprinkle with the remaining coconut.

4. Return to the oven for 15–20 minutes, or until the meringue topping is crisp and golden. Leave to cool in the tin, then dust with cocoa powder, if using, and cut into nine squares.

75 Chocolate ganache cake

Serves
10

Ingredients

oil or melted butter, for greasing
175 g/6 oz butter
175 g/6 oz caster sugar
4 eggs, lightly beaten
250 g/9 oz self-raising flour
1 tbsp cocoa powder
50 g/1¾ oz plain chocolate, melted

Topping

450 ml/16 fl oz double cream
375 g/13 oz plain chocolate, broken into pieces
200 g/7 oz chocolate-flavoured cake covering

1. Preheat the oven to 180°C/350°F/Gas Mark 4. Grease and line a 20-cm/8-inch square cake tin. Beat together the butter and sugar until fluffy. Gradually add the eggs, beating well after each addition. Sift together the flour and cocoa into the cake mixture and fold in carefully. Fold in the melted chocolate. Pour into the prepared tin and bake in the preheated oven for 40 minutes, or until springy to the touch. Leave to cool in the tin for 5 minutes, then transfer to a wire rack to cool completely. Cut the cake into two layers.

2. To make the topping, put the cream in a saucepan and bring to the boil, stirring. Add the chocolate and stir until melted. Pour into a bowl, leave to cool, then chill for 2 hours, or until set and firm. Whisk until fluffy then set aside one third of the topping. Use the remaining topping to sandwich the layers together and spread all over the cake. Melt the cake covering and spread it over a sheet of baking paper. Leave to cool until just set, cut into strips a little wider than the height of the cake, then place around the edge of the cake, overlapping slightly. Pipe the reserved topping in teardrops over the top of the cake, covering it completely. Leave to chill for 1 hour.

#76 Rocky road bars

Makes 8

Ingredients

175 g/6 oz milk chocolate or plain chocolate

55 g/2 oz butter, plus extra for greasing

100 g/3½ oz shortcake biscuits, broken into pieces

85 g/3 oz mini marshmallows

85 g/3 oz walnuts or peanuts

1. Grease and line an 18-cm/7-inch square cake tin with baking paper. Break the chocolate into a heatproof bowl set over a saucepan of gently simmering water and heat until melted. Add the butter and stir until melted and combined. Leave to cool slightly.

2. Stir the broken biscuits, marshmallows and nuts into the chocolate mixture.

3. Pour the chocolate mixture into the prepared tin, pressing down with the back of a spoon. Chill in the refrigerator for at least 2 hours, or until firm. Carefully turn out of the tin and cut into eight pieces.

#77 Mocha-glazed pound cake

Serves 9

Ingredients

300 g/10½ oz plain flour

1 tsp baking powder

250 g/9 oz butter, softened, plus extra for greasing

225 g/8 oz caster sugar

1 tbsp coffee and chicory essence

6 eggs

Glaze

115 g/4 oz plain chocolate, finely chopped

1 tbsp coffee and chicory essence

15 g/½ oz butter

150 ml/5 fl oz double cream

1. Preheat the oven to 180°C/350°F/Gas Mark 4. Grease a 20-cm/8-inch square cake tin and line with baking paper. Sift together the flour and baking powder into a bowl and set aside.

2. Put the butter and sugar in a large bowl and beat with an electric hand-held mixer until pale and creamy. Beat in the coffee and chicory essence, then beat in the eggs, one at a time, adding a spoonful of the flour mixture after each egg. Fold in the remaining flour. Spoon the mixture into the prepared tin and smooth the surface with a palette knife.

3. Bake in the preheated oven for 50 minutes–1 hour, or until risen and golden brown, and a skewer inserted into the centre comes out clean. Leave to cool in the tin for 10 minutes, then turn out onto a wire rack to cool completely.

4. To make the glaze, put the chocolate, coffee and chicory essence and butter in a heatproof bowl. Heat the cream until almost boiling, then pour into the bowl. Stir constantly until the chocolate has melted. Leave to cool and thicken for about 20 minutes, stirring occasionally. Pour the thick glaze over the cake, allowing it to spill down the sides. Leave in a cool place until the glaze has set.

Chocolate cherry cake

Ingredients

oil or melted butter, for greasing

150 g/5½ oz plain flour

2 tbsp cocoa powder

1 tbsp baking powder

175 g/6 oz butter, softened

175 g/6 oz golden caster sugar

3 eggs, beaten

1 tsp vanilla extract

2 tbsp milk

3 tbsp kirsch or brandy (optional)

grated chocolate and fresh whole cherries, to decorate

Filling

450 ml/16 fl oz double or whipping cream

2 tbsp icing sugar

225 g/8 oz fresh dark red cherries, stoned

1. Preheat the oven to 180°C/350°F/Gas Mark 4. Grease 2 x 20-cm/8-inch sandwich cake tins and line the bases with baking paper.

2. Sift the flour, cocoa and baking powder into a large bowl and add the butter, sugar, eggs and vanilla extract. Beat well until the mixture is smooth, then stir in the milk.

3. Divide the mixture between the prepared tins and smooth level. Bake in the preheated oven for 25–30 minutes, or until risen and firm to the touch. Leave to cool in the tins for 2–3 minutes, then turn out onto wire racks to cool completely.

4. When the cakes are cold, sprinkle with the kirsch, if using. To make the filling, whip the cream with the icing sugar until thick, then spread about a third over the top of one of the cakes. Spread the cherries over the cream and place the second cake on top.

5. Spread the remaining cream over the top and sides of the cake and decorate with grated chocolate and fresh whole cherries.

Irish tea cake

Ingredients

175 g/6 oz butter, softened, plus extra for greasing

200 g/7 oz caster sugar

1 tsp vanilla extract or 1 vanilla pod, scraped

2 eggs

85 g/3 oz cream cheese

225 g/8 oz plain flour, plus extra for dusting

1 tsp baking powder

¼ tsp salt

150 ml/5 fl oz buttermilk

125 g/4½ oz sultanas

50 g/1¾ oz icing sugar, sifted

2 tsp fresh lemon juice

1. Preheat the oven to 160°C/325°F/Gas Mark 3. Grease and flour a 900-g/2-lb loaf tin and line the base with baking paper. Put the butter, sugar and vanilla extract into a large bowl and beat until fluffy. Add the eggs, one at a time, beating after each addition until combined. Add the cream cheese and beat until well combined.

2. Sift together the flour, baking powder and salt into a separate bowl. Gradually add the flour mixture to the butter mixture, alternating with the buttermilk, and mix until smooth. Add the sultanas and stir with a wooden spoon until well combined.

3. Transfer the mixture to the prepared tin, smoothing the surface with a palette knife. Bake in the centre of the preheated oven for 1 hour, until golden and a skewer inserted into the centre comes out clean. Remove from the oven and leave to cool in the tin for 10 minutes. Using a palette knife, separate the cake from the sides of the tin and transfer to a wire rack to cool. Meanwhile, combine the sugar and lemon juice in a small bowl and stir until smooth. Spread the icing over the warm cake and leave to cool completely. Cut into slices and serve.

Crème brûlée cheesecake bars

Ingredients

50 g/1¾ oz butter
100 g/3½ oz digestive biscuits, crushed
400 g/14 oz cream cheese
125 g/4½ oz caster sugar
1 tbsp plain flour
2 whole eggs
1 egg yolk
½ tsp vanilla extract
pinch of salt
70 g/2½ oz granulated sugar

1. Line a 20-cm/8-inch square cake tin with baking paper. Melt the butter in a small saucepan, then stir in the biscuit crumbs, mixing well. Press into the base of the prepared tin, pressing down well with the back of the spoon. Chill in the refrigerator while you prepare the topping.

2. Preheat the oven to 150°C/300°F/Gas Mark 2. Place the cream cheese, caster sugar, flour, eggs, egg yolk, vanilla extract and salt in a mixing bowl and beat well until smooth.

3. Pour the mixture into the tin and bake in the preheated oven for 40-45 minutes, until the mixture has set but still has a slight wobble in the centre.

4. Remove from the oven and leave to cool, then chill in the refrigerator for 1–2 hours.

5. Remove the cheesecake from the tin and discard the paper. Cut into 16 squares and place on a flameproof baking tray.

6. To make the topping, sprinkle the granulated sugar evenly over the surface of each square. Use a cook's blowtorch to carefully caramelize the topping. Once hardened, serve immediately.

Chocolate chip flapjacks

Makes
12

Ingredients

115 g/4 oz butter, plus extra
for greasing

60 g/2¼ oz caster sugar

1 tbsp golden syrup

350 g/12 oz rolled oats

85 g/3 oz plain chocolate chips

85 g/3 oz sultanas

1. Preheat the oven to 180°C/350°F/Gas Mark 4. Lightly grease a 20-cm/8-inch shallow, square cake tin.

2. Place the butter, sugar and golden syrup in a saucepan and heat gently, stirring constantly, until the butter and sugar have melted and the mixture is well combined.

3. Remove the pan from the heat and stir in the oats until they are well coated. Add the chocolate chips and sultanas and mix well to combine. Turn into the prepared tin and press down well.

4. Bake in the preheated oven for 30 minutes. Leave to cool slightly, then mark into 12 squares. When almost cold, cut into squares and transfer to a wire rack to cool completely.

Apple crumble squares

Makes
15

Ingredients

175 g/6 oz butter, softened,
plus extra for greasing

125 g/4½ oz caster sugar

1 tsp vanilla extract

2 large eggs, lightly beaten

175 g/6 oz self-raising flour

3 tbsp milk

finely grated zest of ½ lemon

500 g/1 lb 2 oz dessert apples, peeled,
cored and thinly sliced

1 tbsp lemon juice

Topping

115 g/4 oz self-raising flour

85 g/3 oz butter

55 g/2 oz caster sugar

25 g/1 oz ground almonds

icing sugar, for dusting

1. Preheat the oven to 160°C/325°F/Gas Mark 3. Grease a 33 x 23-cm/13 x 9-inch traybake tin, about 5 cm/2 inches deep and line the base with baking paper.

2. Place the butter, sugar and vanilla extract in a large bowl and use an electric hand-held mixer to beat together until pale and creamy. Gradually beat in the eggs.

3. Sift in the flour and fold into the mixture with the milk and lemon zest until thoroughly combined. Spread the mixture in an even layer in the prepared tin.

4. Toss the apples in the lemon juice and arrange over the top of the sponge mixture.

5. To make the topping, place the flour and butter in a bowl and rub the butter into the flour until the mixture resembles coarse breadcrumbs. Stir in the sugar and ground almonds.

6. Scatter the crumble mixture over the apples. Bake in the preheated oven for 45–50 minutes, or until the topping is golden and a skewer inserted into the centre of the cake comes out clean.

7. Leave the cake to cool in the tin, then dust with icing sugar and cut into 15 squares. Serve warm or cold.

#83 Caribbean coconut cake

Ingredients

oil or melted butter, for greasing

280 g/10 oz butter, softened

175 g/6 oz golden caster sugar

3 eggs

175 g/6 oz self-raising flour

1½ tsp baking powder

½ tsp freshly grated nutmeg

55 g/2 oz desiccated coconut

4 tbsp coconut cream

280 g/10 oz icing sugar

5 tbsp pineapple jam

toasted desiccated coconut, to decorate

1. Preheat the oven to 180°C/350°F/Gas Mark 4. Grease 2 x 20-cm/8-inch sandwich cake tins and line the bases with baking paper.

2. Place 175 g/6 oz of the butter in a bowl with the caster sugar and eggs and sift in the flour, baking powder and nutmeg. Beat together until smooth, then stir in the desiccated coconut and 2 tablespoons of the coconut cream. Divide the mixture between the prepared tins and smooth level. Bake in the preheated oven for 25 minutes, or until golden and firm to the touch. Leave to cool in the tins for 5 minutes, then turn out onto wire racks to cool completely.

3. Sift the icing sugar into a bowl, add the remaining butter and coconut cream and beat until smooth. Spread the jam on one of the cakes and top with just under half of the buttercream. Place the other cake on top. Spread the remaining buttercream on top of the cake and sprinkle with toasted desiccated coconut.

#84 Mocha cake

Ingredients

225 g/8 oz self-raising flour

1 tsp baking powder

2 tbsp cocoa powder, plus extra for dusting

310 g/10¾ oz butter, softened, plus extra for greasing

225 g/8 oz soft light brown sugar

4 large eggs, beaten

115 g/4 oz plain chocolate, melted

2 tbsp caster sugar

5 tbsp strong black coffee

250 g/9 oz mascarpone cheese

55 g/2 oz icing sugar

chocolate-coated coffee beans, to decorate

1. Preheat the oven to 180°C/350°F/Gas Mark 4. Grease 2 x 20-cm/8-inch sandwich tins and line with baking paper. Sift together the flour, baking powder and cocoa powder into a large bowl. Add 225 g/8 oz of the butter, the brown sugar and eggs and beat with an electric hand-held mixer for 3–4 minutes, or until the mixture is smooth and creamy. Fold in the melted chocolate. Divide the mixture between the prepared tins and bake in the preheated oven for 25–30 minutes.

2. Place the caster sugar and 3 tablespoons of the coffee in a small saucepan and heat gently for 1–2 minutes. Leave to cool for 10 minutes. Pierce the tops of the warm cakes all over with a skewer and spoon the coffee syrup over the cakes. Leave the cakes to cool in the tins.

3. Place the remaining butter and mascarpone cheese in a bowl and beat together until well blended. Beat in the icing sugar and the remaining coffee until smooth. Remove the cakes from the tins and sandwich together with half the frosting. Swirl the remaining frosting over the top of the cake. Dust with cocoa powder and decorate with chocolate-coated coffee beans.

Nutty granola bars

Makes
16

Ingredients

200 g/7 oz rolled oats
115 g/4 oz chopped hazelnuts
55 g/2 oz plain flour
115 g/4 oz butter, plus extra for greasing
2 tbsp golden syrup
85 g/3 oz light muscovado sugar

1. Preheat the oven to 180°C/350°F/Gas Mark 4. Grease a 23-cm/9-inch square cake tin and line with baking paper. Place the oats, hazelnuts and flour in a large bowl and stir together.

2. Place the butter, syrup and sugar in a saucepan over a low heat and stir until melted. Pour onto the dry ingredients and mix well. Turn the mixture into the prepared tin and smooth the surface with the back of a spoon.

3. Bake in the preheated oven for 20–25 minutes, or until golden and firm to the touch. Mark into 16 pieces and leave to cool in the tin. When completely cooled, cut through with a sharp knife and remove from the tin.

Hot chocolate cheesecake

Serves
10

Ingredients

oil or melted butter, for greasing
150 g/5½ oz plain flour, plus extra for dusting
2 tbsp cocoa powder
55 g/2 oz butter
2 tbsp golden caster sugar
25 g/1 oz ground almonds
1 egg yolk
icing sugar, for dusting
grated chocolate, to decorate

Filling

2 eggs, separated
75 g/2¾ oz golden caster sugar
350 g/12 oz cream cheese
4 tbsp ground almonds
150 ml/5 fl oz double cream
25 g/1 oz cocoa powder, sifted
1 tsp vanilla extract

1. Grease a 20-cm/8-inch round springform cake tin with oil.

2. Sift the flour and cocoa into a bowl and rub in the butter with your fingertips until the mixture resembles fine breadcrumbs. Stir in the sugar and ground almonds. Add the egg yolk and enough water to make a soft dough.

3. Roll out the pastry on a lightly floured work surface and use to line the base and sides of the prepared tin. Leave to chill for 30 minutes. Preheat the oven to 160°C/325°F/Gas Mark 3.

4. To make the filling, put the egg yolks and sugar in a large bowl and whisk until thick and pale. Whisk in the cream cheese, ground almonds, cream, cocoa powder and vanilla extract until well combined.

5. Put the egg whites in a large bowl and whisk until stiff, but not dry. Stir a little of the egg whites into the cheese mixture, then fold in the remainder. Pour into the pastry case.

6. Bake in the preheated oven for 1½ hours, until well risen and just firm to the touch. Carefully remove from the tin, dust with icing sugar and sprinkle with grated chocolate. Serve warm.

#87 Cinnamon brownies

Makes
16

Ingredients

115 g/4 oz plain chocolate, broken into pieces

200 g/7 oz butter, plus extra for greasing

85 g/3 oz pecan nuts halves

250 g/9 oz caster sugar

4 eggs, beaten

225 g/8 oz plain flour

2 tsp ground cinnamon

55 g/2 oz white chocolate, broken into pieces

2 tbsp milk

115 g/4 oz icing sugar

1. Preheat the oven to 180°C/350°F/Gas Mark 4. Grease a 23-cm/9-inch shallow square cake tin.

2. Put the plain chocolate and 175 g/6 oz of the butter into a heatproof bowl set over a saucepan of gently simmering water and heat until melted. Remove from the heat and leave to cool slightly.

3. Reserve 16 pecan nut halves to decorate and chop the rest. Whisk together the caster sugar and eggs until thick and creamy. Fold in the chocolate mixture, flour, cinnamon and chopped nuts.

4. Transfer the mixture to the prepared tin and bake in the preheated oven for 35–40 minutes, or until just firm to the touch. Leave to cool in the tin.

5. Place the remaining butter and the white chocolate in a heatproof bowl set over a saucepan of gently simmering water and heat until melted. Remove from the heat and beat in the milk and icing sugar. Spread over the cooled brownies. Leave to set for 30 minutes, then cut into 16 squares and top each square with a pecan half.

#88 Soured cream cake

Serves
10

Ingredients

225 g/8 oz butter, at room temperature, plus extra for greasing

115 g/4 oz white vegetable fat

600 g/1 lb 5 oz caster sugar

5 eggs

375 g/13 oz plain flour, plus extra for dusting

½ tsp bicarbonate of soda

225 ml/8 fl oz soured cream

4 tbsp milk

1 tsp vanilla extract

vanilla ice cream, to serve (optional)

1. Preheat the oven to 160°C/325°F/Gas Mark 3. Grease and flour a 25-cm/10-inch Bundt tin. Cream together the butter and vegetable fat until light and fluffy. Gradually add the sugar, beating constantly, until light and fluffy. Add the eggs, one at a time, beating after each addition.

2. Mix the flour and bicarbonate of soda together. Mix the soured cream and milk together in a separate bowl. Add one third of the flour mixture to the butter mixture with half of the soured cream mixture. Stir well to combine. Add a further third of the flour mixture and combine. Add the remaining flour mixture, remaining soured cream mixture and the vanilla extract, and mix to combine.

3. Pour the mixture into the prepared tin. Bake in the preheated oven for 1 hour 10 minutes—1 hour 15 minutes, or until a skewer inserted into the cake comes out clean. Leave to cool in the tin for 10 minutes, then turn out onto a wire rack and leave to cool completely. To serve, cut into slices and top each slice with a scoop of ice cream, if using.

#89 Chocolate caraque cake

Serves 12

Ingredients

750 g/1 lb 10 oz plain chocolate, broken into pieces

100 g/3½ oz cocoa powder

300 ml/10 fl oz boiling water

200 g/7 oz butter, softened, plus extra for greasing

500 g/1 lb 2 oz light muscovado sugar

4 eggs, beaten

375 g/13 oz plain flour

¾ tsp bicarbonate of soda

4 tsp vanilla extract

500 ml/18 fl oz double cream

4 tbsp icing sugar

Decoration

200 g/7 oz plain chocolate, chopped

6 tbsp brandy (optional)

rose petals or small edible flowers, to decorate (optional)

1. Preheat the oven to 160°C/325°F/Gas Mark 3. Grease a 20-cm/8-inch round cake tin and line with baking paper. Put 250 g/9 oz of the chocolate into a heatproof bowl set over a saucepan of gently simmering water and heat until melted. Whisk the cocoa powder and water in a bowl until smooth, then stir in the chocolate. In a separate bowl, beat the butter and sugar until pale and creamy, then beat in the eggs, flour, bicarbonate of soda and vanilla extract. Stir in the chocolate mixture then spoon into the prepared tin. Bake in the preheated oven for 2 hours, or until firm. Leave to cool.

2. To make the decoration, place the chocolate in a heatproof bowl set over a saucepan of gently simmering water and heat until melted. Spread a thin layer on a cool slab. Leave in a cool place until the chocolate is set but not brittle.

3. Push the edge of a palette knife or a clean wallpaper scraper across the set chocolate so that the chocolate starts to roll into loose curls. Place the caraque on a baking sheet lined with baking paper and chill in the refrigerator while you finish the cake. Slice the cake in half horizontally. Drizzle the tops of the cake halves with brandy, if using.

4. Place the remaining chocolate in a bowl. Heat the cream and icing sugar in a saucepan and pour over the chocolate. Stir and leave to cool. Use one quarter of this ganache to sandwich the cake layers together, then place the cake on a serving plate. Spread a thin layer of ganache around the sides of the cake with a palette knife to seal in the crumbs. Chill in the refrigerator for 15 minutes. Spread the remaining ganache all over the cake in an even layer, smoothing it so it is as flat or as textured as you like. Scatter the caraque over the cake so the pieces fall at different angles. Scatter with rose petals, if using.

Raisin flapjacks

Makes
14

Ingredients

140 g/5 oz rolled oats

115 g/4 oz demerara sugar

85 g/3 oz raisins

115 g/4 oz butter, melted, plus
extra for greasing

1. Preheat the oven to 190°C/375°F/Gas Mark 5. Grease a
28 x 18-cm/11 x 7-inch shallow baking tin.

2. Combine the oats, sugar, raisins and butter in a mixing bowl,
stirring well. Spoon the mixture into the prepared tin and press down firmly with the back of a
spoon. Bake in the preheated oven for 15–20 minutes, or until golden.

3. Using a sharp knife, mark into 14 bars, then leave to cool in the tin for 10 minutes. Cut into 14
bars, then carefully transfer to a wire rack to cool completely.

91

Raspberry & almond cake

Serves
8

Ingredients

115 g/4 oz self-raising flour

¼ tsp baking powder

2 eggs

115 g/4 oz butter, softened,
plus extra for greasing

115 g/4 oz caster sugar

40 g/1½ oz ground almonds

175 g/6 oz raspberries

2 tbsp flaked almonds

icing sugar, for dusting

1. Preheat the oven to 200°C/400°F/Gas Mark 6. Place
a baking sheet in the oven to heat up. Grease a 23-cm/9-inch
round, shallow cake tin and line the base with baking paper.
Sift together the flour and baking powder into a large bowl. Add the eggs, butter and sugar
and beat with a hand-held electric mixer for 1–2 minutes until pale and creamy. Fold in the
ground almonds.

2. Spoon the mixture into the prepared tin. Gently level the surface and scatter over the raspberries
and flaked almonds. Bake in the preheated oven for 22–25 minutes, or until risen, golden brown and
just firm to the touch.

3. Leave the cake in the tin for 1–2 minutes, then turn out onto a wire rack. Serve warm or cold,
dusted with icing sugar.

Clementine cake

Ingredients

175 g/6 oz butter, softened, plus extra for greasing

200 g/7 oz caster sugar

grated rind and juice of 2 clementines

3 eggs, beaten

175 g/6 oz self-raising flour

3 tbsp ground almonds

3 tbsp single cream

3 white sugar cubes, crushed

1. Preheat the oven to 180°C/350°F/Gas Mark 4. Grease an 18-cm/7-inch round cake tin and line the base with baking paper.

2. Cream together the butter, 175 g/6 oz of the sugar and the grated clementine rind until pale and fluffy. Gradually add the eggs to the mixture, beating thoroughly after each addition. Gently fold in the flour, followed by the ground almonds and cream. Spoon the mixture into the prepared tin. Bake in the preheated oven for 55–60 minutes, or until a skewer inserted in the centre comes out clean. Leave in the tin to cool slightly, then transfer to a wire rack.

3. To make the glaze, put the clementine juice into a small saucepan with the remaining caster sugar. Bring to the boil and simmer for 5 minutes. Drizzle the glaze over the cake until it has been absorbed, then sprinkle with the crushed sugar cubes.

Date, nut & honey slices

Ingredients

250 g/9 oz dates, stoned and chopped

2 tbsp lemon juice

6–7 tbsp cold water

85 g/3 oz pistachio nuts, chopped

2 tbsp clear honey

225 g/8 oz plain flour, plus extra for dusting

25 g/1 oz golden caster sugar

150 g/5½ oz butter

milk, to glaze

1. Preheat the oven to 200°C/400°F/Gas Mark 6. Place the dates, lemon juice and 2 tablespoons of the water in a saucepan and bring to the boil, stirring. Remove from the heat. Stir in the pistachio nuts and 1 tablespoon of the honey. Cover and leave to cool.

2. Place the flour, sugar and butter in a food processor and process to fine crumbs. Mix in just enough of the remaining water to bind to a soft dough.

3. Divide the dough in half and roll out each half on a floured surface to two 30 x 20-cm/12 x 8-inch rectangles. Place one on a baking sheet. Spread the date and nut mixture to within 1 cm/½ inch of the edge. Top with the remaining pastry. Press to seal, trim the edges and mark into 12 slices. Glaze with the milk.

4. Bake in the preheated oven for 20–25 minutes, or until golden. Brush with the remaining honey and turn out onto a wire rack to cool. Cut into slices and serve.

Citrus mousse cake

Serves
12

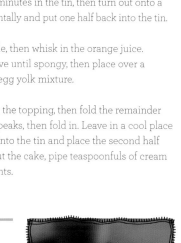

Ingredients

oil or melted butter, for greasing

175 g/6 oz butter

175 g/6 oz caster sugar

4 eggs, lightly beaten

200 g/7 oz self-raising flour

1 tbsp cocoa powder

50 g/1¾ oz orange-flavoured plain chocolate, melted

peeled orange segments, to decorate

Filling

2 eggs, separated

50 g/1¾ oz caster sugar

200 ml/7 fl oz freshly squeezed orange juice

2 tsp powdered gelatine

3 tbsp water

300 ml/10 fl oz double cream

1. Preheat the oven to 180°C/350°F/Gas Mark 4. Grease a 20-cm/8-inch round springform cake tin and line the base with baking paper.

2. Beat the butter and sugar in a bowl until light and fluffy. Gradually add the eggs, beating well after each addition. Sift together the flour and cocoa and fold into the creamed mixture. Fold in the melted chocolate. Pour into the prepared tin and smooth level. Bake in the preheated oven for 40 minutes, or until springy to the touch. Leave to cool for 5 minutes in the tin, then turn out onto a wire rack to cool completely. Cut the cold cake in half horizontally and put one half back into the tin.

3. To make the filling, beat the egg yolks and sugar until pale, then whisk in the orange juice. Sprinkle the gelatine over the water in a small bowl and leave until spongy, then place over a saucepan of hot water and stir until dissolved. Stir into the egg yolk mixture.

4. Whip the cream until it holds its shape, reserve a little for the topping, then fold the remainder into the mousse. Whisk the egg whites until they hold soft peaks, then fold in. Leave in a cool place until starting to set, stirring occasionally. Pour the mixture into the tin and place the second half of the cake on top. Chill in the refrigerator until set. Turn out the cake, pipe teaspoonfuls of cream around the top and decorate the centre with orange segments.

Chocolate mint bars

Makes
16

Ingredients

55 g/2 oz butter, plus extra for greasing

55 g/2 oz caster sugar

115 g/4 oz plain flour

175 g/6 oz icing sugar

1–2 tbsp warm water

½ tsp peppermint extract

2 tsp green edible food colouring (optional)

175 g/6 oz plain chocolate, broken into pieces

1. Preheat the oven to 180°C/350°F/Gas Mark 4. Grease and line the base of a 30 x 20-cm/12 x 8-inch baking tin.

2. Beat the butter and caster sugar together until pale and fluffy. Stir in the flour until the mixture binds together. Knead the mixture to form a smooth dough, then press into the prepared tin. Prick the surface all over with a fork. Bake in the preheated oven for 10–15 minutes, until lightly browned and just firm to the touch. Remove from the oven and leave to cool in the tin.

3. Sift the icing sugar into a bowl. Gradually add the water, then add the peppermint extract and food colouring, if using. Spread the filling over the base, then leave to set.

4. Place the chocolate in a heatproof bowl set over a saucepan of gently simmering water and heat until melted. Remove from the heat, then spread over the filling. Leave to set, then cut into 16 slices.

96 Banana loaf

Serves 8

Ingredients

butter, for greasing

225 g/8 oz self-raising flour

150 g/5½ oz demerara sugar

pinch of salt

½ tsp ground cinnamon

½ tsp grated nutmeg

2 large ripe bananas, peeled

175 ml/6 fl oz orange juice

2 eggs, beaten

4 tbsp rapeseed oil

1. Preheat the oven to 180°C/350°F/Gas Mark 4. Lightly grease and line a 900-g/2-lb loaf tin.

2. Sift the flour, sugar, salt and spices into a large bowl. In a separate bowl, mash the bananas with the orange juice, then stir in the eggs and oil. Pour into the dry ingredients and mix well.

3. Spoon into the prepared tin and bake in the preheated oven for 1 hour, or until a skewer inserted in the centre of the cake comes out clean.

4. Remove from the oven and leave to cool in the tin. Turn the loaf out onto a wire rack to cool completely before cutting into slices to serve.

97 Almond slices

Makes 8

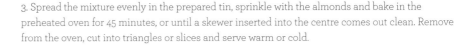

Ingredients

3 eggs

60 g/2¼ oz ground almonds

140 g/5 oz dried milk powder

200 g/7 oz granulated sugar

½ tsp saffron threads

115 g/4 oz butter, plus extra for greasing

1 tbsp flaked almonds

1. Preheat the oven to 160°C/325°F/Gas Mark 3. Lightly beat the eggs together in a mixing bowl and set aside. Grease and line a shallow 20-cm/8-inch square baking tin.

2. Place the ground almonds, milk powder, sugar and saffron in a large mixing bowl and stir to mix well. Melt the butter in a small saucepan over a low heat. Pour the melted butter over the dry ingredients and mix well with a wooden spoon until thoroughly combined. Add the beaten eggs to the mixture and stir to blend well.

3. Spread the mixture evenly in the prepared tin, sprinkle with the almonds and bake in the preheated oven for 45 minutes, or until a skewer inserted into the centre comes out clean. Remove from the oven, cut into triangles or slices and serve warm or cold.

Serves
10

Pineapple upside-down cake

Ingredients

oil or melted butter, for greasing

4 eggs, beaten

200 g/7 oz golden caster sugar

1 tsp vanilla extract

200 g/7 oz plain flour

2 tsp baking powder

125 g/4½ oz butter, melted

Topping

40 g/1½ oz butter

4 tbsp golden syrup

425 g/15 oz canned pineapple rings, drained

4–6 glacé cherries, halved

1. Preheat the oven to 160°C/325°F/Gas Mark 3. Grease a 23-cm/9-inch deep round cake tin and line the base with baking paper.

2. To make the topping, place the butter and golden syrup in a heavy-based saucepan and heat gently until melted. Bring to the boil and boil for 2–3 minutes, stirring, until slightly thickened and toffee-like. Pour the syrup into the base of the prepared tin. Arrange the pineapple rings and glacé cherries in one layer over the syrup.

3. Place the eggs, sugar and vanilla extract in a large heatproof bowl over a saucepan of gently simmering water and whisk with an electric hand-held mixer for about 10–15 minutes, until thick enough to leave a trail when the whisk is lifted. Sift in the flour and baking powder, and fold in lightly and evenly with a metal spoon.

4. Fold the melted butter into the mixture with a metal spoon until evenly mixed. Spoon into the prepared tin and bake in the preheated oven for 1–1¼ hours, or until well risen, firm and golden brown. Leave to cool in the tin for 10 minutes, then carefully turn out onto a serving plate. Serve warm or cold.

Serves
10

Caramel pecan cheesecake

Ingredients

225 g/8 oz digestive biscuits, finely crushed

25 g/1 oz pecan nuts, finely chopped

85 g/3 oz butter, melted, plus extra for greasing

550 g/1 lb 4 oz cream cheese

25 g/1 oz soft light brown sugar

100 g/3½ oz caster sugar

3 large eggs, beaten

1 tsp vanilla extract

300 ml/10 fl oz soured cream

2 tbsp cornflour

4 tbsp dulce du leche

25 g/1 oz pecan nuts, chopped

1. Preheat the oven to 160°C/325°F/Gas Mark 3. Lightly grease a 23-cm/9-inch round springform cake tin.

2. Put the crushed biscuits and the finely chopped nuts into a bowl and stir in the butter. Press into the base of the prepared tin. Chill in the refrigerator while making the filling.

3. Put the cheese, brown sugar and caster sugar into a large bowl and beat together until creamy. Gradually beat in the eggs and vanilla extract, then fold in the soured cream and cornflour. Pour over the biscuit base.

4. Place on a baking sheet and bake in the preheated oven for 45–50 minutes, or until just set (the middle should still wobble slightly). Switch off the oven, open the oven door and leave the cheesecake in the oven until cold. Chill in the refrigerator for 3–4 hours or overnight.

5. Remove the springform tin and transfer the cheesecake to a serving plate. Gently spread the dulce du leche over the top and sprinkle with the nuts to serve.

Small cakes & cookies

#100 Vanilla frosted cupcakes

Makes
12

Ingredients

115 g/4 oz butter, softened
115 g/4 oz golden caster sugar
2 eggs, lightly beaten
115 g/4 oz self-raising flour
1 tbsp milk
crystallized rose petals, to decorate

Frosting

175 g/6 oz butter, softened
2 tsp vanilla extract
2 tbsp milk
300 g/10½ oz icing sugar, sifted

1. Preheat the oven to 180°C/350°F/Gas Mark 4. Line a 12-hole muffin tin with paper cases.

2. Place the butter and sugar in a bowl and beat together until light and fluffy. Gradually beat in the eggs. Sift in the flour and fold in gently using a metal spoon. Fold in the milk. Spoon the mixture into the paper cases. Bake in the preheated oven for 15–20 minutes until golden brown and firm to the touch. Transfer to a wire rack and leave to cool.

3. To make the frosting, put the butter, vanilla extract and milk in a large bowl and beat with an electric hand-held mixer until smooth. Gradually beat in the icing sugar and continue beating for 2–3 minutes until the frosting is very light and creamy. Spoon the frosting into a large piping bag fitted with a large star-shaped nozzle and pipe swirls of frosting on top of each cupcake. Decorate with crystallized rose petals.

#101 Chai tea biscuits

Makes
30

Ingredients

100 g/3½ oz soft light brown sugar
2 tbsp dry chai tea (about 4 tea bags)
¼ tsp salt
125 g/4½ oz wholemeal flour,
plus extra for dusting
1 tsp vanilla extract
115 g/4 oz chilled butter, cut into pieces

1. Preheat the oven to 180°C/350°F/Gas Mark 4 and line 2 baking trays with baking paper.

2. Put the sugar, tea and salt into a food processor and process until the tea has been ground to a fine powder. Add the flour, vanilla extract and butter, and process until well combined and the mixture begins to hold together. If the mixture is too dry, add cold water, ½ teaspoon at a time, and process until the mixture just comes together. Turn out the dough onto a sheet of clingfilm and shape into a log. Wrap tightly and chill in the refrigerator for 15 minutes.

3. Roll out the dough on a lightly floured surface to a thickness of about 3 mm/⅛ inch and cut out 30 rounds using a 6-cm/2½-inch round biscuit cutter. Transfer the biscuits to the prepared trays and bake in the preheated oven for 18–20 minutes, or until they begin to colour.

4. Remove from the oven and transfer the biscuits to wire racks to cool completely before serving.

Cherry & almond loaves

Makes
12

Ingredients

85 g/3 oz lightly salted butter, softened,
plus extra for greasing

70 g/2½ oz caster sugar

1 egg

1 egg yolk

70 g/2½ oz self-raising flour

½ tsp almond extract

55 g/2 oz ground almonds

55 g/2 oz glacé cherries, roughly chopped

2 tbsp flaked almonds

55 g/2 oz icing sugar

2 tsp lemon juice

1. Preheat the oven to 180°C/350°F/Gas Mark 4. Place a 12-hole silicone mini loaf tin on a baking tray or grease 12 individual mini loaf tins and line the bases with baking paper.

2. Put the butter, caster sugar, egg, egg yolk, flour, almond extract and ground almonds in a mixing bowl and beat with an electric hand-held mixer until smooth and creamy. Stir in the cherries.

3. Spoon teaspoons of the mixture into the tin and level with the back of the spoon. Break up the flaked almonds slightly by squeezing them in your hands, then scatter them over the cake mixture. Bake in the preheated oven for 20 minutes (25 minutes if using individual tins), or until risen and just firm to the touch. Leave to cool in the tin for 5 minutes, then transfer to a wire rack to cool completely.

4. Beat together the icing sugar and lemon juice in a small bowl and drizzle over the cakes with a teaspoon. Leave to set before serving.

Chocolate stars

Makes
16

Ingredients

125 g/4½ oz butter, softened,
plus extra for greasing

40 g/1½ oz icing sugar

125 g/4½ oz plain flour

25 g/1 oz cornflour

15 g/½ oz cocoa powder

½ tsp vanilla extract

Icing

100 g/3½ oz icing sugar

2 tsp cocoa powder

2 tbsp milk

1. Preheat the oven to 180°C/350°F/Gas Mark 4. Grease two baking sheets.

2. Put the butter and icing sugar in a bowl and beat together until pale and creamy. Sift in the flour, cornflour and cocoa powder, and beat well until smooth and creamy. Beat in the vanilla extract.

3. Spoon the mixture into a large piping bag fitted with a large star-shaped nozzle and pipe 16 x 7-cm/2¾-inch star shapes onto the prepared baking sheets.

4. Bake in the preheated oven for 15–20 minutes until just firm. Leave to cool on the baking sheets for 5 minutes, then transfer to a wire rack to cool completely.

5. To make the icing, sift the icing sugar and cocoa powder into a bowl and beat in the milk to make a smooth icing. Spoon the icing on top of the biscuits and leave to set.

#104 Melting moments

Ingredients

350 g/12 oz butter, softened
85 g/3 oz icing sugar
½ tsp vanilla extract
300 g/10½ oz plain flour
50 g/1¾ oz cornflour

1. Preheat the oven to 180°C/350°F/Gas Mark 4. Line two large baking sheets with baking paper.

2. Place the butter and icing sugar in a large bowl and beat together until light and fluffy, then beat in the vanilla extract. Sift in the flour and cornflour, and mix thoroughly.

3. Spoon the mixture into a piping bag fitted with a large star-shaped nozzle and pipe 32 biscuits onto the prepared baking sheets, spaced well apart.

4. Bake in the preheated oven for 15–20 minutes, or until golden brown. Leave to cool on the baking sheets.

#105 Frosted berry cupcakes

Ingredients

115 g/4 oz butter, softened
115 g/4 oz caster sugar
2 tsp orange flower water
2 large eggs, beaten
55 g/2 oz ground almonds
115 g/4 oz self-raising flour
2 tbsp milk

Frosting

300 g/10½ oz mascarpone cheese
85 g/3 oz caster sugar
4 tbsp orange juice

Decoration

280 g/10 oz fresh mixed berries
fresh mint leaves
1 egg white
3 tbsp caster sugar

1. Preheat the oven to 180°C/350°F/Gas Mark 4. Line a 12-hole muffin tin with paper cases.

2. Place the butter, sugar and orange flower water in a large bowl and beat together until light and fluffy. Gradually beat in the eggs. Stir in the ground almonds. Sift in the flour and, using a metal spoon, gently fold in with the milk.

3. Divide the mixture between the paper cases. Bake in the preheated oven for 15–20 minutes, or until risen, golden and firm to the touch. Transfer to a wire rack and leave to cool competely.

4. To make the frosting, put the mascarpone cheese, sugar and orange juice in a bowl and beat together until smooth.

5. Swirl the frosting over the top of the cupcakes. Brush the berries and mint leaves with egg white and roll in the sugar to coat. Decorate the cupcakes with the frosted berries and leaves.

#106 Cream tea cupcakes

Makes 10

Ingredients

85 g/3 oz butter, softened
85 g/3 oz caster sugar
1 large egg, lightly beaten
½ tsp vanilla extract
85 g/3 oz self-raising flour
1 tbsp milk
40 g/1½ oz raisins
115 g/4 oz strawberries
1 tbsp strawberry jam
115 g/4 oz clotted cream
icing sugar, for dusting

1. Preheat the oven to 190°C/375°F/Gas Mark 5. Line a 10-hole muffin tin with paper cases.

2. Place the butter and caster sugar in a large bowl and beat together until light and fluffy. Gradually beat in the egg and vanilla extract. Sift in the flour and, using a metal spoon, gently fold in to the mixture with the milk and raisins.

3. Divide the mixture between the paper cases. Bake in the preheated oven for 15–20 minutes, or until risen, golden and firm to the touch. Transfer to a wire rack and leave to cool.

4. Use a serrated knife to cut a round from the top of each cupcake. Hull and slice the strawberries, then gently mix the strawberries and jam together and divide between the cupcakes. Top each with a small dollop of clotted cream. Replace the cupcake tops and dust with icing sugar.

#107 Gingerbread men

Makes 16

Ingredients

450 g/1 lb plain flour,
plus extra for dusting
2 tsp ground ginger
1 tsp bicarbonate of soda
115 g/4 oz butter,
plus extra for greasing
5 tbsp golden syrup
150 g/5½ oz soft light brown sugar
1 large egg, beaten

Decoration

4 tbsp royal icing
48 sugar-coated chocolate drops

1. Preheat the oven to 180°C/350°F/Gas Mark 4. Grease two large baking sheets with butter. Sift together the flour, ginger and bicarbonate of soda into a bowl and mix to combine.

2. Put the butter, golden syrup and sugar into a saucepan and heat gently until syrupy. Add to the flour mixture with the beaten egg and mix to a firm dough.

3. Roll out the dough on a lightly floured work surface to a thickness of 8 mm/³⁄₈ inch and use a shaped cutter to stamp out 16 gingerbread men, re-rolling the dough as necessary. Place on the prepared baking sheets, spaced well apart, and bake in the preheated oven for 10–15 minutes, until golden brown. Leave to cool on the baking sheets for a few minutes, then transfer to a wire rack to cool completely.

4. Spoon the icing into a piping bag fitted with a small, plain nozzle and use to decorate the gingerbread men with faces and bow ties. Attach chocolate drop buttons with a little icing. Leave to set.

#108 Mini ombre cakes

Makes
6

Ingredients

225 g/8 oz self-raising flour
225 g/8 oz butter, softened, plus extra
for greasing
225 g/8 oz caster sugar
4 large eggs
1 tsp vanilla extract
1 tbsp milk
pink food colouring paste
shimmer hundreds
and thousands, to decorate

Frosting

175 g/6 oz butter, softened
6 tbsp double cream
350 g/12 oz icing sugar
pink food colouring paste

1. Preheat the oven to 180°C/350°F/Gas Mark 4. Grease 4 x 20-cm/8-inch round sandwich cake tins and line the bases with baking paper.

2. Sift the flour into a large mixing bowl and add the butter, sugar, eggs, vanilla extract and milk. Beat with an electric hand-held mixer for 1–2 minutes until pale and creamy. Divide the mixture evenly between four bowls.

3. Beat the food colouring paste into three of the bowls of mixture to give three distinctly different shades of colour, from pale pink to very deep pink. Leave the fourth bowl of mixture plain. Spoon each bowl of mixture into a prepared tin and gently level the surface. Bake in the preheated oven for 18–20 minutes, or until risen and just firm to the touch. Leave to cool in the tins for 5 minutes, then turn out onto wire racks and leave to cool completely.

4. To make the frosting, put the butter in a bowl and beat for 1–2 minutes until pale and creamy. Beat in the cream, then gradually sift in the sugar and continue beating for 2–3 minutes, until the frosting is light and fluffy. Beat in a little pink food colouring.

5. To assemble the cakes, use a 6-cm/2½-inch round cutter to stamp six rounds from each sponge. Sandwich four of the different coloured sponge rounds together in a stack with some of the frosting. Start with the darkest sponge at the base and finish with the lightest at the top. Repeat with the remaining rounds and frosting to make six cakes in total. Spoon the remaining frosting into a piping bag fitted with a large star-shaped nozzle. Pipe a rosette on the top of each cake and decorate with shimmer hundreds and thousands.

#109 Chewy flapjack cupcakes

Ingredients

40 g/1½ oz soft tub margarine
40 g/1½ oz demerara sugar
1 tbsp golden syrup
55 g/2 oz rolled oats
55 g/2 oz butter, softened
55 g/2 oz golden caster sugar
1 large egg, lightly beaten
55 g/2 oz self-raising flour

1. Preheat the oven to 190°C/375°F/Gas Mark 5. Line an 8-hole muffin tin with paper cases or put eight double-layer paper cases on a baking tray.

2. Place the margarine, demerara sugar and golden syrup in a small saucepan and heat gently until the margarine has melted. Stir in the oats. Set aside.

3. Put the butter and sugar in a bowl and beat together until light and fluffy. Gradually beat in the egg. Sift in the flour and, using a metal spoon, gently fold into the mixture. Spoon the mixture into the paper cases. Gently spoon the flapjack mixture over the top.

4. Bake the cupcakes in the preheated oven for 20 minutes, or until golden brown. Transfer to a wire rack and leave to cool completely.

#110 Vanilla macaroons

Ingredients

75 g/2¾ oz ground almonds
115 g/4 oz icing sugar
2 large egg whites
50 g/1¾ oz caster sugar
½ tsp vanilla extract

Filling

55 g/2 oz butter, softened
½ tsp vanilla extract
115 g/4 oz icing sugar, sifted

1. Line two baking sheets with baking paper. Place the ground almonds and icing sugar in a food processor and process for 15 seconds. Sift the mixture into a bowl. Place the egg whites in a large bowl and whisk until they hold soft peaks. Gradually whisk in the caster sugar to make a firm, glossy meringue. Whisk in the vanilla extract. Using a spatula, fold the almond mixture into the meringue one third at a time. Continue to cut and fold the mixture until it forms a shiny batter with a thick, ribbon-like consistency.

2. Pour the mixture into a piping bag fitted with a 1-cm/½-inch plain nozzle. Pipe 32 small rounds onto the prepared baking sheets. Tap the sheets firmly on a work surface to remove air bubbles. Leave to stand at room temperature for 30 minutes. Meanwhile, preheat the oven to 160°C/325°F/Gas Mark 3. Bake in the preheated oven for 10–15 minutes. Leave to cool for 10 minutes, then carefully peel the macaroons off the baking paper. Leave to cool completely.

3. To make the filling, beat the butter and vanilla extract in a bowl until pale and fluffy. Gradually beat in the icing sugar until smooth and creamy. Use to sandwich pairs of the macaroons together.

Berry muffins

Makes
12

Ingredients

150 g/5½ oz frozen mixed berries

280 g/10 oz plain white flour

1 tbsp baking powder

⅛ tsp salt

115 g/4 oz caster sugar

2 medium eggs

250 ml/9 fl oz buttermilk

6 tbsp sunflower oil, plus extra
for greasing

1 tsp vanilla extract

icing sugar, for dusting

1. Preheat the oven to 200°C/400°F/Gas Mark 6. Grease a 12-hole muffin tin or line with paper cases. Cut any large berries, such as strawberries, into small pieces.

2. Sift together the flour, baking powder and salt into a large bowl and stir in the caster sugar. Lightly beat the eggs in a large jug, then beat in the buttermilk, oil and vanilla extract. Make a well in the centre of the dry ingredients, pour in the beaten liquid ingredients and add the berries. Stir gently until just combined; do not over-mix. Spoon into the paper cases. Bake in the preheated oven for about 20 minutes, until well risen, golden brown and firm to the touch.

3. Leave the muffins to cool in the tin for 5 minutes, then serve warm or transfer to a wire rack to cool completely. Dust with icing sugar just before serving.

112 Red velvet crinkle cookies

Makes
22

Ingredients

115 g/4 oz butter, softened

200 g/7 oz light muscovado sugar

2 eggs, beaten

2 tsp red liquid food colouring

280 g/10 oz plain flour

1 tsp baking powder

¼ tsp bicarbonate of soda

40 g/1½ oz cocoa powder

25 g/1 oz icing sugar

1. Put the butter and sugar into a large bowl and beat with an electric hand-held mixer until pale and fluffy. Gradually beat in the eggs, then beat in the food colouring.

2. Sift together the flour, baking powder, bicarbonate of soda and cocoa powder into the mixture. Stir with a wooden spoon to make a soft dough. Cover and chill in the refrigerator for 30–40 minutes, or until the dough is firm enough to shape.

3. Preheat the oven to 190°C/375°F/Gas Mark 5. Line two large baking sheets with baking paper.

4. Divide the dough into 22 pieces, then shape each piece into a ball. Sift the icing sugar onto a plate. Roll each ball of dough in the sugar to coat it completely, then place the balls on the baking sheets. Flatten each ball with your fingertips to a 6-cm/2½-inch round.

5. Bake in the preheated oven for 14–16 minutes, or until just set. Leave to cool on the baking sheets for 5 minutes, then transfer to wire racks to cool completely. Sprinkle any remaining icing sugar over the cookies.

#113 Pina colada cupcakes

Makes 12

Ingredients

190 g/6¾ oz plain flour

1½ tsp baking powder

¼ tsp salt

115 g/4 oz butter, softened

200 g/7 oz caster sugar

2 large eggs

2 tbsp white rum

125 ml/4 fl oz milk

85 g/3 oz canned pineapple, drained and crushed with a fork

4 large egg whites

200 g/7 oz granulated sugar

¼ tsp cream of tartar

1 tbsp coconut extract

2 tbsp coconut cream

60 g/2¼ oz toasted desiccated coconut

12 cocktail umbrellas, to decorate

1. Preheat the oven to 180°C/350°F/Gas Mark 4 and line a 12-hole muffin tin with paper cases.

2. Sift together the flour, baking powder and salt in a bowl. Put the butter and caster sugar into a separate bowl and beat until pale and fluffy. Add the eggs, one at a time, beating after each addition. Add the rum, milk and half of the flour mixture, and beat until combined. Add the remaining flour mixture and stir. Mix in the pineapple.

3. Spoon the mixture into the paper cases and bake in the preheated oven for 20 minutes, until risen and golden. Leave to cool in the tin for 1–2 minutes, then transfer to a wire rack to cool completely.

4. To make the frosting, put the egg whites, granulated sugar and cream of tartar in a heatproof bowl set over a saucepan of gently simmering water and whisk until the sugar has completely dissolved. Remove from the heat and whisk the mixture for 4–5 minutes, or until it holds stiff peaks. Add the coconut extract and coconut cream and stir until just combined. Spoon the frosting into a piping bag fitted with a star-shaped nozzle and pipe onto the cupcakes.

5. Sprinkle with toasted desiccated coconut and decorate each cupcake with a cocktail umbrella.

#114 Snickerdoodles

Makes 40

Ingredients

225 g/8 oz butter, softened

140 g/5 oz caster sugar, plus extra for dusting

2 large eggs, lightly beaten

1 tsp vanilla extract

400 g/14 oz plain flour

1 tsp bicarbonate of soda

½ tsp freshly grated nutmeg

55 g/2 oz pecan nuts, finely chopped

2 tbsp ground cinnamon

salt

1. Put the butter and sugar into a bowl and mix well with a wooden spoon, then beat in the eggs and vanilla extract. Sift the flour, bicarbonate of soda, nutmeg and a pinch of salt into the mixture, add the nuts and stir until thoroughly combined. Shape the dough into a ball, wrap in clingfilm and chill in the refrigerator for 30–60 minutes. Preheat the oven to 190°C/375°F/Gas Mark 5. Line three baking sheets with baking paper.

2. Mix a little caster sugar with the cinnamon in a shallow dish. Scoop up 40 tablespoons of the dough and roll into balls. Roll each ball in the cinnamon mixture to coat and place on the prepared baking sheets, spaced well apart.

3. Bake in the preheated oven for 10–12 minutes, until golden brown. Leave to cool on the baking sheets for a few minutes, then transfer to wire racks to cool completely.

#115 Chocolate chip cookies

Makes
8

Ingredients

175 g/6 oz plain flour, sifted

1 tsp baking powder

125 g/4½ oz margarine, melted, plus
extra for greasing

85 g/3 oz light muscovado sugar

55 g/2 oz caster sugar

½ tsp vanilla extract

1 egg, beaten

125 g/4½ oz plain chocolate chips

1. Preheat the oven to 190°C/375°F/Gas Mark 5. Lightly grease two baking sheets.

2. Place all of the ingredients in a large mixing bowl and beat until well combined. Place tablespoons of the mixture on the prepared baking sheets, spaced well apart.

3. Bake in the preheated oven for 10–12 minutes, or until golden brown. Transfer to a wire rack and leave to cool.

#116 Chocolate whoopie pies

Makes
10

Ingredients

175 g/6 oz plain flour

1½ tsp bicarbonate of soda

40 g/1½ oz cocoa powder

large pinch of salt

85 g/3 oz butter, softened

85 g/3 oz white vegetable fat

150 g/5½ oz soft dark brown sugar

1 large egg, beaten

1 tsp vanilla extract

150 ml/5 fl oz milk

Filling

225 g/8 oz white marshmallows

4 tbsp milk

115 g/4 oz white vegetable fat

55 g/2 oz icing sugar, sifted

1. Preheat the oven to 180°C/350°F/Gas Mark 4. Line three large baking sheets with baking paper. Sift together the flour, bicarbonate of soda, cocoa powder and salt.

2. Place the butter, vegetable fat and sugar in a large bowl and beat with an electric hand-held mixer until pale and fluffy. Beat in the egg and vanilla extract, followed by half the flour mixture and then the milk. Stir in the remaining flour mixture and mix until thoroughly incorporated.

3. Pipe 20 mounds of the mixture onto the prepared baking sheets, spaced well apart. Bake in the preheated oven, one sheet at a time, for 12–14 minutes until risen and just firm to the touch. Leave to cool for 5 minutes, then transfer to a wire rack to cool completely.

4. To make the filling, place the marshmallows and milk in a heatproof bowl set over a saucepan of gently simmering water and heat until the marshmallows have melted, stirring occasionally. Remove from the heat and leave to cool.

5. Place the vegetable fat and icing sugar in a bowl and beat together until smooth and creamy. Add to the marshmallow and beat for 1–2 minutes until fluffy.

6. Spread the filling over the flat side of 10 of the cakes, then sandwich with the remaining cakes.

Molten chocolate cupcakes

Makes
9

Ingredients

175 g/6 oz soft margarine
175 g/6 oz caster sugar
3 large eggs
250 g/9 oz self-raising flour
3 tbsp cocoa powder
175 g/6 oz plain chocolate, broken into 9 pieces
icing sugar, for dusting

1. Preheat the oven to 190°C/375°F/Gas Mark 5. Line a 9-hole muffin tin with paper cases.

2. Put the margarine, caster sugar, eggs, flour and cocoa powder in a large bowl and beat with an electric hand-held mixer until just smooth.

3. Spoon half of the mixture into the paper cases. Use a teaspoon to make an indentation in the centre of each cake. Place a piece of chocolate in each indentation, then spoon the remaining cake mixture on top.

4. Bake the cupcakes in the preheated oven for 20 minutes, or until well risen and springy to the touch. Leave to cool for 2–3 minutes before serving warm, dusted with icing sugar.

Rosewater biscuits

Makes
40

Ingredients

225 g/8 oz butter, softened
225 g/8 oz caster sugar
1 large egg, lightly beaten
1 tbsp rosewater
280 g/10 oz plain flour
1 tsp baking powder
pinch of salt

Icing

1 egg white
250 g/9 oz icing sugar
2 tsp plain flour
2 tsp rosewater
a few drops of pink food colouring

1. Place the butter and sugar in a large bowl and beat together until light and fluffy, then beat in the egg and rosewater. Sift the flour, baking powder and salt into the mixture and stir until combined. Shape the dough into a log, wrap in clingfilm and chill in the refrigerator for 1–2 hours.

2. Preheat the oven to 190°C/375°F/Gas Mark 5. Line three baking sheets with baking paper. Unwrap the dough, cut into thin slices with a sharp serrated knife and place on the baking sheets, spaced well apart. Bake in the preheated oven for 10–12 minutes, or until light golden brown. Leave to cool on the baking sheets for 10 minutes, then transfer to wire racks to cool completely.

3. To make the icing, use a fork to lightly beat the egg white in a bowl. Sift in half of the icing sugar and stir well, then sift in the remaining icing sugar and the flour and mix in enough rosewater to make a smooth, easy-to-spread icing. Stir in a few drops of pink food colouring. Leave the biscuits on the racks and gently spread the icing over the top. Leave to set.

Toasted marshmallow cupcakes

Makes
12

Ingredients

100 g/3½ oz butter or margarine

100 g/3½ oz caster sugar

2 eggs

25 g/1 oz cocoa powder, sifted

85 g/3 oz self-raising flour, sifted

1 tsp baking powder

12 marshmallows

silver dragées, to decorate

1. Preheat the oven to 200°C/400°F/Gas Mark 6. Line a 12-hole muffin tin with paper cases.

2. Place the butter, sugar, eggs, cocoa powder, flour and baking powder in a mixing bowl and beat well for 3–4 minutes until smooth and creamy.

3. Divide the mixture between the paper cases and bake in the preheated oven for 15–20 minutes, until well risen and the tops bounce back when lightly pressed with your fingertip. Transfer to a wire rack.

4. Place the marshmallows in a small saucepan and heat very gently until they are molten. Alternatively, heat them in a microwave for a few seconds on the lowest setting.

5. Top each cake with a little of the marshmallow, smoothing it with a teaspoon. Use a cook's blowtorch or a very hot grill to gently toast the top of the cakes. Scatter over some silver dragées, leave to set, then serve.

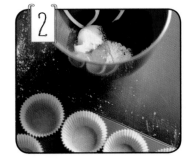
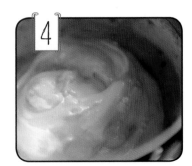

#120 Viennese fingers

Ingredients

100 g/3½ oz butter, plus extra
for greasing
25 g/1 oz golden caster sugar
½ tsp vanilla extract
100 g/3½ oz self-raising flour
100 g/3½ oz plain chocolate, broken
into pieces

1. Preheat the oven to 160°C/325°F/Gas Mark 3. Lightly grease two baking sheets.

2. Place the butter, sugar and vanilla extract in a bowl and cream together until pale and fluffy. Stir in the flour, mixing to a fairly stiff dough. Place the mixture in a piping bag fitted with a large star-shaped nozzle and pipe 16 x 6-cm/2½-inch fingers onto the prepared baking sheets, spaced well apart. Bake in the preheated oven for 10–15 minutes, until golden brown. Leave to cool on the baking sheets for 5 minutes, then transfer to wire racks to cool completely.

3. Place the chocolate in a small heatproof bowl set over a saucepan of gently simmering water and heat until melted. Remove from the heat. Dip one end of each biscuit into the chocolate to coat, then place on a sheet of baking paper and leave to set.

#121 Chocolate chip muffins

Ingredients

300 g/10½ oz self-raising flour
1½ tsp baking powder
85 g/3 oz butter, chilled
and diced
85 g/3 oz caster sugar
150 g/5½ oz milk chocolate,
chopped into chunks
2 large eggs, beaten
200 ml/7 fl oz buttermilk
1 tsp vanilla extract

1. Preheat the oven to 200°C/400°F/Gas Mark 6. Line a 12-hole muffin tin with paper cases.

2. Sift together the flour and baking powder into a large bowl. Add the butter and rub in to make fine breadcrumbs. Stir in the sugar and the chocolate chunks.

3. Beat together the eggs, buttermilk and vanilla extract. Make a well in the centre of the dry ingredients and pour in the beaten liquid ingredients. Stir gently until just combined; do not over-mix.

4. Divide the mixture evenly between the paper cases. Bake in the preheated oven for 20–25 minutes, or until risen, golden and just firm to the touch. Leave to cool for 5 minutes, then transfer to a wire rack to cool completely.

#122 Mini blueberry muffins

Makes
18

Ingredients

125 g/4½ oz self-raising flour

½ tsp baking powder

70 g/2½ oz caster sugar

85 g/3 oz blueberries

2 tsp vanilla extract

1 egg

125 ml/4 fl oz buttermilk

2 tbsp vegetable oil

vanilla sugar, for dusting

1. Preheat the oven to 190°C/375°F/Gas Mark 5. Cut out 18 x 9-cm/3½-inch squares of baking paper. Push the squares into two 12-hole mini muffin tins, creasing the squares to fit so that they form paper cases. Don't worry if they lift out of the sections slightly; the weight of the muffin mixture will hold them in place.

2. Sift the flour and baking powder into a mixing bowl. Stir in the sugar and blueberries. In a separate mixing bowl, beat together the vanilla extract, egg, buttermilk and oil with a fork until evenly combined.

3. Tip the buttermilk mixture into the flour. Using a metal spoon, gently fold the ingredients together until just combined; do not over-mix.

4. Spoon the mixture into the paper cases; it should be level with the top of the tin. Sprinkle with a little vanilla sugar and bake in the preheated oven for 15 minutes, or until risen and just firm to the touch. Leave the muffins in the tin for 2 minutes, then transfer them to wire racks to cool. Serve warm or cold, dusted with extra vanilla sugar.

#123 Mini coffee & maple Bundt cakes

Makes
4

Ingredients

115 g/4 oz butter, softened, plus extra for greasing

115 g/4 oz caster sugar

2 eggs, beaten

175 g/6 oz self-raising flour, sifted, plus extra for dusting

1 tbsp coffee and chicory essence

4 tbsp buttermilk

Icing

115 g/4 oz icing sugar

2 tbsp maple syrup

1–2 tsp water

1. Preheat the oven to 180°C/350°F/Gas Mark 4. Thoroughly grease 4 x 200-ml/7-fl oz Bundt tins, then dust each with a little flour, tipping out any excess.

2. Put the butter and sugar into a bowl and beat together until pale and creamy. Gradually beat in the eggs, then fold in half the flour. Fold in the coffee and chicory essence and buttermilk, followed by the remaining flour. Divide the mixture between the prepared tins. Place on a baking sheet and bake in the preheated oven for 25–30 minutes, or until risen and firm to the touch. Leave to cool in the tins for 5 minutes, then turn out onto a wire rack to cool completely.

3. To make the icing, sift the sugar into a bowl and stir in the maple syrup and water, then mix until smooth. Drizzle over the cakes and leave to set.

87

Mango cakes

Makes
12

Ingredients

70 g/2½ oz dried mango, finely chopped

finely grated rind of 1 orange, plus 3 tbsp juice

25 g/1 oz creamed coconut, finely grated

85 g/3 oz lightly salted butter, softened, plus extra for greasing

70 g/2½ oz caster sugar

1 egg

85 g/3 oz self-raising flour

icing sugar, for dusting

1. Grease and line the bases of 12 individual loaf tins. Put the mango and orange juice in a small bowl and leave to stand, covered, for 2–3 hours, or until the orange juice is mostly absorbed.

2. Preheat the oven to 180°C/350°F/Gas Mark 4. Put the coconut, butter, sugar, egg, flour and orange rind in a mixing bowl and beat with an electric hand-held mixer until smooth and pale. Stir in the mango and any unabsorbed orange juice.

3. Spoon the mixture into the tins with a teaspoon and level with the back of the spoon. Bake in the preheated oven for 25 minutes, or until risen and just firm to the touch. Leave to cool in the tins for 5 minutes, then transfer to a wire rack to cool completely. Lightly dust with icing sugar and serve.

Raspberry daiquiri cupcakes

Makes
12

Ingredients

190 g/6¾ oz plain flour

1½ tsp baking powder

¼ tsp salt

115 g/4 oz butter, softened

250 g/9 oz caster sugar

2 large eggs

125 ml/4 fl oz milk

4 tbsp rum

finely grated rind and juice of 1 lime

350 g/12 oz fresh raspberries, puréed

1 tbsp cornflour

pink sugar crystals, to decorate

Frosting

115 g/4 oz butter, softened

250 g/9 oz icing sugar

1 tsp raspberry extract

2 tbsp double cream

pinch of salt

1. Preheat the oven to 180°C/350°F/Gas Mark 4 and line a 12-hole muffin tin with paper cases.

2. Sift together the flour, baking powder and salt into a bowl. Put the butter and 200 g/7 oz of the caster sugar into a separate bowl and beat until pale and fluffy. Add the eggs, one at a time, beating after each addition. Add half of the flour mixture, the milk, half of the rum and the lime rind and juice, and beat until incorporated. Add the remaining flour mixture and mix. Spoon into the paper cases and bake in the preheated oven for 20 minutes, until risen and golden. Leave to cool in the tin for 1–2 minutes, then transfer to a wire rack to cool completely.

3. Put the raspberry purée and the remaining caster sugar in a saucepan and bring to the boil, stirring frequently. Put the remaining rum and the cornflour into a small bowl and whisk together. Pour into the boiling raspberry mixture and cook for a further 1–2 minutes, stirring, until thick. Remove from the heat, leave to cool, then chill.

4. To make the frosting, beat the butter in a bowl until pale and creamy. Add the icing sugar, raspberry extract, cream, salt and 2 tablespoons of the raspberry mixture. Beat well to combine. Spoon into a piping bag fitted with a star-shaped nozzle.

5. Use an apple corer to remove the centre of each cupcake and spoon the remaining raspberry filling into each hole. Pipe the frosting onto the cupcakes, then sprinkle with the sugar crystals.

Blueberry cheesecake whoopie pies

Ingredients

250 g/9 oz plain flour
1 tsp bicarbonate of soda
large pinch of salt
115 g/4 oz butter, softened
150 g/5½ oz caster sugar
1 large egg, beaten
1 tsp vanilla extract
4 tbsp soured cream
3 tbsp milk
55 g/2 oz sweetened dried blueberries
icing sugar, for dusting

Filling

225 g/8 oz full-fat soft cheese
2 tsp finely grated lemon rind
6 tbsp soured cream
40 g/1½ oz icing sugar, sifted

1. Preheat the oven to 180°C/350°F/Gas Mark 4. Line three large baking sheets with baking paper. .

2. Sift together the flour, bicarbonate of soda and salt. Place the butter and sugar in a large bowl and beat until pale and fluffy. Beat in the egg and vanilla extract, followed by half the flour mixture, then beat in the soured cream and milk. Stir in the remaining flour mixture and mix until thoroughly incorporated. Stir in the blueberries.

3. Pipe or spoon 24 mounds of the mixture onto the prepared baking sheets, spaced well apart. Bake in the preheated oven, one sheet at a time, for 10–12 minutes until risen and just firm to the touch. Leave to cool for 5 minutes, then carefully transfer to a wire rack and leave to cool completely.

4. To make the filling, place the soft cheese, lemon rind, soured cream and icing sugar in a bowl and beat together until smooth.

5. To assemble, spread or pipe the filling on the flat side of 12 of the cakes. Top with the remaining cakes and lightly dust with icing sugar.

Black & white cookies

Ingredients

115 g/4 oz butter, softened, plus extra for greasing
1 tsp vanilla extract
175 g/6 oz caster sugar
2 eggs, beaten
300 g/10½ oz plain flour
½ tsp baking powder
200 ml/7 fl oz milk

Icing

225 g/8 oz icing sugar
125 ml/4 fl oz double cream
½ tsp vanilla extract
75 g/2¾ oz plain chocolate, broken

1. Preheat the oven to 190°C/375°F/Gas Mark 5. Grease three baking sheets. Place the butter, vanilla extract and caster sugar in a large bowl and beat until light and fluffy. Beat in the eggs.

2. Sift in the flour and baking powder and fold into the mixture, loosening with milk as you go until the dry ingredients have been incorporated and the mix has a dropping consistency. Drop heaped tablespoons of the mixture on the prepared baking sheets, spaced well apart. Bake in the preheated oven for 15 minutes, then transfer to wire racks to cool.

3. To make the icing, put the icing sugar in a bowl and mix in half the cream and the vanilla extract to a thick but spreadable consistency. Using a palette knife, spread half of each biscuit with white icing. Place the chocolate in a bowl set over a saucepan of gently simmering water and heat until melted. Remove from the heat and stir in the remaining cream. Spread the dark icing over the uncoated biscuit halves.

#128 Orange blossom & pistachio friands

Makes 8

Ingredients

115 g/4 oz butter, plus extra for greasing

70 g/2½ oz pistachio nuts

55 g/2 oz plain flour

150 g/5½ oz icing sugar, plus extra
for dusting

55 g/2 oz ground almonds

3 large egg whites

2 tsp orange blossom water

pinch of salt

1. Preheat the oven to 200°C/400°F/Gas Mark 6. Thoroughly grease an 8-hole silicone friand mould, then place the mould on a baking sheet.

2. Melt the butter in a small saucepan, then set aside to cool for 10 minutes. Put 55 g/2 oz of the pistachio nuts into a food processor or blender and process until finely ground. Roughly chop the remaining nuts and set aside.

3. Sift together the flour and sugar into a large bowl and stir in the ground pistachio nuts and ground almonds. Put the egg whites, orange blossom water and salt into a large, grease-free bowl and beat with an electric hand-held mixer for 1–2 minutes, until foamy and floppy, but not stiff.

4. Pour the egg whites and melted butter into the dry ingredients and mix well to make a thick mixture. Spoon the mixture evenly into the prepared mould and scatter over the reserved pistachio nuts.

5. Bake in the preheated oven for 15–18 minutes, or until risen, golden and just firm to the touch. Leave to cool in the mould for 2–3 minutes, then carefully turn out onto a wire rack and leave to cool completely. Serve dusted with icing sugar.

#129 Raspberry ripple cupcakes

Makes
32

Ingredients

175 g/6 oz plain flour
1 tbsp baking powder
1 tbsp cornflour
175 g/6 oz butter, softened
175 g/6 oz caster sugar
3 eggs, beaten
1 tsp almond extract
200 g/7 oz fresh raspberries
vanilla sugar, for sprinkling

1. Preheat the oven to 190°C/375°F/Gas Mark 5. Line two 16-hole muffin tins with paper cases or put 32 double-layer paper cases on baking trays.

2. Sift the flour, baking powder and cornflour into a large bowl and add the butter, caster sugar, eggs and almond extract. Beat well until the mixture is smooth. Mash the raspberries lightly with a fork, then fold into the mixture. Spoon the mixture into the paper cases.

3. Bake the cupcakes in the preheated oven for 15-20 minutes, or until golden brown and firm to the touch. Transfer the cupcakes to a wire rack and leave to cool.

4. Sprinkle with vanilla sugar before serving.

#130 Coffee & walnut puddings

Makes
6

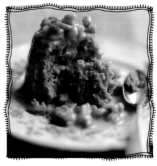

Ingredients

1 tbsp instant coffee powder
150 g/5½ oz self-raising flour
1 tsp ground cinnamon
55 g/2 oz butter, softened, plus extra for greasing
55 g/2 oz brown sugar
2 large eggs, beaten
55 g/2 oz walnuts, finely chopped

Sauce

25 g/1 oz walnuts, roughly chopped
55 g/2 oz butter
55 g/2 oz brown sugar

1. Preheat the oven to 190°C/375°F/Gas Mark 5. Grease six small pudding basins. Dissolve the coffee powder in 2 tablespoons of boiling water and set aside. Sift the flour and cinnamon into a bowl. Place the butter and sugar in a separate bowl and beat together until creamy. Gradually beat in the eggs, adding a little of the flour mixture if it starts to curdle. Fold in half of the flour and cinnamon mixture, then fold in the remaining mixture, alternating with the coffee and walnuts.

2. Divide the mixture evenly between the prepared basins. Place a piece of greased foil over each basin and secure with an elastic band. Stand the basins in a roasting tin and pour in boiling water to reach halfway up the sides of the basins. Cover the tin with a tent of foil, folding it under the rim.

3. Bake in the preheated oven for 30-40 minutes, or until well risen and firm to the touch. Meanwhile, make the sauce. Place all the ingredients in a saucepan over a low heat and stir until melted and blended. Bring to a simmer, then remove from the heat. Turn out the sponges onto a serving plate, spoon over the hot sauce and serve.

Cappuccino soufflés

Ingredients

butter, for greasing

6 tbsp whipping cream

2 tsp instant espresso
coffee granules

2 tbsp coffee liqueur

3 large eggs, separated,
plus 1 extra egg white

2 tbsp golden caster sugar,
plus extra for coating

150 g/5½ oz plain chocolate, melted
and cooled

cocoa powder, for dusting

1. Preheat the oven to 190°C/375°F/Gas Mark 5. Lightly grease 6 x 175-ml/6-fl oz ramekins and dust with caster sugar. Place the cream in a small, heavy-based saucepan and heat gently. Stir in the coffee until it has dissolved, then stir in the liqueur. Divide the mixture between the prepared ramekins.

2. Place the egg whites in a clean, grease-free bowl and whisk until they hold soft peaks, then gradually whisk in the sugar until stiff but not dry. Stir the egg yolks and melted chocolate together in a separate bowl, stir in a little egg white, then gradually fold in the remainder.

3. Divide the egg mixture between the ramekins, then place them on a baking sheet and bake in the preheated oven for 15 minutes, or until just set. Dust with cocoa powder and serve.

Lamingtons

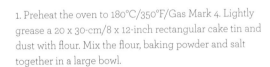

Ingredients

280 g/10 oz plain flour,
plus extra for dusting

3 tsp baking powder

¼ tsp salt

140 g/5 oz butter, softened,
plus extra for greasing

150 g/5½ oz granulated sugar

1 tsp vanilla extract or 1 vanilla
pod, scraped

2 eggs

125 ml/4 fl oz milk

Icing

200 g/7 oz icing sugar

30 g/1 oz cocoa powder

125 ml/4 fl oz milk

25 g/1 oz butter

280 g/10 oz desiccated coconut

1. Preheat the oven to 180°C/350°F/Gas Mark 4. Lightly grease a 20 x 30-cm/8 x 12-inch rectangular cake tin and dust with flour. Mix the flour, baking powder and salt together in a large bowl.

2. Put the butter, sugar and vanilla extract into a separate bowl and whisk until pale and fluffy. Gradually add the eggs, flour mixture and milk, making alternate additions and stirring carefully.

3. Spread the mixture evenly in the prepared tin and bake in the preheated oven for 30–40 minutes, until a cocktail stick inserted in the centre of the cake comes out clean. Remove from the oven, transfer to a wire rack and leave to cool for 5 minutes. Cut the cake into 8–10 rectangles and chill in the refrigerator overnight.

4. To make the icing, mix together the icing sugar and cocoa powder in a bowl. Heat the milk in a saucepan, then add the butter and stir until melted. Pour the warm liquid into the sugar mixture, stirring well until thickened but still runny. Using a fork, dip the cake rectangles in the icing to cover them completely, then place them on a wire rack set over a piece of baking paper. Put the coconut into a shallow bowl, then add the cakes, one at a time, and turn in the coconut until completely covered.

133 Indulgent almond cupcakes

Makes
12

Ingredients

100 g/3½ oz butter, softened
100 g/3½ oz caster sugar
2 eggs, lightly beaten
¼ tsp almond extract
4 tbsp single cream
175 g/6 oz plain flour
1½ tsp baking powder
70 g/2½ oz ground almonds

Frosting

115 g/4 oz butter, softened
225 g/8 oz icing sugar
a few drops of almond extract
25 g/1 oz toasted flaked almonds

1. Preheat the oven to 180°C/350°F/Gas Mark 4. Line a
12-hole muffin tin with paper cases.

2. Place the butter and sugar in a large bowl and beat together
until light and fluffy. Gradually beat in the eggs, then add the almond extract and cream. Sift in
the flour and baking powder and fold into the mixture, then fold in the ground almonds. Spoon the
mixture into the paper cases.

3. Bake in the preheated oven for 25 minutes, or until golden brown and firm to the touch. Transfer
the cupcakes to a wire rack and leave to cool.

4. To make the frosting, place the butter in a large bowl and beat until creamy. Sift in the icing
sugar. Add the almond extract and beat together until smooth. Spread the frosting on top of each
cake, swirling with a knife. Sprinkle the flaked almonds over the top.

134 Jam rings

Makes
15

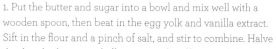

Ingredients

225 g/8 oz butter, softened
140 g/5 oz caster sugar, plus extra
for sprinkling
1 egg yolk, lightly beaten
2 tsp vanilla extract
280 g/10 oz plain flour
1 egg white, lightly beaten
salt

Filling

55 g/2 oz butter, softened
100 g/3½ oz icing sugar
5 tbsp strawberry jam or raspberry jam

1. Put the butter and sugar into a bowl and mix well with a
wooden spoon, then beat in the egg yolk and vanilla extract.
Sift in the flour and a pinch of salt, and stir to combine. Halve
the dough, shape into balls, wrap in clingfilm and chill in the refrigerator for 30–60 minutes.

2. Preheat the oven to 190°C/375°F/Gas Mark 5. Line two baking sheets with baking paper.
Roll out the dough between two sheets of baking paper. Stamp out 30 cookies with a 7-cm/2¾-inch
fluted round cutter and put 15 on a prepared baking sheet, spaced well apart. Use a 4-cm/1½-inch
plain round cutter to stamp out the centres of the remaining cookies to make rings. Put the rings
on the other baking sheet, spaced well apart. Bake in the preheated oven for 7 minutes, then brush
the rings with beaten egg white and sprinkle with caster sugar. Bake for a further 5–8 minutes.
Leave to cool on the baking sheets for 5–10 minutes, then transfer to wire racks to cool completely.

3. To make the filling, beat the butter and icing sugar together in a bowl until smooth. Spread the
buttercream on the whole cookies. Top with a little jam. Place the rings on top and press together.

#135 Chocolate chip cupcakes

Makes 8

Ingredients

100 g/3½ oz soft tub margarine

100 g/3½ oz caster sugar

2 large eggs

100 g/3½ oz self-raising flour, sifted

100 g/3½ oz plain chocolate chips

1. Preheat the oven to 190°C/375°F/Gas Mark 5. Line an 8-hole muffin tin with paper cases or put eight double-layer paper cases on a baking tray.

2. Put the margarine, sugar, eggs and flour in a large bowl and beat with an electric hand-held mixer until just smooth. Fold in the chocolate chips. Spoon the mixture into the paper cases.

3. Bake the cupcakes in the preheated oven for 20–25 minutes, or until well risen and golden brown. Transfer to a wire rack to cool.

#136 German baumkuchen

Makes 20

Ingredients

6 egg yolks, separated

200 g/7 oz softened butter, plus extra for greasing

100 g/3½ oz icing sugar

10 g/¼ oz vanilla sugar

100 g/3½ oz plain flour

50 g/1¾ oz cornflour

pinch of salt

115 g/4 oz caster sugar

200 g/7 oz plain chocolate, broken into pieces

15 g/½ oz white vegetable fat

1. Preheat the grill to medium and grease a 25-cm/10-inch round springform cake tin.

2. Put the egg yolks, butter, icing sugar, vanilla sugar, flour and cornflour into a large bowl and mix to combine. Put the egg whites and salt into a separate bowl and whisk, gradually adding the caster sugar, until they hold soft peaks. Carefully fold into the flour mixture.

3. Spread a thin layer of the mixture on the base of the prepared tin and place under the preheated grill for 1 minute, or until golden brown. Remove from the grill, spread another thin layer of batter over the first layer and return to the grill. Repeat until all the mixture has been used up. Turn out the cake onto a wire rack and leave to cool.

4. Meanwhile, put the chocolate into a bowl set over a saucepan of gently simmering water, add the vegetable fat and stir until melted. Cut the cake into bite-sized triangles and use a fork to dip the wider ends in the chocolate mixture. Transfer to a wire rack and leave to cool.

#137 Pineapple ginger creams

Makes
15

Ingredients

225 g/8 oz butter, softened

140 g/5 oz caster sugar

1 egg yolk, lightly beaten

2 tsp vanilla extract

280 g/10 oz plain flour

100 g/3½ oz ready-to-eat dried pineapple, finely chopped

salt

cocoa powder, for dusting

icing sugar, for dusting

Filling

150 ml/5 fl oz Greek-style yogurt

1 tbsp golden syrup

1 tbsp ground ginger

1. Put the butter and sugar into a bowl and mix well with a wooden spoon, then beat in the egg yolk and vanilla extract. Sift the flour and a pinch of salt into the mixture, add the pineapple and stir until thoroughly combined. Halve the dough, shape into balls, wrap in clingfilm and chill in the refrigerator for 30–60 minutes.

2. Preheat the oven to 190°C/375°F/Gas Mark 5. Line two baking sheets with baking paper.

3. Unwrap the dough and roll out between two sheets of baking paper. Stamp out 30 cookies with a 6-cm/2½-inch fluted round cutter and put them on the prepared baking sheets, spaced well apart. Bake in the preheated oven for 10–15 minutes, until light golden brown. Leave to cool on the baking sheets for 5–10 minutes, then carefully transfer to wire racks to cool completely.

4. To make the filling, beat the yogurt, golden syrup and ginger in a bowl until thoroughly combined. Sandwich the cookies together with the ginger cream. Cover half of each cookie with a piece of paper and dust the exposed half with sifted cocoa powder. Cover the cocoa-dusted half of each cookie with a piece of paper and dust the exposed half with sifted icing sugar.

#138 Raspberry crumble muffins

Makes
12

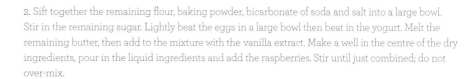

Ingredients

330 g/11¾ oz plain flour

120 g/4¼ oz butter

140 g/5 oz caster sugar

1 tbsp baking powder

½ tsp bicarbonate of soda

pinch of salt

2 eggs

250 ml/9 fl oz natural yogurt

1 tsp vanilla extract

150 g/5½ oz frozen raspberries

1. Preheat the oven to 200°C/400°F/Gas Mark 6. Line a 12-hole muffin tin with paper cases. Sift 50 g/1¾ oz of the flour into a bowl. Cut 35 g/1¼ oz of the butter into small pieces, add to the flour and rub it in with your fingertips until the mixture resembles fine breadcrumbs. Stir in 25 g/1 oz of the sugar and set aside.

2. Sift together the remaining flour, baking powder, bicarbonate of soda and salt into a large bowl. Stir in the remaining sugar. Lightly beat the eggs in a large bowl then beat in the yogurt. Melt the remaining butter, then add to the mixture with the vanilla extract. Make a well in the centre of the dry ingredients, pour in the liquid ingredients and add the raspberries. Stir until just combined; do not over-mix.

3. Spoon the mixture into the paper cases. Scatter the crumble mixture over each muffin and press down lightly. Bake in the preheated oven for about 20 minutes, until risen, golden and firm to the touch. Leave to cool in the tin for 5 minutes, then transfer to a wire rack to cool completely.

Raspberry & pink peppercorn macaroons

Makes
20

Ingredients

175 g/6 oz icing sugar
125 g/4½ oz ground almonds
3 egg whites
70 g/2½ oz caster sugar
1–2 tsp natural pink food colouring
raspberry flavouring (optional)

Filling

150 g/5½ oz butter, softened
70 g/2½ oz icing sugar
1–2 tbsp raspberry jam
1 tsp crushed pink peppercorns

1. Preheat the oven to 140°C/275°F/Gas Mark 1. Line two baking trays with baking paper.

2. Place the icing sugar and ground almonds in a blender or food processor and blend until very fine and evenly ground. Sift into a bowl.

3. Place the egg whites in a mixing bowl and whisk with an electric mixer until they hold soft peaks. Gradually add the sugar, 1 teaspoon at a time, until the mixture is smooth and glossy. Beat in the food colouring and raspberry flavouring, if using, until evenly distributed.

4. Fold the ground almond and sugar mixture into the egg whites, one third at a time, until the mixture is well combined. Spoon into a piping bag fitted with a 1-cm/½-inch plain nozzle.

5. Pipe 40 small rounds, about 3 cm/1¼ inches in diameter, onto the prepared trays. Sharply tap the trays on the work surface and leave to stand at room temperature for 15–20 minutes until a skin forms on the rounds. Bake the macaroons in the preheated oven for 15 minutes, then leave to cool on the trays.

6. To make the filling, beat together the butter and icing sugar until smooth. Beat in the raspberry jam and the peppercorns. Pipe a little buttercream into the macaroons, sandwich together and serve immediately.

#140 Giant choc chunk cookies

Ingredients

115 g/4 oz butter, softened
125 g/4½ oz caster sugar
125 g/4½ oz soft light brown sugar
2 large eggs, lightly beaten
1 tsp vanilla extract
280 g/10 oz plain flour
1 tsp bicarbonate of soda
300 g/10½ oz chocolate chunks

1. Preheat the oven to 180°C/350°F/Gas Mark 4. Line four large baking sheets with baking paper.

2. Place the butter, caster sugar and brown sugar in a large bowl and beat together until pale and creamy. Whisk the eggs and vanilla extract into the mixture until smooth. Sift in the flour and bicarbonate of soda and beat together until well mixed. Stir in the chocolate chunks.

3. Drop 12 large spoonfuls of the mixture onto the prepared baking sheets, spaced well apart. Bake in the preheated oven for 15–20 minutes, or until set and golden brown. Leave to cool on the baking sheets for 2–3 minutes, then transfer to a wire rack to cool completely.

#141 Lemon meringue cupcakes

Makes 4

Ingredients

85 g/3 oz butter, softened, plus extra for greasing
85 g/3 oz caster sugar
finely grated rind and juice of ½ lemon
1 large egg, lightly beaten
85 g/3 oz self-raising flour
2 tbsp lemon curd

Topping

2 egg whites
115 g/4 oz caster sugar

1. Preheat the oven to 190°C/375°F/Gas Mark 5. Grease 4 x 200-ml/7-fl oz ovenproof teacups or ramekins.

2. Place the butter, caster sugar and lemon rind in a large bowl and beat together until light and fluffy. Gradually beat in the egg. Sift in the flour and, using a metal spoon, fold into the mixture with the lemon juice.

3. Spoon the mixture into the teacups. Put the teacups on a baking sheet. Bake in the preheated oven for 15 minutes, or until risen, golden and firm to the touch. Do not switch off the oven.

4. While the cupcakes are baking, make the topping. Put the egg whites in a grease-free bowl and whisk with an electric hand-held mixer until stiff. Gradually whisk in the sugar to make a stiff and glossy meringue.

5. Spread the lemon curd over the hot cupcakes, then swirl over the meringue. Return the cupcakes to the oven for 4–5 minutes, until the meringue is golden. Serve immediately.

142 Pistachio & almond tuiles

Makes
6

Ingredients

1 egg white

55 g/2 oz golden caster sugar

25 g/1 oz plain flour

25 g/1 oz pistachio nuts,
finely chopped

25 g/1 oz ground almonds

½ tsp almond extract

40 g/1½ oz butter,
melted and cooled

1. Preheat the oven to 160°C/325°F/Gas Mark 3. Line two baking trays with baking paper.

2. Lightly whisk the egg white with the sugar, then stir in the flour, pistachio nuts, ground almonds, almond extract and butter, mixing to a soft paste.

3. Place six walnut-sized spoonfuls of the mixture on the prepared trays and use the back of the spoon to spread as thinly as possible. Bake in the preheated oven for 10–15 minutes, until the biscuits are pale golden.

4. Quickly lift each biscuit with a palette knife and place over the side of a rolling pin to shape into a curve. When set, transfer to a wire rack to cool.

143 Lemon butterfly cupcakes

Makes
12

Ingredients

115 g/4 oz self-raising flour

½ tsp baking powder

115 g/4 oz butter, softened

115 g/4 oz caster sugar

2 eggs, beaten

finely grated rind of ¾ lemon

2–4 tbsp milk

icing sugar, for dusting

Filling

55 g/2 oz butter

115 g/4 oz icing sugar

1 tbsp lemon juice

1. Preheat the oven to 190°C/375°F/Gas Mark 5. Line a 12-hole muffin tin with paper cases.

2. Sift the flour and baking powder into a bowl. Add the butter, caster sugar, eggs, lemon rind and enough milk to give a medium-soft consistency. Beat until smooth, then divide between the paper cases and bake in the preheated oven for 15–20 minutes, or until well risen and golden. Transfer to a wire rack to cool completely.

3. To make the filling, place the butter in a bowl. Sift in the icing sugar and add the lemon juice. Beat well until smooth and creamy.

4. Use a sharp-pointed vegetable knife to cut a round from the top of each cake, then cut each round in half. Spoon a little buttercream filling on top of each cake and press the two semi-circular pieces into it to resemble wings. Dust the cakes with icing sugar just before serving.

99

#144 White chocolate & raspberry muffins

Makes 12

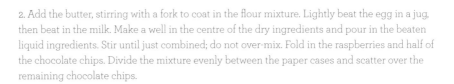

Ingredients

250 g/9 oz plain flour

1 tbsp baking powder

115 g/4 oz caster sugar

85 g/3 oz butter, chilled and coarsely grated

1 large egg, beaten

175 ml/6 fl oz milk

175 g/6 oz raspberries

140 g/5 oz white chocolate chips

1. Preheat the oven to 200°C/400°F/Gas Mark 6. Line a 12-hole muffin tin with paper cases. Sift the flour and baking powder into a large bowl and stir in the sugar.

2. Add the butter, stirring with a fork to coat in the flour mixture. Lightly beat the egg in a jug, then beat in the milk. Make a well in the centre of the dry ingredients and pour in the beaten liquid ingredients. Stir until just combined; do not over-mix. Fold in the raspberries and half of the chocolate chips. Divide the mixture evenly between the paper cases and scatter over the remaining chocolate chips.

3. Bake in the preheated oven for 20–25 minutes, or until risen, golden and just firm to the touch. Leave to cool for 5 minutes, then transfer to a wire rack to cool completely.

#145 Treacle & spice drizzles

Makes 25

Ingredients

200 g/7 oz butter, softened

2 tbsp black treacle

140 g/5 oz caster sugar

1 egg yolk, lightly beaten

280 g/10 oz plain flour

1 tsp ground cinnamon

½ tsp grated nutmeg

½ tsp ground cloves

2 tbsp chopped walnuts

salt

Icing

115 g/4 oz icing sugar

1 tbsp hot water

a few drops of yellow food colouring

a few drops of pink food colouring

1. Put the butter, treacle and sugar into a bowl and mix well with a wooden spoon, then beat in the egg yolk. Sift together the flour, cinnamon, nutmeg, cloves and a pinch of salt into the mixture, add the walnuts and stir until thoroughly combined. Halve the dough, shape into balls, wrap in clingfilm and chill in the refrigerator for 30–60 minutes.

2. Preheat the oven to 190°C/375°F/Gas Mark 5. Line two baking sheets with baking paper. Unwrap the dough and roll out between two sheets of baking paper to a thickness of 5 mm/¼ inch. Stamp out 25 rounds with a 6-cm/2½-inch fluted cutter and put them on the prepared baking sheets.

3. Bake in the preheated oven for 10–15 minutes, until firm. Leave to cool on the baking sheets for 5–10 minutes, then carefully transfer to wire racks to cool completely.

4. To make the icing, sift the icing sugar into a bowl, then gradually stir in the hot water until the icing has the consistency of thick cream. Spoon half of the icing into a separate bowl. Stir a few drops of yellow food colouring into one bowl and a few drops of pink food colouring into the other. Leaving the cookies on the racks, use teaspoons to drizzle the yellow icing over them in one direction and the pink icing over them at right angles. Leave to set.

#146 Hokey pokey biscuits

Makes
15

Ingredients

125 g/4½ oz butter

100 g/3½ oz granulated sugar

1 tbsp golden syrup

1 tbsp milk

175 g/6 oz plain flour, plus extra for dusting

1 tsp bicarbonate of soda

200 g/7 oz white chocolate, melted

55 g/2 oz walnuts, very finely chopped

1. Preheat the oven to 180°C/350°F/Gas Mark 4. Line a large baking tray with baking paper.

2. Put the butter, sugar, golden syrup and milk into a saucepan and heat, stirring constantly, until the butter is melted and the mixture is just below boiling point. Remove from the heat and leave to cool to lukewarm. Sift together the flour and bicarbonate of soda into a bowl, add to the cooled mixture and stir well.

3. Roll heaped tablespoons of the mixture into balls. Place the balls on the prepared tray, then flatten them with a floured fork to make 7.5-cm/3-inch rounds.

4. Bake in the preheated oven for 15–20 minutes, or until golden brown. Leave to cool on the tray for 1–2 minutes, then carefully transfer to a wire rack to cool completely.

5. Dip the biscuits halfway vertically into the melted chocolate and sprinkle the chocolate with the chopped nuts. Transfer to greaseproof paper to set.

#147 Pistachio & lime cupcakes

Makes
16

Ingredients

85 g/3 oz unsalted pistachio nuts, plus extra, roughly chopped, to decorate

115 g/4 oz butter, softened

140 g/5 oz golden caster sugar

140 g/5 oz self-raising flour

2 eggs, lightly beaten

4 tbsp Greek-style yogurt

Frosting

115 g/4 oz butter, softened

2 tbsp lime juice cordial

200 g/7 oz icing sugar

1. Preheat the oven to 180°C/350°F/Gas Mark 4. Line two 8-hole muffin tins with paper cases or put 16 double-layer paper cases on a baking tray.

2. Put the nuts in a food processor or blender and process for a few seconds until finely ground. Add the butter, sugar, flour, eggs and yogurt, and process until evenly mixed. Spoon the mixture into the paper cases and bake in the preheated oven for 20–25 minutes, or until well risen and springy to the touch. Transfer to a wire rack and leave to cool completely.

3. To make the frosting, put the butter and cordial in a bowl and beat until light and fluffy. Sift in the icing sugar and beat until smooth. Swirl the frosting over each cupcake and decorate with the chopped nuts.

#148 Caramel appletini cupcakes

Makes 12

Ingredients

190 g/6¾ oz plain flour
1½ tsp baking powder
1 tsp ground ginger
1 tsp ground cinnamon
⅛ tsp ground nutmeg
250 g/8 oz butter, softened
200 g/7 oz caster sugar
1 tsp vanilla extract
2 large eggs
4 tbsp apple sauce
2 tbsp apple juice
4 tbsp apple-flavoured vodka
200 g/7 oz soft dark brown sugar
90 ml/3 fl oz double cream
190 g/6¾ oz icing sugar
salt

Decoration

green food colouring
55 g/2 oz marzipan
30 g/1 oz brown ready-to-roll
fondant icing

1. Preheat the oven to 180°C/350°F/Gas Mark 4 and line a 12-hole cupcake tin with paper cases.

2. Sift together the flour, baking powder, ginger, cinnamon, nutmeg and ¼ teaspoon of salt into a bowl. Put half of the butter and the caster sugar into a separate bowl and beat until pale and fluffy. Add the vanilla extract, then add the eggs, one at a time, beating after each addition. Add half of the flour mixture and the apple sauce, apple juice and half of the vodka, and beat to incorporate. Mix in the remaining flour mixture. Spoon the mixture into the paper cases and bake in the preheated oven for 20 minutes, until risen and golden. Leave to cool in the tin for 1–2 minutes, then transfer to a wire rack to cool completely.

3. To make the frosting, melt the remaining butter in a small saucepan over a medium heat. Add the brown sugar, cream and a pinch of salt and cook, stirring constantly, for about 4 minutes, until the sugar has dissolved completely. Remove from the heat, stir in the remaining vodka and leave to cool for 30 minutes.

4. Pour the caramel sauce into a mixing bowl, reserving 125 ml/4 fl oz for decoration. Add the icing sugar to the bowl and beat until fully incorporated. Spoon the frosting into a piping bag fitted with a star-shaped nozzle and pipe onto the cupcakes.

5. To decorate, add 1–2 drops of green food colouring to the marzipan and knead until the colour is evenly incorporated. Roll the marzipan into 12 balls. Pinch off small pieces of the brown fondant icing to make apple stems and press into the top of a marzipan ball. Repeat for the 11 remaining balls. To serve, drizzle the cupcakes with the reserved caramel sauce and place a marzipan apple on top of each.

#149 Mini Victoria sponge cakes

Makes
12

Ingredients

70 g/2½ oz lightly salted butter, softened, plus extra for greasing

70 g/2½ oz caster sugar

70 g/2½ oz self-raising flour

1 egg

1 egg yolk

1 tsp vanilla extract

Decoration

150 ml/5 fl oz double cream

6 tbsp strawberry jam

85 g/3 oz icing sugar

1 tbsp lemon juice

1. Preheat the oven to 180°C/350°F/Gas Mark 4. Grease a 12-hole mini muffin tin and line the base with baking paper. Put the butter, caster sugar, flour, egg, egg yolk and vanilla extract in a mixing bowl, and beat with an electric hand-held mixer until smooth and creamy.

2. Using a teaspoon, spoon the mixture into the prepared tin and level with the back of the spoon. Bake in the preheated oven for 15 minutes, or until risen and just firm to the touch. Leave to cool in the tin for 5 minutes, then transfer to a wire rack to cool completely.

3. To decorate, whip the cream until it holds soft peaks. Cut the cakes in half horizontally. Press 2 tablespoons of the jam through a small sieve into a bowl. Put the sieved jam in a small paper piping bag and snip off the tip. Sandwich the cakes together with the remaining jam and cream.

4. Beat together the icing sugar and lemon juice until smooth. Spoon over the cakes, spreading just to the edges. Pipe dots of jam on top of each cake and draw a wooden skewer through them, to decorate.

#150 Caramel fudge whoopie pies

Makes
10

Ingredients

250 g/9 oz plain flour

2 tsp baking powder

large pinch of salt

115 g/4 oz butter, softened

85 g/3 oz soft dark brown sugar

2 tbsp golden syrup

1 large egg, beaten

1 tsp vanilla extract

125 ml/4 fl oz milk

25 g/1 oz chopped fudge, to decorate

Filling

125 g/4½ oz butter, softened

115 g/4 oz icing sugar

5 tbsp dulce de leche

1. Preheat the oven to 180°C/350°F/Gas Mark 4. Line three large baking sheets with baking paper. Sift together the plain flour, baking powder and salt.

2. Place the butter and sugar in a large bowl and beat with an electric hand-held mixer until pale and fluffy. Beat in the golden syrup, egg and vanilla extract, then beat in half of the flour mixture and the milk. Stir in the remaining flour mixture and mix until thoroughly incorporated. Pipe 20 mounds of the mixture onto the prepared baking sheets, spaced well apart. Bake, one sheet at a time, in the preheated oven for 10–12 minutes, until risen and just firm to the touch. Leave to cool for 5 minutes, then transfer to a wire rack and leave to cool completely.

3. To make the filling, beat the butter for 2–3 minutes until pale and creamy. Gradually beat in the icing sugar, beating for 2–3 minutes until very light and fluffy. Stir in the dulce de leche.

4. To assemble, pipe two thirds of the buttercream on the flat side of 10 of the cakes. Thinly spread the remaining buttercream on the top of the remaining cakes. Sandwich the cakes together and decorate with the chopped fudge.

#151 Mango, coconut & ginger cookies

Makes 30

Ingredients

225 g/8 oz butter, softened

140 g/5 oz caster sugar

1 egg yolk, lightly beaten

55 g/2 oz stem ginger, chopped, plus
2 tsp syrup from the jar

280 g/10 oz plain flour

55 g/2 oz ready-to-eat dried mango,
chopped

100 g/3½ oz desiccated coconut

salt

1. Put the butter and sugar into a bowl and mix well with a wooden spoon, then beat in the egg yolk and ginger syrup. Sift together the flour and a pinch of salt into the mixture, add the stem ginger and mango, and stir until thoroughly combined.

2. Spread out the coconut in a shallow dish. Shape the dough into a log and roll it in the coconut to coat. Wrap in clingfilm and chill in the refrigerator for 30–60 minutes.

3. Preheat the oven to 190°C/375°F/Gas Mark 5. Line two baking sheets with baking paper. Unwrap the log and cut it into 5-mm/¼-inch slices with a sharp serrated knife and put them on the prepared baking sheets, spaced well apart. Bake in the preheated oven for 12–15 minutes. Leave to cool on the baking sheets for 5–10 minutes, then carefully transfer to wire racks to cool completely.

#152 Salted caramel pies

Makes 4

Ingredients

235 g/8½ oz butter

175 g/6 oz digestive biscuits,
finely crushed

300 g/10½ oz caster sugar

4 tbsp water

¼ tsp sea salt crystals

125 ml/4 fl oz double cream

Topping

150 ml/5 fl oz double cream

chocolate curls or shavings

1. Melt 85 g/3 oz of the butter in a pan over a low heat. Place the crushed biscuits in a bowl and stir in the melted butter. Divide the mixture between four tartlet tins and press down firmly into the base and up the sides of each tin. Chill in the refrigerator for 30 minutes.

2. Place the sugar and water in a heavy-based saucepan. Heat gently, stirring, until the sugar has dissolved. Bring the syrup to the boil and boil, without stirring, until the liquid is a golden toffee colour. Remove from the heat and leave to cool for 2 minutes, then carefully stir in the remaining butter and half the salt.

3. Gradually whisk in the cream and continue whisking until the mixture is smooth and glossy. Transfer to a heatproof bowl and leave to cool and thicken, stirring occasionally. Stir in the remaining salt. Spoon the cooled caramel into the tartlet cases.

4. To make the topping, whip the cream until it holds soft peaks. Drop large spoonfuls on top of the caramel filling, scatter over the chocolate curls and serve.

Cherry sundae cupcakes

Ingredients

200 g/7 oz butter, softened,
or soft margarine

175 g/6 oz caster sugar

3 eggs, beaten

1 tsp vanilla extract

200 g/7 oz plain flour

1½ tsp baking powder

55 g/2 oz glacé cherries, chopped

85 g/3 oz plain chocolate,
broken into pieces

1 tbsp golden syrup

Decoration

600 ml/1 pint double cream

2 tbsp toasted chopped
mixed nuts

pink shimmer sugar

12 maraschino cherries

1. Preheat the oven to 160°C/325°F/Gas Mark 3. Line a
12-hole muffin tin with paper cases.

2. Place 175 g/6 oz of the butter and the caster sugar in a large
bowl and beat together until light and fluffy. Gradually beat in the eggs and vanilla extract. Sift in
the flour and baking powder and, using a metal spoon, fold in gently. Fold in the glacé cherries.

3. Divide the mixture evenly between the paper cases. Bake in the preheated oven for 25–30
minutes, or until risen, golden and firm to the touch. Transfer to a wire rack and leave to cool.

4. Place the chocolate, remaining butter and the golden syrup in a heatproof bowl set over a
saucepan of simmering water and heat until melted. Remove from the heat and stir until smooth.
Leave to cool, stirring occasionally, for 20–30 minutes.

5. To decorate, whip the cream until it holds firm peaks. Spoon into a piping bag fitted with
a large, star-shaped nozzle and pipe swirls of cream on top of each cupcake. Drizzle over the
chocolate sauce and sprinkle with the chopped nuts and shimmer sugar. Top each cupcake with a
maraschino cherry.

Boston bun

Ingredients

115 g/4 oz cold mashed potatoes

225 g/8 oz granulated sugar

150 g/5½ oz raisins

250 g/9 oz plain flour

3 tsp baking powder

1 tsp ground cinnamon

250 ml/9 fl oz milk

Icing

185 g/6½ oz icing sugar

2 tsp lemon juice

30 g/1 oz butter, melted,
plus extra for greasing

3 tsp desiccated coconut

1. Preheat the oven to 180°C/350°F/Gas Mark 4. Lightly grease
a 20-cm/8-inch round cake tin. Put the potatoes and sugar into
a large bowl and beat together. Add the raisins and beat the
mixture until smooth.

2. Sift together the flour, baking powder and cinnamon into a separate bowl, then add to the potato
mixture alternately with the milk.

3. Transfer the mixture to the prepared tin, using a palette knife to spread it evenly. Bake in the
preheated oven for 40–50 minutes. Transfer to a wire rack to cool in the tin.

4. Carefully remove the cake from the tin and transfer to a serving plate. To make the icing, mix the
sugar, lemon juice, butter and coconut together. Use a spoon to press the mixture through a sieve,
then spread it over the top of the cake in a thick layer. Cut into slices and serve.

#155 Lavender cookies

Makes 40

Ingredients

225 g/8 oz butter, softened
175 g/6 oz caster sugar
1 large egg, lightly beaten
250 g/9 oz plain flour
2 tsp baking powder
1 tbsp dried lavender, chopped

1. Preheat the oven to 190°C/375°F/Gas Mark 5. Line two baking sheets with baking paper

2. Put the butter and sugar into a bowl and mix well with a wooden spoon, then beat in the egg. Sift together the flour and baking powder into the mixture, add the lavender and stir until thoroughly combined.

3. Put tablespoons of the mixture on the prepared baking sheets, spaced well apart. Bake in the preheated oven for 15 minutes, until golden brown. Leave to cool on the baking sheets for 5–10 minutes, then carefully transfer to wire racks to cool completely.

#156 Pastry cream biscuits

Makes 15

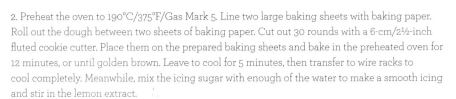

Ingredients

225 g/8 oz butter, softened
140 g/5 oz caster sugar
1 egg, separated
2 tsp vanilla extract
280 g/10 oz plain flour
pinch of salt
225 g/8 oz icing sugar, sifted
3–4 tbsp lukewarm water
¼ tsp lemon extract
redcurrants and caster sugar, to decorate

Filling

2 egg yolks, lightly beaten
4 tbsp caster sugar
1 heaped tbsp plain flour
1 tbsp cornflour
300 ml/10 fl oz milk
a few drops of vanilla extract
1 egg white

1. Place the butter and sugar in a large bowl and beat together. Lightly beat the egg yolk and then beat into the mixture with the vanilla extract. Sift in the flour and salt and stir until thoroughly combined. Halve the dough, wrap in clingfilm and chill in the refrigerator for 45 minutes.

2. Preheat the oven to 190°C/375°F/Gas Mark 5. Line two large baking sheets with baking paper. Roll out the dough between two sheets of baking paper. Cut out 30 rounds with a 6-cm/2½-inch fluted cookie cutter. Place them on the prepared baking sheets and bake in the preheated oven for 12 minutes, or until golden brown. Leave to cool for 5 minutes, then transfer to wire racks to cool completely. Meanwhile, mix the icing sugar with enough of the water to make a smooth icing and stir in the lemon extract.

3. To make the filling, beat the egg yolks and sugar together. Sift in the flour and cornflour and beat well. Stir in 3 tablespoons of the milk and the vanilla extract. Bring the remaining milk to the boil, then whisk it into the mixture. Return to the pan and bring to the boil, stirring, then remove from the heat and beat until cool.

4. Whisk the egg white to stiff peaks. Spoon a little of the cream filling into a bowl, fold in the egg white, then fold into the remaining filling. Heat for 2 minutes, then leave to cool and use to sandwich the biscuits together. Dip the redcurrants into the egg white and roll in caster sugar. Spread the lemon icing over the biscuits and decorate with the frosted redcurrants.

Makes
10

Ingredients

250 g/9 oz plain flour
2 tsp baking powder
large pinch of salt
225 g/8 oz butter, softened
150 g/5½ oz caster sugar
finely grated rind of 1 lemon
1 large egg, beaten
100 ml/3½ fl oz milk
2 tbsp lemon juice
200 g/7 oz icing sugar, sifted
4 tbsp lemon curd
1 tbsp yellow sugar sprinkles,
to decorate

Icing

115 g/4 oz icing sugar
1–2 tbsp lukewarm water

1. Preheat the oven to 180°C/350°F/Gas Mark 4. Line three large baking sheets with baking paper. Sift together the plain flour, baking powder and salt.

2. Place half of the butter, the caster sugar and lemon rind in a large bowl and beat until pale and fluffy. Beat in the egg, then beat in half of the flour mixture and the milk. Stir in the remaining flour mixture and mix until thoroughly incorporated. Pipe 20 mounds of the mixture onto the prepared baking sheets, spaced well apart. Bake in the preheated oven, one sheet at a time, for 10–12 minutes. Leave to cool for 5 minutes, then transfer to a wire rack and leave to cool completely.

3. Put the remaining butter and the lemon juice in a bowl and beat for 2–3 minutes until pale and creamy. Gradually beat in the icing sugar. Beat for 2–3 minutes until very light and fluffy.

4. To make the icing, sift the icing sugar into a bowl and gradually stir in enough water to make a smooth icing that is thick enough to coat the back of a wooden spoon. To assemble, spread or pipe the buttercream on the flat side of 10 of the cakes and pipe the lemon curd over the remaining cakes. Sandwich the cakes together. Spoon the icing over the whoopie pies and decorate with the sugar sprinkles.

158 Apple streusel cupcakes

Makes
14

Ingredients

50 g/1¾ oz plain flour
135 g/4¾ oz demerara sugar
¾ tsp ground cinnamon
½ tsp freshly grated nutmeg
90 g/3¼ oz butter, softened
½ tsp bicarbonate of soda
280 g/10 oz apple sauce
1 large egg
175 g/6 oz self-raising flour

1. Preheat the oven to 180°C/350°F/Gas Mark 4. Line 14 holes in a muffin tin with paper cases.

2. To make the topping, put the plain flour, 85 g/3 oz demerara sugar, ½ teaspoon cinnamon and the nutmeg in a bowl. Cut 55 g/2 oz butter into small pieces, then add to the bowl and rub it in with your fingertips until the mixture resembles fine breadcrumbs. Set aside.

3. Add the bicarbonate of soda to the apple sauce and stir until dissolved. Place the remaining butter and demerara sugar in a large bowl and beat together until light and fluffy. Lightly beat the egg in a separate bowl, then add to the butter mixture. Sift in the self-raising flour and remaining cinnamon, and fold into the mixture, adding the apple sauce a spoonful at a time.

4. Spoon the mixture into the paper cases. Scatter the topping over the cupcakes and press down gently. Bake in the preheated oven for 20 minutes, or until risen, golden and firm to the touch. Transfer to a wire rack and leave to cool.

Pear & ginger Bundt cakes with whisky & muscovado glaze

Ingredients

250 g/9 oz pears, peeled, cored and cubed

1 tbsp dark muscovado sugar

125 g/4½ oz butter, softened, plus extra for greasing

175 g/6 oz caster sugar

2 eggs, beaten

100 ml/3½ fl oz soured cream

175 g/6 oz plain flour, sifted, plus extra for dusting

1 tsp baking powder

1 tsp ground ginger

pinch of salt

4 tbsp finely chopped crystallized ginger

2 tsp vanilla extract

Glaze

2 tbsp whisky

50 g/1¾ oz dark muscovado sugar

1. Preheat the oven to 180°C/350°F/Gas Mark 4. Grease a 12-hole mini Bundt tin and lightly dust with flour, shaking out any excess.

2. Place the pears in a small saucepan with a splash of cold water and the muscovado sugar. Cook over a low heat for 3–4 minutes, until the pears are soft, but not mushy. Drain through a sieve, reserving the cooking juices, and leave to cool.

3. Place the butter and caster sugar in a mixing bowl and beat until light and fluffy. Gradually beat in the eggs, adding a spoonful of the flour if the mixture curdles. Stir in the soured cream.

4. Mix the flour with the baking powder, ground ginger, salt and 2 tablespoons of the crystallized ginger, then gently fold into the mixture with the vanilla extract and the cooked pears.

5. Spoon the mixture into the prepared tin and bake in the preheated oven for 25–30 minutes until risen and golden. Leave to cool in the tin for a few minutes, then transfer to a wire rack to cool completely.

6. To make the glaze, place the reserved cooking juices in a small saucepan with the whisky and sugar, bring to the boil and boil hard for 2–3 minutes until slightly reduced and thickened. Spoon over the tops of the cakes and scatter over the remaining crystallized ginger.

#160 White chocolate & macadamia nut cookies

Makes 16

Ingredients

115 g/4 oz butter, softened, plus extra for greasing

115 g/4 oz soft light brown sugar

1 tbsp golden syrup

175 g/6 oz self-raising flour

55 g/2 oz macadamia nuts, roughly chopped

55 g/2 oz white chocolate, chopped into chunks

1. Preheat the oven to 180°C/350°F/Gas Mark 4. Grease two large baking sheets.

2. Put the butter and sugar into a bowl and beat together until pale and creamy, then beat in the golden syrup. Sift in the flour, add the nuts and mix to form a rough dough.

3. Roll the dough into 16 even-sized balls and place on the prepared baking sheets, spaced well apart. Slightly flatten each ball with your fingertips and top with the chocolate chunks, pressing them lightly into the dough.

4. Bake in the preheated oven for 12–14 minutes, or until just set and pale golden. Leave to cool on the baking sheets for 5 minutes, then transfer to wire racks to cool completely.

#161 Maple & bacon cupcakes

Makes 12

Ingredients

8 unsmoked streaky bacon rashers

55 g/2 oz soft light brown sugar

190 g/6¾ oz plain flour

1½ tsp baking powder

¼ tsp salt

115 g/4 oz butter, softened

100 g/3½ oz caster sugar

125 ml/4 fl oz maple syrup

1 tsp vanilla extract

2 large eggs

125 ml/4 fl oz milk

Frosting

4 large egg whites

200 g/7 oz granulated sugar

¼ tsp cream of tartar

2 tbsp maple syrup

2 tsp maple extract

1. Preheat the oven to 180°C/350°F/Gas Mark 4 and line a 12-hole muffin tin with paper cases.

2. Line a baking sheet with foil. Place the bacon on the prepared sheet and sprinkle with half of the brown sugar. Turn and repeat. Bake in the preheated oven for 25–30 minutes, until the bacon is crisp. Do not switch off the oven. Transfer to kitchen paper and leave to cool. Reserve four whole rashers of bacon and crumble the remaining rashers.

3. Sift together the flour, baking powder and salt into a bowl. Put the butter and caster sugar into a separate bowl and beat until pale and fluffy. Add the maple syrup and vanilla extract, then add the eggs, one at a time, beating after each addition. Add half of the flour mixture and the milk, and beat until combined. Add the remaining flour mixture and mix. Stir in the crumbled bacon. Spoon the mixture into the paper cases and bake in the oven for 20 minutes, until risen and golden. Leave to cool in the tin for 1–2 minutes, then transfer to a wire rack to cool completely.

4. To make the frosting, put the egg whites, sugar and cream of tartar in a heatproof bowl set over a saucepan of gently simmering water and whisk until the sugar is completely dissolved. Remove from the heat and whisk for 4–5 minutes, or until the mixture holds stiff peaks. Add the maple syrup and maple extract, and whisk to combine. Spoon the frosting into a piping bag fitted with a star-shaped nozzle and pipe onto the cupcakes. Break the reserved bacon into 12 pieces and place on top of the cupcakes.

Coconut & pineapple macaroons

Makes
16

Ingredients

50 g/1¾ oz ground almonds

25 g/1 oz desiccated coconut, finely ground

115 g/4 oz icing sugar

2 large egg whites

50 g/1¾ oz caster sugar

2 tbsp toasted desiccated coconut, to decorate

Filling

55 g/2 oz butter

2 tsp pineapple juice

115 g/4 oz icing sugar, sifted

2 canned pineapple rings, drained and finely chopped

1. Place the ground almonds, ground coconut and icing sugar in a food processor and process for 15 seconds, then sift into a bowl. Line two baking sheets with baking paper.

2. Place the egg whites in a large bowl and whisk until they hold soft peaks. Gradually whisk in the caster sugar until you have a firm, glossy meringue. Using a spatula, fold the almond mixture into the meringue one third at a time. Continue to cut and fold the mixture until it forms a shiny batter with a thick, ribbon-like consistency.

3. Pour the mixture into a piping bag fitted with a 1-cm/½-inch plain nozzle. Pipe 32 small rounds onto the prepared baking sheets. Tap the baking sheets firmly on a work surface to remove air bubbles. Sprinkle over the toasted coconut. Leave to stand at room temperature for 30 minutes. Meanwhile, preheat the oven to 160°C/325°F/Gas Mark 3. Bake the macaroons in the preheated oven for 10–15 minutes. Leave to cool for 10 minutes, then carefully peel the macaroons off the baking paper. Transfer to wire racks and leave to cool completely.

4. To make the filling, beat the butter and pineapple juice in a bowl until pale and fluffy. Gradually beat in the icing sugar until smooth and creamy, then fold in the chopped pineapple. Use to sandwich pairs of macaroons together.

Strawberry & cream whoopie pies

Makes
12

Ingredients

250 g/9 oz plain flour

1 tsp bicarbonate of soda

large pinch of salt

115 g/4 oz butter, softened

150 g/5½ oz caster sugar

1 large egg, beaten

2 tsp rosewater

150 ml/5 fl oz buttermilk

300 ml/10 fl oz double cream

4 tbsp icing sugar, sifted, plus extra for dusting

3 tbsp strawberry jam

225 g/8 oz strawberries, sliced

1. Preheat the oven to 180°C/350°F/Gas Mark 4. Line three large baking sheets with baking paper. Sift together the flour, bicarbonate of soda and salt into a bowl.

2. Place the butter and sugar in a large bowl and beat until pale and fluffy. Beat in the egg and rosewater, then beat in half the flour mixture and the buttermilk. Stir in the remaining flour mixture and mix until thoroughly incorporated. Pipe or spoon 24 mounds of the mixture onto the prepared baking sheets, spaced well apart to allow for spreading. Bake in the preheated oven, one sheet at a time, for 10–12 minutes until risen and just firm to the touch. Leave to cool for 5 minutes, then transfer to wire racks and leave to cool completely.

3. Place the cream in a bowl and whip until it holds firm peaks. Fold in the icing sugar. To assemble, spread the strawberry jam on the flat side of 12 of the cakes, followed by the whipped cream and strawberries. Top with the remaining cakes and dust with icing sugar.

#164 Cinnamon & berry cookies

Makes 30

Ingredients

225 g/8 oz butter, softened
140 g/5 oz caster sugar
1 egg yolk, lightly beaten
2 tsp vanilla extract
280 g/10 oz plain flour
1 tsp ground cinnamon
55 g/2 oz dried blueberries
55 g/2 oz dried cranberries
55 g/2 oz pine nuts, chopped
salt

1. Preheat the oven to 190°C/375°F/Gas Mark 5. Line two baking sheets with baking paper.

2. Put the butter and sugar in a bowl and mix well, then beat in the egg yolk and vanilla extract. Sift together the flour, cinnamon and a pinch of salt into the mixture, add the blueberries and cranberries, and stir to combine.

3. Spread out the pine nuts in a shallow dish. Scoop up tablespoons of the mixture, roll into balls and roll the balls in the pine nuts to coat. Place on the prepared baking sheets, spaced well apart, and flatten slightly. Bake in the preheated oven for 10–15 minutes. Leave to cool on the baking sheets for 5–10 minutes, then carefully transfer to wire racks to cool completely.

#165 Toffee chocolate puffs

Makes 12

Ingredients

375 g/13 oz ready-rolled puff pastry
140 g/5 oz plain chocolate, broken into pieces
300 ml/10 fl oz double cream
50 g/1¾ oz caster sugar
4 egg yolks
4 tbsp ready-made toffee sauce
whipped cream and cocoa powder, to decorate

1. Line the base of a 12-hole muffin tin with discs of baking paper. Cut out 12 x 5-cm/2-inch rounds from the edge of the pastry and cut the remaining pastry into 12 strips. Roll the strips to half their thickness and line the sides of each hole with one strip. Place a pastry disc in each base and press together to seal and make a tart case. Prick the bases and chill in the refrigerator for 30 minutes.

2. Preheat the oven to 200°C/400°F/Gas Mark 6. While the pastry is chilling, place the chocolate in a heatproof bowl set over a saucepan of gently simmering water and heat until melted. Leave to cool slightly, then stir in the cream.

3. Place the sugar and egg yolks in a bowl and beat together, then mix well with the melted chocolate. Place a teaspoon of toffee sauce in each pastry case, then divide the chocolate mixture between the tarts. Bake in the preheated oven for 20–25 minutes, turning the tin around halfway through cooking, until just set. Leave to cool in the tin, then remove carefully, decorate with whipped cream, dust with cocoa powder and serve.

#166 Tiramisù cupcakes

Makes 12

Ingredients

115 g/4 oz butter, softened

115 g/4 oz soft light brown sugar

2 eggs, beaten

115 g/4 oz self-raising flour, sifted

½ tsp baking powder

2 tsp instant coffee granules

25 g/1 oz icing sugar

4 tbsp water

2 tbsp finely grated plain chocolate, for dusting

Frosting

225 g/8 oz mascarpone cheese

85 g/3 oz caster sugar

2 tbsp Marsala or sweet sherry

1. Preheat the oven to 180°C/350°F/Gas Mark 4. Line a 12-hole muffin tin with paper cases.

2. Place the butter, brown sugar, eggs, flour and baking powder in a bowl and beat until pale and creamy. Divide the mixture between the paper cases. Bake in the preheated oven for 15–20 minutes, or until risen, golden and firm to the touch.

3. Place the coffee granules, icing sugar and water in a saucepan and heat gently, stirring, until the coffee and sugar have dissolved. Boil for 1 minute, then leave to cool for 10 minutes. Brush the coffee syrup over the top of the warm cupcakes. Transfer the cupcakes to a wire rack and leave to cool completely.

4. To make the frosting, put the mascarpone cheese, sugar and Marsala in a bowl and beat together until smooth. Spread over the top of the cakes. Holding a star template over the tops of the cupcakes, sprinkle the grated chocolate over the frosting.

#167 Apricot & pecan cookies

Makes 30

Ingredients

225 g/8 oz butter, softened

140 g/5 oz caster sugar

1 egg yolk, lightly beaten

2 tsp vanilla extract

280 g/10 oz plain flour

grated rind of 1 orange

55 g/2 oz ready-to-eat dried apricots, chopped

100 g/3½ oz pecan nuts, finely chopped

salt

1. Put the butter and sugar into a bowl and mix well with a wooden spoon, then beat in the egg yolk and vanilla extract. Sift the flour and a pinch of salt into the mixture, add the orange rind and apricots, and stir until thoroughly combined.

2. Shape the dough into a log. Spread out the nuts in a shallow dish. Roll the log in the nuts until well coated, then wrap in clingfilm and chill in the refrigerator for 30–60 minutes.

3. Preheat the oven to 190°C/375°F/Gas Mark 5. Line two baking sheets with baking paper. Unwrap the dough and cut into 5-mm/¼-inch slices with a sharp serrated knife. Put the slices on the prepared baking sheets, spaced well apart.

4. Bake in the preheated oven for 10–12 minutes. Leave to cool on the baking sheets for 5–10 minutes, then carefully transfer to wire racks to cool completely.

#168 Lemon jumbles

Ingredients

75 g/2¾ oz butter, softened, plus extra for greasing

115 g/4 oz caster sugar

grated rind of 1 lemon

1 egg, lightly beaten

4 tbsp lemon juice

350 g/12 oz plain flour, plus extra for dusting

1 tsp baking powder

1 tbsp milk

icing sugar, for dusting

1. Preheat the oven to 160°C/325°F/Gas Mark 3. Grease several baking sheets and line with baking paper.

2. In a mixing bowl, cream together the butter, caster sugar and lemon rind until pale and fluffy. Add the egg and lemon juice, a little at a time, beating well after each addition.

3. Sift the flour and baking powder into the creamed mixture and blend together. Add the milk, mixing to form a firm dough.

4. Turn out the dough onto a lightly floured work surface and divide into 40 equal-sized pieces. Roll each piece into a sausage shape with your hands and twist in the middle to make an 'S' shape or curls.

5. Place the biscuits on the prepared baking sheets and bake in the preheated oven for 15–20 minutes. Transfer to wire racks and leave to cool completely. Generously dust with icing sugar just before serving.

169 Rose petal cupcakes

Makes 12

Ingredients

115 g/4 oz butter, softened

115 g/4 oz caster sugar

2 eggs, lightly beaten

1 tbsp milk

a few drops of essence of rose oil

¼ tsp vanilla extract

175 g/6 oz self-raising flour, sifted

crystallized rose petals, to decorate

Frosting

85 g/3 oz butter, softened

175 g/6 oz icing sugar

pink food colouring

1. Preheat the oven to 200°C/400°F/Gas Mark 6. Line a 12-hole muffin tin with paper cases, or put 12 double-layer paper cases on a baking tray.

2. Put the butter and sugar in a bowl and beat until light and fluffy. Gradually add the eggs, beating well after each addition. Stir in the milk, rose oil and vanilla extract then, using a metal spoon, fold in the flour. Spoon the mixture into the paper cases and bake the cupcakes in the preheated oven for 12–15 minutes, until well risen and golden brown. Transfer to a wire rack and leave to cool completely.

3. To make the frosting, put the butter in a large bowl and beat until fluffy. Sift in the icing sugar and mix well together. Add a few drops of pink food colouring to complement the rose petals.

4. Put a blob of frosting on top of each cupcake and decorate with 1–2 crystallized rose petals and mix well.

170 Clubs & spades

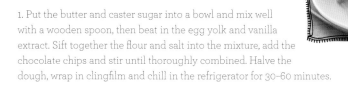

Makes 15

Ingredients

225 g/8 oz butter, softened

140 g/5 oz caster sugar

1 egg yolk, lightly beaten

2 tsp vanilla extract

280 g/10 oz plain flour

pinch of salt

100 g/3½ oz plain chocolate chips

Filling

55 g/2 oz butter, softened

1 tsp golden syrup

85 g/3 oz icing sugar

1 tbsp cocoa powder

1. Put the butter and caster sugar into a bowl and mix well with a wooden spoon, then beat in the egg yolk and vanilla extract. Sift together the flour and salt into the mixture, add the chocolate chips and stir until thoroughly combined. Halve the dough, wrap in clingfilm and chill in the refrigerator for 30–60 minutes.

2. Preheat the oven to 190°C/375°F/Gas Mark 5. Line two baking sheets with baking paper.

3. Unwrap the dough halves and roll out between two sheets of baking paper. Stamp out 30 cookies with a 6-cm/2½-inch square fluted cutter and put 15 of them on one of the prepared baking sheets, spaced well apart. Using small club- and spade-shaped cutters, stamp out the centres of the remaining cookies, then place the cookies on the other baking sheet, spaced well apart. Bake in the preheated oven for 10–15 minutes, until light golden brown. Leave to cool on the baking sheets for 5–10 minutes, then carefully transfer to wire racks to cool completely.

4. To make the filling, put the butter and golden syrup into a bowl. Sift in the icing sugar and cocoa powder. Beat until smooth and spread over the whole cookies. Top with the cut-out cookies.

#171 Coffee fudge cupcakes

Ingredients

175 g/6 oz plain white flour

1 tbsp baking powder

225 g/8 oz butter, softened

175 g/6 oz caster sugar

3 eggs, beaten

1½ tsp coffee extract

4 tbsp milk

115 g/4 oz light muscovado sugar

400 g/14 oz icing sugar, sifted

chocolate-covered coffee beans, to decorate

1. Preheat the oven to 190°C/375°F/Gas Mark 5. Line three muffin tins with 28 paper cases.

2. Sift the flour and baking powder into a large bowl and add 175 g/6 oz of the butter, the caster sugar, eggs and 1 teaspoon of the coffee extract. Beat until smooth, then beat in 2 tablespoons of the milk. Spoon into the paper cases and bake in the preheated oven for 15–20 minutes, or until golden brown and firm to the touch. Transfer to a wire rack and leave to cool.

3. Place the remaining butter, muscovado sugar, remaining milk and coffee extract in a saucepan over a medium heat and stir until melted and smooth. Bring to the boil and boil, stirring, for 2 minutes. Remove from the heat and beat in the icing sugar. Stir until smooth and thick, then spoon into a piping bag fitted with a large star-shaped nozzle. Pipe a swirl of frosting on top of each cupcake and top with a coffee bean.

#172 Blueberry & orange biscuits

Ingredients

225 g/8 oz butter, softened

140 g/5 oz caster sugar

1 egg yolk, lightly beaten

1 tsp orange extract

280 g/10 oz plain flour

100 g/3½ oz dried blueberries

100 g/3½ oz cream cheese

grated rind of 1 orange

40 g/1½ oz macadamia nuts, finely chopped

salt

1. Put the butter and sugar into a bowl and mix well with a wooden spoon, then beat in the egg yolk and orange extract. Sift the flour and a pinch of salt into the mixture, add the blueberries and stir until thoroughly combined. Shape the dough into a log, wrap in clingfilm and chill in the refrigerator for 30–60 minutes.

2. Preheat the oven to 190°C/375°F/Gas Mark 5. Line two baking sheets with baking paper.

3. Unwrap the dough and cut into 5-mm/¼-inch slices with a sharp serrated knife. Put them on the prepared baking sheets, spaced well apart.

4. Bake in the preheated oven for 10–15 minutes, until golden brown. Leave to cool on the baking sheets for 5–10 minutes, then carefully transfer to wire racks to cool completely.

5. Just before serving, beat the cream cheese in a bowl and stir in the orange rind. Spread the mixture over the biscuits and sprinkle with the chopped nuts.

Carrot cakes

Ingredients

150 g/5½ oz lightly salted butter, softened, plus extra for greasing

150 g/5½ oz light muscovado sugar

3 eggs

150 g/5½ oz self-raising flour

½ tsp baking powder

½ tsp ground mixed spice

85 g/3 oz ground almonds

finely grated rind of 1 lemon

150 g/5½ oz carrots, grated

85 g/3 oz sultanas, roughly chopped

150 g/5½ oz cream cheese

40 g/1½ oz unsalted butter, softened

115 g/4 oz icing sugar, plus extra for dusting

2 tbsp lemon juice

60 g/2¼ oz marzipan

orange food colouring

fresh dill sprigs, to decorate

1. Preheat the oven to 180°C/350°F/Gas Mark 4. Grease a 25 x 20-cm/10 x 8-inch baking tin. Line with baking paper and grease the paper. Put the salted butter, muscovado sugar, eggs, flour, baking powder, mixed spice, almonds and lemon rind in a mixing bowl and beat until smooth and creamy. Stir in the carrots and sultanas.

2. Tip the mixture into the tin and level the surface. Bake in the preheated oven for 35 minutes, or until risen and just firm to the touch. Leave to cool in the tin for 10 minutes, then transfer to a wire rack to cool completely.

3. Beat together the cream cheese, unsalted butter, icing sugar and lemon juice until creamy. Colour the marzipan deep orange with the food colouring. Roll it into a sausage shape on a surface lightly dusted with icing sugar, then divide it into 20 pieces and form each piece into a small carrot shape, marking shallow grooves with a knife.

4. Using a palette knife, spread the frosting over the cake, taking it almost to the edges. Trim the crusts from the cake to neaten it, then cut it into 20 squares. Place a marzipan carrot on each square and add a small sprig of dill to form a carrot top.

Lemon crunch cupcakes

Ingredients

175 g/6 oz butter, softened

175 g/6 oz golden caster sugar

175 g/6 oz self-raising flour, sifted

1 tsp baking powder

3 large eggs

3 tbsp lemon curd

100 g/3½ oz granulated sugar

grated rind and juice of 1 lemon

1. Preheat the oven to 180°C/350°F/Gas Mark 4. Line a 12-hole muffin tin with paper cases.

2. Put the butter, caster sugar, flour, baking powder and eggs in a large bowl and beat until thoroughly combined. Fold in the lemon curd. Spoon the mixture into the paper cases.

3. Bake the cupcakes in the preheated oven for 20 minutes, or until risen and golden brown. Meanwhile, mix the granulated sugar and lemon juice and rind together in a bowl.

4. Remove the cupcakes from the oven and leave for 2 minutes, then spread some of the lemon mixture over each cupcake. Leave to cool in the tin – the topping will go crisp on cooling.

#175 Garibaldi biscuits

Makes 24

Ingredients

140 g/5 oz plain flour

100 g/3½ oz icing sugar,
plus extra for dusting

1 tsp finely grated lime zest

115 g/4 oz butter, softened,
plus extra for greasing

pinch of salt

1. Preheat the oven to 180°C/350°F/Gas Mark 4. Lightly grease a baking tray. Put the flour, sugar and lime zest into a medium-sized bowl and mix to combine. Add the butter and salt, and beat to a smooth dough.

2. Turn out onto a lightly floured work surface, roll out into a large rectangle and cut into about three wide strips. Use your hands to roll the strips into tubes, then cut them into 2-cm/¾-inch pieces. Roll into 24 small balls, then place on the prepared tray. Pinch with your fingers to create a ridged shape on each biscuit, then bake in the preheated oven for about 15 minutes, until golden brown.

3. Remove from the oven, sprinkle with sugar and serve.

#176 Coffee crumb cakes

Makes 18

Ingredients

85 g/3 oz plain flour

125 g/4½ oz lightly salted butter,
cut into pieces, plus extra for greasing

½ tsp ground mixed spice

1½ tsp ground espresso coffee

175 g/6 oz caster sugar

1 egg

5 tbsp soured cream

125 g/4½ oz self-raising flour

Icing

85 g/3 oz icing sugar

1 tbsp strong espresso coffee

1. Preheat the oven to 180°C/350°F/Gas Mark 4. Grease an 18-cm/7-inch shallow, loose-based square cake tin. Line with baking paper and grease the paper.

2. Put the plain flour, 70 g/2½ oz of the butter, the mixed spice and coffee in a food processor and process until the mixture starts to resemble coarse breadcrumbs. Add 70 g/2½ oz of the caster sugar and process again briefly. Tip the mixture into a mixing bowl.

3. Put the remaining butter and caster sugar, the egg, soured cream and self-raising flour in the food processor and blend until smooth and creamy, then tip into the prepared tin and level the surface. Sprinkle the crumb mixture in an even layer on top. Bake in the preheated oven for 30–35 minutes, or until risen, firm to the touch and a skewer inserted in the centre comes out clean. Leave in the tin for 10 minutes, then transfer to a wire rack to cool.

4. To make the icing, put all but 2 tablespoons of the icing sugar in a small mixing bowl and add the coffee. Beat to a smooth paste that falls in a thick trail from the spoon, adding a little more icing sugar if necessary. Cut the cake into three even-sized pieces, then cut across to make 18 rectangular pieces. Drizzle with the icing.

Gingerbread & vanilla whoopie pies

Ingredients

1 egg

70 g/2½ oz light muscovado sugar

1 tbsp black treacle

40 g/1½ oz lightly salted butter, melted

5 tbsp milk

150 g/5 oz plain flour

½ tsp bicarbonate of soda

1½ tsp ground ginger

½ tsp ground mixed spice

Filling

100 g/3½ oz cream cheese

15 g/½ oz unsalted butter, softened

1 tsp vanilla extract

55 g/2 oz icing sugar, plus extra for dusting

1 tsp boiling water

1. Preheat the oven to 180°C/350°F/Gas Mark 4. Line two baking trays with baking paper. Put the egg, sugar and treacle in a mixing bowl and beat until thick and foamy. Beat in the butter and milk. Sift the flour, bicarbonate of soda, ginger and mixed spice into the bowl and stir with a wooden spoon to make a soft paste.

2. Spoon 28 teaspoons of the mixture onto the prepared trays, spaced well apart, flattening them slightly. Bake in the preheated oven for 10 minutes, or until risen and firm to the touch, switching over the trays halfway through cooking. Leave to cool on the trays for 5 minutes, then transfer to wire racks to cool completely.

3. To make the filling, put the cream cheese, butter, vanilla extract and icing sugar in a mixing bowl and beat until smooth and creamy. Beat in the boiling water. Use the filling to sandwich the whoopie pies together in pairs. Leave in a cool place to firm up for a couple of hours, then dust with icing sugar and serve.

Macadamia & maple cupcakes

Ingredients

85 g/3 oz butter, softened

55 g/2 oz soft light brown sugar

2 tbsp maple syrup

1 large egg, lightly beaten

85 g/3 oz self-raising flour

55 g/2 oz macadamia nuts, chopped

1 tbsp milk

Frosting

25 g/1 oz butter, softened

2 tbsp maple syrup

85 g/3 oz icing sugar, sifted

85 g/3 oz full-fat soft cheese

2 tbsp chopped macadamia nuts

1. Preheat the oven to 190°C/375°F/Gas Mark 5. Put 10 paper paper cases in a muffin tray or put 10 double-layer paper cases on a baking tray.

2. Put the butter, sugar and maple syrup in a bowl and beat together until light and fluffy. Gradually beat in the egg. Sift in the flour and, using a metal spoon, fold into the mixture with the nuts and milk. Spoon the mixture into the paper cases.

3. Bake the cupcakes in the preheated oven for 20 minutes, or until golden brown and firm to the touch. Transfer to a wire rack and leave to cool completely.

4. To make the frosting, beat the butter and maple syrup together until smooth. Fold in the icing sugar and beat in thoroughly. Gently beat in the soft cheese. Swirl the icing on the top of the cupcakes and sprinkle over the chopped nuts.

Apple cider funnel cookies in cinnamon sugar

Makes
20

Ingredients

275 ml/9 fl oz cider or apple juice

70 g/2½ oz butter

1 tbsp sugar

150 g/5½ oz plain flour, sifted

pinch of salt

4 whole eggs and 2 egg whites, beaten

1 tsp bicarbonate of soda

1 tsp vanilla extract

vegetable oil, for deep-frying

4 tbsp icing sugar mixed with 1 tsp ground cinnamon, to serve

1. Place the cider in a medium-sized saucepan with the butter and sugar and bring to the boil. Stir in the flour and salt and beat with a wooden spoon until a dough forms. Remove from the heat and leave to cool for 1–2 minutes.

2. Gradually add the eggs, beating thoroughly between each addition. Beat in the bicarbonate of soda and the vanilla extract.

3. Heat enough oil for deep-frying in a large saucepan or deep-fryer to 180–190°C/350–375°F, or until a cube of bread browns in 30 seconds.

4. Using a piping bag fitted with a 3-mm/⅛-inch plain nozzle, pipe the dough into the hot oil to make a lattice shape. Fry for about 30 seconds, then turn and cook until puffed and golden. Cook 1–2 cookies at a time, being careful not to overcrowd the pan. After cooking each batch, reheat the oil to the correct temperature before cooking the next.

5. Drain the cookies on kitchen paper, then quickly roll them in the cinnamon sugar and serve immediately. Dust with a little extra sugar on top, if liked.

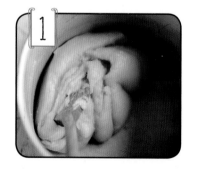

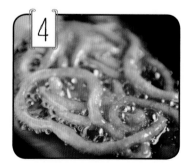

#180 Cranberry muffins

Makes 10

Ingredients

175 g/6 oz self-raising white flour
55 g/2 oz self-raising wholemeal flour
1 tsp ground cinnamon
½ tsp bicarbonate of soda
1 egg
70 g/2½ oz fine-cut marmalade
150 ml/5 fl oz skimmed milk
5 tbsp vegetable oil
115 g/4 oz eating apple, peeled, cored and finely diced
115 g/4 oz cranberries, thawed if frozen
1 tbsp rolled oats

1. Preheat the oven to 200°C/400°F/Gas Mark 6. Line a 10-hole muffin tin with paper cases. Sift together the flours, cinnamon and bicarbonate of soda into a large bowl, tipping in any husks that remain in the sieve.

2. Lightly beat the egg with the marmalade in a large jug, then beat in the milk and oil. Make a well in the centre of the dry ingredients and pour in the beaten liquid ingredients. Stir gently until just combined; do not over-mix. Stir in the apple and cranberries. Divide the mixture between the paper cases and sprinkle the oats over the top of the muffins. Bake in the preheated oven for about 20 minutes, or until well risen, golden brown and firm to the touch.

3. Leave to cool in the tin for 5 minutes, then serve warm or transfer to a wire rack and leave to cool.

#181 Lemon iced cookies

Makes 45

Ingredients

115 g/4 oz butter, softened
85 g/3 oz caster sugar
1 egg yolk
1 tsp finely grated lemon zest
150 g/5½ oz plain flour

Icing

150 g/5½ oz icing sugar
1 tbsp lukewarm water
1 tbsp lemon juice
pink and yellow food colouring

1. Preheat the oven to 190°C/375°F/Gas Mark 5. Put the butter and sugar into a bowl and beat with a wooden spoon until pale and creamy. Beat in the egg yolk and lemon zest, then stir in the flour. Mix to a soft dough.

2. Use a cookie press fitted with a disc of your choice to stamp out 45 cookies onto three non-stick baking sheets (re-filling the press when necessary). Alternatively, roll the dough into small balls or shapes of your choice and gently flatten onto the baking sheets.

3. Bake in the preheated oven for 8–10 minutes, until golden around the edges. Leave to cool on the baking sheets for a few minutes, then transfer to wire racks to cool completely.

4. To make the icing, sift the icing sugar into a bowl and stir in the water and lemon juice to make a smooth icing. Divide the icing equally between two bowls. Colour one pink and the other yellow. Spoon into paper piping bags, snip the ends and pipe decorations on the cookies. Leave to set.

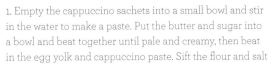

#182 Cappuccino cookies

Ingredients

2 sachets instant cappuccino

1 tbsp hot water

225 g/8 oz butter, softened

140 g/5 oz caster sugar

1 egg yolk, lightly beaten

280 g/10 oz plain flour

pinch of salt

Decoration

175 g/6 oz white chocolate, broken into pieces

cocoa powder, for dusting

1. Empty the cappuccino sachets into a small bowl and stir in the water to make a paste. Put the butter and sugar into a bowl and beat together until pale and creamy, then beat in the egg yolk and cappuccino paste. Sift the flour and salt into the mixture and stir until thoroughly combined. Halve the dough, shape into balls, wrap in clingfilm and chill in the refrigerator for 30–60 minutes.

2. Preheat the oven to 190°C/375°F/Gas Mark 5. Line two baking sheets with baking paper. Unwrap the dough and roll out between two sheets of baking paper. Stamp out 30 cookies with a 6-cm/2½-inch round cutter and put them on the prepared baking sheets.

3. Bake in the preheated oven for 10–12 minutes, or until golden. Leave to cool completely. Put the chocolate into a heatproof bowl set over a saucepan of gently simmering water and heat until melted. Remove and leave to cool, then spoon the chocolate over the cookies. Dust lightly with cocoa powder and leave to set.

#183 Blueberry cupcakes with soured cream frosting

Ingredients

175 g/6 oz plain white flour

1 tbsp baking powder

175 g/6 oz butter, softened

175 g/6 oz caster sugar

3 eggs, beaten

1 tsp vanilla extract

finely grated rind of ½ orange

150 g/5½ oz fresh blueberries

Frosting

3 tbsp soured cream

150 g/5½ oz icing sugar, sifted

1. Preheat the oven to 190°C/375°F/Gas Mark 5. Line three muffin tins with 30 paper cases or put 30 double-layer paper cases on baking trays.

2. Sift the flour and baking powder into a large bowl and add the butter, caster sugar, eggs and vanilla extract. Beat well until the mixture is smooth, then stir in the orange rind and 100 g/3½ oz of the blueberries.

3. Divide the mixture between the paper cases. Bake in the preheated oven for 15–20 minutes, or until risen, golden brown and firm to the touch. Transfer to wire racks to cool completely.

4. To make the frosting, stir the soured cream into the icing sugar and mix well until smooth. Spoon a little frosting on top of each cupcake and top with a blueberry. Leave to set.

#184 Sugar cookies

Ingredients

115 g/4 oz butter, softened,
plus extra for greasing

55 g/2 oz caster sugar,
plus extra for sprinkling

1 tsp finely grated lemon rind

1 egg yolk

175 g/6 oz plain flour,
plus extra for dusting

1. Place the butter and sugar in a bowl and beat together until pale and creamy. Beat in the lemon rind and egg yolk. Sift in the flour and mix to a soft dough. Turn out onto a floured work surface and knead until smooth, adding a little more flour, if necessary. Halve the dough, shape into balls, wrap in clingfilm and chill in the refrigerator for 1 hour.

2. Preheat the oven to 180°C/350°F/Gas Mark 4. Lightly grease two large baking sheets.

3. Roll out the dough on a lightly floured work surface to a thickness of 5 mm/¼ inch. Using 7-cm/2¾-inch flower-shaped and heart-shaped cutters stamp out 20 cookies, re-rolling the dough as necessary. Place on the prepared baking sheets and sprinkle with sugar. Bake in the preheated oven for 10–12 minutes, or until pale golden. Leave to cool on the baking sheets for 2–3 minutes, then transfer to a wire rack to cool completely.

#185 Peanut partners

Ingredients

225 g/8 oz butter, softened

140 g/5 oz caster sugar

1 egg yolk, lightly beaten

280 g/10 oz plain flour

1 tsp ground ginger

2 tsp finely grated lemon rind

3 tbsp smooth peanut butter

3 tbsp icing sugar

salt

whole or chopped roasted peanuts,
to decorate

1. Put the butter and sugar into a bowl and mix well with a wooden spoon, then beat in the egg yolk. Sift together the flour, ginger and a pinch of salt into the mixture, add the lemon rind and stir until thoroughly combined. Halve the dough, shape into balls, wrap in clingfilm and chill in the refrigerator for 30–60 minutes.

2. Preheat the oven to 190°C/375°F/Gas Mark 5. Line two baking sheets with baking paper.

3. Unwrap the dough and roll out between two sheets of baking paper to 3 mm/⅛ inch thick. Stamp out 30 rounds with a 6-cm/2½-inch cutter and place on the prepared baking sheets, spaced well apart.

4. Bake for 10–15 minutes, until golden brown. Leave to cool on the baking sheets for 5–10 minutes, then carefully transfer to wire racks to cool completely.

5. Beat together the peanut butter and icing sugar in a bowl, adding a little water if necessary. Spread the cookies with the peanut butter mixture and decorate with whole or chopped peanuts.

186 Black Forest whoopie pies

Makes 10

Ingredients

250 g/9 oz plain flour

1 tsp bicarbonate of soda

25 g/1 oz cocoa powder

large pinch of salt

115 g/4 oz butter, softened

150 g/5½ oz soft dark brown sugar

1 large egg, beaten

1 tsp vanilla extract

4 tbsp soured cream

3 tbsp milk

55 g/2 oz dried and sweetened sour cherries, chopped

cocoa powder, to dust

Filling

300 ml/10 fl oz double cream

2 tbsp cherry liqueur (optional)

6 tbsp cherry jam

55 g/2 oz plain chocolate, grated

1. Preheat the oven to 180°C/350°F/Gas Mark 4. Line three large baking sheets with baking paper. Sift together the flour, bicarbonate of soda, cocoa powder and salt.

2. Place the butter and sugar in a large bowl and beat until pale and fluffy. Whisk in the egg and vanilla extract, then beat in half of the flour mixture, the soured cream and milk. Stir in the remaining flour mixture and mix until thoroughly incorporated. Stir in the dried cherries.

3. Pipe 20 mounds of the mixture onto the prepared baking sheets, spaced well apart. Bake in the preheated oven, one sheet at a time, for 10-12 minutes until risen and just firm to the touch. Leave to cool for 5 minutes then transfer to a wire rack and leave to cool completely.

4. To make the filling, place the cream and cherry liqueur, if using, in a bowl and whip until it holds firm peaks. Spread the cherry jam on the flat side of 10 of the cakes. Top with the whipped cream and the grated chocolate. Top with the remaining cakes, then dust with cocoa powder.

187 Spiced apple pie cupcakes

Makes 12

Ingredients

190 g/6½ oz plain flour

1 tsp ground mixed spice

75 g/2¾ oz butter

40 g/1½ oz caster sugar

70 g/2½ oz demerara sugar

1 egg, lightly beaten

1½ tsp baking powder

1 large cooking apple, peeled, cored and finely chopped

1 tbsp orange juice

1. Preheat the oven to 180°C/350°F/Gas Mark 4. Line a 12-hole muffin tin with paper cases. Place 40 g/1½ oz of the flour, ½ teaspoon of the mixed spice, 25 g/1 oz of the butter and the caster sugar in a large bowl and rub in with your fingertips until the mixture resembles fine breadcrumbs. Set aside.

2. Place the remaining butter and the demerara sugar in a large bowl and beat together until light and fluffy, then gradually beat in the egg. Sift in the remaining flour, baking powder and remaining mixed spice, and fold into the mixture, then fold in the chopped apple and orange juice. Spoon the mixture into the paper cases. Cover the top of each cupcake with the reserved rubbed-in mixture and press down gently.

3. Bake in the preheated oven for 30 minutes. Leave to cool in the tin for 2-3 minutes and serve warm, or leave to cool for 10 minutes, then transfer to a wire rack to cool completely.

#188 Gingerbread cupcakes

Makes 30

Ingredients

175 g/6 oz plain flour
1 tbsp baking powder
2 tsp ground ginger
1 tsp ground cinnamon
175 g/6 oz butter, softened
175 g/6 oz dark muscovado sugar
3 eggs, lightly beaten
1 tsp vanilla extract
chopped crystallized ginger, to decorate

Frosting

85 g/3 oz butter, softened
3 tbsp orange juice
150 g/5½ oz icing sugar

1. Preheat the oven to 190°C/375°F/Gas Mark 5. Line three mini muffin tins with 30 paper cases.

2. Sift the flour, baking powder, ground ginger and cinnamon into a large bowl. Add the butter, muscovado sugar, eggs and vanilla extract and beat until smooth.

3. Spoon the mixture into the paper cases. Bake in the preheated oven for 15–20 minutes, or until risen, golden and firm to the touch. Transfer to wire racks and leave to cool.

4. To make the frosting, place the butter and orange juice in a bowl and beat until smooth. Sift in the icing sugar and continue beating until light and fluffy. Spoon the frosting into a piping bag fitted with a star-shaped nozzle. Pipe a little swirl of frosting on top of each cupcake and scatter over the crystallized ginger.

Vanilla swirled brownies

Ingredients

85 g/3 oz lightly salted butter, plus extra for greasing

100 g/3½ oz plain chocolate, roughly chopped

1 egg

1 egg yolk

100 g/3½ oz light muscovado sugar

40 g/1½ oz self-raising flour

¼ tsp baking powder

85 g/3 oz milk chocolate, roughly chopped

milk chocolate curls, for sprinkling

Frosting

150 g/5½ oz mascarpone cheese

4 tbsp icing sugar

1 tsp vanilla extract

1. Preheat the oven to 190°C/375°F/Gas Mark 5. Grease a 12-hole mini muffin tin and line the bases with baking paper.

2. Put the butter and plain chocolate in a heatproof bowl set over a saucepan of gently simmering water and heat until melted. Leave the mixture to cool slightly.

3. Put the egg, egg yolk and sugar in a mixing bowl and beat with an electric hand-held mixer until the mixture begins to turn frothy. Stir in the melted chocolate. Sift the flour and baking powder into the bowl, scatter in the milk chocolate and stir to combine. Using a teaspoon, spoon the mixture into the prepared tin. Bake in the preheated oven for 12–15 minutes, or until the crust feels dry but gives a little when gently pressed. Leave to cool in the tin for 10 minutes, then transfer to a wire rack to cool.

4. To make the frosting, put the mascarpone cheese, icing sugar and vanilla extract in a small bowl and beat until smooth and creamy. Put the mixture in a piping bag fitted with a 1-cm/½-inch star-shaped nozzle and pipe swirls over the cakes. Sprinkle with chocolate curls.

Marzipan ring cups

Ingredients

125 g/4½ oz butter, softened

30 g/1 oz caster sugar

½ tsp almond extract

125 g/4½ oz plain flour, sifted

1 tbsp milk (optional)

40 g/1½ oz marzipan

4 tsp apricot jam, warmed

icing sugar, sifted, for dusting

1. Preheat the oven to 190°C/375°F/Gas Mark 5. Line an 8-hole muffin tin with paper cases.

2. Place the butter, sugar and almond extract in a food processor and process until pale and fluffy. Add the flour and process to a soft dough, adding milk if needed to achieve a good piping consistency. Spoon the mixture into a piping bag fitted with a large star-shaped nozzle. Pipe the mixture in a spiral around the sides of each case, leaving a dip in the centre. Cut the marzipan into eight cubes and press one cube into the centre of each cup.

3. Bake in the preheated oven for 15–20 minutes, until pale and golden. Transfer to a wire rack and leave to cool completely, then spoon a little jam into the centre of each. Dust with icing sugar just before serving.

#191 Double chocolate muffins

Ingredients

15 g/½ oz cocoa powder

70 g/2½ oz self-raising flour

¼ tsp baking powder

25 g/1 oz light muscovado sugar

85 g/3 oz milk chocolate, roughly chopped

1 egg

3 tbsp milk

40 g/1½ oz lightly salted butter, melted

40 g/1½ oz plain chocolate, roughly chopped

1. Preheat the oven to 190°C/375°F/Gas Mark 5. Line a 12-hole mini muffin tin with paper cases. Sift the cocoa powder, flour and baking powder into a mixing bowl. Stir in the sugar and milk chocolate. In a separate mixing bowl, mix the egg, milk and butter with a fork until combined. Tip into the flour mixture and gently fold in until just combined; do not over-mix.

2. Spoon the mixture into the paper cases; it should be level with the top of the tin. Bake in the preheated oven for 15 minutes, or until risen and just firm to the touch. Leave to cool in the tin for 2 minutes, then transfer to a wire rack to cool completely.

3. Put the plain chocolate in a heatproof bowl set over a saucepan of gently simmering water and heat until melted. Use a teaspoon to drizzle it over the muffins and serve warm or cold.

#192 Iced baby Bundt cakes

Ingredients

200 g/7 oz plain flour, plus extra for sprinkling

1 tsp baking powder

1 tsp ground cinnamon, plus extra for sprinkling

125 g/4½ oz caster sugar

60 g/2¼ oz walnuts, finely chopped

2 small dessert apples, peeled, cored and finely grated

6 tbsp vegetable oil, plus extra for greasing

3 eggs

150 ml/5 fl oz buttermilk

Icing

3 tbsp natural yogurt

150 g/5½ oz icing sugar, sifted

1. Preheat the oven to 180°C/350°F/Gas Mark 4. Brush 2 x 75-ml/2½-fl oz mini Bundt tins with oil. Sprinkle a little flour into the tins and tilt to coat the bases and sides, shaking out any excess.

2. Sift the flour, baking powder and cinnamon into a bowl. Stir in the sugar, walnuts and apples.

3. In a separate mixing bowl, beat together the oil, eggs and buttermilk. Add to the dry ingredients and stir to form a soft paste.

4. Using a teaspoon, spoon the mixture into the prepared tins and level with the back of the spoon. Bake in the preheated oven for 15–20 minutes, or until risen and just firm to the touch. Leave to cool in the tins for 5 minutes, then transfer to a wire rack to cool completely.

5. To make the icing, put the yogurt into a bowl and add the icing sugar. Beat together well until smooth. Spoon a little of the icing onto the top of each cake, easing it slightly down the sides with the back of the spoon. Lightly sprinkle the tops of the cakes with cinnamon.

Ingredients

175 g/6 oz plain flour

1 tbsp baking powder

1 tbsp custard powder

175 g/6 oz butter, softened

175 g/6 oz golden caster sugar

3 eggs, beaten

1 tsp vanilla extract

70 g/2½ oz raspberry jam

icing sugar, for dusting

1. Preheat the oven to 190°C/375°F/Gas Mark 5. Line three muffin tins with 28 paper cases or put 28 double-layer paper cases on baking trays.

2. Sift the flour, baking powder and custard powder into a large bowl and add the butter, caster sugar, eggs and vanilla extract. Beat well until smooth.

3. Divide the mixture between the paper cases and place ½ teaspoon of jam in the centre of each cupcake, without pressing down.

4. Bake in the preheated oven for 15–20 minutes, or until risen, golden brown and firm to the touch. Transfer the cupcakes to a wire rack to cool completely. Dust with icing sugar just before serving.

194 Coconut kisses

Makes
24

Ingredients

butter, for greasing

200 g/7 oz desiccated coconut

60 g/2¼ oz plain flour

4 egg yolks

1 egg white,
plus extra for brushing

2 tbsp coconut milk

225 g/8 oz soft light brown sugar

1 tsp vanilla extract or 1 vanilla pod, scraped

glacé cherries, to decorate

1. Preheat the oven to 180°C/350°F/Gas Mark 4. Line a baking tray with baking paper and grease the paper.

2. Put all the ingredients into a large bowl and mix to a firm dough. Divide the dough into 24 pieces and roll each piece into a ball.

3. Place the balls on the prepared tray, brush with egg white and bake in the preheated oven for 15 minutes, until the tops are golden brown. Remove from the oven and transfer to a wire rack to cool. Decorate with cherries and serve.

#195 Oaty raisin & nut cookies

Ingredients

55 g/2 oz raisins, chopped

125 ml/4 fl oz orange juice

225 g/8 oz butter, softened

140 g/5 oz caster sugar

1 egg yolk, lightly beaten

2 tsp vanilla extract

225 g/8 oz plain flour

55 g/2 oz rolled oats

55 g/2 oz hazelnuts, chopped, plus extra whole nuts, to decorate

salt

1. Preheat the oven to 190°C/375°F/Gas Mark 5. Line two baking sheets with baking paper. Put the raisins in a bowl, add the orange juice and leave to soak for 10 minutes.

2. Put the butter and sugar into a bowl and mix well, then beat in the egg yolk and vanilla extract. Sift the flour and a pinch of salt into the mixture and add the oats and hazelnuts. Drain the raisins, discarding the orange juice, and add them to the mixture.

3. Put 30 tablespoons of the mixture on the prepared baking sheets, spaced well apart. Flatten slightly and place a whole hazelnut in the centre of each cookie. Bake in the preheated oven for 12–15 minutes, until golden brown. Leave to cool on the baking sheets for a few minutes, then transfer to wire racks to cool completely.

#196 Chocolate & cream cheese cupcakes

Makes
12

Ingredients

175 g/6 oz plain flour

20 g/¾ oz cocoa powder

¾ tsp bicarbonate of soda

200 g/7 oz caster sugar

50 ml/2 fl oz sunflower oil

175 ml/6 fl oz water

2 tsp white vinegar

½ tsp vanilla extract

150 g/5½ oz full-fat cream cheese

1 egg, lightly beaten

100 g/3½ oz plain chocolate chips

1. Preheat the oven to 180°C/350°F/Gas Mark 4. Line a 12-hole muffin tin with paper cases.

2. Sift the flour, cocoa powder and bicarbonate of soda into a large bowl. Stir 150 g/5½ oz of the caster sugar into the flour mixture. Add the oil, water, vinegar and vanilla extract, and stir well until combined.

3. Place the remaining caster sugar, cream cheese and egg in a large bowl and beat together until well mixed. Stir in the chocolate chips.

4. Spoon the cocoa mixture into the paper cases and top each with a spoonful of the cream cheese mixture. Bake in the preheated oven for 20–25 minutes, or until risen and firm to the touch. Transfer to a wire rack and leave to cool completely.

197 Rhubarb & ginger muffins

Makes 12

Ingredients

oil, for greasing

250 g/9 oz rhubarb

200 g/7 oz plain flour

2 tsp baking powder

115 g/4 oz caster sugar

2 eggs

100 ml/3½ fl oz milk

125 g/4½ oz butter, melted and cooled

3 tbsp raisins

2 pieces of stem ginger in syrup, drained and chopped

1. Preheat the oven to 180°C/350°F/Gas Mark 4. Line a 12-hole muffin tin with paper cases. Chop the rhubarb into 1-cm/½-inch lengths.

2. Sift together the flour and baking powder into a large bowl. Stir in the sugar. Lightly beat the eggs in a large jug, then beat in the milk and melted butter. Make a well in the centre of the dry ingredients and pour in the beaten liquid ingredients. Stir in the rhubarb, raisins and ginger until just combined; do not over-mix. Spoon the mixture into the paper cases. Bake in the preheated oven for 15–20 minutes, until well risen, golden brown and firm to the touch.

3. Leave the muffins to cool in the tin for 5 minutes, then serve warm or transfer to a wire rack to cool completely.

198 Chocolate & nut cakes

Makes 4

Ingredients

55 g/2 oz butter, plus extra for greasing

3 tbsp icing sugar

55 g/2 oz sponge fingers

25 g/1 oz ground hazelnuts

180 g/6½ oz plain chocolate

2 eggs, separated

1 tbsp brandy

1 tbsp crème de cacao

4 tsp water

2½ tbsp caster sugar

grated rind and juice of 1 orange

1. Preheat the oven to 180°C/350°F/Gas Mark 4. Grease four dariole moulds or ramekins. Beat the butter in a large bowl until light and fluffy, gradually add the icing sugar and beat thoroughly. Break the sponge fingers into pieces and stir into the butter mixture with the hazelnuts. Grate 55 g/2 oz of the chocolate and combine with the butter mixture. Add the egg yolks, brandy and crème de cacao, and mix well.

2. Beat the egg whites until they hold stiff peaks, fold carefully into the mixture and divide evenly between the moulds. Cover with greased foil and place in a roasting tin. Pour in hot water to come halfway up the sides of the moulds. Place in the preheated oven and bake for 45 minutes, or until the mixture has set.

3. To make the sauce, put the water, caster sugar and orange rind and juice into a small saucepan, and bring to the boil. Reduce the heat and simmer for 3 minutes. Break the remaining chocolate into a heatproof bowl and heat over a saucepan of gently simmering water until melted. Slowly stir in the syrup. Turn out the cakes onto plates, then pour over the sauce and serve warm.

#199 Biscotti

Makes
30

Ingredients

225 g/8 oz butter, softened
140 g/5 oz caster sugar
finely grated rind of 1 lemon
1 egg yolk, lightly beaten
2 tsp brandy
280 g/10 oz plain flour
pinch of salt
85 g/3 oz pistachio nuts
icing sugar, for dusting

1. Put the butter, caster sugar and lemon rind into a bowl and mix well with a wooden spoon, then beat in the egg yolk and brandy. Sift together the flour and salt into the mixture and stir in the pistachio nuts until thoroughly combined. Shape the mixture into a log, flatten slightly, wrap in clingfilm and chill in the refrigerator for 30–60 minutes.

2. Preheat the oven to 190°C/375°F/Gas Mark 5. Line two baking sheets with baking paper. Unwrap the log and cut it slightly on the diagonal into 30 x 5-mm/¼-inch slices with a sharp serrated knife. Put them on the prepared baking sheets, spaced well apart.

3. Bake in the preheated oven for 10 minutes, or until golden brown. Leave to cool on the baking sheets for 5–10 minutes, then transfer to wire racks to cool completely. Dust with icing sugar just before serving.

#200 Salted caramel cupcakes

Makes
12

Ingredients

190 g/6¾ oz plain flour
1½ tsp baking powder
¼ tsp salt
115 g/4 oz butter, softened
100 g/3½ oz caster sugar
110 g/3¾ oz soft dark brown sugar
1 tsp vanilla extract
1 tsp coffee extract
2 large eggs
125 ml/4 fl oz milk
1 tsp sea salt flakes, to decorate

Frosting

115 g/4 oz butter
220 g/7¾ oz soft dark
brown sugar
90 ml/3 fl oz double cream
½ tsp salt
190 g/6¾ oz icing sugar

1. Preheat the oven to 180°C/350°F/Gas Mark 4 and line a 12-hole muffin tin with paper cases.

2. Sift together the flour, baking powder and salt into a bowl. Put the butter, caster sugar and brown sugar into a separate bowl and beat until pale and fluffy. Add the vanilla extract and coffee extract, then add the eggs one at a time, beating between each addition. Add half of the flour mixture and the milk, and beat until incorporated. Add the remaining flour mixture and mix to combine.

3. Spoon the mixture into the paper cases and bake in the preheated oven for 20 minutes, until risen and golden. Leave to cool in the tin for 1–2 minutes, then transfer to a wire rack to cool completely.

4. To make the frosting, melt the butter in a small saucepan over a medium heat. Add the brown sugar, cream and salt, and cook, stirring constantly, for about 4 minutes, or until the sugar has completely dissolved. Remove from the heat and set aside to cool.

5. Add the icing sugar to the caramel sauce and beat until fully incorporated. Spoon into a piping bag fitted with a star-shaped nozzle and pipe onto the cupcakes. To decorate, sprinkle the cupcakes with the sea salt flakes.

132

#201 Chocolate mint cookies

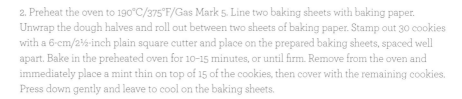

Ingredients

225 g/8 oz butter, softened

140 g/5 oz caster sugar

1 egg yolk, lightly beaten

2 tsp vanilla extract

250 g/9 oz plain flour

25 g/1 oz cocoa powder

pinch of salt

55 g/2 oz glacé cherries, finely chopped

15 after-dinner mint thins

115 g/4 oz plain chocolate, broken into pieces

55 g/2 oz white chocolate, broken into pieces

1. Put the butter and sugar into a bowl and beat together until pale and creamy, then beat in the egg yolk and vanilla extract. Sift together the flour, cocoa powder and salt into the mixture, add the cherries and stir until thoroughly combined. Halve the dough, shape into balls, wrap in clingfilm and chill in the refrigerator for 30–60 minutes.

2. Preheat the oven to 190°C/375°F/Gas Mark 5. Line two baking sheets with baking paper. Unwrap the dough halves and roll out between two sheets of baking paper. Stamp out 30 cookies with a 6-cm/2½-inch plain square cutter and place on the prepared baking sheets, spaced well apart. Bake in the preheated oven for 10–15 minutes, or until firm. Remove from the oven and immediately place a mint thin on top of 15 of the cookies, then cover with the remaining cookies. Press down gently and leave to cool on the baking sheets.

3. Melt the plain chocolate in a heatproof bowl set over a saucepan of gently simmering water, then leave to cool. Put the cookies on a wire rack, spoon the plain chocolate over them and leave to set. Melt the white chocolate in a heatproof bowl set over a saucepan of gently simmering water then leave to cool. Drizzle over the cookies and leave to set.

#202 Pina colada whoopie pies

Ingredients

225 g/8 oz plain flour

2 tsp baking powder

large pinch of salt

55 g/2 oz desiccated coconut

115 g/4 oz butter, softened

150 g/5½ oz caster sugar

1 large egg, beaten

100 ml/3½ fl oz milk

25 g/1 oz crystallized pineapple

300 ml/10 fl oz double cream

2 tbsp white rum

115 g/4 oz icing sugar

1–2 tbsp pineapple juice

toasted coconut shavings, to decorate

1. Preheat the oven to 180°C/350°F/Gas Mark 4. Line three large baking sheets with baking paper. Sift together the flour, baking powder and salt. Stir in the coconut.

2. Place the butter and caster sugar in a large bowl and beat until pale and fluffy. Beat in the egg, half of the flour mixture and the milk. Stir in the remaining flour mixture and mix well. Finely chop and fold in the pineapple. Pipe 24 mounds of the mixture onto the prepared baking sheets, spaced well apart. Bake in the preheated oven, one sheet at a time, for 10–12 minutes until risen and just firm to the touch. Leave to cool for 5 minutes then transfer to a wire rack to cool completely. Put the cream and rum in a bowl and whip until the mixture holds firm peaks.

3. Sift the icing sugar into a bowl and stir in enough pineapple juice to make a smooth icing. Spread the rum cream on the flat side of 12 of the cakes. Top with the remaining cakes. Spoon the icing over the pies, letting it drip down the sides. Decorate with toasted coconut shavings.

Pastries
& fancies

203 Madeleines

Ingredients

3 eggs

1 egg yolk

1 tsp vanilla extract

140 g/5 oz caster sugar

140 g/5 oz plain flour

1 tsp baking powder

140 g/5 oz butter, melted and cooled, plus extra for greasing

1. Preheat the oven to 190°C/375°F/Gas Mark 5. Lightly grease 30 holes in three standard-sized madeleine tins.

2. Place the eggs, egg yolk, vanilla extract and sugar in a large bowl and whisk with an electric hand-held mixer until very pale and thick.

3. Sift in the flour and baking powder and fold in lightly and evenly using a metal spoon. Fold in the melted butter. Spoon the mixture into the prepared tins, filling to about three-quarters full. Bake in the preheated oven for 8–10 minutes, until risen and golden.

4. Carefully remove the cakes from the tins and transfer to wire racks to cool completely. They are best served the day they are made.

204 Simple doughnuts

Ingredients

3 tbsp easy-blend dried yeast

225 ml/8 fl oz lukewarm milk

250 g/9 oz plain flour, plus extra for dusting

2 tbsp caster sugar

½ tsp salt

3 egg yolks

1 tsp vanilla extract

55 g/2 oz butter, softened

oil, for greasing and deep-frying

200 g/7 oz icing sugar

3–4 tbsp water

1. Dissolve the yeast in the milk. Add 200 g/7 oz of the flour into the mixture and set aside for 30 minutes.

2. Add the caster sugar, salt, egg yolks and vanilla extract to the bowl of a stand mixer fitted with a paddle attachment and mix on a low speed until smooth. Add the butter and milk mixture, and mix slowly. Replace the paddle attachment with a dough hook and add the remaining flour. Mix slowly until the dough is smooth. Chill in the refrigerator for 1 hour.

3. Lightly grease a baking tray. Roll out the dough on a floured surface to a thickness of about 1 cm/½ inch. Use a doughnut cutter to cut out 12 doughnuts.

4. Place the doughnuts on the prepared tray, cover with clingfilm and leave in a warm place until the doughnuts have risen to nearly double their original size and spring back when touched.

5. Heat enough oil for deep-frying in a large saucepan or deep-fryer to 180–190°C/350–375°F, or until a cube of bread browns in 30 seconds. Carefully place the doughnuts, one at a time, into the hot oil and fry for 2 minutes, or until golden brown. Remove with a slotted spoon, drain on kitchen paper and leave to cool.

6. Place the icing sugar in a bowl, mix in the water until smooth and pour over the doughnuts.

205 Raisin apple turnovers

Makes
6

Ingredients

oil, for greasing and brushing
1 cooking apple, peeled, cored and diced
2 tbsp raisins
2 tbsp soft light brown sugar
6 sheets frozen filo pastry, thawed
whipped cream, to serve

1. Preheat the oven to 190°C/375°F/Gas Mark 5. Grease a baking tray.

2. Place the apple, raisins and brown sugar in a large bowl and toss to mix well.

3. To make the turnovers, lay a sheet of filo on a work surface and brush with oil. Lay a second sheet on top and brush with oil. Lay a third sheet on top. Using kitchen scissors, cut the stack lengthways into three long strips.

4. Place a heaped tablespoon of the apple mixture at one end of one of the strips, leaving about 5 cm/2 inches at the end. Fold the uncovered end over the filling at a 45-degree angle. Continue folding end over end to form a triangular, fully enclosed bundle. Repeat with the remaining two strips and set the triangles on the baking tray. Repeat with the remaining pastry and filling.

5. Lightly brush the turnovers with oil. Bake in the preheated oven for about 15 minutes, or until the turnovers are lightly coloured and crisp. Serve warm or at room temperature with a dollop of whipped cream.

206 Cinnamon rolls

Makes
12

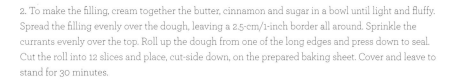

Ingredients

225 g/8 oz strong white flour
½ tsp salt
10 g/¼ oz easy-blend dried yeast
25 g/1 oz butter, cut into small pieces, plus extra for greasing
1 egg, lightly beaten
125 ml/4 fl oz lukewarm milk
2 tbsp maple syrup, for glazing

Filling

50 g/2 oz butter, softened
2 tsp ground cinnamon
50 g/1¾ oz soft light brown sugar
50 g/1¾ oz currants

1. Grease a baking sheet. Sift the flour and salt into a mixing bowl. Stir in the yeast. Rub in the butter with your fingertips until the mixture resembles breadcrumbs. Add the egg and milk, and mix to form a dough. Shape the dough into a ball, place in a greased bowl, cover with clingfilm and leave to stand in a warm place for about 40 minutes, or until doubled in size. Lightly knock back the dough for 1 minute, then roll out to a 30 x 23-cm/12 x 9-inch rectangle.

2. To make the filling, cream together the butter, cinnamon and sugar in a bowl until light and fluffy. Spread the filling evenly over the dough, leaving a 2.5-cm/1-inch border all around. Sprinkle the currants evenly over the top. Roll up the dough from one of the long edges and press down to seal. Cut the roll into 12 slices and place, cut-side down, on the prepared baking sheet. Cover and leave to stand for 30 minutes.

3. Meanwhile, preheat the oven to 190°C/375°F/Gas Mark 5. Bake the rolls in the preheated oven for 20–30 minutes, or until well risen. Brush with maple syrup and leave to cool slightly before serving.

137

#207 Churros

Ingredients

225 ml/8 fl oz water

85 g/3 oz butter, diced

2 tbsp dark muscovado sugar

finely grated rind of 1 small orange

pinch of salt

175 g/6 oz plain flour, well sifted

1 tsp ground cinnamon, plus extra
for dusting

1 tsp vanilla extract

2 eggs

oil, for deep-frying

caster sugar, for dusting

1. Heat the water, butter, muscovado sugar, orange rind and salt in a heavy-based saucepan over a medium heat until the butter has melted. Add the flour, cinnamon and vanilla extract, then remove from the heat and beat rapidly until the mixture pulls away from the sides of the pan. Leave to cool slightly, then beat in the eggs, one at a time, beating well after each addition, until the mixture is thick and smooth. Spoon into a piping bag fitted with a large star-shaped nozzle.

2. Heat enough oil for deep-frying in a deep-fryer or heavy-based saucepan to 180–190°C/350–375°F, or until a cube of bread browns in 30 seconds. Pipe 13-cm/5-inch lengths about 7.5 cm/3 inches apart into the hot oil. Fry for 2–3 minutes, turning frequently, until crisp and golden. Remove with a slotted spoon and drain on kitchen paper. Keep warm while frying the remaining mixture. Dust the churros with caster sugar and cinnamon, and serve.

#208 Coconut brownie pie pops

Ingredients

55 g/2 oz plain chocolate, broken
into pieces

25 g/1 oz butter, plus extra for greasing

1 egg, beaten

40 g/1½ oz light muscovado sugar

70 g/2½ oz plain flour, plus extra
for dusting

25 g/1 oz desiccated coconut

500 g/1 lb 2 oz ready-made sweet
shortcrust pastry

2 tsp cold water

14 cake pop sticks

1. Put the chocolate and butter into a heatproof bowl set over a saucepan of gently simmering water and heat until melted. Remove from the heat, stir until smooth, then leave to cool for 10 minutes.

2. Put the egg into a bowl, reserving 1 tablespoon. Add the sugar and beat to combine. Beat in the chocolate mixture. Sift in the flour and fold in with the coconut. The mixture should be quite stiff.

3. Preheat the oven to 190°C/375°F/Gas Mark 5. Grease two large baking sheets. Roll out half the pastry on a lightly floured work surface to a thickness of 3 mm/⅛ inch. Using a 7-cm/2¾-inch round cutter, stamp out 14 rounds and transfer to the prepared baking sheets.

4. Put a heaped teaspoon of the chocolate mixture in the centre of each round and flatten slightly. Push a cake pop stick into the chocolate filling. Roll out the remaining pastry and stamp out a further 14 rounds. Lightly brush the pastry edges around the filling with a little water then top with the rounds, pressing together firmly. Crimp and seal the edges of each pie with the tines of a fork.

5. Mix the cold water into the reserved egg and brush over the tops of the pies. Bake in the preheated oven for 16–18 minutes, or until pale golden. Leave to cool on the baking sheets for 5 minutes, then carefully transfer to a wire rack and leave to cool completely.

#209 Mini florentines

Makes 40

Ingredients

85 g/3 oz butter, plus extra for greasing

plain flour, for dusting

75 g/2¾ oz caster sugar

2 tbsp sultanas or raisins

2 tbsp chopped glacé cherries

2 tbsp chopped stem ginger

25 g/1 oz sunflower seeds

100 g/3½ oz flaked almonds

2 tbsp double cream

175 g/6 oz plain chocolate or milk chocolate, broken into pieces

1. Preheat the oven to 180°C/350°F/Gas Mark 4. Grease and flour two baking trays. Place the butter in a small saucepan and heat gently until melted. Add the sugar, stir until dissolved, then bring the mixture to the boil. Remove from the heat and stir in the sultanas, cherries, ginger, sunflower seeds and almonds. Mix well, then beat in the cream.

2. Place 40 small teaspoons of the fruit and nut mixture on the prepared trays, spaced well apart. Bake in the preheated oven for 10–12 minutes, or until light golden in colour. Remove from the oven and, while still hot, use a round biscuit cutter to pull in the edges to form perfect rounds. Leave to cool and go crisp before removing from the baking trays.

3. Put the chocolate in a heatproof bowl set over a saucepan of gently simmering water and heat until melted. Spread most of the chocolate on a sheet of baking paper. When the chocolate is on the point of setting, place the biscuits flat-side down on the chocolate and leave to harden.

4. Cut around the florentines and remove the paper. Spread a little more chocolate on the coated sides and use a fork to mark waves in the chocolate. Leave to set.

#210 Berry & plum crumbles

Makes 8

Ingredients

450 g/1 lb red plums, halved, stoned and diced

115 g/4 oz raspberries

25 g/1 oz light muscovado sugar

3 tbsp water

ready-made custard, to serve

Topping

85 g/3 oz plain flour

20 g/¾ oz porridge oats

20 g/¾ oz barley flakes

40 g/1½ oz light muscovado sugar

40 g/1½ oz butter, chilled and diced

1. Preheat the oven to 180°C/350°F/Gas Mark 4. Put the plums, raspberries, sugar and the water into a heavy-based saucepan over a low heat. Cover and simmer for 5 minutes, or until the fruit has softened.

2. To make the topping, put the flour, oats, barley flakes and sugar into a mixing bowl and stir. Rub in the butter with your fingertips until the mixture resembles fine breadcrumbs.

3. Spoon the fruit mixture into 8 x 150-ml/5-fl oz metal pudding basins and stand them on a baking tray. Sprinkle the topping on top.

4. Bake in the preheated oven for 15 minutes, or until golden. Leave to cool for 5–10 minutes, then serve topped with small spoonfuls of custard.

#211 Chocolate éclairs

Makes 12

Ingredients

Pastry
150 ml/5 fl oz water

70 g/2½ oz butter, cut into small pieces, plus extra for greasing

100 g/3½ oz plain flour, sifted

2 eggs

Filling
2 eggs, lightly beaten

4 tbsp caster sugar

2 tbsp cornflour

300 ml/10 fl oz milk

½ tsp vanilla extract

Icing
25 g/1 oz butter

1 tbsp milk

1 tbsp cocoa powder

55 g/2 oz icing sugar

50 g/1¾ oz milk chocolate, broken into pieces

1. Preheat the oven to 200°C/400°F/Gas Mark 6. Lightly grease a baking sheet.

2. To make the pastry, place the water in a saucepan, add the butter and gently heat until melted. Bring to a rolling boil, then remove the pan from the heat and add the flour, beating well until the mixture leaves the sides of the pan. Leave to cool slightly, then gradually beat in the eggs to form a smooth, glossy mixture. Spoon into a large piping bag fitted with a 1-cm/½-inch plain nozzle. Sprinkle the prepared baking sheet with a little water. Pipe 12 x 7.5-cm/3-inch éclairs onto the baking sheet, spaced well apart. Bake in the preheated oven for 30–35 minutes, or until crisp and golden. Make a small slit in the side of each éclair to allow the to steam escape. Transfer to a wire rack and leave to cool.

3. Meanwhile, make the filling. Whisk the eggs and sugar until thick and creamy, then fold in the cornflour. Heat the milk until almost boiling and pour onto the eggs, whisking constantly. Return to the pan and cook over a low heat, stirring until thick. Remove the pan from the heat and stir in the vanilla extract. Cover with baking paper and leave to cool.

4. To make the icing, melt the butter with the milk in a saucepan. Remove from the heat and stir in the cocoa and sugar. Split the éclairs lengthways and pipe in the filling. Spread the icing over the top of the éclairs. Place the chocolate in a heatproof bowl set over a saucepan of gently simmering water and heat until melted. Drizzle over the chocolate icing and leave to set. Serve immediately.

140

#212 Chocolate ginger macaroons

Makes 16

Ingredients

75 g/2¾ oz ground almonds

115 g/4 oz icing sugar

1 tsp ground ginger

2 large egg whites

50 g/1¾ oz caster sugar

Filling

25 g/1 oz butter

1 tbsp stem ginger syrup

85 g/3 oz plain chocolate, broken into pieces

4 tbsp double cream

1 piece stem ginger, finely chopped

1. Line two baking sheets with baking paper. Place the ground almonds, icing sugar and ground ginger in a food processor and process for 15 seconds. Sift the mixture into a bowl.

2. Place the egg whites in a large bowl and whisk until they hold soft peaks. Gradually whisk in the caster sugar to make a firm, glossy meringue. Fold the almond mixture into the meringue one third at a time, cutting and folding the mixture until it forms a shiny batter with a thick, ribbon-like consistency. Pour into a piping bag fitted with a 1-cm/½-inch plain nozzle. Pipe 32 small rounds onto the prepared baking sheets. Tap the baking sheets firmly on a work surface to remove air bubbles. Leave at room temperature for 30 minutes. Preheat the oven to 160°C/325°F/Gas Mark 3. Bake in the preheated oven for 10–15 minutes. Leave to cool for 10 minutes, then peel the macaroons off the baking paper. Leave to cool completely.

3. To make the filling, put the butter, ginger syrup and chocolate in a heatproof bowl set over a saucepan of gently simmering water and heat until the butter and chocolate are melted. Remove from the heat and stir in the cream and stem ginger. Leave to cool for 20 minutes, stirring occasionally. Use to sandwich pairs of macaroons together.

#213 Apple pie

Serves 10

Ingredients

350 g/12 oz plain flour, plus extra for dusting

pinch of salt

85 g/3 oz butter or margarine, diced

85 g/3 oz white vegetable fat, diced

6 tbsp cold water

750 g–1 kg/1 lb 10 oz–2 lb 4 oz cooking apples, peeled, cored and sliced

125 g/4½ oz caster sugar, plus extra for sprinkling

½–1 tsp ground cinnamon, mixed spice or ground ginger

beaten egg or milk, for glazing

1. Sift the flour and salt into a bowl. Add the butter and vegetable fat and rub in with your fingertips until the mixture resembles fine breadcrumbs. Add the water and gather the mixture together into a dough. Wrap in clingfilm and chill in the refrigerator for 30 minutes. Preheat the oven to 220°C/425°F/Gas Mark 7. Thinly roll out almost two thirds of the pastry on a lightly floured surface and use to line a deep 23-cm/9-inch pie dish.

2. Place the apples, sugar and cinnamon in a bowl and mix together. Pack the mixture into the pastry case. Add 1–2 tablespoons of water, if needed. Roll out the remaining pastry to make a lid. Dampen the edges of the pie rim with water and position the lid, firmly pressing the edges together. Trim and crimp the edges. Use the trimmings to cut out leaf shapes, dampen and attach to the top of the pie. Glaze with beaten egg, make 1–2 slits in the top and place the pie dish on a baking sheet.

3. Bake in the preheated oven for 20 minutes, then reduce the temperature to 180°C/350°F/Gas Mark 4 and bake for a further 30 minutes, or until light golden brown. Serve hot or cold, sprinkled with sugar.

#214 Baby blueberry brûlées

Ingredients

125 g/4½ oz blueberries

4 egg yolks

1 tsp vanilla extract

100 g/3½ oz caster sugar

300 ml/10 fl oz double cream

1. Preheat the oven to 160°C/325°F/Gas Mark 3. Put 12 x 50-ml/2-fl oz ovenproof dishes in a large roasting tin and divide the blueberries between them.

2. Put the egg yolks, vanilla and 40 g/1½ oz of the sugar into a jug and mix with a fork until smooth and creamy. Pour the cream into a small, heavy-based saucepan, bring to the boil, then gradually mix into the yolks. Strain through a sieve into the jug and pour over the blueberries. Pour warm water into the roasting tin to come halfway up the sides of the dishes. Bake in the preheated oven for 15 minutes, until the custard is just set with a slight wobble in the centre.

3. Leave to cool for 5–10 minutes, then chill in the refrigerator for 3–4 hours. Sprinkle the remaining sugar over the dishes in an even layer, then place under a hot grill to caramelize the sugar and serve immediately.

#215 Latticed cherry pie

Serves 8–10

Ingredients

140 g/5 oz plain flour, plus extra for dusting

¼ tsp baking powder

¾ tsp mixed spice

½ tsp salt

200 g/7 oz caster sugar

55 g/2 oz butter, chilled and diced, plus extra for greasing

1 egg, beaten, plus extra for glazing

ice cream, to serve

Filling

900 g/2 lb stoned fresh cherries, or canned cherries, drained

½ tsp almond extract

2 tsp cherry brandy

2 tbsp cornflour

2 tbsp water

25 g/1 oz melted butter

1. To make the pastry, sift the flour with the baking powder into a large bowl. Stir in ½ teaspoon of the mixed spice, the salt and 50 g/1¾ oz of the sugar. Rub in the diced butter until the mixture resembles fine breadcrumbs. Make a well in the centre, pour in the egg and mix into a dough. Cut the dough in half and roll each half into a ball. Wrap in clingfilm and chill in the refrigerator for 30 minutes.

2. Preheat the oven to 220°C/425°F/Gas Mark 7. Grease a 23-cm/9-inch pie dish. Roll out the dough into 2 x 30-cm/12-inch rounds. Use one round to line the prepared dish.

3. To make the filling, put half the cherries and all the remaining sugar in a saucepan. Bring to a simmer and stir in the almond extract, brandy and remaining mixed spice. Mix the cornflour and water into a paste in a bowl. Stir the paste into the pan, then boil until the mixture thickens. Stir in the remaining cherries, pour into the pastry case, then drizzle with the melted butter. Cut the remaining pastry into 1-cm/½-inch wide strips. Lay the strips over the filling, crossing to form a lattice. Trim and seal the edges with water. Use your fingers to crimp around the rim, then glaze the top with the beaten egg.

4. Cover the pie with foil, then bake in the preheated oven for 30 minutes. Discard the foil, then bake for a further 15 minutes, or until golden. Serve with ice cream.

216 Profiteroles

Ingredients

70 g/2½ oz butter, plus extra for greasing
200 ml/7 fl oz water
100 g/3½ oz plain flour
3 eggs, beaten
300 ml/10 fl oz double cream
3 tbsp caster sugar
1 tsp vanilla extract

Sauce

125 g/4½ oz plain chocolate, broken
into pieces
35 g/1¼ oz butter
6 tbsp water
2 tbsp brandy

1. Preheat the oven to 200°C/400°F/Gas Mark 6. Grease two large baking sheets.

2. Put the butter and water in a saucepan and bring to the boil. Meanwhile, sift the flour into a bowl. Remove the pan from the heat and beat in the flour until smooth. Leave to cool for 5 minutes. Beat in enough of the eggs to give the mixture a soft, dropping consistency. Transfer to a piping bag fitted with a 1-cm/½-inch plain nozzle. Pipe small balls onto the prepared baking sheets. Bake in the preheated oven for 25 minutes. Remove from the oven. Pierce each ball with a skewer to let the steam escape.

3. Whip together the cream, sugar and vanilla extract. Cut the pastry balls across the middle, then fill with the cream.

4. To make the sauce, place the chocolate, butter and water together in a heatproof bowl set over a saucepan of gently simmering water and heat, stirring constantly, until smooth. Stir in the brandy.

5. Pile the profiteroles into individual serving dishes, pour over the sauce and serve.

217 Coffee madeleines

Ingredients

1 large egg
50 g/1¾ oz caster sugar
1 tsp coffee and chicory essence
55 g/2 oz self-raising flour, plus extra
for dusting
40 g/1½ oz butter, melted, plus extra
for greasing

Icing

85 g/3 oz icing sugar, sifted
4–5 tsp strong black coffee, cooled

1. Preheat the oven to 190°C/375°F/Gas Mark 5. Thoroughly grease a 12-hole madeleine tin, then lightly dust with flour, tipping out any excess. Put the egg, sugar and coffee and chicory essence into a heatproof bowl set over a saucepan of gently simmering water. Beat with an electric hand-held mixer until the mixture is thick and pale and leaves a trail on the surface when the whisk is lifted.

2. Sift in half the flour and gently fold in, then pour over half the butter and fold in until just incorporated. Repeat with the remaining flour and butter. Spoon the mixture into the prepared tin, taking care not to overfill each hole. Bake in the preheated oven for 8–10 minutes, or until risen and springy to the touch. Leave in the tin for 5 minutes, then turn out onto a wire rack and leave to cool.

3. To make the icing, put the sugar and coffee in a small bowl and beat together until smooth. Dip each madeleine in the icing to coat just half. Transfer to a wire rack and leave to set.

#218 One-roll fruit tart

Ingredients

175 g/6 oz plain flour, plus extra for dusting

100 g/3½ oz butter, diced, plus extra for greasing

1 tbsp water

1 egg, separated

600 g/1 lb 5 oz prepared fruit, such as rhubarb, gooseberries or plums

85 g/3 oz soft light brown sugar

1 tbsp ground ginger

crushed sugar cubes, for sprinkling

1. Place the flour in a large bowl, add the butter and rub in with your fingertips until the mixture resembles breadcrumbs. Add the water and mix to a soft dough. Cover and chill in the refrigerator for 30 minutes.

2. Preheat the oven to 200°C/400°F/Gas Mark 6. Grease a large baking sheet. Roll out the dough on a lightly floured work surface to a 35-cm/14-inch round. Transfer to the prepared baking sheet and brush with the beaten egg yolk.

3. Mix the fruit with the sugar and ginger and pile it into the centre of the pastry. Turn in the edges of the pastry Brush the surface of the pastry with the egg white and sprinkle with the crushed sugar cubes. Bake in the preheated oven for 35 minutes, or until golden brown. Transfer to a serving plate and serve warm.

#219 Powdered doughnuts

Ingredients

250 g/9 oz self-raising flour, plus extra for dusting

1½ tsp baking powder

½ tsp mixed spice

½ tsp salt

55 g/2 oz caster sugar

1 large egg, beaten

100 ml/3½ fl oz milk

25 g/1 oz butter, melted and slightly cooled

½ tsp vanilla extract

oil, for deep-frying

115 g/4 oz icing sugar, plus extra if needed, for dusting

1. Sift together the flour, baking powder and mixed spice into a large bowl. Stir in the salt and sugar. Make a well in the centre.

2. Put the egg, milk, butter and vanilla extract into a jug, mix together and pour into the well. Mix to a medium-soft dough, adding a little extra flour if the dough is too sticky to handle. Cover and chill in the refrigerator for 30 minutes.

3. Roll out the dough on a lightly floured surface to a thickness of 15 mm/⅝ inch. Use a 7.5-cm/ 3-inch doughnut cutter to stamp out eight doughnuts

4. Heat enough oil for deep-frying in a large saucepan or deep-fryer to 180–190°C/350–375°F, or until a cube of bread browns in 30 seconds. Add the doughnuts, 3–4 at a time, and fry, turning frequently, for 3–4 minutes, or until crisp and deep golden. Remove and drain on kitchen paper. Leave to cool for 10 minutes.

5. Sift the icing sugar into a shallow bowl and toss the doughnuts in it to coat thoroughly. Serve immediately, before the icing sugar dissolves into the warm doughnuts – if this does happen, just dust liberally with more icing sugar.

#220 Cream palmiers

Ingredients

40 g/1½ oz granulated sugar

225 g/8 oz ready-made puff pastry

400 ml/14 fl oz whipping cream or double cream

1 tbsp icing sugar, sifted

a few drops of vanilla extract

2 tbsp strawberry jam

1. Preheat the oven to 220°C/425°F/Gas Mark 7. Dust the work surface with half the sugar and roll out the pastry to a 25 x 30-cm/10 x 12-inch rectangle.

2. Sprinkle the remaining sugar over the pastry and gently roll over it with the rolling pin. Roll the two short sides of the pastry into the centre until they meet, moisten the edges that meet with a little water and press together gently. Cut across the roll into 16 even-sized slices.

3. Place the slices, cut-side down, on a dampened baking tray. Use a rolling pin to flatten each one slightly.

4. Bake in the preheated oven for 15–18 minutes until crisp and golden brown, turning the palmiers over halfway through cooking. Transfer to a wire rack to cool.

5. Whip the cream with the icing sugar and vanilla extract until it holds soft peaks Sandwich the palmiers together with the jam and whipped cream.

#221 Coconut doughnuts

Ingredients

175 g/6 oz self-raising flour

1 tsp baking powder

115 g/4 oz caster sugar

¼ tsp salt

150 ml/5 fl oz coconut milk

1 egg, lightly beaten

25 g/1 oz butter, melted, plus extra for greasing

100 g/3½ oz desiccated coconut

5 tbsp seedless raspberry jam, warmed

1. Preheat the oven to 190°C/375°F/Gas Mark 5. Grease a 6-hole doughnut tin.

2. Sift together the flour and baking powder into a bowl and stir in the sugar and salt. Make a well in the centre. Mix the coconut milk, egg and butter together, pour into the well and mix until smooth. Stir in 25 g/1 oz of the coconut.

3. Spoon the mixture into a large piping bag fitted with a plain nozzle. Pipe half the mixture into the doughnut holes. Bake in the preheated oven for 10–15 minutes, until risen, golden and just firm to the touch. Leave to cool in the tin for 5 minutes, then turn out onto a wire rack. Rinse and regrease the tin and repeat with the remaining mixture to make 12 doughnuts in total.

4. Sprinkle the remaining coconut over a large flat plate. Brush the warm doughnuts all over with the warmed jam and dip in the coconut to coat completely. Serve warm or cold.

Tempura-style pear fritters with caramel dipping sauce

Ingredients

100 g/3½ oz cornflour

150 g/5½ oz plain flour

chilled soda water or sparkling mineral water

3–4 pears

juice of ½ lemon

oil, for deep-frying

1–2 tbsp caster sugar mixed with ½ tsp cinnamon, to serve

Sauce

70 g/2½ oz butter

60 g/2¼ oz soft dark brown sugar

40 g/1½ oz caster sugar

50 g/1¾ oz golden syrup

90 ml/3 fl oz double cream

pinch of salt

1. To make the sauce, put the butter, brown sugar, caster sugar and golden syrup into a medium-sized saucepan and heat gently until simmering. Simmer for 3–4 minutes, then stir in the cream and salt and continue to simmer until warmed through. Transfer to a jug, cover with foil and set aside until ready to serve the pears.

2. Sift together the cornflour and plain flour into a bowl, then gradually whisk in enough soda water to make a batter that will coat the back of a teaspoon. Don't over-beat or the batter will be heavy. Leave to stand while you prepare the fruit.

3. Peel the pears and cut in half lengthways. Remove the cores neatly, using a melon baller or a teaspoon. Slice the pears to a maximum thickness of 5 mm/¼ inch. Place in a bowl with the lemon juice and toss to coat.

4. Heat enough oil for deep-frying in a large saucepan or deep-fryer to 180–190°C/350–375°F, or until a cube of bread browns in 30 seconds.

5. When ready to cook, dip each pear slice in the batter, allowing the excess to drip off. Place 2–3 slices in the pan and cook for 3–4 minutes until the fruit is tender and the batter is golden and crisp. Don't overcrowd the pan. After cooking each batch, reheat the oil to the correct temperature before cooking the next batch.

6. Drain on kitchen paper, then sprinkle over the cinnamon sugar and serve immediately with the warm caramel sauce on the side.

#223 Raspberry coconut ice

Makes 20

Ingredients

oil, for greasing

325 g/11½ oz icing sugar, sifted, plus extra if needed

325 g/11½ oz sweetened desiccated coconut

400 g/14 oz canned sweetened full-fat condensed milk

1 tsp vanilla extract

55 g/2 oz raspberries

½ tsp pink food colouring

1 tsp raspberry extract

1. Lightly grease a 20-cm/8-inch square baking tin. Line the base with baking paper. Put half of the icing sugar and half of the coconut into a mixing bowl and put the remainder into a second bowl. Stir the contents of each bowl, then make a well in the centre. Add half of the condensed milk and half of the vanilla extract to each bowl and stir. Press the contents of one bowl into the prepared tin and level with a spatula.

2. Put the raspberries into a blender and process to a purée. Push through a sieve into a bowl to remove the seeds. Add the purée, food colouring and raspberry extract to the remaining coconut mixture. Add more sifted icing sugar if the mixture is too wet. Spread the pink layer over the white layer, cover, then chill in the refrigerator for 3 hours, or until set.

3. Lift the coconut ice out of the tin, peel off the paper and cut into 20 squares.

#224 Lemon meringue pies

Makes 12

Ingredients

100 g/3½ oz butter, plus extra for greasing

2 tbsp golden syrup

300 g/10½ oz digestive biscuits, crushed

grated rind and juice of 3 lemons

200 g/7 oz caster sugar

40 g/1½ oz cornflour

3 eggs, separated

1. Preheat the oven to 180°C/350°F/Gas Mark 4. Lightly grease a 12-hole muffin tin.

2. Put the butter and syrup in a small saucepan and heat until the butter has just melted. Take the pan off the heat, stir in the crushed biscuits, then divide the mixture between the sections of the prepared tin. Press it firmly over the base and sides of the tin with the back of a teaspoon. Line the cases with baking paper and baking beans, then bake in the preheated oven for 8–10 minutes, or until slightly darker in colour. Leave to cool and harden in the tin for 10–15 minutes. Remove the paper and beans. Do not switch off the oven.

3. Put the lemon rind in a separate, larger saucepan. Make the juice up to 450 ml/16 fl oz with cold water. Add this liquid to the rind and bring just to the boil. In a mixing bowl, stir together 85 g/3 oz of the sugar, the cornflour and egg yolks until a thick paste forms, then gradually stir in the boiling lemon juice until smooth. Pour the liquid back into the saucepan and cook over a medium heat, stirring constantly, for a few minutes, until it is very thick and smooth. Spoon into the cases.

4. Whisk the egg whites in a large clean mixing bowl until they hold stiff peaks, then gradually whisk in the remaining sugar, a teaspoon at a time, for a further 1–2 minutes, or until the meringue is very thick and glossy. Spoon or pipe the meringue on top of the pies. Bake in the preheated oven for 10–12 minutes, or until the meringue peaks are golden and just cooked through. Leave to cool and firm up in the tin, then loosen with a round-bladed knife and transfer to a plate.

225 Hot cross buns

Makes 14

Ingredients

125 ml/4 fl oz lukewarm water

40 g/1½ oz fresh yeast

500 g/1 lb 2 oz strong white flour, plus extra for dusting

2 tsp milk, plus extra for brushing

2 eggs

60 g/2¼ oz sugar

½ tsp salt

85 g/3 oz butter, softened, plus extra for greasing

100 g/3½ oz sultanas

½ tsp cinnamon

½ tsp mixed spice

pinch of nutmeg

60 g/2¼ oz plain flour

1 tsp icing sugar

4 tbsp water

butter and marmalade, to serve

1. Pour the water into a large bowl, crumble in the yeast, stir in 100 g/3½ oz of the strong flour, then cover the bowl with a tea towel and leave to stand for 20 minutes.

2. Add the milk, eggs, sugar, salt and the remaining flour and knead using the dough hook of a food processor or electric whisk until smooth. Stir in the butter, sultanas, cinnamon, mixed spice and nutmeg. Cover with a damp tea towel and leave to rise for about 1 hour, until doubled in size.

3. Meanwhile, mix together the plain flour, icing sugar and water in a small bowl.

4. Grease two large baking trays. Turn out the dough onto a lightly floured work surface, knock back, then divide into 14 pieces. Roll each piece into a ball and place the balls on the prepared trays. Fill a disposable piping bag with the flour mixture, cut off the tip and pipe a cross on each ball, then gently brush some milk over the tops of the buns. Leave to rise for 40 minutes, then brush with milk again.

5. Meanwhile, preheat the oven to 190°C/375°F/Gas Mark 5. Bake the buns in the preheated oven for 15–20 minutes, until golden. Serve warm with butter and marmalade.

226 Baked pumpkin doughnuts

Makes 6

Ingredients

115 g/4 oz self-raising flour

½ tsp baking powder

½ tsp salt

1½ tsp ground cinnamon

½ tsp grated nutmeg

50 g/1¾ oz butter, softened, plus extra for greasing

50 g/1¾ oz soft light brown sugar

1 large egg, beaten

1 tsp vanilla extract

2 tbsp milk

115 g/4 oz canned pumpkin purée

115 g/4 oz icing sugar

1–2 tsp maple syrup

1. Preheat the oven to 190°C/375°F/Gas Mark 5. Grease a 6-hole doughnut tin.

2. Sift together the flour and baking powder into a bowl and stir in the salt, 1 teaspoon of the cinnamon and the nutmeg. Put the butter and brown sugar into a separate bowl and beat together until pale and creamy. Gradually beat in the egg, vanilla extract and 1 tablespoon of the milk. Fold in the flour mixture and pumpkin purée. Spoon the mixture into a large piping bag fitted with a plain nozzle and pipe into the prepared tin. Bake in the preheated oven for 15 minutes, until risen, golden and just firm to the touch. Leave to cool for 5 minutes, then turn out onto a wire rack to cool completely.

3. Sift the icing sugar and remaining cinnamon into a bowl, add the remaining milk and the maple syrup, and stir until smooth. Dip the top of each doughnut in the glaze and leave to set.

#227 Chocolate & caramel cups

Makes
12

Ingredients

150 g/5½ oz plain chocolate, broken into pieces

115 g/4 oz granulated sugar

4 tbsp water

12 small walnut halves

25 g/1 oz butter

125 ml/4 fl oz double cream

1. Line a 12-hole mini muffin tin with petit four cases. Line a baking tray with baking paper. Put the chocolate into a heatproof bowl set over a saucepan of gently simmering water and heat until melted. Put a spoonful of melted chocolate into each paper case, then brush it up the sides. Chill for 30 minutes, then brush on a second layer of chocolate. Cover and chill in the refrigerator.

2. Combine the sugar and water in a small saucepan and heat until the sugar has dissolved. Boil rapidly, without stirring, for 4–5 minutes, until the caramel is deep golden. Remove from the heat and quickly stir in the walnuts. Transfer to the prepared baking tray.

3. Add the butter to the remaining caramel, then gradually stir in the cream. Leave to cool, then cover and chill in the refrigerator for 1½ hours, or until thick. To serve, pipe the caramel into the chocolate cups, chill, then decorate with the candied walnuts.

#228 Crème brûlée tartlets

Makes
6

Ingredients
Pastry

175 g/6 oz plain flour, plus extra for dusting

40 g/1½ oz caster sugar

pinch of salt

140 g/5 oz butter, plus extra for greasing

1–2 tsp cold water

Filling

4 egg yolks

50 g/1¾ oz caster sugar

400 ml/14 fl oz single cream

1 tsp vanilla extract or 1 vanilla pod, scraped

demerara sugar, for sprinkling

1. To make the pastry, sift together the flour, sugar and salt into a bowl. Gradually add the butter, then add the water and mix to a smooth dough using the dough hook of an electric mixer. Wrap the pastry in clingfilm and chill in the refrigerator for at least 1 hour.

2. Preheat the oven to 180°C/350°F/Gas Mark 4. Grease 6 x 10-cm/4-inch tartlet tins. Turn out the pastry onto a work surface lightly dusted with flour and roll out to a thickness of 5 mm/¼ inch, then use to line the prepared tins. Re-roll and cut out the trimmings if necessary. Ease the pastry into the prepared tins, pressing it up the sides. Trim the excess, then prick the pastry several times with a fork. Line the pastry cases with baking paper and fill with baking beans. Bake in the middle of the preheated oven for 10 minutes, then remove the beans and paper, and bake for a further 10 minutes until golden brown.

3. Meanwhile, put the egg yolks and the sugar into a bowl and whisk until foaming. Heat the cream and vanilla extract in a saucepan over a medium heat. Do not allow it to boil. Whisk in the egg and sugar mixture and cook without boiling, until thickened. Remove from the heat and leave to cool, then pour into the pastry cases. Leave to cool completely, then chill in the refrigerator overnight.

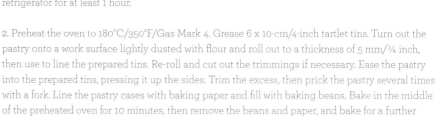

4. Sprinkle a generous layer of demerara sugar over the chilled tartlets and heat with a cook's blowtorch until the surface has caramelized. Alternatively, place the tartlets under a hot grill until the surface has caramelized. Serve immediately.

#229 Jam doughnuts

Ingredients

oil, for greasing and deep-frying

450 g/1 lb strong white flour, plus extra for dusting

55 g/2 oz butter, cut into pieces

2 tbsp caster sugar, plus extra for dusting

½ tsp salt

2¼ tsp easy-blend dried yeast

1 egg, lightly beaten

175 ml/6 fl oz lukewarm milk

150 g/5½ oz seedless strawberry or raspberry jam

1. Lightly grease a large bowl and two baking trays. Place the flour in a large bowl, add the butter and rub it in until the mixture resembles breadcrumbs. Stir in the sugar, salt and yeast. Make a well in the centre and add the egg and milk, then mix to form a soft, pliable dough. Knead well for 10 minutes.

2. Place in the greased bowl and cover. Leave in a warm place to rise for about 1 hour, or until doubled in size. Knead the dough on a floured work surface, then divide into 10 pieces. Shape each piece into a ball and place on the prepared baking trays. Cover and leave in a warm place for 45 minutes, or until doubled in size.

3. Heat enough oil for deep-frying in a large saucepan or deep-fryer to 180–190°C/350–375°F, or until a cube of bread browns in 30 seconds. Deep-fry the doughnuts, in batches, for 2–3 minutes on each side. Remove with a slotted spoon, drain on kitchen paper and dust with sugar.

4. To fill the doughnuts, spoon the jam into a piping bag fitted with a plain nozzle. Insert a sharp knife into each doughnut and twist to make a hole. Push the point of the nozzle into the hole and pipe in some jam.

#230 Chocolate filo parcels

Ingredients

85 g/3 oz ground hazelnuts

1 tbsp finely chopped fresh mint

125 ml/4 fl oz soured cream

2 eating apples, peeled and grated

55 g/2 oz plain chocolate, melted

9 sheets filo pastry, about 15 cm/ 6 inches square

55–85 g/2–3 oz butter, melted, plus extra for greasing

icing sugar, sifted, for dusting

1. Preheat the oven to 190°C/375°F/Gas Mark 5. Grease a baking tray. Mix the nuts, mint and soured cream in a bowl. Add the apples, stir in the chocolate and mix well.

2. Cut each pastry sheet into four squares. Brush one square with butter, then place a second square on top and brush with butter. Place 1 tablespoon of the chocolate mixture in the centre, bring up the corners and twist together. Repeat until all of the pastry and filling has been used.

3. Place the parcels on the prepared baking tray and bake in the preheated oven for about 10 minutes, until crisp and golden. Remove from the oven and leave to cool slightly. Dust with icing sugar and serve.

#231 Pain au chocolat cinnamon rolls

Makes
12

Ingredients

100 g/3½ oz plain chocolate, broken into pieces

320 g/11 oz ready-rolled puff pastry

25 g/1 oz butter, melted

2 tbsp caster sugar

1½ tsp ground cinnamon

icing sugar, for dusting (optional)

1. Put the chocolate into a heatproof bowl set over a saucepan of gently simmering water and heat until melted. Remove from the heat, stir until smooth, then leave to cool for 15 minutes, stirring occasionally.

2. Unroll the pastry and place on a board. Generously brush with some of the melted butter. Leave to stand for 10 minutes, then spread the cooled chocolate all over the buttered pastry. Mix together the sugar and cinnamon and scatter over the chocolate.

3. Roll up the pastry, Swiss roll-style, from one long side then brush all over with more of the melted butter. Chill in the refrigerator for 15 minutes. Preheat the oven to 220°C/425°F/Gas Mark 7. Use the remaining melted butter to grease a 12-hole muffin tin.

4. Using a serrated knife, slice the pastry roll into 12 even-sized rounds. Place the rounds, cut-side up, in the prepared tin.

5. Bake in the preheated oven for 15–20 minutes, or until risen and golden brown. Leave to cool in the tin for 5 minutes, then transfer to a wire rack. Dust with icing sugar if using, and serve warm or cold.

#232 Raspberry & chocolate cake

Serves 10

Ingredients

225 g/8 oz butter, plus extra for greasing

250 g/9 oz plain chocolate, broken into pieces

1 tbsp strong black coffee

5 eggs

90 g/3¼ oz golden caster sugar

90 g/3¼ oz plain flour, sifted

1 tsp ground cinnamon

150 g/5½ oz fresh raspberries, plus extra to serve

cocoa powder, for dusting

whipped cream, to serve

1. Preheat the oven to 160°C/325°F/Gas Mark 3. Grease a 23-cm/9-inch round cake tin and line with baking paper.

2. Put the butter, chocolate and coffee in a heatproof bowl set over a saucepan of gently simmering water and heat until melted. Stir and leave to cool slightly.

3. Put the eggs and sugar in a bowl and beat until thick and pale. Gently fold in the chocolate mixture. Sift the flour and cinnamon into a bowl, then fold into the chocolate mixture. Pour into the prepared tin and sprinkle the raspberries evenly over the top.

4. Bake in the preheated oven for 35–45 minutes, until the cake is well risen and springy to the touch. Leave to cool in the tin for 15 minutes before turning out onto a large plate. Dust with cocoa and serve with raspberries and whipped cream.

#233 Summer fruit tartlets

Makes 12

Ingredients

200 g/7 oz plain flour, plus extra for dusting

85 g/3 oz icing sugar, sifted

55 g/2 oz ground almonds

115 g/4 oz butter, diced

1 egg yolk

1 tbsp milk

fresh summer berries, to decorate

Filling

225 g/8 oz cream cheese

icing sugar, to taste, plus extra, sifted, for dusting

1. Sift the flour and icing sugar into a bowl. Stir in the almonds. Add the butter, rubbing it in until the mixture resembles breadcrumbs. Add the egg yolk and milk and work in until the dough binds together. Wrap in clingfilm and chill in the refrigerator for 30 minutes. Meanwhile, preheat the oven to 200°C/400°F/Gas Mark 6.

2. Roll out the dough on a lightly floured surface and use it to line 12 deep tartlet tins. Prick the bases and press a piece of foil into each.

3. Bake in the preheated oven for 10–15 minutes, or until light golden brown. Remove the foil and bake for a further 2–3 minutes. Transfer to a wire rack to cool.

4. To make the filling, place the cream cheese and icing sugar in a bowl and mix together. Place a spoonful of filling in each tartlet and arrange the berries on top. Dust with icing sugar and serve.

234 Chelsea buns

Makes
6

Ingredients

½ tsp easy-blend dried yeast

150 ml/5 fl oz lukewarm milk

30 g/1 oz granulated sugar

280 g/10 oz plain flour, plus extra for dusting

¼ tsp salt

30 g/1 oz butter, plus extra for greasing

½ tsp mixed spice

30 g/1 oz sultanas

30 g/1 oz mixed peel

1 egg, beaten

30 g/1 oz caster sugar, for sprinkling

1. Preheat the oven to 200°C/400°F/Gas Mark 6. Lightly grease a baking tray. Combine the yeast in a bowl with the milk and a small amount of the granulated sugar and set aside for 10 minutes.

2. Meanwhile, sift together the flour and salt into a mixing bowl, add the butter and rub in, then add the yeast mixture and beat well. Cover and set aside until the mixture doubles in size.

3. Turn out the dough onto a lightly floured work surface, lightly knead and roll out to a 25-cm/10-inch square. Sprinkle with the remaining granulated sugar, the mixed spice, sultanas and mixed peel, and roll into a sausage shape. Cut into six slices and lay the slices flat on the prepared tray. Leave to stand until doubled in size. Brush with the beaten egg, then bake in the preheated oven for 20 minutes, or until golden. Sprinkle with the caster sugar and serve.

235 Peanut butter & jam macaroons

Makes
16

Ingredients

50 g/1¾ oz ground almonds

25 g/1 oz natural roasted peanuts, finely ground

115 g/4 oz icing sugar

2 large egg whites

50 g/1¾ oz caster sugar

1 tbsp salted peanuts, finely chopped

Filling

4 tbsp peanut butter

2 tbsp seedless raspberry jam

1. Place the ground almonds, ground peanuts and icing sugar in a food processor and process for 15 seconds. Sift into a bowl. Line two baking sheets with baking paper.

2. Place the egg whites in a large bowl and whisk until they hold soft peaks. Gradually whisk in the caster sugar to make a firm, glossy meringue.

3. Using a spatula, fold the almond mixture into the meringue one third at a time. When all the dry ingredients are thoroughly incorporated, continue to cut and fold the mixture until it forms a shiny batter with a thick, ribbon-like consistency.

4. Pour the mixture into a piping bag fitted with a 1-cm/½-inch plain nozzle. Pipe 32 small rounds onto the prepared baking sheets. Tap the baking sheets firmly onto a work surface to remove air bubbles. Sprinkle over the chopped peanuts. Leave to stand at room temperature for 30 minutes. Meanwhile, preheat the oven to 160°C/325°F/Gas Mark 3.

5. Bake in the preheated oven for 10–15 minutes. Leave to cool for 10 minutes, then carefully peel the macaroons off the baking paper. Leave to cool completely.

6. Sandwich pairs of macaroons together with the peanut butter and jam to serve.

236 Mini chocolate éclairs

Makes
36

Ingredients

55 g/2 oz butter, plus extra for greasing
150 ml/5 fl oz water
70 g/2½ oz plain flour
pinch of salt
2 eggs, beaten
a few drops of vanilla extract
350 ml/12 fl oz double cream
2 tbsp icing sugar, sifted
4 tbsp Irish cream liqueur

Topping

25 g/1 oz butter, diced
100 g/3½ oz plain chocolate, roughly chopped
1 tbsp icing sugar, sifted
2 tsp milk

1. Preheat the oven to 200°C/400°F/Gas Mark 6. Lightly grease two baking trays with butter. Put the butter and water into a heavy-based saucepan and heat gently until the butter has melted. Increase the heat and bring to the boil, then remove from the heat. Sift in the flour and salt, then return to the heat and stir until the mixture makes a smooth ball that leaves the sides of the pan clean. Leave to cool for at least 15 minutes.

2. Gradually beat in the eggs, beating well after each addition, until the mixture is smooth. Stir in the vanilla extract. Spoon the mixture into a large piping bag fitted with a 15-mm/⅝-inch plain nozzle, then pipe 4-cm/1½-inch long éclairs onto the prepared baking trays. Bake in the preheated oven for 10–12 minutes, until well risen and crisp on the outside. Make a slit in the side of each éclair to allow the steam to escape, then return to the oven for 2 minutes. Leave to cool.

3. Pour the cream into a large mixing bowl, add the icing sugar and liqueur, and whisk it to soft peaks. Spoon into a piping bag fitted with a star-shaped nozzle, then pipe into the éclairs.

4. To make the topping, put all the ingredients in a heatproof bowl set over a saucepan of gently simmering water and heat until melted, smooth and glossy, stirring once or twice. Spoon this over the éclairs, leave to set for 15 minutes, then transfer to a serving plate.

237 Blueberry tarts

Makes
24

Ingredients

300 g/10½ oz blueberries
2 tsp cornflour
55 g/2 oz caster sugar
4 tsp water
55 g/2 oz plain flour, plus extra for dusting
grated rind of 1 lemon
40 g/1½ oz butter, diced, plus extra for greasing
325 g/11½ oz ready-made sweet shortcrust pastry, chilled

1. Preheat the oven to 190°C/375°F/Gas Mark 5. Lightly grease 2 x 12-hole mini muffin tins. Put half the blueberries in a small saucepan with the cornflour, half the caster sugar and the water. Cook, uncovered, over a medium heat, stirring constantly, for 2–3 minutes, or until the juices begin to run and the sauce thickens. Remove from the heat and add the remaining blueberries.

2. To make the streusel topping, put the flour, lemon rind, butter and remaining sugar in a medium mixing bowl. Toss together, then rub with your fingertips until it resembles fine breadcrumbs.

3. Thinly roll out the pastry on a lightly floured surface. Using a fluted cookie cutter, stamp out 24 x 6-cm/2½-inch rounds. Press into the prepared tins. Spoon the blueberry filling into the cases, then sprinkle the tops of the tarts with the streusel mixture. Bake in the preheated oven for 15 minutes, or until the topping is pale gold. Leave to cool in the tins for 10 minutes, then loosen with a round-bladed knife and transfer to a wire rack to cool. Serve warm or cold.

Lemon poppy seed madeleines

Makes
36

Ingredients

oil, for greasing

3 eggs

1 egg yolk

finely grated rind of 1 lemon

140 g/5 oz golden caster sugar

140 g/5 oz plain flour

1 tsp baking powder

140 g/5 oz butter, melted and cooled

1 tbsp poppy seeds

1. Preheat the oven to 190°C/375°F/Gas Mark 5. Lightly grease three 12-hole madeleine tins.

2. Whisk together the eggs, egg yolk, lemon rind and sugar in a large bowl until very pale and thick. Sift in the flour and baking powder and fold in lightly using a metal spoon. Fold in the melted butter and poppy seeds.

3. Spoon the mixture into the tins and bake in the preheated oven for 10 minutes, until well risen.

4. Turn out the cakes and cool on wire racks, then serve while very fresh.

239 Cider doughnuts

Makes
12

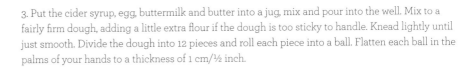

Ingredients

225 ml/8 fl oz sweet cider or apple juice

250 g/9 oz self-raising flour, plus extra for dusting

1½ tsp baking powder

1 tsp ground cinnamon

¼ tsp salt

55 g/2 oz soft light brown sugar

1 large egg, beaten

4 tbsp buttermilk

25 g/1 oz butter, melted and slightly cooled

oil, for deep-frying

55 g/2 oz granulated sugar

1. Pour the cider into a saucepan and bring to the boil. Boil for 10–15 minutes, until reduced to about 4 tablespoons of syrup. Leave to cool.

2. Sift together the flour, baking powder and half the cinnamon into a large bowl. Stir in the salt and brown sugar. Make a well in the centre.

3. Put the cider syrup, egg, buttermilk and butter into a jug, mix and pour into the well. Mix to a fairly firm dough, adding a little extra flour if the dough is too sticky to handle. Knead lightly until just smooth. Divide the dough into 12 pieces and roll each piece into a ball. Flatten each ball in the palms of your hands to a thickness of 1 cm/½ inch.

4. Heat enough oil for deep-frying in a large saucepan or deep-fryer to 180–190°C/350–375°F, or until a cube of bread browns in 30 seconds. Add the doughnuts, four at a time, and fry, turning frequently, for 3–4 minutes, or until crisp and deep golden. Remove and drain on kitchen paper.

5. Mix together the granulated sugar and the remaining cinnamon in a shallow dish and roll each hot doughnut in the mixture to coat. Serve warm or cold.

240 Peach crumb pie

Ingredients

Pastry
200 g/7 oz plain flour,
plus extra for dusting

100 g/3½ oz butter, diced

1 egg yolk

1 tsp lemon juice

1–2 tbsp iced water

Topping
115 g/4 oz self-raising flour

70 g/2½ oz butter, diced

55 g/2 oz demerara sugar

Filling
600 g/1 lb 5 oz just ripe peaches, halved,
stoned and sliced

25 g/1 oz caster sugar

1 tbsp cornflour

1. To make the pastry, sift the flour into a bowl and add the butter. Rub the butter into the flour until the mixture resembles fine breadcrumbs. Mix together the egg yolk and lemon juice with 1 tablespoon of the water. Stir into the flour mixture and mix to a firm dough, adding more water if necessary. Knead lightly until smooth, then wrap in clingfilm and chill in the refrigerator for 30 minutes.

2. Roll out the pastry on a lightly floured work surface and use to line a 23-cm/9-inch pie dish. Prick the base all over with a fork. Chill in the refrigerator for 15 minutes. Preheat the oven to 200°C/400°F/Gas Mark 6 and preheat a baking sheet. Line the pastry case with baking paper and baking beans. Place on the baking sheet and bake in the preheated oven for 10 minutes. Remove the paper and beans and bake for a further 5–6 minutes, or until light golden. Reduce the oven temperature to 190°C/375°F/Gas Mark 5.

3. To make the crumb topping, place the flour and butter in a bowl and rub in the butter with your fingertips until crumbly. Stir in the sugar.

4. To make the filling, place the peach slices in a bowl with the sugar and cornflour, and toss well to mix. Transfer to the pastry case, then sprinkle over the crumb topping. Bake in the preheated oven for 25–30 minutes, or until the topping is golden. Serve warm or cold.

241 Mexican sopapillas

Ingredients

2 tsp easy-blend dried yeast

3 tbsp lukewarm water

150 ml/5 fl oz milk

85 g/3 oz granulated sugar, plus extra
for sprinkling

1 tsp salt

25 g/1 oz butter

1 egg, beaten

500 g/1 lb 2 oz plain flour, plus
extra for dusting

oil, for deep-frying

1. Put the yeast into a large bowl with the water, stir to dissolve and leave to stand in a warm place. Put the milk, sugar and salt into a saucepan over a medium heat, bring to the boil, then add the butter and stir. Remove from the heat and leave to cool slightly. Stir into the yeast mixture, add the egg and mix to combine, then gradually mix in the flour. Cover the bowl with a damp tea towel and leave to rise for 1–2 hours.

2. Turn out the dough onto a lightly floured surface and knock back, then leave to rise for 20 minutes. Roll out the dough to a thickness of 1 cm/½ inch, then cut into 20 x 5-mm/8 x ¼-inch strips.

3. Heat enough oil for deep-frying in a large saucepan or deep-fryer to 180–190°C/350–375°F, or until a cube of bread browns in 30 seconds. Drop small batches of the dough strips into the oil and fry for 3–5 minutes, until light brown, turning to cook on both sides.

4. Remove from the oil and drain on kitchen paper. Sprinkle with sugar and serve immediately.

Makes
12

Cocoa & cinnamon madeleines with white chocolate

Ingredients

100 g/3½ oz plain flour, sifted, plus extra for dusting

2 eggs

50 g/1¾ oz soft light brown sugar

50 g/1¾ oz caster sugar

100 g/3½ oz butter, melted, plus extra for greasing

1 tsp baking powder

½ tsp ground cinnamon

2 tbsp cocoa powder, sifted

1 tsp vanilla extract

100 g/3½ oz white chocolate, broken into pieces, to decorate

1. Preheat the oven to 200°C/400°F/Gas Mark 6. Lightly grease a 12-hole madeleine tin and dust with flour.

2. Place the eggs, brown sugar and caster sugar in a mixing bowl and beat well until the mixture is light and frothy.

3. Lightly fold in the flour, butter, baking powder, cinnamon, cocoa powder and vanilla extract. Leave to stand for 20 minutes.

4. Divide the mixture between the holes in the prepared tin and bake in the preheated oven for 8-10 minutes until well risen. Leave to cool in the tin for 1-2 minutes, then transfer to a wire rack to cool completely.

5. To decorate, place the chocolate in a heatproof bowl set over a saucepan of gently simmering water and heat until melted. Dip the end of each madeleine in the melted chocolate and leave to set on a baking sheet. Eat on the day of making.

243 Spiced doughnut holes

Makes
18

Ingredients

125 ml/4 fl oz lukewarm milk

1 egg

2 tbsp natural yogurt

1 tsp vanilla extract

225 g/8 oz plain flour

2 tsp baking powder

½ tsp salt

70 g/2½ oz caster sugar,
plus extra for sprinkling

1 tsp grated nutmeg

25 g/1 oz butter

oil, for deep-frying

1. Mix the milk, egg, yogurt and vanilla extract together in a bowl.

2. Using a stand mixer fitted with a paddle attachment, mix the flour, baking powder, salt, sugar and nutmeg together. Slowly add the butter and blend. Slowly add the milk mixture until the mixture is smooth, thick and resembles biscuit dough. Leave to rest in the mixer for 20 minutes.

3. Heat enough oil for deep-frying in a large saucepan or deep-fryer to 180–190°C/350–375°F, or until a cube of bread browns in 30 seconds. Drop the dough, 1 tablespoon at a time, into the hot oil. Fry for 1 minute, or until golden brown. Remove with a slotted spoon and drain on kitchen paper.

4. Sprinkle with caster sugar and serve.

244 Green tea macaroons

Makes
16

Ingredients

75 g/2¾ oz ground almonds

115 g/4 oz icing sugar, plus extra
for dusting

2 tsp green tea leaves

2 large egg whites

50 g/1¾ oz caster sugar

green food colouring paste or liquid

Filling

55 g/2 oz butter, softened

finely grated rind and juice of ½ lemon

115 g/4 oz icing sugar, sifted

1. Place the ground almonds, icing sugar and green tea in a food processor and process for 15 seconds. Sift the mixture into a bowl. Line two baking sheets with baking paper.

2. Place the egg whites in a large bowl and whisk until they hold soft peaks. Gradually whisk in the sugar to make a firm, glossy meringue. Whisk in enough food colouring to give a pale green colour.

3. Using a spatula, fold the almond mixture into the meringue one third at a time. When all the dry ingredients are thoroughly incorporated, continue to cut and fold the mixture until it forms a shiny batter with a thick, ribbon-like consistency.

4. Pour the mixture into a piping bag fitted with a 1-cm/½-inch plain nozzle. Pipe 32 small rounds onto the prepared baking sheets. Tap the baking sheets firmly on a work surface to remove air bubbles. Leave at room temperature for 30 minutes. Preheat the oven to 160°C/325°F/Gas Mark 3.

5. Bake in the preheated oven for 10–15 minutes. Leave to cool for 10 minutes, then carefully peel the macaroons off the baking paper, then transfer to wire racks and leave to cool completely.

6. To make the filling, beat the butter and lemon juice and rind in a bowl until pale and fluffy. Gradually beat in the icing sugar until smooth and creamy. Use to sandwich pairs of macaroons together. Dust with icing sugar.

245 Mini cranberry florentines

Makes
48

Ingredients

70 g/2½ oz muscovado sugar

55 g/2 oz clear honey

100 g/3½ oz butter, plus extra for greasing

50 g/1¾ oz desiccated coconut

70 g/2½ oz flaked almonds

1 tbsp finely chopped candied peel

1 tbsp finely chopped crystallized stem ginger

100 g/3½ oz dried cranberries

50 g/1¾ oz plain flour, plus extra for dusting

250 g/9 oz plain chocolate, roughly chopped

1. Preheat the oven to 180°C/350°F/Gas Mark 4. Lightly grease 4 x 12-hole mini muffin tins, then lightly dust with flour.

2. Put the sugar, honey and butter into a heavy-based saucepan. Heat gently, stirring, until the sugar has dissolved, tilting the pan to mix the ingredients together. Stir in the coconut, almonds, candied peel, crystallized ginger, cranberries and flour.

3. Put small teaspoons of the mixture into the prepared tins. Bake in the preheated oven for 10–12 minutes, or until golden brown. Leave to cool in the tins for 1 hour. Using a palette knife, transfer to wires rack to firm up.

4. Meanwhile, put the chocolate in a heatproof bowl set over a saucepan of gently simmering water and heat until melted.

5. Dip each florentine into the melted chocolate so the base is covered. Place on a wire rack, coated-side up, and leave to set for 1 hour, before serving.

246 Pistachio & almond tarts

Makes
12

Ingredients

225 g/8 oz ready-made sweet shortcrust pastry, chilled

plain flour, for dusting

50 g/1¾ oz butter, softened, plus extra for greasing

50 g/1¾ oz caster sugar

1 egg yolk

50 g/1¾ oz ground almonds

a few drops of almond extract or orange flower water

1½ tbsp flaked almonds

1 tbsp pistachio nuts, thinly sliced

sifted icing sugar, to decorate

1. Preheat the oven to 180°C/350°F/Gas Mark 4. Lightly grease a 12-hole mini muffin tin.

2. Thinly roll out the pastry on a lightly floured work surface. Using a fluted cookie cutter, stamp out 12 x 6-cm/2½-inch rounds. Press these gently into the prepared tin, re-rolling the trimmings as needed.

3. Meanwhile, put the butter and caster sugar in a mixing bowl and beat together until light and fluffy. Beat in the egg yolk, then beat in the ground almonds. Flavour with a little almond extract.

4. Spoon the frangipane into the pastry cases. Sprinkle the almonds and pistachio nuts over the top and press them lightly into the filling. Bake in the preheated oven for 15 minutes, or until the almonds are golden. Leave to cool in the tin for 10 minutes, then loosen with a round-bladed knife and transfer to a wire rack to cool. Serve warm or cold, dusted with sifted icing sugar.

Fig tartlets

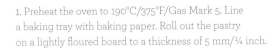

Serves
4

Ingredients

250 g/9 oz ready-made puff pastry

plain flour, for dusting

8 fresh ripe figs

1 tbsp caster sugar

½ tsp ground cinnamon

milk, for brushing

vanilla ice cream, to serve

1. Preheat the oven to 190°C/375°F/Gas Mark 5. Line a baking tray with baking paper. Roll out the pastry on a lightly floured board to a thickness of 5 mm/¼ inch.

2. Using a saucer as a guide, cut out 4 x 15-cm/6-inch rounds and place on the prepared baking tray. Use a sharp knife to score a line around each round, about 1 cm/½ inch from the edge. Prick the centre of each round all over with a fork.

3. Cut the figs into quarters and arrange eight quarters over the centre of each pastry round. Mix together the sugar and cinnamon and sprinkle over the figs.

4. Brush the edges of the pastry with milk and bake in the preheated oven for 15–20 minutes, until risen and golden brown. Serve the tartlets warm with ice cream.

248 Honey, walnut & ricotta pies

Makes
24

Ingredients

oil, for greasing

325 g/11½ oz ready-made sweet shortcrust pastry, chilled

plain flour, for dusting

125 g/4½ oz walnut pieces

225 g/8 oz ricotta cheese

2 egg yolks

5 tbsp runny orange blossom honey

large pinch of ground cinnamon

115 g/4 oz granulated sugar

1 tbsp water

200 g/7 oz Greek yogurt, to serve

1. Preheat the oven to 180°C/350°F/Gas Mark 4. Lightly grease 2 x 12-hole mini muffin tins and a baking tray.

2. Thinly roll out the pastry on a lightly floured work surface. Using a fluted cookie cutter, stamp out 24 x 6 cm/2½-inch rounds. Press these gently into the prepared tins, re-rolling the trimmings as needed.

3. Lightly toast half the walnut pieces in a dry frying pan. Leave to cool, then roughly chop. Lightly whisk the ricotta cheese, egg yolks, 4 tablespoons of the honey and the cinnamon together in a bowl until just mixed. Stir in the toasted walnuts. Spoon the filling into the cases and bake in the preheated oven for 20 minutes, or until the filling is golden brown. Leave to cool in the tin for 10 minutes.

4. Meanwhile, put the sugar, remaining honey and the water into a pan and gently heat, without stirring, until the sugar has dissolved. Tilt the pan to mix any remaining grains of sugar into the syrup. Add the remaining walnuts and cook over a medium heat, without stirring, for about 5 minutes, or until the syrup turns a rich golden brown. Tilt the pan to mix if needed, then quickly pour the praline onto the prepared tray and leave to cool and harden.

5. Loosen the pies with a round-bladed knife and transfer to a plate. Top with yogurt. Loosen the praline from the baking tray with a knife, cut into thin shards and press pieces of it into the yogurt.

#249 Cinnamon & apple fritters with blackberry sauce

Makes 30

Ingredients

8 small dessert apples
150 g/5½ oz blackberries
125 ml/4 fl oz water
6 tbsp caster sugar
150 g/5½ oz plain flour
pinch of ground cinnamon
1 egg, separated
150 ml/5 fl oz milk
1 litre/1¾ pints sunflower oil

1. Peel, quarter, core and dice two of the apples and put them into a heavy-based saucepan with the blackberries, water and 1 tablespoon of the sugar. Cover and simmer for 5–10 minutes, or until the apples are soft. Purée using a hand-held blender, then press through a sieve into a serving bowl. Cover with clingfilm and set aside. Peel and core the remaining apples, cut them into thin rings, then put them in a polythene bag with 40 g/1½ oz of the flour. Seal the bag, then shake to thinly coat the apples with the flour.

2. Put the remaining flour into a mixing bowl. Stir in 1 tablespoon of the sugar, the cinnamon and the egg yolk. Gradually whisk in the milk until smooth. Whisk the egg white in a separate large, bowl until it holds soft peaks. Fold into the flour mixture.

3. Half fill a saucepan with oil. Heat to 160°C/325°F on a sugar thermometer, or until bubbles form when a little batter is dropped into the oil. Line a plate with kitchen paper. Shake any excess flour from the apple slices, then dip them into the batter and remove them using two forks. Drain off the excess batter, then carefully add 4–5 apple slices to the hot oil and cook for 2–3 minutes, or until golden. Lift out of the oil with a slotted spoon, transfer to the prepared plate and leave to drain while you cook the remaining apples. Sprinkle the remaining sugar over the fritters and serve with the blackberry sauce for dipping.

#250 Brandy snaps

Makes 20

Ingredients

85 g/3 oz butter
85 g/3 oz golden caster sugar
3 tbsp golden syrup
85 g/3 oz plain flour
1 tsp ground ginger
1 tbsp brandy
finely grated rind of ½ lemon

Filling

150 ml/5 fl oz double cream
1 tbsp icing sugar
1 tbsp brandy (optional)

1. Preheat the oven to 160°C/325°F/Gas Mark 3. Line three large baking trays with baking paper. Put the butter, sugar and golden syrup into a saucepan and gently heat, stirring occasionally, until smooth. Remove from the heat and leave to cool slightly. Sift the flour and ginger into the pan and whisk until smooth, then stir in the brandy and lemon rind. Drop 20 small spoonfuls of the mixture onto the prepared trays, spaced well apart.

2. Bake in the preheated oven, one tray at a time, for 10–12 minutes, or until golden brown. Remove from the oven, leave to cool for about 30 seconds, then lift each snap with a palette knife and wrap around the handle of a wooden spoon. If the snaps become too firm to wrap, return to the oven for 30 seconds. When firm, remove from the spoon and transfer to a wire rack to cool completely.

3. To make the filling, whip the cream with the icing sugar and the brandy, if using, until thick. Chill in the refrigerator until required. Just before serving, pipe the mixture into both ends of each snap.

#251 Funfetti cinnamon buns

Ingredients

450 g/1 lb strong white flour, plus extra for dusting

¼ tsp salt

1½ tsp easy-blend dried yeast

40 g/1½ oz caster sugar

55 g/2 oz butter, melted

1 egg, beaten

200 ml/7 fl oz lukewarm milk

oil, for greasing

Filling

50 g/1¾ oz butter, softened

50 g/1¾ oz caster sugar

1 tsp ground cinnamon

1 tbsp multi-coloured hundreds and thousands, plus extra for sprinkling

Frosting

25 g/1 oz butter, softened

85 g/3 oz full-fat soft cheese, at room temperature

70 g/2½ oz icing sugar, sifted

1. Sift together the flour and salt into a large bowl. Stir in the yeast and sugar and make a well in the centre. Beat together the butter, egg and milk in a jug, then pour into the well. Mix to a soft dough, then turn out onto a floured work surface and knead for 5–6 minutes until smooth and elastic, adding a little more flour if the dough is too sticky. Place the dough in a clean bowl, cover with oiled clingfilm and leave in a warm place for about 1¼ hours, or until the dough has doubled in size. Grease a 23-cm/9-inch square shallow cake tin.

2. Turn out the dough onto a floured work surface and lightly knead for 1 minute. Roll out to a 40 x 23-cm/16 x 9-inch rectangle. To make the filling, spread the butter over the dough, then sprinkle with the sugar, cinnamon and hundreds and thousands.

3. Roll up the dough from one side, then use a sharp knife to slice it into 16 rounds. Arrange the rounds, cut-side up, in the prepared tin. Cover loosely with oiled clingfilm and leave to stand in a warm place for about 30 minutes, or until almost doubled in size. Preheat the oven to 200°C/400°F/Gas Mark 6.

4. Bake in the preheated oven for 15–20 minutes, or until risen and golden. Leave to cool in the tin for 15 minutes, then carefully turn out onto a wire rack.

5. To make the frosting, beat together the butter and soft cheese until smooth, then beat in the icing sugar. Spread over the warm buns, then scatter over some hundreds and thousands. Serve warm or cold.

252 Rich chocolate pies

Makes
8

Ingredients

Pastry

225 g/8 oz plain flour, plus extra
for dusting

115 g/4 oz butter, diced

2 tbsp icing sugar

1 egg yolk

2–3 tbsp cold water

Filling

250 g/9 oz plain chocolate,
broken into pieces

115 g/4 oz butter

50 g/1¾ oz icing sugar

300 ml/10 fl oz double cream

grated chocolate, to decorate

1. To make the pastry, sift the flour into a large bowl. Add the butter and rub it in with your fingertips until the mixture resembles breadcrumbs. Add the icing sugar, egg yolk and enough water to form a soft dough. Wrap the dough in clingfilm and chill in the refrigerator for 15 minutes. Roll out the pastry on a lightly floured surface and use to line 8 x 10-cm/4-inch shallow tartlet cases. Chill for 30 minutes.

2. Preheat the oven to 200°C/400°F/Gas Mark 6. Prick the cases with a fork and line with crumpled foil. Bake in the preheated oven for 10 minutes, then remove the foil and bake for a further 5–10 minutes. Transfer to a wire rack to cool. Reduce the oven temperature to 160°C/325°F/Gas Mark 3.

3. To make the filling, place the chocolate, butter and icing sugar in a heatproof bowl set over a saucepan of gently simmering water and heat until melted. Remove from the heat and stir in 200 ml/7 fl oz of the double cream. Remove the cases from the tins and place on a baking sheet. Fill each case with the chocolate. Bake for 5 minutes. Leave to cool, then chill until required. To serve, whip the remaining cream and pipe into the centre of each tart. Decorate with grated chocolate.

253 Chilli & chocolate churros

Makes
16

Ingredients

85 g/3 oz plain chocolate,
broken into pieces

100 ml/3½ fl oz double cream

½ tsp vanilla extract

1 tsp dried chilli flakes, crushed

100 g/3½ oz butter, diced

225 ml/8 fl oz water

140 g/5 oz plain flour, sifted

large pinch of salt

2 large eggs, beaten

½ small red chilli, deseeded and very
finely chopped

oil, for deep-frying

4 tbsp caster sugar

2 tsp cocoa powder, sifted

1. Put the chocolate and cream into a heatproof bowl set over a saucepan of gently simmering water and heat until the chocolate is melted. Remove from the heat and stir until smooth, then stir in the vanilla extract and chilli flakes. Keep warm.

2. Put the butter and water into a large saucepan over a low heat and heat until the butter has melted. Bring to the boil, remove from the heat and tip in the flour and salt. Beat thoroughly until the mixture is smooth and comes away from the sides of the pan. Leave to cool for 5 minutes, then gradually beat in the eggs to make a thick and glossy paste. Beat in the chilli.

3. Heat enough oil for deep-frying in a large saucepan to 180–190°C/350–375°F, or until a cube of bread browns in 30 seconds. Spoon the paste into a large piping bag fitted with a large star-shaped nozzle and pipe 4 x 10-cm/4-inch lengths into the oil. Fry for 2–3 minutes, turning, until crisp and golden. Remove with a slotted spoon. Drain on kitchen paper and repeat with the remaining mixture.

4. Mix together the sugar and cocoa powder on a flat plate and toss the warm churros in the mixture to coat. Serve immediately with the chocolate sauce for dipping.

#254 Coconut cream pie

Serves
8–10

Ingredients

250 g/9 oz ready-made sweet shortcrust pastry, thawed, if frozen

2 eggs

55 g/2 oz caster sugar

1 tsp vanilla extract

2 tbsp plain flour, plus extra for dusting

2 tbsp cornflour

150 ml/5 fl oz milk

200 ml/7 fl oz coconut milk

25 g/1 oz desiccated coconut

400 ml/14 fl oz double cream

2 tbsp toasted desiccated coconut, to decorate

1. Preheat the oven to 200°C/400°F/Gas Mark 6. Roll out the pastry on a lightly floured surface and use to line a 20–23-cm/8–9-inch pie dish. Trim and crimp the edges. Prick the base with a fork and chill in the refrigerator for 15 minutes. Line with baking paper and baking beans, and bake in the preheated oven for 10 minutes. Remove the paper and beans and bake for a further 6–8 minutes, or until golden. Leave to cool.

2. Whisk together the eggs, sugar and vanilla extract in a bowl. Blend the flour and cornflour to a paste with 4 tablespoons of milk, then whisk into the egg mixture. Heat the remaining milk and coconut milk in a saucepan until almost boiling and pour onto the egg mixture, stirring constantly. Return to the pan and heat slowly, whisking until smooth and thick. Stir in the coconut. Cover with dampened baking paper and leave to cool completely. Spread the filling in the pastry case. Whip the cream until it holds soft peaks and spread over the top of the filling. Sprinkle over the toasted coconut and serve.

#255 Chocolate blueberry pies

Makes
10

Ingredients

175 g/6 oz plain flour

40 g/1½ oz cocoa powder

55 g/2 oz caster sugar

pinch of salt

125 g/4½ oz butter, diced

1 egg yolk

1–2 tbsp cold water

200 g/7 oz blueberries

2 tbsp crème de cassis

10 g/¼ oz icing sugar, sifted

Filling

140 g/5 oz plain chocolate, broken into pieces

225 ml/8 fl oz double cream

150 ml/5 fl oz soured cream

1. Put the flour, cocoa, sugar and salt in a large bowl and rub in the butter until the mixture resembles breadcrumbs. Add the egg and a little cold water to form a dough. Wrap the dough in clingfilm and chill in the refrigerator for 30 minutes. Remove the dough from the refrigerator, roll out and use to line 10 tartlet tins. Freeze for 30 minutes. Meanwhile, put the blueberries, crème de cassis and icing sugar in a saucepan and warm through so that the berries become shiny, but do not burst. Leave to cool.

2. Preheat the oven to 180°C/350°F/Gas Mark 4. Bake the pastry cases in the oven for 15–20 minutes. Leave to cool.

3. To make the filling, put the chocolate in a heatproof bowl set over a saucepan of gently simmering water, then leave to cool slightly. Whip the double cream until stiff, then fold in the soured cream and melted chocolate.

4. Transfer the tartlet cases to a serving plate and divide the chocolate filling between them, smoothing the surface with a palette knife, then top with the blueberries and serve.

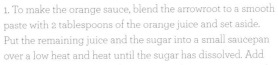

#256 Lemon churros with orange dipping sauce

Ingredients

100 g/3½ oz butter, diced

300 ml/10 fl oz water

140 g/5 oz plain flour, sifted

large pinch of salt

2 large eggs, beaten

finely grated rind of 1 large lemon

oil, for deep-frying

icing sugar, for dusting

Orange sauce

1 tbsp arrowroot

300 ml/10 fl oz fresh orange juice

40 g/1½ oz caster sugar

1. To make the orange sauce, blend the arrowroot to a smooth paste with 2 tablespoons of the orange juice and set aside. Put the remaining juice and the sugar into a small saucepan over a low heat and heat until the sugar has dissolved. Add the blended arrowroot and simmer gently, stirring constantly, for 4–5 minutes, until just thickened. Remove from the heat, cover and keep warm.

2. Put the butter and water into a large saucepan over a medium heat and heat until the butter has melted. Bring to the boil, remove from the heat and tip in the flour and salt. Beat thoroughly until the mixture is smooth and comes away from the sides of the pan. Leave to cool for 5 minutes, then gradually beat in the eggs to make a thick and glossy paste. Beat in the lemon rind.

3. Heat enough oil for deep-frying in a large saucepan or deep-fryer to 180–190°C/350–375°F, or until a cube of bread browns in 30 seconds. Spoon the paste into a large piping bag fitted with a large star nozzle and pipe 4–5 short loops of the paste into the hot oil. Fry, turning frequently, for 2–3 minutes, until crisp and golden. Remove with a slotted spoon and drain on kitchen paper. Keep warm while frying the remaining mixture.

4. Thickly dust the hot churros with icing sugar and serve immediately with the orange sauce.

#257 Chocolate meringue kisses

Ingredients

3 egg whites

1 tsp raspberry vinegar

150 g/5½ oz caster sugar

1 tsp cornflour

2 tbsp cocoa powder, sifted

200 g/7 oz plain chocolate, roughly chopped

1. Preheat the oven to 160°C/325°F/Gas Mark 3. Line three baking trays with baking paper.

2. Whisk the egg whites in a large, clean mixing bowl until they hold stiff peaks. Gradually whisk in the vinegar and sugar, until thick and glossy. Using a large metal spoon, gently fold in the cornflour and cocoa. Spoon into a piping bag fitted with a large star-shaped nozzle and pipe 40 x 2.5-cm/1-inch 'kisses' onto the prepared trays. Put the trays in the preheated oven, then reduce the temperature to 120°C/250°F/Gas Mark ½. Bake for 45 minutes, or until crisp on the outside. Transfer to a wire rack, leave to cool for 1 hour, then peel off the paper.

3. Meanwhile, put the chocolate in a heatproof bowl set over a saucepan of gently simmering water and heat until melted. Line the baking trays with more baking paper. Dip the bases of the meringues in the melted chocolate and place them, coated-side up, on the prepared trays. Leave to set for 1 hour before serving.

#258 Cherry & almond bakes

Makes
18

Ingredients

55 g/2 oz butter, softened, plus extra for greasing

55 g/2 oz caster sugar

55 g/2 oz self-raising flour

25 g/1 oz ground almonds

1 egg

a few drops of almond extract

18 fresh cherries, stalked and stoned, or 18 canned cherries

25 g/1 oz flaked almonds

icing sugar, sifted, for dusting

1. Preheat the oven to 180°C/350°F/Gas Mark 4. Lightly grease 18 sections of 2 x 12-hole mini muffin tins.

2. Put the butter, sugar, flour and ground almonds into a mixing bowl, then stir. Add the egg and almond extract and beat together with a wooden spoon until smooth.

3. Spoon the mixture into the prepared tins, then lightly press a cherry into the centre of each cake. Sprinkle with the flaked almonds. Bake in the preheated oven for 12–15 minutes, or until risen and firm to the touch.

4. Leave the cakes in the tins for 5 minutes, then remove and transfer to wire racks. Serve warm, dusted with sifted icing sugar.

#259 Lemon tart

Serves
8–10

Ingredients
Pastry

3 tbsp water

1 tbsp caster sugar

⅛ tsp salt

1 tbsp vegetable oil

90 g/3¼ oz butter, softened

150 g/5½ oz plain flour, plus extra for dusting

lemon and lime slices, to decorate

Filling

2 eggs

2 egg yolks

125 ml/4 fl oz freshly squeezed lemon juice

grated rind of 1 lemon

100 g/3½ oz caster sugar

85 g/3 oz butter, diced

1. Preheat the oven to 200°C/400°F/Gas Mark 6. To make the pastry, mix the water, sugar, salt, oil, butter and flour together. Chill in the refrigerator for 20 minutes.

2. Roll out the dough on a lightly floured work surface to a thickness of 5 mm/¼ inch. Place in a 23-cm/9-inch round flan tin, trimming the edge. Prick with a fork and bake for 15 minutes until golden brown. Remove from the oven and leave to cool in the tin. Do not switch off the oven.

3. Meanwhile, to make the filling, beat together the eggs and egg yolks and set aside. Put the lemon juice, lemon zest, sugar and butter into a saucepan over a medium heat and heat until the butter has melted. Reduce the heat, add the beaten egg and cook, stirring constantly until the mixture has thickened and bubbles are beginning to form.

4. Pour the lemon and egg mixture through a sieve set over the pastry case, evenly spreading the mixture with the back of a spoon. Return to the oven for 5 minutes. Remove from the oven and leave to cool. Serve cold, decorated with lemon and lime slices.

#260 Baklava pastries

Makes
30

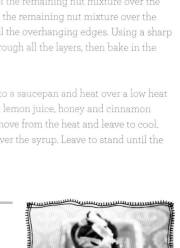

Ingredients

400 g/14 oz finely chopped mixed nuts,
such as walnuts, almonds and
pistachio nuts

450 g/1 lb filo pastry sheets

175 g/6 oz butter, melted, plus extra
for greasing

2 tbsp caster sugar

1 tsp ground cinnamon

Syrup

325 g/11½ oz caster sugar

300 ml/10 fl oz water

1 tbsp lemon juice

3 tbsp clear honey

2 small cinnamon sticks

1. Preheat the oven to 180°C/350°F/Gas Mark 4. Grease a baking tray. Spread the nuts on the prepared tray. Bake in the preheated oven for 5–10 minutes. Do not switch off the oven.

2. Meanwhile, place a layer of filo pastry in a 25 x 35-cm/10 x 14-inch baking tin. Brush with melted butter. Continue layering and brushing until there are 5–7 layers of pastry in the tin.

3. Mix the nuts with the sugar and cinnamon. Sprinkle a third of the nut mixture over the pastry, then cover with 2–3 buttered layers of pastry. Sprinkle half of the remaining nut mixture over the pastry and cover with 2–3 layers of buttered pastry. Sprinkle the remaining nut mixture over the pastry, cover with 5–7 layers of buttered pastry and fold in all the overhanging edges. Using a sharp knife, cut the baklava into diamond shapes, cutting right through all the layers, then bake in the preheated oven for 25–30 minutes until golden brown.

4. Meanwhile, prepare the syrup. Put the sugar and water into a saucepan and heat over a low heat until the sugar has dissolved. Bring to the boil, then add the lemon juice, honey and cinnamon sticks. Reduce the heat and simmer for 10 minutes, then remove from the heat and leave to cool. Remove the baklava from the oven and immediately pour over the syrup. Leave to stand until the pastry has fully absorbed the syrup.

#261 Mississippi mud pies

Makes
6

Ingredients

butter, for greasing

225 g/8 oz ready-made sweet shortcrust
pastry, chilled

plain flour, for dusting

100 g/3½ oz plain chocolate, roughly
chopped

4 tbsp icing sugar

125 ml/4 fl oz semi-skimmed milk

1 egg

225 ml/8 fl oz double cream

1 tsp vanilla extract

white and dark chocolate curls,
to decorate

1. Lightly grease a 6-hole muffin tin. Thinly roll out the pastry on a lightly floured surface. Use a plain cutter to stamp out 6 x 10-cm/4-inch rounds. Press gently into the prepared tin, prick the base of each with a fork, then chill in the refrigerator for 15 minutes. Preheat the oven to 190°C/375°F/Gas Mark 5. Line the pastry cases with baking paper and baking beans. Bake in the preheated oven for 10 minutes. Remove the paper and beans and cook for a further 2–3 minutes until crisp and dry.

2. Meanwhile, put the plain chocolate in a heatproof bowl set over a saucepan of gently simmering water and heat until melted. Beat together 2 tablespoons of the sugar, the milk and egg in a jug. Remove the chocolate from the heat and gradually stir in the milk mixture until smooth. Pour into the cases and leave to cool. Transfer to the refrigerator for 2 hours, or until the filling has set. Whip the cream with the remaining icing sugar and the vanilla extract until it holds soft peaks. Transfer the pies to a plate. Spoon the cream over the top and decorate with the chocolate curls.

White chocolate & passion fruit éclairs

Makes 10

Ingredients

50 g/1¾ oz butter

150 ml/5 fl oz cold water

60 g/2¼ oz plain flour, sifted

pinch of salt

2 large eggs, beaten

200 ml/7 fl oz double cream

2 passion fruit

Topping

200 g/7 oz white chocolate, broken into pieces

yellow writing icing

1. Preheat the oven to 200°C/400°F/Gas Mark 6. Line two baking trays with baking paper.

2. Place the butter and water in a medium-sized saucepan and bring to the boil. Add the flour and salt and beat well until the mixture starts to come away from the sides of the pan. Remove from the heat and leave to cool for 1–2 minutes.

3. Gradually beat in the eggs until the mixture is smooth and glossy. Transfer to a piping bag fitted with a 2.5-cm/1-inch nozzle and pipe 10 x 8-cm/3¼-inch lengths of the mixture onto the prepared trays.

4. Bake in the preheated oven for 15 minutes, then remove from the oven and use a fine skewer to make a slit along the length of each éclair to allow the steam to escape. Return to the oven and bake for a further 10 minutes, then transfer to a wire rack to cool.

5. Whip the cream until it just holds stiff peaks. Cut the passion fruit in half and use a teaspoon to remove the flesh. Stir into the cream and use either a piping bag or a teaspoon to fill the éclairs with the mixture.

6. To make the topping, place the chocolate in a heatproof bowl set over a saucepan of gently simmering water and heat until melted. Use a teaspoon to spread the melted chocolate evenly over the filled éclairs. To create a feathered effect, pipe 2–3 straight lines lengthways on the chocolate with the writing icing. Carefully drag a cocktail stick backwards and forwards across the lines at regular intervals. Leave to stand for 30 minutes before serving.

#263 Spiced pear strudel

Serves
6

Ingredients

85 g/3 oz butter, melted, plus extra for greasing

3 firm ripe pears, peeled, cored and diced

finely grated rind and juice of ½ lemon

75 g/2¾ oz demerara sugar

1 tsp ground allspice

55 g/2 oz sultanas

55 g/2 oz ground almonds

6 sheets filo pastry

icing sugar, sifted, for dusting

1. Preheat the oven to 200°C/400°F/Gas Mark 6 and grease a baking tray. Mix together the pears, lemon rind and juice, sugar, allspice, sultanas and half the almonds.

2. Place two sheets of filo pastry, slightly overlapping, on a clean tea towel. Brush with melted butter and sprinkle with a third of the remaining almonds. Top with two more sheets, butter and almonds. Repeat once. Spread the pear mixture down one long side, to within 2.5 cm/1 inch of the edge.

3. Roll the pastry over to enclose the filling and roll up, using the tea towel to lift. Tuck the ends under. Brush with a little melted butter and bake in the preheated oven for 20–25 minutes until golden and crisp. Lightly dust the strudel with icing sugar. Serve warm or cold, cut into thick slices.

#264 Yum yums

Makes
16

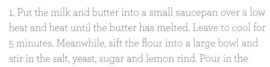

Ingredients

175 ml/6 fl oz milk

25 g/1 oz butter

350 g/12 oz strong white flour, plus extra for dusting and kneading

½ tsp salt

1½ tsp easy-blend dried yeast

40 g/1½ oz caster sugar

2 tsp finely grated lemon rind

1 egg, beaten

oil, for deep-frying and greasing

Glaze

175 g/6 oz icing sugar

4 tbsp lemon juice

1. Put the milk and butter into a small saucepan over a low heat and heat until the butter has melted. Leave to cool for 5 minutes. Meanwhile, sift the flour into a large bowl and stir in the salt, yeast, sugar and lemon rind. Pour in the milk mixture and the egg and mix to a soft dough. Turn out the dough onto a floured surface and knead for 5–6 minutes, until smooth and elastic. Put the dough into a bowl, cover and leave in a warm place for 1 hour, or until doubled in size. Line two large baking sheets with baking paper.

2. Knock back the dough and roll out to a 25 x 31 cm/10 x 12½ inch rectangle. Cut the dough into 16 short strips and tightly twist each strip 2–3 times. Place on the prepared baking sheets and cover with lightly oiled clingfilm. Leave to stand in a warm place for 10 minutes, until puffy.

3. Heat enough oil for deep-frying in a large saucepan or deep-fryer to 180–190°C/350–375°F, or until a cube of bread browns in 30 seconds. Add the doughnuts, 2–3 at a time, and fry on each side for 1–2 minutes, or until golden. Remove with a slotted spoon and drain on kitchen paper.

4. To make the glaze, mix the icing sugar and lemon juice together until smooth. When the doughnuts are just cool enough to handle, dip each one in the lemon glaze to coat. Transfer to a wire rack and leave to set.

#265 Red berry pies

Makes 24

Ingredients

butter, for greasing

350 g/12 oz mixed strawberries, raspberries and redcurrants

2 tsp cornflour

3 tbsp caster sugar, plus extra for sprinkling

grated rind of ½ lemon

450 g/1 lb ready-made sweet shortcrust pastry, chilled

plain flour, for dusting

1 egg yolk mixed with 1 tbsp water, for glazing

whipped cream, to serve

1. Preheat the oven to 180°C/350°F/Gas Mark 4. Lightly grease 2 x 12-hole mini muffin tins.

2. Roughly chop the strawberries and break up any large raspberries. Put all the fruit in a mixing bowl and stir in the cornflour, sugar and lemon rind.

3. Thinly roll out the pastry on a lightly floured surface. Using a fluted cookie cutter, stamp out 24 x 6-cm/2½-inch rounds. Press gently into the prepared tins. Reserve some trimmings for decoration. Brush the top edges of the pie cases with a little glaze, then spoon in the filling.

4. Thinly roll out the reserved pastry on a lightly floured surface. Cut 48 x 1-cm/½-inch wide strips and arrange two strips over each pie, pressing the edges together well to seal. Use a cookie cutter to cut small stars and arrange these over the strips. Brush glaze over the pastry and sprinkle with sugar.

5. Bake in the preheated oven for 15 minutes, or until golden. Leave to cool in the tins for 10 minutes, then transfer to wire racks to cool. Serve warm or cold with whipped cream.

#266 Strawberry shortcake

Serves 8–10

Ingredients

250 g/9 oz self-raising flour

50 g/1¾ oz butter, diced, plus extra for greasing

50 g/1¾ oz caster sugar

125–150 ml/4–5 fl oz milk

Topping

4 tbsp milk

500 g/1 lb 2 oz mascarpone cheese

5 tbsp caster sugar

500 g/1 lb 2 oz strawberries, hulled and quartered

finely grated rind of 1 orange

fresh mint leaves, to decorate

1. Preheat the oven to 200°C/400°F/Gas Mark 6. Lightly grease a 20-cm/8-inch loose-based round cake tin.

2. Sift the flour into a large bowl, add the butter and rub in with your fingertips until the mixture resembles fine breadcrumbs. Add the sugar and stir in enough milk to make a soft, smooth dough. Gently press the dough into the prepared tin. Bake in the preheated oven for 15–20 minutes until risen, firm to the touch and golden brown. Leave to cool in the tin for 5 minutes, then turn out onto a wire rack and leave to cool completely.

3. To make the topping, put the milk, mascarpone cheese and 3 tablespoons of the sugar into a bowl and whisk until smooth and fluffy. Put the strawberries into a separate bowl and sprinkle with the remaining sugar and the orange rind. Spread the mascarpone mixture over the cake and pile the strawberries on top. Spoon over any juices left over from the strawberries in the bowl, scatter with mint leaves and serve.

#267 Baked lemon cheesecake

Serves
8–10

Ingredients

55 g/2 oz butter, plus extra for greasing

175 g/6 oz gingernut biscuits, crushed

finely grated rind and juice of 3 lemons

300 g/10½ oz ricotta cheese

200 g/7 oz Greek-style yogurt

4 eggs

1 tbsp cornflour

100 g/3½ oz caster sugar

strips of lemon zest, to decorate

icing sugar, for dusting

1. Lightly grease a 20-cm/8-inch round springform cake tin and line the base with baking paper.

2. Melt the butter and stir in the crushed biscuits. Press into the base of the prepared tin. Chill in the refrigerator until firm. Preheat the oven to 180°C/350°F/Gas Mark 4.

3. Meanwhile, put the lemon rind and juice, ricotta cheese, yogurt, eggs, cornflour and caster sugar into a bowl and whisk until smooth. Carefully pour into the prepared tin. Bake in the preheated oven for 40–45 minutes, or until just firm and golden brown.

4. Leave to cool completely in the tin, then run a knife around the edge to loosen and turn out onto a serving plate. Decorate with lemon zest and dust with icing sugar.

#268 Stollen

Serves
8

Ingredients

150 ml/5 fl oz lukewarm milk

55 g/2 oz caster sugar

2 tsp active dried yeast

350 g/12 oz strong white bread flour

½ tsp salt

115 g/4 oz butter, softened

1 medium egg, beaten

40 g/1½ oz currants

55 g/2 oz sultanas

55 g/2 oz chopped mixed peel

55 g/2 oz glacé cherries

25 g/1 oz blanched almonds, chopped

grated rind of ½ lemon

175 g/6 oz marzipan, shaped into a 23-cm/9-inch sausage

oil or melted butter, for greasing

115 g/4 oz icing sugar, sifted

1 tbsp water

1. Pour the warm milk into a small bowl, add 1 teaspoon of the caster sugar, sprinkle over the yeast, and whisk thoroughly. Set aside for 10 minutes until frothy.

2. Set aside 2 tablespoons of the flour and sift the remainder into a large mixing bowl with the salt and remaining caster sugar. Make a well in the centre, pour in the yeast mixture, then add the butter and beaten egg. Mix well to a soft dough.

3. Mix in the currants, sultanas, mixed peel, cherries, almonds and lemon rind, then transfer the dough to a work surface and knead for 5 minutes, until smooth and elastic. Place in a clean bowl, cover with clingfilm and leave to stand in a warm place for 1½–2 hours, until doubled in size.

4. Sprinkle the reserved flour onto a work surface and turn out the dough onto it. Knock back, then knead until smooth and elastic. Roll out to a 25 x 20-cm/10 x 8-inch rectangle and place the marzipan in the centre. Grease a baking sheet. Fold the dough over the marzipan and place, seam-side down, on the prepared baking sheet. Cover and set aside until doubled in size. Meanwhile, preheat the oven to 190°C/375°F/Gas Mark 5.

5. Bake in the preheated oven for 35–40 minutes, until risen and golden. Transfer to a wire rack to cool slightly. Mix the icing sugar with the water and spread it thinly over the warm stollen. Cut into slices and serve.

#269 Raspberry cheesecakes

Ingredients

55 g/2 oz butter

115 g/4 oz digestive biscuits, crushed

3 tbsp water

2 tsp powdered gelatine

150 g/5½ oz raspberries, plus 24 to decorate

150 ml/5 fl oz double cream

150 ml/5 fl oz ready-made custard

¼ tsp vanilla extract

1. Melt the butter in a saucepan, then stir in the biscuit crumbs. Divide between 2 x 6-hole silicone muffin tins, pressing into the base of the holes with the back of a teaspoon. Chill in the refrigerator.

2. Put the water in a small heatproof bowl, sprinkle the gelatine over the surface and set aside for 5 minutes. Meanwhile, purée the raspberries in a blender and press through a sieve into a bowl to remove the seeds. Set the bowl of gelatine in a saucepan of gently simmering water and heat for about 5 minutes, stirring from time to time, until clear.

3. Pour the cream into a large mixing bowl and whip until it holds soft peaks. Fold in the custard and vanilla. Stir 1½ tablespoons of the gelatine into the raspberry purée and fold the remainder into the cream mixture. Spoon the cream mixture into the tins, level the surface using the back of a teaspoon, then spoon the raspberry purée on top. Swirl the two mixtures together using the handle of the teaspoon. Cover and chill in the refrigerator for at least 3 hours, until set.

4. Loosen the cheesecakes using a round-bladed knife, then turn them out onto individual plates by pressing underneath. Decorate each cake with two raspberries and serve.

#270 Chocolate 'ice-cream' cones

Ingredients

125 g/4½ oz milk chocolate, roughly chopped

200 g/7 oz plain chocolate, roughly chopped

4 tbsp water

2 egg whites

25 g/1 oz caster sugar

200 ml/7 fl oz double cream

2 tbsp vanilla sugar

chocolate and rainbow-coloured sugar sprinkles, to decorate

1. Line a baking tray with baking paper. Cut 8 x 18-cm/7-inch rounds of baking paper Fold the rounds in half, then cut them in half just to one side of the fold. Shape each semi-circle into a cone of double thickness paper. Secure in place with sticky tape.

2. Put the milk chocolate in a heatproof bowl set over a saucepan of gently simmering water and heat until melted. Divide the chocolate between each cone, then spread it up the sides with a pastry brush. Invert onto the prepared baking tray and chill for at least 30 minutes.

3. Put the plain chocolate and water in a heatproof bowl set over a saucepan of gently simmering water and heat until melted. Whisk the egg whites until they hold soft peaks. Whisk in the caster sugar, a little at a time. Fold in the chocolate. Spoon the mousse into the cones and chill for 1 hour. Whip the cream with the vanilla sugar until only just peaking. Put it into a small piping bag fitted with a 1-cm/½-inch star-shaped nozzle. Peel the paper from the cones and pipe swirls of cream on top. Scatter with sprinkles and serve.

Ingredients

50 g/1¾ oz butter

150 ml/5 fl oz water

70 g/2½ oz plain flour, sifted

pinch of salt

2 eggs, beaten

300 ml/10 fl oz double cream

1 tsp rosewater

200 g/7 oz small raspberries

Icing

200 g/7 oz icing sugar, sifted

½ tsp rosewater

1½–2 tbsp lukewarm water

a few drops of pink liquid food colouring

1. Preheat the oven to 220°C/425°F/Gas Mark 7. Line a large baking sheet with baking paper. Put the butter and water into a saucepan and heat gently until the butter has melted. Bring to a rolling boil, remove from the heat and quickly beat in the flour and salt until the mixture forms a ball that leaves the side of the pan. Transfer to a bowl and leave to cool for 5 minutes.

2. Gradually beat in the eggs to make a smooth glossy mixture with a soft dropping consistency. Spoon into a piping bag fitted with a 1.5-cm/⅝-inch plain nozzle and pipe 12 x 12-cm/4½-inch éclairs onto the prepared baking sheet. Sprinkle a little water around the éclairs.

3. Bake in the preheated oven for 20 minutes, or until golden. Remove from the oven and use the tip of a knife to pierce a hole in each éclair. Return to the oven for a further 5 minutes. Transfer to a wire rack and leave to cool.

4. Put the cream into a bowl with the rosewater and whip until it holds soft peaks. To make the icing, sift the icing sugar into a bowl and stir in the rosewater with enough of the water to make a thick, spreadable icing. Remove 2 tablespoons of the icing and add enough food colouring to tint it deep pink. Spoon it into a paper piping bag.

5. Split the éclairs lengthways and fill with small spoonfuls of the cream and the raspberries. Gently spread the white icing over the tops of the éclairs. Snip the end off the paper piping bag and pipe three thin lines of pink icing along the length of each éclair. Drag the tip of a cocktail stick backwards and forwards through the icing to create a feathered effect. Leave to set.

#272 Mint chocolate macaroons

Makes
16

Ingredients

75 g/2¾ oz ground almonds

115 g/4 oz icing sugar

2 large egg whites

50 g/1¾ oz caster sugar

1 tsp peppermint extract

green food colouring paste or liquid

2 tbsp chocolate sugar strands

Filling

55 g/2 oz butter, softened

55 g/2 oz icing sugar

55 g/2 oz milk chocolate, melted and cooled for 15 minutes

1. Place the ground almonds and icing sugar in a food processor and process for 15 seconds. Sift into a bowl. Line two baking sheets with baking paper. Place the egg whites in a large bowl and whisk until they hold soft peaks. Gradually whisk in the caster sugar to make a firm, glossy meringue. Whisk in the peppermint extract and enough green food colouring to give a bright green colour.

2. Use a spatula to fold the almond mixture into the meringue one third at a time, cutting and folding the mixture until it forms a shiny batter with a thick, ribbon-like consistency. Pour into a piping bag fitted with a 1-cm/½-inch plain nozzle. Pipe 32 small rounds onto the prepared baking sheets. Tap the baking sheets firmly onto a work surface to remove air bubbles. Top with the chocolate sugar strands. Leave at room temperature for 30 minutes. Preheat the oven to 160°C/325°F/Gas Mark 3. Bake in the preheated oven for 10–15 minutes. Leave to cool for 10 minutes, then carefully peel the macaroons off the baking paper. Transfer to a wire rack and leave to cool completely.

3. To make the filling, beat the butter until pale and fluffy. Sift in the icing sugar and beat until smooth and creamy, then fold in the chocolate. Use to sandwich pairs of macaroons together.

#273 Chocolate mousse

Serves
4–6

Ingredients

225 g/8 oz plain chocolate, chopped

2 tbsp brandy, Grand Marnier or Cointreau

4 tbsp water

30 g/1 oz unsalted butter, diced

3 large eggs, separated

¼ tsp cream of tartar

55 g/2 oz sugar

125 ml/4 fl oz double cream

1. Place the chocolate, brandy and water in a small saucepan over low heat and melt, stirring, until smooth. Remove the pan from the heat and beat in the butter. Beat the egg yolks into the chocolate mixture, one after another, until blended, then cool slightly.

2. Meanwhile, using an electric hand-held mixer on low speed, beat the egg whites in a clean, grease-free bowl until frothy, then gradually increase the mixer's speed and beat until soft peaks form. Sprinkle the cream of tartar over the surface, then add the sugar, tablespoon by tablespoon, and continue beating until stiff peaks form. Beat several tablespoons of the egg whites into the chocolate mixture to loosen.

3. In another bowl, whip the cream until soft peaks form. Spoon the cream over the chocolate mixture, then spoon the remaining whites over the cream. Use a large spoon or spatula to fold the chocolate into the cream and egg whites. Either spoon the chocolate mousse into a large serving bowl or divide between individual glasses. Cover the glasses with clingfilm and chill the mousse for at least 3 hours before serving.

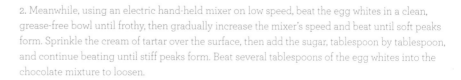
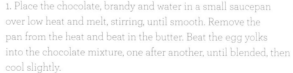

#274 Chocolate-dipped strawberries

Makes 24

Ingredients

100 g/3½ oz plain chocolate, roughly chopped

100 g/3½ oz white chocolate, roughly chopped

24 large strawberries

1. Line a baking tray with baking paper. Put the plain chocolate and white chocolate into two separate heatproof bowls set over saucepans of gently simmering water and heat until melted.

2. Dip the pointed end of each strawberry into one of the melted chocolates and transfer it to the prepared tray. Leave to cool for 1 hour, or until set.

3. Put each strawberry in a liqueur glass or on a plate and serve immediately.

#275 Semla buns

Makes 14-16

Ingredients

300 ml/10 fl oz milk, plus extra for brushing

1 tbsp ground cardamom

50 g/1¾ oz fresh yeast

1 egg

150 g/5½ oz softened butter

140 g/5 oz caster sugar

½ tsp salt

600 g/1 lb 5 oz plain flour, plus extra for dusting

1 egg yolk

icing sugar, for dusting

Filling

400 g/14 oz marzipan paste

dash of milk

400 ml/14 fl oz whipped cream

1. Gently heat the milk with the cardamom in a saucepan, then remove from the heat, crumble in the yeast and stir to dissolve. Break the egg into a bowl and gradually beat in the butter. Add the sugar and salt. Sift the flour into a large bowl and add the egg and butter mixture. Add the yeast mixture and knead until a smooth, elastic dough forms. Cover with a damp tea towel and leave to rise for about 1 hour until doubled in size.

2. Preheat the oven to 200°C/400°F/Gas Mark 6. Dust a baking tray with flour. Divide the dough into 14-16 pieces, roll each piece into a ball and place on the prepared baking sheet. Dust with flour, then cover and leave to rise for a further 10 minutes.

3. Whisk the egg yolk with a little milk and brush over the surface of the buns. Bake in the middle of the preheated oven for 6-7 minutes. Remove from the oven and leave to cool.

4. Cut off the top of the buns horizontally and set aside. Use your fingers to hollow out the buns, reserving the crumbs. To make the filling, mix the reserved crumbs with the marzipan paste and milk to a soft paste. Spoon the paste into the buns, pipe over the whipped cream and place a reserved top on each bun. Dust with icing sugar and serve.

276 Croissants

Ingredients

500 g/1 lb 2 oz strong white flour,
plus extra for dusting

40 g/1½ oz caster sugar

1 tsp salt

2¼ tsp easy-blend dried yeast

300 ml/10 fl oz lukewarm milk,
plus extra if needed

300 g/10½ oz butter, softened,
plus extra for greasing

1 egg, lightly beaten with 1 tbsp milk,
for glazing

1. Stir the dry ingredients into a large bowl, make a well in the centre and add the milk. Mix to a soft dough, adding more milk if too dry. Knead on a lightly floured surface for 5–10 minutes, or until smooth and elastic. Place in a large, greased bowl covered in clingfilm in a warm place until doubled in size. Meanwhile, flatten the butter with a rolling pin between two sheets of greaseproof paper to form a rectangle about 5 mm/¼ inch thick, then chill in the refrigerator. Preheat the oven to 200°C/400°F/Gas Mark 6.

2. Knead the dough for 1 minute. Remove the butter from the refrigerator. Roll out the dough on a floured surface to 46 x 15 cm/18 x 6 inches. Place the butter in the centre, fold up the sides and squeeze the edges together. With the short end of the dough towards you, fold the top third down towards the centre. Fold the bottom third up. Rotate 90° clockwise so that the fold is to your left. Roll out to a rectangle and fold again. Repeat the rolling process twice more. Cut the dough in half. Roll out one half into a 5-mm/¼-inch thick triangle (keep the other half refrigerated). Cut out 12 triangles using a card template with an 18-cm/7-inch base and 20-cm/8-inch sides. Repeat with the refrigerated dough.

3. Brush lightly with the egg glaze. Roll into croissant shapes, starting at the base and tucking the points under. Brush again with the glaze. Place on an ungreased baking tray and leave to double in size. Bake in the preheated oven for 15–20 minutes, or until golden brown.

277 Baked ring doughnuts

Ingredients

225 g/8 oz self-raising flour

1½ tsp baking powder

175 g/6 oz caster sugar

½ tsp salt

150 ml/5 fl oz milk

2 eggs, beaten

½ tsp vanilla extract

40 g/1½ oz butter, melted,
plus extra for greasing

Coating

4 tbsp caster sugar

2–3 tsp ground cinnamon

1. Preheat the oven to 190°C/375°F/Gas Mark 5. Grease a 6-hole doughnut tin.

2. Sift together the flour and baking powder into a bowl and stir in the sugar and salt. Make a well in the centre. Mix together the milk, eggs, vanilla extract and butter and pour into the well. Mix until smooth.

3. Spoon the mixture into a large piping bag fitted with a plain nozzle. Pipe some of the mixture into the prepared tin, filling each hole about two-thirds full. Bake in the preheated oven for 10–15 minutes, or until risen, golden and just firm to the touch. Leave to cool in the tin for 5 minutes, then turn out onto a wire rack. Repeat with the remaining mixture, rinsing and greasing the pan each time, to make 16 doughnuts in total.

4. To make the sugar coating, mix together the sugar and cinnamon on a plate. Gently toss each warm doughnut in the cinnamon sugar to coat completely. Serve warm or cold.

#278 Key lime pies

Makes 24

Ingredients

4 tbsp golden syrup

70 g/2½ oz butter, plus extra
for greasing

175 g/6 oz digestive biscuits, crushed

150 ml/5 fl oz double cream

grated rind of 2 limes

200 g/7 oz canned sweetened
condensed milk

4 tbsp freshly squeezed lime juice

extra lime zest, to decorate

1. Preheat the oven to 180°C/350°F/Gas Mark 4. Lightly grease 2 x 12-hole mini muffin tins. Put the syrup and butter in a small saucepan. Heat gently, uncovered, stirring, until the butter has just melted. Remove from the heat and stir in the crushed biscuits. Divide the mixture between the prepared tins, pressing it over the base and sides with the back of a teaspoon. Bake in the preheated oven for 6 minutes, or until slightly darker in colour. Reshape the centre if needed with the back of a spoon. Leave to cool in the tins for 10–15 minutes.

2. Meanwhile, pour the cream into a bowl, add the lime rind and whisk until beginning to thicken. Gradually whisk in the condensed milk, then the lime juice, whisking until it has thickened. Pipe or spoon the lime cream into the cases. Chill for at least 30 minutes. Lift the pies out of the tins and decorate with lime zest curls.

#279 South African milk tarts

Makes 12

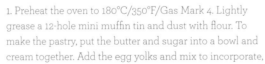

Ingredients

40 g/1½ oz butter, melted

225 g/8 oz caster sugar

3 egg yolks

140 g/5 oz plain flour

1 tsp baking powder

¼ tsp salt

1 tsp vanilla extract

1 litre/1¾ pints milk

3 egg whites

1 tbsp cinnamon sugar

strawberries and icing sugar, to decorate

Pastry

225 g/8 oz butter, plus extra for greasing

55 g/2 oz caster sugar

2 egg yolks

2 tbsp whipping cream

300 g/10½ oz plain flour, plus extra
for dusting

1. Preheat the oven to 180°C/350°F/Gas Mark 4. Lightly grease a 12-hole mini muffin tin and dust with flour. To make the pastry, put the butter and sugar into a bowl and cream together. Add the egg yolks and mix to incorporate, then add the cream and mix until combined. Using a palette knife, carefully fold in the flour to make a dough. Leave to chill for 1 hour.

2. Roll out the pastry on a floured surface, then use a 5-cm/2-inch round cutter to cut out 12 rounds. Use the rounds to line the holes in the prepared tin, then line with baking paper, fill with baking beans and bake in the preheated oven for 10 minutes. Remove from the oven and increase the oven temperature to 190°C/375°F/Gas Mark 5. Remove the paper and beans.

3. Put the butter and sugar into a large bowl and beat together until smooth. Add the egg yolks, one at a time, and beat until smooth. Sift in the flour, baking powder and salt and stir until well mixed. Add the vanilla extract and milk and stir. Put the egg whites into a separate bowl and whisk until they hold stiff peaks. Carefully fold into the butter and sugar mixture, then pour into the pastry cases and sprinkle over the cinnamon sugar.

4. Bake for 25 minutes, then remove from oven and leave to cool. Halve the strawberries. Place a strawberry half on each tart, dust with icing sugar and serve.

#280 Raspberry & strawberry pavlovas

Ingredients

2 egg whites

115 g/4 oz caster sugar

½ tsp cornflour

½ tsp white wine vinegar

Topping

300 ml/10 fl oz double cream

finely grated rind and juice of 1 lime

3 tbsp strawberry jam

200 g/7 oz raspberries

200 g/7 oz small strawberries, hulled and sliced

1. Preheat the oven to 140°C/275°F/Gas Mark 1. Line a large baking tray with baking paper. Whisk the egg whites in a large, clean mixing bowl until they hold stiff peaks. Whisk in the sugar a tablespoonful at a time, then whisk for a further 1–2 minutes, until the meringue is thick and glossy.

2. Mix the cornflour and vinegar together in a small bowl until smooth, then fold it into the meringue. Spoon 20 mounds of the mixture onto the prepared tray, leaving a little space between each mound. Spread the mounds into 5-cm/2-inch rounds, then make a small dip in the centre of each using the back of a teaspoon. Bake in the preheated oven for 25–30 minutes, or until the meringues are a very pale biscuit colour and can easily be lifted off the paper. If they stick to the paper, cook them for a few minutes longer, then retest. Leave to cool on the paper.

3. To make the topping, pour the cream into a large mixing bowl and whip until it holds soft peaks, then fold in the lime rind. Spoon a dollop of the cream on each pavlova, then transfer to a plate.

4. Put the jam and lime juice in a small, heavy-based saucepan and gently heat until the jam has just melted. Stir in the raspberries and strawberries, leave to cool slightly, then spoon over the pavlovas and serve.

#281 Chocolate cake doughnuts

Ingredients

125 ml/4 fl oz lukewarm milk

1 egg

1 tsp vanilla extract

30 g/1 oz cocoa powder

225 g/8 oz plain flour

½ tsp bicarbonate of soda

½ tsp baking powder

½ tsp salt

100 g/3½ oz caster sugar

25 g/1 oz butter

oil, for deep-frying

40 g/1½ oz plain chocolate, broken into pieces

40 g/1½ oz white chocolate, broken into pieces

1. Blend the milk, egg and vanilla extract in a bowl. Using a stand mixer with a paddle attachment, mix the cocoa powder, flour, bicarbonate of soda, baking powder, salt and sugar together. Add the butter and blend. Slowly add the milk mixture and mix until smooth and thick. Leave to rest in the mixer for 20 minutes. Roll out on a floured surface to a thickness of 1 cm/½ inch. Use a doughnut cutter to stamp out 14 doughnuts.

2. Heat enough oil for deep-frying in a large saucepan to 180–190°C/350–375°F, or until a cube of bread browns in 30 seconds. Carefully place the doughnuts, two to three at a time, into the oil. Fry for 2 minutes on each side, or until crisp. Do not overcrowd the pan. Remove with a slotted spoon and drain on kitchen paper.

3. Place the plain chocolate and white chocolate in separate heatproof bowls set over saucepans of simmering water and heat until melted. Drizzle over the doughnuts in a pattern.

#282 Orange & almond custard tarts

Makes
12

Ingredients

oil or butter, for greasing
250 ml/9 fl oz double cream
175 ml/6 fl oz milk
1 vanilla pod, scraped, or 1 tsp
vanilla extract
finely grated zest of 1 orange
4 egg yolks
2 tbsp cornflour
100 g/3½ oz caster sugar
150 g/5½ oz ready-made puff pastry
1–2 tbsp plain flour, for dusting
25 g/1 oz flaked almonds

1. Preheat the oven to 190°C/375°F/Gas Mark 5. Lightly grease a 12-hole muffin tin.

2. Place the cream, milk, vanilla seeds and orange zest in a saucepan and gently heat until simmering. Place the egg yolks, cornflour and sugar in a heatproof bowl and beat together until smooth. Gradually pour in the hot milk mixture, stirring constantly.

3. Return the mixture to the pan and warm through until thick, whisking constantly to prevent it catching on the base of the pan. Remove from the heat and cover the surface with clingfilm to prevent a skin forming. Leave to cool.

4. Meanwhile, roll out the pastry on a lightly floured surface to a very thin rectangle. Roll up tightly into a sausage shape and cut into 12 rounds. Roll out each round to a diameter of about 9 cm/3½ inches and press into a hole in the prepared tin.

5. Divide the custard between the prepared pastry cases and scatter a few flaked almonds over one half of each.

6. Bake in the preheated oven for 18–20 minutes until the tarts are golden, covering with foil if the almonds start to brown too quickly.

#283 Maple & pecan pie

Serves
8–10

Ingredients

175 g/6 oz plain flour, plus extra
for dusting

170 g/5¾ oz butter, diced

1 tbsp caster sugar

1 egg, beaten with 1 tbsp cold water

200 g/7 oz pecan nuts

85 g/3 oz soft light brown sugar

150 ml/5 fl oz maple syrup

5 tbsp golden syrup

3 large eggs, beaten

1 tsp vanilla extract

1. Sift the flour into a bowl, add 85 g/3 oz of the butter and rub in until the mixture resembles breadcrumbs. Stir in the caster sugar and egg and water mixture, and mix to a firm dough. Turn out onto a lightly floured surface and lightly knead until smooth. Roll out and use to line a 24-cm/9½-inch loose-based tart tin. Prick with a fork and chill in the refrigerator for 30 minutes. Preheat the oven to 200°C/400°F/Gas Mark 6. Place the tin on a baking sheet, line with baking paper and baking beans and bake in the preheated oven for 10 minutes. Remove the paper and beans and bake for a further 5 minutes. Reduce the oven temperature to 180°C/350°F/Gas Mark 4.

2. Chop half the nuts. Place the remaining butter, the brown sugar, maple syrup and golden syrup in a saucepan and heat over a low heat until melted. Leave to cool for 5 minutes, then beat in the eggs and vanilla extract. Stir in the chopped nuts. Pour into the pastry case and scatter over the remaining nuts. Bake for 35–45 minutes, until just set.

#284 Blueberry cheesecake macaroons

Makes
16

Ingredients

75 g/2¾ oz ground almonds

115 g/4 oz icing sugar

2 large egg whites

50 g/1¾ oz caster sugar

½ tsp vanilla extract

blue liquid food colouring

Filling

115 g/4 oz soft cheese

2 tbsp soured cream

1 tbsp icing sugar

85 g/3 oz fresh blueberries,
lightly crushed

1. Place the ground almonds and icing sugar in a food processor and process for 15 seconds. Sift the mixture into a bowl. Line two baking sheets with baking paper.

2. Place the egg whites in a large bowl and whisk until they hold soft peaks. Gradually whisk in the caster sugar to make a firm, glossy meringue. Whisk in the vanilla extract and enough food colour to give a bright blue colour.

3. Using a spatula, fold the almond mixture into the meringue one third at a time, cutting and folding the mixture until it forms a shiny batter with a thick, ribbon-like consistency.

4. Pour the mixture into a piping bag fitted with a 1-cm/½-inch plain nozzle. Pipe 32 small rounds onto the prepared baking sheets. Tap the baking sheets firmly on a work surface to remove air bubbles. Leave at room temperature for 30 minutes. Preheat the oven to 160°C/325°F/Gas Mark 3.

5. Bake in the preheated oven for 10–15 minutes. Leave to cool for 10 minutes, then carefully peel the macaroons off the baking paper. Transfer to wire racks and leave to cool completely.

6. To make the filling, beat together the soft cheese, soured cream and icing sugar until smooth. Fold in the crushed blueberries. Use to sandwich pairs of macaroons together.

184

285 French crullers

Ingredients

55 g/2 oz butter
125 ml/4 fl oz water
2 tsp caster sugar
115 g/4 oz self-raising flour
large pinch of salt
2 eggs
1 egg white
oil, for deep-frying
225 g/8 oz icing sugar
4 tbsp milk

1. Put the butter, water and sugar into a large saucepan over a medium heat and heat until the butter has melted. Bring to the boil, remove from the heat and tip in the flour and salt. Beat thoroughly until the mixture is smooth and comes away from the sides of the pan. Return to the heat and cook, stirring constantly, for a further 1 minute.

2. Leave to cool for 5 minutes, then gradually beat in the eggs and egg white to make a thick, glossy paste. Line a baking sheet with baking paper. Spoon the paste into a large piping bag fitted with a large star-shaped nozzle and pipe 8 x 8-cm/3¼-inch rings onto the prepared baking sheet. Place in the freezer for 1 hour.

3. Heat enough oil for deep-frying in a large saucepan or deep-fryer to 180–190°C/350–375°F, or until a cube of bread browns in 30 seconds. Carefully remove the semi-frozen rings from the baking sheet, add to the hot oil in batches of 2–3 and fry on each side for 2–3 minutes, until crisp and deep golden brown. Remove with a slotted spoon and drain on kitchen paper.

4. Sift the icing sugar into a large bowl and beat in the milk until smooth. Dip the warm crullers in the glaze to coat completely and transfer to a wire rack to set.

286 Chocolate fondants with toffee sauce

Ingredients

150 g/5½ oz butter
cocoa powder, for dusting
150 g/5½ oz plain chocolate, roughly chopped
2 eggs, plus 2 egg yolks
125 g/4½ oz caster sugar
25 g/1 oz plain flour
icing sugar, sifted, for dusting

Sauce

55 g/2 oz butter
55 g/2 oz light muscovado sugar
1 tbsp clear honey
150 ml/5 fl oz double cream

1. Melt 25 g/1 oz of the butter in a small saucepan, brush it inside 10 x 125-ml/4-fl oz ovenproof ramekins, then dust with cocoa powder. Put the chocolate and the remaining butter in a heatproof bowl set over a saucepan of gently simmering water and heat until melted. Put the eggs, egg yolks and caster sugar into a mixing bowl and whisk together until thick and frothy. Sift in the flour, then gently fold it in. Fold the melted chocolate mixture into the egg mixture until smooth. Pour it into the prepared ramekins, cover and chill in the refrigerator for at least 1 hour.

2. To make the sauce, put the butter, sugar and honey into a saucepan and gently heat for 3–4 minutes, or until the butter has melted and the sugar dissolved, then boil for 1–2 minutes, stirring, until it begins to thicken. Remove from the heat and stir in the cream, then set aside and keep warm. Preheat the oven to 180°C/350°F/Gas Mark 4. Leave the ramekins to stand at room temperature for 10 minutes, then bake in the preheated oven for 10–12 minutes, until the tops are crusty and the centres still slightly soft. Dust with sifted icing sugar and serve with the sauce.

#287 Cinnamon waffle bites

Ingredients

115 g/4 oz butter, plus extra for greasing

100 g/3½ oz plain flour

150 ml/5 fl oz single cream

2 egg yolks

½ tsp cinnamon

pinch of ground cloves

seeds from 1 vanilla pod

3 egg whites

2 tbsp caster sugar, plus extra for sprinkling

1 x waffle maker

1. Melt the butter in a small saucepan. Sift the flour into a bowl and gradually stir in the cream, egg yolks, spices, vanilla seeds and 2½ tablespoons of the melted butter.

2. Put the egg whites and half of the sugar in a bowl and beat until light and fluffy. Gradually add the remaining sugar and continue beating until they hold stiff peaks. Fold a third of the egg white into the cream mixture, then mix in the rest.

3. Preheat a waffle maker and lightly grease with butter. Pour a little batter into the waffle maker, spread out and cook over a medium heat until golden yellow. Continue cooking until the batter is used up, transferring the cooked waffles to a wire rack.

4. Brush the waffle bites with the remaining butter, sprinkle with sugar and serve.

#288 Mini chocolate-dipped doughnuts

Ingredients

500 g/1 lb 2 oz self-raising flour, plus extra for dusting

1 tsp baking powder

90 g/3¼ oz caster sugar

2 eggs

2 tbsp sunflower oil, plus extra for deep frying

200 ml/7 fl oz milk

100 g/3½ oz plain chocolate, roughly chopped

1. Sift the flour and baking powder into a large bowl. Add the sugar and stir. Put the eggs, oil and milk into a separate bowl and lightly whisk together, then pour into the flour mixture. Using a wooden spoon, work the ingredients together into a smooth ball, then turn out onto a lightly floured surface.

2. Using a floured rolling pin, roll out the dough to a thickness of just over 1 cm/½ inch. Dust a 4-cm/1½-inch and a 1-cm/½-inch round fondant cutter with flour. Use the larger cutter to cut out rounds of dough, then use the smaller one to cut out the centres. Re-roll the trimmings to make more doughnuts.

3. Heat enough oil for deep-frying in a deep saucepan to 180–190°C/350–375°F, or until a cube of bread browns in 30 seconds. Line a plate with kitchen paper. Carefully lower 2–3 doughnut rings into the oil and fry for 3–4 minutes, until golden and cooked through. Transfer to the prepared plate to drain and cool. Repeat until all of the doughnuts are cooked.

4. Put the chocolate in a heatproof bowl set over a saucepan of gently simmering water and heat until melted. Dip the top of the doughnuts in the chocolate and transfer to a wire rack to set for 1 hour. Serve immediately.

#289 Blueberry profiteroles

Makes 12

Ingredients

125 ml/4 fl oz milk
55 g/2 oz butter
125 g/4½ oz plain flour
pinch of salt
3 eggs, beaten
300 ml/10 fl oz double cream
280 g/10 oz blueberries
25 g/1 oz caster sugar
1 tsp lemon juice
55 g/2 oz blackberries
icing sugar, for dusting

1. Preheat the oven to 200°C/400°F/Gas Mark 6. Line a baking sheet with baking paper.

2. Put the milk and butter into a medium-sized saucepan and bring to the boil. Add the flour and salt and beat with a wooden spoon until a smooth ball of dough forms. Leave to cool for 10–15 minutes.

3. Use a wooden spoon to beat the eggs, a little at a time, into the dough until a smooth, glossy paste forms. Spoon into a piping bag fitted with a large star-shaped nozzle and pipe 12 x 5-cm/ 2-inch balls onto the prepared baking sheet. Bake in the preheated oven for about 20–25 minutes. Place a baking sheet sprinkled with hot water on the floor of the oven to help the profiteroles rise better. Leave the profiteroles to cool and cut in half horizontally.

4. Whip the cream until it holds stiff peaks. Purée 225 g/8 oz of the blueberries with the sugar and lemon juice and gently fold into the cream. Spoon into a piping bag fitted with a large nozzle and pipe onto the bottom halves of the profiteroles. Sprinkle with the remaining blueberries and the blackberries. Top with the top halves of the profiteroles and dust with the icing sugar to serve.

#290 Strawberry éclairs

Makes 16–18

Ingredients

55 g/2 oz butter, plus extra for greasing
150 ml/5 fl oz water
60 g/2¼ oz plain flour, sifted
2 eggs, beaten
200 g/7 oz strawberries, hulled
2 tbsp icing sugar
140 g/5 oz mascarpone cheese

1. Preheat the oven to 220°C/425°F/Gas Mark 7. Grease two baking trays. Heat the butter and water in a saucepan until boiling. Remove from the heat, quickly tip in the flour and beat until smooth. Transfer to a bowl. Gradually beat in the eggs until glossy. Spoon into a piping bag fitted with a large plain nozzle and pipe 16–18 x 9-cm/3½-inch fingers onto the prepared trays.

2. Bake in the preheated oven for 12–15 minutes, until golden brown. Cut a horizontal slit in the side of each éclair to release steam. Bake for a further 2 minutes, then transfer to wire racks to cool.

3. Purée half the strawberries with the icing sugar. Finely chop the remaining strawberries and stir into the mascarpone cheese. Pipe the mascarpone mixture into the éclairs. Serve the éclairs with the strawberry purée spooned over. The éclairs are best eaten within 1 hour of filling.

#291 Salted caramel mini éclairs

Makes
30

Ingredients

50 g/1¾ oz butter

150 ml/5 fl oz water

70 g/2½ oz plain flour, sifted

pinch of salt

2 eggs, beaten

300 ml/10 fl oz double cream

2 tsp coffee and chicory extract

1 sheet edible gold leaf or 1 tbsp gold
hundreds and thousands

Glaze

150 g/5½ oz granulated sugar

3 tbsp cold water

70 g/2½ oz lightly salted butter

pinch of sea salt

4 tbsp double cream

1. Preheat the oven to 220°C/425°F/Gas Mark 7. Line two large baking sheets with baking paper. Put the butter and water into a saucepan and heat gently until the butter has melted. Bring to a rolling boil, remove from the heat and quickly beat in the flour and salt until the mixture forms a ball that leaves the side of the pan clean. Transfer to a bowl and leave to cool for 5 minutes.

2. Gradually beat in the eggs to form a smooth, glossy mixture with a soft dropping consistency. Spoon into a piping bag fitted with a 1-cm/½-inch plain nozzle and pipe 15 x 7-cm/2¾-inch mini éclairs onto each prepared baking sheet. Sprinkle a little water around the éclairs and bake in the preheated oven for 15 minutes, or until golden. Remove from the oven and use the tip of a knife to pierce a hole in the end of each éclair. Return to the oven for a further 5 minutes. Transfer to a wire rack and leave to cool completely.

3. To make the glaze, put the sugar and water into a heavy-based saucepan. Heat gently, stirring, until the sugar has dissolved, then bring to the boil and continue boiling, without stirring, until a deep golden caramel forms. Remove from the heat and leave to stand for 2 minutes, then stir in the butter and salt. Use a balloon whisk to whisk in the double cream until a smooth caramel sauce forms. Pour into a heatproof bowl and leave to cool and thicken for about 30 minutes, stirring occasionally.

4. To assemble the éclairs, put the cream into a bowl with the coffee and chicory extract and whip until it holds soft peaks. Spoon into a piping bag fitted with a 5-mm/¼-inch plain nozzle. Use the tip of a knife to make the holes in each éclair a little larger. Pipe the cream into the éclairs through the holes. Gently dip the top of each filled éclair in the caramel and transfer to wire racks. Use the tip of a fine paintbrush to dot a few tiny specks of gold leaf on the caramel. Leave in a cool place until set.

#292 Tarte tatin

Ingredients

200 g/7 oz caster sugar

150 g/5½ oz butter

800 g/1 lb 12 oz Cox or Golden Delicious apples

350 g/12 oz ready-made puff pastry

1. Place a 20-cm/8-inch ovenproof frying pan over a low heat, add the sugar and heat until it starts to caramelize, then stir in the butter to make a light toffee sauce. Remove from the heat.

2. Peel and core the apples and cut them into eighths vertically. Lay them in the pan on top of the toffee sauce, cut-side up. They should fill the pan. Fill any large gaps with a few more apple pieces. Place the pan over a medium heat and cover. Simmer, without stirring, for 5-10 minutes until the apples have soaked up some of the sauce, then remove from the heat.

3. Preheat the oven to 190°C/375°F/Gas Mark 5. Roll out the pastry so that it will thickly cover the pan, with extra over-hanging the sides. Lay it on top of the apples and tuck the edges down inside between the fruit and the pan until it is sealed. Bake in the preheated oven for 25–35 minutes, making sure the pastry doesn't burn, until puffed and golden. Remove from the oven and leave to rest for 30–60 minutes.

4. To serve, place a plate on top of the pan. Quickly turn it over and lift off the pan. Serve warm.

#293 Cinnamon orange fritters

Ingredients

250 g/9 oz plain flour

1 tsp easy-blend dried yeast

1½ tbsp caster sugar

125 ml/4 fl oz lukewarm milk

1 egg, beaten

finely grated rind of 1 small orange

1 tsp orange flower water

40 g/1½ oz butter, melted

oil, for deep frying

cinnamon sugar, for dusting

orange slices or segments, to serve

1. Sift the flour into a bowl and stir in the yeast and sugar.

2. Add the milk, egg, orange rind, flower water and butter and mix to a soft dough, kneading until smooth.

3. Cover and leave in a warm place until doubled in size. Roll out on a lightly floured surface to a thickness of 1 cm/½ inch, and cut into 8 x 7.5-cm/3-inch squares.

4. Heat enough oil for deep-frying in a large saucepan to 180–190°C/350–375°F, or until a cube of bread browns in 30 seconds. Add the fritters in batches and fry until golden brown. Remove with a slotted spoon and drain on kitchen paper.

5. Sprinkle with cinnamon sugar and serve hot with orange slices.

#294 Tea cakes

Ingredients

4 tsp dried yeast

85 g/3 oz caster sugar

325 ml/11 fl oz lukewarm milk

450 g/1 lb strong white flour, plus extra for dusting

1 tsp salt

1 tsp mixed spice

115 g/4 oz currants

25 g/1 oz mixed peel, chopped

55 g/2 oz butter, melted, plus extra for greasing

1 egg, beaten

1. Add the yeast and 1 teaspoon of the sugar to 300 ml/10 fl oz of the milk. Mix well and leave in a warm place for 15 minutes until frothy. Sift the flour, salt and spice into a large mixing bowl and add the currants, peel and all but 2 tablespoons of the remaining sugar. Make a well in the centre of the dry ingredients and pour in the yeast mixture, butter and egg. Mix well with a wooden spoon and then mix by hand. Turn out onto a lightly floured surface and lightly knead until smooth and elastic. Return the dough to the bowl, cover with clingfilm and leave to rise in a warm place for 40–45 minutes until doubled in size. Lightly knead and shape into 10–12 buns.

2. Preheat the oven to 220°C/425°F/Gas Mark 7. Grease two baking trays. Place the buns on the prepared trays, cover with a damp tea towel and leave to rise for 30–40 minutes. Bake in the preheated oven for 18–20 minutes until golden brown. Meanwhile, mix the remaining sugar and milk together. Transfer the buns to a wire rack and glaze with the sugar mixture while still hot.

#295 Honey & nut mini doughnuts

Ingredients

115 g/4 oz self-raising flour

½ tsp baking powder

pinch of salt

55 g/2 oz butter, softened, plus extra for greasing

55 g/2 oz caster sugar

1 egg, beaten

6 tbsp milk

40 g/1½ oz pistachio nuts, finely chopped

Glaze

85 g/3 oz icing sugar

1 tbsp clear honey, warmed

2 tsp milk

1. Preheat the oven to 190°C/375°F/Gas Mark 5. Grease a 12-hole mini doughnut tin. Sift together the flour, baking powder and salt into a bowl.

2. Put the butter and sugar into a bowl and beat together until pale and fluffy. Gradually beat in the egg, then stir in half the flour mixture. Beat in the milk, then fold in the remaining flour mixture and three quarters of the chopped nuts.

3. Spoon the mixture into a large, disposable piping bag. Snip off the end and pipe half the filling into the doughnut holes, filling each one about two-thirds full.

4. Bake in the preheated oven for 8–10 minutes, until risen, pale golden and just firm to the touch. Leave to cool in the tin for 2–3 minutes, then transfer to a wire rack. Rinse and re-grease the tin and repeat with the remaining mixture.

5. To make the glaze, sift the icing sugar into a bowl and stir in the warm honey and milk until smooth. Dip the top of each doughnut into the glaze, then sprinkle with the remaining nuts.

#296 Spiced apple macaroons

Ingredients

75 g/2¾ oz ground almonds

115 g/4 oz icing sugar

1 tsp ground cinnamon

2 large egg whites

50 g/1¾ oz caster sugar

½ tsp freshly grated nutmeg

Filling

450 g/1 lb cooking apples, peeled, cored and chopped

3 tbsp caster sugar

1 tbsp water

1. Place the ground almonds, icing sugar and cinnamon in a food processor and process for 15 seconds. Sift the mixture into a bowl. Line two baking sheets with baking paper.

2. Place the egg whites in a large bowl and whisk until holding soft peaks. Gradually whisk in the caster sugar to make a firm, glossy meringue. Using a spatula, fold the almond mixture into the meringue one third at a time. When all the dry ingredients are thoroughly incorporated, continue to cut and fold the mixture until it forms a shiny batter with a thick, ribbon-like consistency.

3. Pour the mixture into a piping bag fitted with a 1-cm/½-inch plain nozzle. Pipe 32 small rounds onto the prepared baking sheets. Tap the baking sheets firmly on a work surface to remove air bubbles. Sprinkle over the grated nutmeg. Leave at room temperature for 30 minutes. Preheat the oven to 160°C/325°F/Gas Mark 3. Bake in the preheated oven for 10–15 minutes. Leave to cool for 10 minutes, then carefully peel the macaroons off the baking paper. Leave to cool completely.

4. To make the filling, put the apples, sugar and water in a small saucepan over a low heat. Cover and simmer for 10 minutes, until soft. Mash with a fork to make a purée, then leave to cool. Use to sandwich pairs of macaroons together.

#297 Canadian butter tarts

Ingredients

1 egg

100 g/3½ oz soft light brown sugar

2 tsp golden syrup

1 tbsp butter

1 tsp vanilla extract

125 g/4½ oz sultanas

Pastry

300 g/10½ oz plain flour, plus extra for dusting

1 tsp salt

225 g/8 oz vegetable fat

1 egg

3 tbsp cold water

1. To make the pastry, sift together the flour and salt into a large bowl, then rub in the vegetable fat until the mixture resembles breadcrumbs. Mix together the egg and water in a separate bowl and add to the flour mixture, working it in until smooth. Wrap the pastry in clingfilm and chill in the refrigerator for 30 minutes.

2. Preheat the oven to 200°C/400°F/Gas Mark 6. Turn out the pastry onto a lightly floured work surface, roll out and use a 7.5-cm/3-inch cutter to cut out 16 rounds, re-rolling the trimmings if necessary. Press the rounds into 16 tartlet tins and trim the edges.

3. Put the egg, sugar, golden syrup, butter and vanilla extract into a saucepan and heat over a medium heat, stirring constantly, until the butter has melted. Divide the sultanas between the tartlet cases. Pour over the filling so that the pastry cases are almost filled. Bake in the preheated oven for 10 minutes, until light golden brown. Remove from the oven and serve hot or cold.

Baked blueberry doughnuts

Ingredients

200 g/7 oz self-raising flour

1 tsp baking powder

115 g/4 oz caster sugar

¼ tsp salt

125 ml/4 fl oz buttermilk

2 large eggs, beaten

1½ tsp vanilla extract

25 g/1 oz butter, melted, plus extra for greasing

125 g/4½ oz small fresh blueberries

115 g/4 oz icing sugar

2 tbsp milk

1. Preheat the oven to 190°C/375°F/Gas Mark 5. Grease a 6-hole doughnut tin. Sift together the flour and baking powder into a bowl and stir in the sugar and salt. Make a well in the centre. Put the buttermilk, eggs, ½ teaspoon of the vanilla extract and the butter into a jug, mix together and pour into the well. Mix until smooth, then gently fold in the blueberries.

2. Using a teaspoon, carefully spoon half the mixture into the prepared tin, filling the holes about two-thirds full. Bake in the preheated oven for 12–15 minutes, or until risen, golden and just firm to the touch. Leave to cool in the tin for 5 minutes, then turn out onto a wire rack to cool completely. Rinse and re-grease the tin and repeat with the remaining mixture.

3. Sift the icing sugar into a bowl and beat in the milk and the remaining vanilla extract until smooth. Spoon the glaze over the doughnuts, letting it run down the sides. Leave to set.

Chocolate peanut butter pie

Ingredients

225 g/8 oz bourbon biscuits, crushed

25 g/1 oz plain chocolate, grated

70 g/2½ oz butter, melted

175 g/6 oz cream cheese

140 g/5 oz smooth peanut butter

25 g/1 oz caster sugar

200 ml/7 fl oz double cream

chopped roasted peanuts, to decorate

Topping

115 g/4 oz plain chocolate, broken into pieces

1 tbsp golden syrup

25 g/1 oz butter

100 ml/3½ fl oz double cream

1. Preheat the oven to 180°C/350°F/Gas Mark 4. Put the crushed biscuits into a bowl and stir in the chocolate and butter. Press the mixture into the base and up the sides of a 23-cm/9-inch tart tin. Bake in the preheated oven for 10 minutes, or until just set. Leave to cool.

2. Put the cream cheese and peanut butter into a bowl and beat together until smooth. Beat in the sugar, then gradually beat in the cream. Spoon the mixture into the biscuit case and gently level the surface. Chill in the refrigerator for 30 minutes.

3. To make the topping, put the chocolate, syrup and butter into a heatproof bowl set over a saucepan of simmering water and heat until melted. Remove from the heat and stir in the cream until smooth. Leave to cool for 10–20 minutes, until thickened, then gently spread over the filling. Chill in the refrigerator for at least 1 hour before serving.

4. To serve, remove the pie from the tin and decorate with chopped roasted peanuts.

Saffron & cardamom macaroons

Makes 16

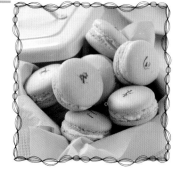

Ingredients

75 g/2¾ oz ground almonds

115 g/4 oz icing sugar

2 large egg whites

¼ tsp saffron strands, crushed, plus extra strands to decorate

50 g/1¾ oz caster sugar

yellow food colouring paste or liquid

Filling

55 g/2 oz butter, softened

seeds from 4 cardamom pods, finely crushed

115 g/4 oz icing sugar, sifted

1. Place the ground almonds and icing sugar in a food processor and process for 15 seconds. Sift the mixture into a bowl. Line two baking sheets with baking paper.

2. Place the egg whites and crushed saffron strands in a large bowl and whisk until they hold soft peaks. Gradually whisk in the caster sugar to make a firm, glossy meringue. Whisk in enough food colouring to give a pale yellow colour. Using a spatula, fold the almond mixture into the meringue one third at a time, cutting and folding the mixture until it forms a shiny batter with a thick, ribbon-like consistency.

3. Pour the mixture into a piping bag fitted with a 1-cm/½-inch plain nozzle. Pipe 32 small rounds onto the prepared baking sheets. Tap the baking sheets firmly on a work surface to remove air bubbles. Sprinkle over the extra saffron strands. Leave at room temperature for 30 minutes. Preheat the oven to 160°C/325°F/Gas Mark 3. Bake in the preheated oven for 10–15 minutes. Leave to cool for 10 minutes, then carefully peel the macaroons off the baking paper. Leave to cool completely.

4. To make the filling, beat the butter and cardamom seeds in a bowl until pale and fluffy. Gradually beat in the icing sugar until smooth and creamy. Use to sandwich pairs of macaroons together.

Pear & pecan strudel

Serves 4

Ingredients

2 ripe pears

55 g/2 oz butter

55 g/2 oz fresh white breadcrumbs

55 g/2 oz pecan nuts, chopped

25 g/1 oz light muscovado sugar

finely grated rind of 1 orange

100 g/3½ oz filo pastry, thawed if frozen

6 tbsp orange blossom honey

2 tbsp orange juice

icing sugar, for dusting

Greek-style yogurt, to serve (optional)

1. Preheat the oven to 200°C/400°F/Gas Mark 6. Peel, core and chop the pears. Melt 1 tablespoon of the butter in a frying pan and gently fry the breadcrumbs until golden. Transfer to a bowl and add the pears, nuts, muscovado sugar and orange rind. Put the remaining butter in a small saucepan and heat until melted.

2. Reserve one sheet of filo pastry, keeping it well wrapped, and brush the remaining filo sheets with a little melted butter. Spoon some of the nut filling onto the first filo sheet, leaving a 2.5-cm/1-inch margin around the edge. Build up the strudel by placing more buttered filo sheets on top of the first, spreading each one with nut filling as you build up the layers. Drizzle the honey and orange juice over the top.

3. Fold the short ends over the filling, then roll up, starting at a long side. Carefully lift onto a baking sheet, with the join facing up. Brush with any remaining melted butter and crumple the reserved sheet of filo pastry around the strudel. Bake for 25 minutes, or until golden and crisp. Sift over some icing sugar and serve warm with Greek-style yogurt, if using.

Something different

#302 Cinnamon sugared nuts

Serves 12

Ingredients

1 egg white
1 tbsp water
½ tsp vanilla extract
125 g/4½ oz pecan nuts
115 g/4 oz whole unblanched almonds
70 g/2½ oz cashew nuts
55 g/2 oz granulated sugar
55 g/2 oz light muscovado sugar
1½ tsp ground cinnamon
pinch of salt

1. Preheat the oven to 150°C/300°F/Gas Mark 2. Line a large baking tray with baking paper.

2. Put the egg white, water and vanilla extract into a bowl and beat with a fork until just frothy. Add the pecan nuts, almonds and cashew nuts and stir to coat thoroughly in the mixture. Mix the granulated sugar, muscovado sugar, cinnamon and salt together and stir into the nuts. Mix well to completely coat the nuts. Spread in a single layer on the prepared tray.

3. Bake in the preheated oven for 35–40 minutes, turning 2–3 times with a fork, until all the nuts are crisp and golden. Leave to cool completely on the baking tray, then serve or store in an airtight container for up to 2 weeks.

#303 Lime & chilli sorbet lollies

Makes 8

Ingredients

100 g/3½ oz caster sugar
1 red chilli, deseeded and very finely chopped
400 ml/14 fl oz water
4 large limes
8 very thin slices from a small lime

1. Put the sugar, chilli and water in a saucepan. Place over a medium-low heat, stirring, for 6–8 minutes, or until the sugar has dissolved. Increase the heat to medium–high and bring the mixture to the boil, then remove from the heat.

2. Finely grate the rind of two of the limes into the mixture and stir. Cover and leave to cool for about 1 hour, until completely cool.

3. Squeeze the juice from the four limes and stir it into the mixture.

4. Pour the mixture into 8 x 60-ml/2-fl oz ice pop moulds and place a lime slice in each mould. Insert the ice-pop sticks and freeze for 5–6 hours, or until firm.

5. To unmould the ice pops, dip the frozen moulds in warm water for a few seconds and gently release the pops while holding the sticks.

#304 Banana & pecan wontons

Ingredients

cooking spray
1 medium banana, mashed
30 g/1 oz pecan nut pieces
3 tbsp soft light brown sugar
16 square or round wonton wrappers
1 egg, beaten

Sauce

15 g/½ oz unsalted butter
100 g/3½ oz soft light brown sugar
2 tbsp whisky
5 tbsp milk
½ tsp vanilla extract

1. Preheat the oven to 200°C/400°F/Gas Mark 6. Line a large baking tray with baking paper and spray it with cooking spray.

2. In a medium-sized bowl, combine the banana, pecan nut pieces and brown sugar and stir to mix well. Lay out the wonton wrappers on a work surface and coat the edges with the beaten egg. Put 1 tablespoon of filling in the centre of each wonton wrapper. Fold the wonton wrappers over to form semicircles or triangles and press to seal the edges. Transfer the wontons to the prepared baking tray and bake in the preheated oven for 5 minutes, or until crisp and lightly coloured. Remove from the oven and leave to cool on the tray while you make the sauce.

3. To make the sauce, combine the butter, brown sugar and whisky in a small saucepan set over a medium–high heat. Cook, swirling the pan, until the sugar has completely dissolved. Add the milk and bring to the boil. Heat for a further 5 minutes, until the mixture has thickened.

4. Remove from the heat and stir in the vanilla extract. Serve the wontons warm with the sauce drizzled over the top.

#305 Double ginger cupcakes

Ingredients

175 g/6 oz plain flour
1 tbsp baking powder
2 tsp ground ginger
175 g/6 oz butter, softened
175 g/6 oz light muscovado sugar
3 eggs, beaten
25 g/1 oz crystallized stem ginger, finely chopped
200 g/7 oz ricotta cheese
85 g/3 oz icing sugar, sifted
finely grated rind of 1 tangerine
diced crystallized ginger, to decorate

1. Preheat the oven to 190°C/375°F/Gas Mark 5. Put 12 paper cases in a muffin tin or put 12 double-layer paper cases on a baking tray.

2. Sift the flour, baking powder and ground ginger into a large bowl. Add the butter, muscovado sugar and eggs, and beat well until smooth. Stir in the crystallized stem ginger.

3. Spoon the mixture into the paper cases. Bake in the preheated oven for 15–20 minutes, or until well risen and springy to the touch. Transfer to a wire rack to cool completely.

4. Mix together the ricotta cheese, icing sugar and tangerine rind until smooth. Spoon a little of the frosting onto each cupcake and spread over the surface to cover. Decorate with the diced crystallized ginger and leave to set.

306 Cookie pops

Ingredients

125 g/4½ oz butter, softened,
plus extra for greasing

100 g/3½ oz soft light brown sugar

100 g/3½ oz caster sugar

1 egg, lightly beaten

½ tsp vanilla extract

250 g/9 oz self-raising flour

pinch of salt

2–3 tbsp mini sugar-coated
chocolate drops

24 lollipop sticks

1. Preheat the oven to 180°C/350°F/Gas Mark 4. Lightly grease three large baking sheets.

2. Beat together the butter, brown sugar and caster sugar until pale and creamy, then gradually beat in the egg and vanilla extract. Sift in the flour and salt and stir to make a soft dough. Lightly knead until smooth, then halve the dough, shape into balls, wrap in clingfilm and chill in the refrigerator for 30 minutes.

3. Divide the dough into 24 pieces and roll each piece into a ball. Place on the prepared baking sheets, spaced well apart. Push a lollipop stick into each ball at a slight angle. Lightly flatten the balls with your fingertips and top each with 4–5 chocolate drops. Bake in the preheated oven for 12–14 minutes, or until light golden. Leave to cool on the baking sheets for about 5 minutes, then carefully transfer to wire racks to cool completely.

307 Strawberry rosé jellies

Makes
8

Ingredients

150 g/5½ oz small strawberries, hulled and sliced

1½ tbsp caster sugar

3 tbsp water

2 tsp powdered gelatine

200 ml/7 fl oz rosé wine

Topping

1½ tbsp caster sugar

2 tbsp rosé wine

finely grated rind of 1 lemon

150 ml/5 fl oz double cream

1. Put the strawberries and sugar into a mixing bowl and mix together using a metal spoon.

2. Put the water in a small heatproof bowl, then sprinkle the gelatine over the surface, making sure the powder is absorbed. Set aside for 5 minutes. Set the bowl of gelatine over a saucepan of gently simmering water and heat for about 5 minutes, stirring occasionally, until the gelatine has completely dissolved.

3. Divide the sugar-coated strawberries between eight small champagne or liqueur glasses. Pour the wine into a jug and stir in the gelatine, then pour it into the glasses. Cover and chill in the fridge for 4 hours, or until the jelly has set.

4. To make the topping, put the sugar, wine and half the lemon rind in a small bowl and stir. Pour the cream into a large bowl and whip until it holds soft peaks. Add the wine mixture and whisk briefly, until the cream has thickened again. Spoon the lemon cream into the centre of the jellies, then decorate with the remaining lemon rind.

308 Raspberry ripple ice cream

Serves
6–8

Ingredients

300 ml/10 fl oz milk

1 vanilla pod

210 g/7½ oz caster sugar

3 egg yolks

350 g/12 oz fresh raspberries

6 tbsp water

300 ml/10 fl oz whipping cream

1. Pour the milk into a heavy-based saucepan, add the vanilla pod and place over a low heat. Slowly bring to a simmer and remove from the heat. Leave to infuse for 30 minutes. Put 85 g/3 oz of the sugar and the egg yolks in a bowl and whisk together until pale and the mixture leaves a trail when the whisk is lifted. Remove the vanilla pod, then add the milk to the sugar mixture and whisk. Return to the rinsed-out saucepan and cook over a low heat for 10–15 minutes. Do not allow the mixture to boil. Remove from the heat and submerge the base of the pan in a bowl of ice-cold water. Leave to cool for at least 1 hour, stirring occasionally to prevent a skin forming.

2. Meanwhile, put the raspberries in a heavy-based saucepan with the remaining sugar and the water. Heat gently, until the sugar has dissolved and the raspberries are very soft. Pass through a nylon sieve into a bowl and leave to cool. Meanwhile, whip the cream until it holds its shape.

3. Fold the whipped cream into the milk mixture and freeze, uncovered, for 1–2 hours, or until it begins to set around the edges. Tip into a bowl and stir with a fork until smooth. Transfer half the mixture to another container. Pour over half the raspberry purée then repeat the layers. Return to the container and freeze for a further 2–3 hours, or until completely frozen. Remove the ice cream from the freezer and place in the refrigerator for 15–20 minutes to soften before serving.

309 Pistachio apricot nougat

Makes
16

Ingredients

edible rice paper

250 g/9 oz caster sugar

125 ml/4 fl oz liquid glucose

85 g/3 oz runny honey

2 tbsp water

pinch of salt

1 egg white

½ tsp vanilla extract

60 g/2¼ oz butter, softened and diced

50 g/1¾ oz pistachio nuts, roughly chopped

50 g/1¾ oz ready-to-eat dried apricots, finely chopped

1. Line a 18-cm/7-inch square loose-based cake tin with clingfilm, leaving an overhang. Line the base with rice paper. Put the sugar, glucose, honey, water and salt into a heavy-based saucepan. Heat gently until the sugar has dissolved, tilting the pan to mix the ingredients together. Increase the heat and boil for 8 minutes, or until the mixture reaches 121°C/250°F on a sugar thermometer.

2. Whisk the egg white until it holds stiff peaks, gradually pouring in a quarter of the hot syrup in a thin stream. Place the remaining syrup over a gentle heat for 2 minutes, or until the mixture reaches 143°C/290°F on a sugar thermometer. Gradually whisk the syrup into the egg white. Add the vanilla and butter and beat for a further 5 minutes. Add the nuts and apricots and stir. Pour the mixture into the tin and level with a palette knife. Cover with rice paper and chill in the refrigerator for 8–10 hours, or until fairly firm. Lift the nougat out of the tin and cut into 16 squares.

310 Double chocolate brownie mix

Makes
6

Ingredients

750 g/1 lb 10 oz plain flour

1½ tsp salt

600 g/1 lb 5 oz soft light
brown sugar

800 g/1 lb 12 oz granulated sugar

350 g/12 oz cocoa powder

450 g/1 lb toasted hazelnuts, chopped

525 g/1 lb 3 oz mini plain chocolate chips

6 x 475-ml/16-fl oz wide-mouthed
preserving jars, sterilized

1. Evenly divide all of the ingredients between the jars in layers, starting with the flour. Place the lids on the jars and secure tightly.

2. Attach a gift tag to each jar with these instructions:

How to prepare Double Chocolate Brownies

You will need:
2 large eggs
2 tbsp milk
1 tsp vanilla extract
115 g/4 oz butter, melted, plus extra for greasing

Preheat the oven to 180°C/350°F/Gas Mark 4 and grease a 23 x 33-cm/9 x 13-inch rectangular cake tin. Transfer the brownie mix from the jar to a large mixing bowl. Put the eggs, milk and vanilla extract into a separate bowl and mix to combine. Add the egg mixture to the dry ingredients and mix until well combined. Stir in the melted butter and mix to combine.

Transfer the batter to the prepared tin and bake in the preheated oven for about 20 minutes, until the top is dry and a cocktail stick inserted in the centre comes out almost clean. Place the tin on a wire rack and leave to cool completely. Serve at room temperature.

Baked Alaskas

Ingredients

4 tbsp sultanas or raisins

3 tbsp dark rum or ginger wine

4 square slices ginger cake

4 scoops vanilla ice cream or rum and raisin ice cream

3 egg whites

175 g/6 oz granulated sugar or caster sugar

1. Preheat the oven to 230°C/450°F/Gas Mark 8. Mix the sultanas with the rum in a small bowl.

2. Place the cake slices on a baking sheet, spaced well apart, and scatter a tablespoon of the soaked sultanas on each slice.

3. Place a scoop of ice cream in the centre of each slice and place in the freezer.

4. Meanwhile, whisk the egg whites in a clean, grease-free bowl until they hold soft peaks. Gradually whisk the sugar into the egg whites, a tablespoon at a time, until the mixture holds stiff peaks.

5. Remove the ice cream-topped cake slices from the freezer and spoon the meringue over the ice cream. Spread to cover the ice cream completely.

6. Bake in the preheated oven for 5 minutes, or until starting to brown. Serve immediately.

Buttermilk pralines

Ingredients

385 g/13½ oz granulated sugar

55 g/2 oz soft light brown sugar

1 tsp bicarbonate of soda

225 ml/8 fl oz buttermilk

1 tsp vanilla extract

1 tbsp lightly salted butter, plus extra for greasing

200 g/7 oz pecan nut halves

1. Grease a sheet of baking paper and set aside. Grease a large, heavy-based saucepan.

2. Put the granulated sugar, brown sugar, bicarbonate of soda, and buttermilk into the pan and mix to combine. Slowly bring to the boil over a low heat, stirring constantly, until the sugar has dissolved. Cover, increase the heat to medium, and cook for 2–3 minutes to wash down the sugar crystals from the sides of pan. Uncover and continue to cook, stirring occasionally, until a teaspoon of the mixture forms a ball when dropped into cold water.

3. Remove from the heat and add the vanilla extract, butter and nuts. Beat vigorously with a wooden spoon until the mixture is just glossy and beginning to thicken. Working quickly, drop tablespoons of the mixture onto the prepared baking paper, then leave to cool completely.

#313 Espresso truffles

Ingredients

300 g/10½ oz plain chocolate, roughly chopped

2 tbsp double cream

1 tbsp cold strong espresso coffee

2 tbsp coffee liqueur

55 g/2 oz butter, softened and diced

edible gold leaf, to decorate

1. Put 100 g/3½ oz of the chocolate and the cream in a heatproof bowl set over a saucepan of gently simmering water and heat until melted. Remove from the heat, add the espresso, coffee liqueur and butter and whisk for 3–4 minutes, or until thickened. Transfer to an airtight container and chill in the refrigerator for 6–8 hours, or until firm.

2. Line a baking tray with baking paper. Roll teaspoons of the mixture into truffle-sized balls using the palms of your hands. Place on the prepared tray, cover with clingfilm and freeze for 6–8 hours.

3. Put the remaining chocolate in a heatproof bowl set over a saucepan of gently simmering water and heat until melted. Using two forks, dip each truffle into the chocolate to coat evenly. Return to the tray and chill in the refrigerator for 1–2 hours, or until firm. Top each truffle with edible gold leaf.

#314 Share-sized sundae

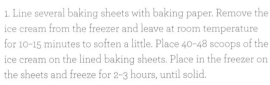

Ingredients

4 litres/7 pints good-quality ice cream

450 ml/15 fl oz double cream

2 bananas

225 g/8 oz strawberries

8 tbsp chocolate dessert sauce

175 g/6 oz ready-made chocolate brownies, cut into small chunks

25 g/1 oz mini marshmallows

115 g/4 oz mixed sweets, such as gummy bears, jelly beans, sugar-coated chocolate drops

6 tbsp raspberry dessert sauce

1–2 tbsp sugar strands

2 tbsp chocolate flakes

few maraschino cherries

1. Line several baking sheets with baking paper. Remove the ice cream from the freezer and leave at room temperature for 10–15 minutes to soften a little. Place 40–48 scoops of the ice cream on the lined baking sheets. Place in the freezer on the sheets and freeze for 2–3 hours, until solid.

2. When you are ready to assemble the sundae, whip the cream until it holds soft peaks. Spoon into a large piping bag fitted with a large star-shaped nozzle.

3. Peel and slice the bananas and hull and halve the strawberries. Warm the chocolate sauce in a bowl set over a saucepan of simmering water for 5–10 minutes.

4. Remove the ice cream from the freezer and pile into the serving bowl together with the fruit, brownies, marshmallows and nearly all the sweets. Drizzle with the raspberry sauce. Pipe rosettes of cream all over the sundae. Scatter over the remaining sweets and the sugar strands. Top with chocolate flakes and maraschino cherries and pour over the chocolate sauce. Serve immediately.

315 Chocolate chip ice cream

Serves
4–6

Ingredients

300 ml/10 fl oz milk

1 vanilla pod

85 g/3 oz caster sugar

3 egg yolks

300 ml/10 fl oz whipping cream

115 g/4 oz milk chocolate, roughly chopped

ice cream cones, to serve

1. Pour the milk into a heavy-based saucepan, add the vanilla pod and bring almost to the boil. Remove from the heat and leave to infuse for 30 minutes.

2. Put the sugar and egg yolks in a large bowl and whisk until pale and the mixture leaves a trail when the whisk is lifted. Remove the vanilla pod from the milk, then slowly add the milk to the sugar mixture, stirring all the time with a wooden spoon. Strain the mixture into the rinsed-out pan and cook over a low heat for 10–15 minutes, stirring all the time, until the mixture thickens enough to coat the back of the wooden spoon. Do not allow it to boil. Remove the custard from the heat, cover and leave to cool for at least 1 hour, stirring occasionally to prevent a skin forming. Meanwhile, whip the cream until it holds its shape. Keep in the refrigerator until ready to use.

3. If using an ice-cream maker, fold the whipped cream into the cold custard, then churn the mixture following the manufacturer's instructions. Just before the ice cream freezes, add the chocolate pieces. Alternatively, freeze the custard in a freezerproof container, uncovered, for 1–2 hours, until beginning to set around the edges. Tip into a bowl and stir with a fork until smooth. Fold in the whipped cream and chocolate pieces. Return to the freezer and freeze for a further 2–3 hours, or until firm. Scoop the ice cream into cones to serve.

316 Blood orange polenta tart

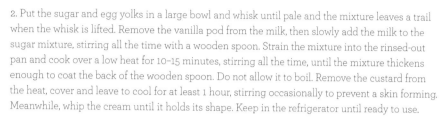

Serves
8

Ingredients

cooking spray

250 g/9 oz cooked polenta

55 g/2 oz soft light brown sugar,
plus 1 tbsp extra

3 blood oranges or small navel oranges

Filling

4 eggs

140 g/5 oz caster sugar

150 ml/5 fl oz orange juice

1 tbsp lemon juice

125 ml/4 fl oz semi-skimmed milk

½ tsp vanilla extract

1 tsp finely grated orange rind

1. Preheat the oven to 180°C/350°F/Gas Mark 4. Spray a 23-cm/9-inch springform tart tin with cooking spray.

2. To make the case, combine the cooked polenta with 55 g/2 oz of the brown sugar in a medium-sized bowl and mix well. Spread the mixture into a thin layer in the prepared tart tin and bake in the preheated oven for about 20 minutes, or until it begins to colour.

3. To make the filling, whisk together the eggs, sugar, orange juice, lemon juice, milk and vanilla extract. Stir in the orange rind, then pour the mixture into the polenta case and smooth level. Bake in the preheated oven for about 15 minutes, or until the filling begins to set.

4. While the tart is baking, slice the oranges into thin rounds using a serrated knife. When the filling is partly set, remove the tart from the oven and arrange the orange slices on top. Sprinkle the remaining tablespoon of brown sugar over the top and return the tart to the oven. Bake for a further 6–8 minutes, or until the filling is mostly set. Remove from the oven and set the tin on a wire rack to cool. Slice the tart into wedges and serve.

317 Honeycomb brittle

Serves
10

Ingredients

oil, for greasing
175 g/6 oz caster sugar
100 g/3½ oz golden syrup
100 g/3½ oz butter, diced
2 tsp bicarbonate of soda

1. Lightly grease a 20-cm/8-inch square baking tin.

2. Put the sugar, syrup and butter into a large, heavy-based saucepan. Heat gently until the sugar has dissolved, tilting the pan to mix the ingredients together. Increase the heat and boil rapidly for 4–5 minutes, or until the mixture turns a light golden colour.

3. Add the bicarbonate of soda and stir for a few seconds. Take care as the mixture will expand and bubble.

4. Pour the mixture into the prepared tin. Leave to cool for 5 minutes, or until set. Break the brittle into shards. Store in an airtight container in a cool, dry place for up to 2 weeks.

318 Cranberry amaretti creams

Makes
10

Ingredients

85 g/3 oz granulated sugar
2 tsp cornflour
large pinch of ground cinnamon
large pinch of ground ginger
125 ml/4 fl oz water
200 g/7 oz frozen cranberries
150 g/5½ oz full-fat soft cheese
3 tbsp caster sugar
200 ml/7 fl oz double cream
4 tsp orange juice or Cointreau
55 g/2 oz amaretti biscuits, crushed

1. Put the granulated sugar, cornflour, cinnamon and ginger into a heavy-based saucepan, then gradually mix in the water until smooth. Add the cranberries and cook for 5–8 minutes, stirring occasionally, until they are soft and the mixture has thickened. Cover and leave to cool.

2. Put the soft cheese and caster sugar into a mixing bowl and stir, then gradually whisk in the cream until smooth. Stir in the orange juice and then the biscuit crumbs. Spoon the mixture into a disposable paper or polythene piping bag. Spoon the cranberry mixture into a separate disposable piping bag. Snip off the tips.

3. Pipe the amaretti cream into 10 shot glasses until they are one-quarter full. Pipe over half the cranberry mixture, then repeat the layers. Cover and chill.

319 Baked apples

Ingredients

4 cooking apples
1 tbsp lemon juice
50 g/1¾ oz blueberries
50 g/1¾ oz raisins
25 g/1 oz mixed nuts, chopped and toasted
½ tsp ground cinnamon
2 tbsp soft light brown sugar
275 ml/9 fl oz red wine
2 tsp cornflour
4 tsp water
double cream, to serve (optional)

1. Preheat the oven to 200°C/400°F/Gas Mark 6. Using a sharp knife, score a line around the centre of each apple. Core the apples, then brush the centres with the lemon juice to prevent discoloration. Transfer them to a small roasting tin.

2. Place the blueberries and raisins in a bowl, then add the nuts, cinnamon and sugar. Mix together well. Pile the mixture into the centres of the apple, then pour over the wine.

3. Transfer the stuffed apples to the preheated oven and bake for 40–45 minutes, or until tender. Remove from the oven, then lift the apples out of the tin, set aside and keep warm.

4. Blend the cornflour with the water, then add the mixture to the cooking juices in the tin. Transfer to the hob and cook over a medium heat, stirring, until thickened. Remove from the heat and pour over the apples. Serve the apples with cream, if using.

320 Lemon buttermilk sorbet

Ingredients

1 tbsp finely grated lemon zest
4 tbsp fresh lemon juice
1 tbsp fresh lime juice
200 g/7 oz caster sugar
500 ml/17 fl oz buttermilk

1. If you are using an ice-cream maker, freeze the insert of your ice-cream maker for at least 24 hours.

2. Combine the lemon zest, lemon juice, lime juice and sugar in a medium-sized bowl and whisk until the sugar is fully dissolved. Add the buttermilk and whisk to combine. Cover and chill in the refrigerator for at least 3–4 hours, or overnight.

3. If you are using an ice-cream maker, transfer the mixture to the frozen insert of your ice-cream maker and churn according to the manufacturer's instructions for about 30–60 minutes, or until firm. Transfer to a freezerproof container, cover and store in the freezer. Alternatively, pour the mixture into a freezerproof container, cover with clingfilm and freeze for about 2 hours, or until it has begun to harden around the edges. Beat until smooth to get rid of any ice crystals. Freeze again, repeat the process twice, then freeze until completely firm.

4. Serve straight from the freezer.

Makes
6

Zebra puddings with hot chocolate fudge sauce

Ingredients

125 ml/4 fl oz vegetable oil, plus extra for greasing

125 g/4½ oz caster sugar

4 tbsp milk

2 eggs, beaten

150 g/5½ oz self-raising flour, sifted, plus extra for dusting

½ tsp baking powder

15 g/½ oz cocoa powder, sifted

Sauce

300 ml/10 fl oz double cream

200 g/7 oz plain chocolate, chopped

1 tbsp golden syrup

25 g/1 oz butter

1. Lightly grease 6 x 175-ml/6-fl oz dariole moulds or ramekin dishes and dust with flour. Preheat the oven to 180°C/350°F/Gas Mark 4.

2. Place the oil, sugar, milk and eggs in a mixing bowl and gently whisk to combine. Divide the mixture between two bowls.

3. Add 100 g/3½ oz of the flour to one bowl together with half the baking powder and fold to combine. Add the remaining flour and baking powder together with the cocoa to the other bowl and mix well. Make sure that both mixtures have the same consistency; pourable but not runny. If they need to be looser, add a little more milk.

4. Begin to build the sponge mixtures in the moulds. Pour a little of the vanilla mixture into each of the moulds to cover the base. Pour a little of the chocolate mixture into the centre of each, then repeat with the vanilla mix. Alternate and repeat until all the mixture has been used, always pouring into the centre to form a 'zebra' pattern. Place the moulds on a baking tray and bake in the preheated oven for 20–25 minutes, until well risen and a skewer inserted in the middle of the cakes comes out clean. Leave in the moulds until ready to serve.

5. To make the sauce, heat the cream in a saucepan until just below boiling point. Stir in the chocolate, golden syrup and butter, and mix gently until the chocolate has melted and combined with the other ingredients. The sauce should be smooth and glossy.

6. Pour the sauce over the warm puddings and serve immediately.

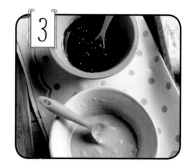
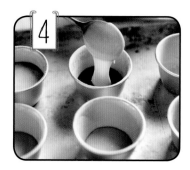

322 Mini toffee apples

Ingredients

3 large red apples

juice of 1 lemon

100 g/3½ oz caster sugar

175 ml/6 fl oz water

15 g/½ oz butter

a few drops of red food colouring

12 lollipop sticks

1. Put a bowl of iced water in the refrigerator. Use a melon scoop to scoop out 12 balls from the apples, making sure each ball has some red skin on it. Push a lollipop stick into each ball through the red skin. Squeeze over the lemon juice to prevent discoloration and set aside.

2. Put the sugar, water and butter into a heavy-based saucepan. Gently heat until the sugar has dissolved, tilting the pan to mix the ingredients together. Increase the heat and boil rapidly for 12–15 minutes until the mixture reaches 160°C/320°F on a sugar thermometer and is deep golden. Remove from the heat, stir in the food colouring and allow the bubbles to subside.

3. Remove the bowl of iced water from the refrigerator. Working as quickly as possible, dip the apples into the toffee one at a time, rotating them a few times to get an even coating, then drop them into the iced water for 30 seconds. Serve immediately.

323 Champagne sorbet

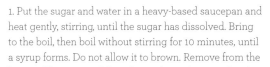

Ingredients

225 g/8 oz caster sugar

300 ml/10 fl oz water

½ bottle pink or white champagne or sparkling wine

juice of ½ lemon

1 egg white

1. Put the sugar and water in a heavy-based saucepan and heat gently, stirring, until the sugar has dissolved. Bring to the boil, then boil without stirring for 10 minutes, until a syrup forms. Do not allow it to brown. Remove from the heat and leave to cool for at least 1 hour, then stir the champagne and lemon juice into the syrup.

2. If using an ice-cream maker, churn the mixture following the manufacturer's instructions. When the mixture begins to freeze, whisk the egg white until stiff but not dry, then add to the mixture and continue churning. Alternatively, freeze in a freezerproof container, uncovered, for 3–4 hours, or until mushy. Turn the mixture into a bowl and stir with a fork until smooth. Lightly whisk the egg white until it holds stiff peaks, then fold into the mixture. Return to the container and freeze for a further 3–4 hours, or until firm.

3. To store, cover the container with a suitable lid. Remove the sorbet from the freezer and place in the refrigerator for 15–20 minutes before serving.

324 Mojito pops

Makes
8

Ingredients

juice of 6 limes

600 ml/1 pint chilled soda water

50 g/1¾ oz fresh mint leaves

3 limes, cut into wedges

100 g/3½ oz caster sugar

2 tbsp white rum

8 ice pop moulds

8 ice pop sticks

1. Put the lime juice and soda water into a measuring jug and stir together well.

2. Stir in the mint leaves, lime wedges, sugar and rum. Using a 'muddler' or thick wooden spoon or mallet, mash together all the ingredients until well blended.

3. Pour the mixture into 8 x 100-ml/3½-fl oz ice pop moulds. Divide the lime wedges and mint leaves evenly between them. Insert the ice pop sticks and freeze for 10–12 hours, or until firm.

4. To unmould the ice pops, dip the frozen moulds in warm water for a few seconds and gently release the pops while holding the sticks.

325 Grilled stone fruit

Serves
6

Ingredients

375 g/13 oz low-fat ricotta cheese

2 tsp freshly grated orange rind

3 firm, ripe peaches, stoned and quartered

3 firm, ripe nectarines, stoned and quartered

3 ripe plums, apricots or figs, stoned and halved or quartered

2 tbsp orange blossom honey

2 tbsp flaked almonds

1. In a medium-sized bowl, stir together the ricotta cheese and orange rind.

2. Preheat the grill to medium-high and grill the fruit, cut-side down, turning once or twice, for about 5 minutes, or until they are softened and beginning to caramelize.

3. To serve, spoon the ricotta into six small glasses or dessert bowls. Top each with some grilled fruit, drizzle with the honey and sprinkle the almonds over the top. Serve immediately.

#326 Toffee popcorn

Ingredients

25 g/1 oz butter

55 g/2 oz popping corn

Coating

40 g/1½ oz butter

55 g/2 oz soft dark brown sugar

2 tbsp golden syrup

1. Melt the butter in a large, heavy-based saucepan. Sprinkle in the corn and swirl the pan to coat the corn evenly.

2. Cover the pan with a tight-fitting lid, reduce the heat to low and leave the corn to pop. Shake the pan a couple of times to move the unpopped pieces to the bottom. As soon as the popping stops, remove from the heat and leave to stand, covered.

3. To make the coating, melt the butter in a heavy-based saucepan. Add the sugar and syrup and cook over a high heat, stirring constantly, for 1-2 minutes, or until the sugar has dissolved.

4. Pour the coating over the popped corn, cover the pan and shake well. Leave to cool slightly, then serve.

#327 Indulgent whisky fudge

Ingredients

oil, for greasing

250 g/9 oz soft light brown sugar

100 g/3½ oz butter, diced

400 g/14 oz canned sweetened condensed milk

2 tbsp glucose syrup

150 g/5½ oz plain chocolate, roughly chopped

60 ml/2 fl oz Scotch whisky

25 g/1 oz walnut pieces

1. Lightly grease a 20-cm/8-inch square baking tin. Line it with baking paper, snipping diagonally into the corners, then pressing the paper into the tin so that the base and sides are lined.

2. Put the sugar, butter, condensed milk and glucose into a heavy-based saucepan. Heat gently, stirring, until the sugar has dissolved.

3. Increase the heat and boil for 12–15 minutes, or until the mixture reaches 116°C/240°F on a sugar thermometer. As the temperature rises, stir the fudge occasionally so the sugar doesn't stick and burn. Remove the fudge from the heat. Add the chocolate and whisky and stir until the chocolate has melted and the mixture is smooth.

4. Preheat the grill to medium–hot. Put the walnuts on a baking tray and toast them under the grill for 2–3 minutes, or until brown, then roughly chop.

5. Pour the mixture into the prepared tin, smooth the surface with a spatula and sprinkle over the walnuts. Leave to cool for 1 hour. Cover with clingfilm, then chill in the refrigerator for 1–2 hours, or until firm. Lift the fudge out of the tin, peel off the paper and cut into 16 small squares.

328 Chocolate mint swirls

Ingredients

300 ml/10 fl oz double cream

150 g/5½ oz mascarpone cheese

2 tbsp icing sugar

1 tbsp crème de menthe

175 g/6 oz plain chocolate, broken, plus extra to decorate

1. Place the cream in a large mixing bowl and whip until it holds soft peaks. Fold in the mascarpone cheese and icing sugar, then place about one third of the mixture in a smaller bowl. Stir the crème de menthe into the smaller bowl.

2. Put the plain chocolate in a heatproof bowl set over a saucepan of gently simmering water until melted. Stir the melted chocolate into the remaining mascarpone mixture.

3. Place alternate tablespoons of the two mixtures into six serving glasses, then swirl the mixture together to give a decorative effect. Chill until required.

4. To make the piped chocolate decorations, melt a small amount of chocolate and place in a paper piping bag. Place a sheet of greaseproof paper on a cutting board and pipe squiggles, stars or flower shapes onto it with the melted chocolate. Alternatively, to make curved decorations, pipe decorations onto a long strip of baking paper, then carefully place the strip over a rolling pin securing with sticky tape. Let the chocolate set, then carefully remove from the baking paper.

5. Decorate each dessert with the piped chocolate decorations and serve. The desserts can be decorated and then chilled, if preferred.

329 Refrigerator cookies

Ingredients

325 g/11½ oz plain flour

2 tbsp cocoa powder

½ tsp bicarbonate of soda

1 tsp ground ginger

½ tsp ground cinnamon

125 ml/4 fl oz treacle

4 tbsp boiling water

115 g/4 oz butter, softened

4 tbsp caster sugar

icing sugar, for dusting

1. Sift together the flour, cocoa powder, bicarbonate of soda, ginger and cinnamon into a bowl, then set aside. Mix the treacle with the water and set aside.

2. Put the butter into a large bowl and beat with an electric hand-held mixer until creamy. Slowly add the caster sugar and continue beating until light and fluffy. Gradually add the flour mixture, alternating it with the treacle mixture to form a soft dough. Scrape equal amounts of the dough onto two pieces of clingfilm and roll into logs, each about 19 cm/7½ inches long and 4 cm/1½ inches thick. Chill in the refrigerator for 2 hours, then transfer to the freezer for at least 2 hours.

3. Preheat the oven to 180°C/350°F/Gas Mark 4 and line one or two baking sheets with baking paper. Unwrap the logs and cut into 5-mm/¼-inch slices and place on the prepared baking sheets. Bake in the preheated oven for 12 minutes. Remove from the oven, leave to cool on the sheets for 3 minutes, then transfer to wire racks, dust with icing sugar and leave to cool completely.

#330 Giant frosted cupcake

Serves
12–14

Ingredients

200 g/7 oz self-raising flour,
plus extra for dusting

200 g/7 oz plain flour

350 g/12 oz butter, softened,
plus extra for greasing

350 g/12 oz caster sugar

6 large eggs

2 tbsp milk

Filling & topping

200 g/7 oz unsalted butter, softened

400 g/14 oz icing sugar, plus extra for
dusting

1 tsp vanilla extract

2 tbsp apricot jam, warmed and strained

500 g /1 lb 2 oz pink ready-to-roll
fondant icing

1 glacé cherry

pink and red sugar-coated chocolate drops

1. Preheat the oven to 160°C/325°F/Gas Mark 3. Thoroughly grease both halves of a giant cupcake mould with butter, then lightly dust with flour, tipping out any excess. Place on a baking sheet and set aside.

2. Sift the self-raising flour and plain flour into a large bowl and add the remaining ingredients. Beat with an electric hand-held mixer until pale and creamy. Divide the mixture between the prepared moulds, making a slight dip in the centre of each. Bake in the preheated oven for 1 hour 20 minutes, or until risen, golden and a skewer inserted into each cake comes out clean. Remove the top cake from the oven, and bake the base cake for a further 10 minutes. Remove the base cake from the oven, leave both cakes in the moulds for 10–15 minutes, then carefully turn out onto a wire rack and leave to cool completely.

3. Meanwhile, to make the filling and topping, place the butter in a large bowl and beat until pale. Gradually beat in the icing sugar and vanilla extract, beating constantly until pale and creamy.

4. Trim the top of each cake to give a level surface. Place the base cake upside down on a board and brush all over with the jam. Roll out the fondant icing on a surface dusted with icing sugar to a 28-cm/11-inch round. Drape the icing over the base cake, smoothing the sides. Carefully lift the cake and place it upright on a cake board. Fold the edges of the fondant over the top of the cake, trimming any excess. Spread a layer of the buttercream filling over the top of the base cake, then spoon the remainder into a large piping bag. Position the top cake firmly on the base cake. Pipe the buttercream all over the top cake, working in one continuous swirl from the base to the top, then smooth. Top with a glacé cherry and sugar-coated chocolate drops.

Brownie sundae

Serves
6

Ingredients

175 g/6 oz plain chocolate, broken into pieces

175 g/6 oz butter, plus extra for greasing

175 g/6 oz soft light brown sugar

3 eggs, beaten

115 g/4 oz self-raising flour

6 large scoops of vanilla ice cream, to serve

6 fresh cherries or maraschino cherries

1 tbsp pecan nuts, chopped, to decorate

Sauce

55 g/2 oz plain chocolate, broken into pieces

55 g/2 oz soft light brown sugar

55 g/2 oz butter

3 tbsp milk

1. Preheat the oven to 180°C/350°F/Gas Mark 4. Grease a 20-cm/8-inch square cake tin and line with baking paper.

2. Place the chocolate and butter in a large, heatproof bowl set over a saucepan of simmering water and heat until melted. Leave to cool for 5 minutes, then whisk in the sugar and eggs. Sift in the flour and fold in. Pour the mixture into the prepared tin and bake in the preheated oven for 35–40 minutes, or until risen and just firm to the touch. Leave to cool in the tin for 15 minutes, then turn out onto a wire rack to cool completely.

3. To make the sauce, place all the ingredients in a saucepan and heat gently, stirring constantly, until melted. Bring to the boil and bubble for 1 minute. Remove from the heat and leave to cool.

4. To serve, cut the brownie into six rectangles, place each one on a serving plate and top with a large scoop of ice cream. Spoon over the warm sauce and decorate with the cherries and chopped pecan nuts.

332 Mango & rice tart

Serves
12

Ingredients

200 g/7 oz jasmine rice

140 g/5 oz granulated sugar

350 ml/12 fl oz water

100 ml/3½ fl oz coconut milk

1 tsp salt

2–3 ripe mangos, peeled and thinly sliced

Pastry

200 g/7 oz plain flour, plus extra for dusting

75 g/2¾ oz caster sugar

1 tsp vanilla extract

2 egg yolks

100 g/3½ oz butter, diced, plus extra for greasing

2 tbsp water

1. To make the pastry, sift together the flour and sugar into a large bowl and add the vanilla extract and egg yolks. Add the butter and water and knead until a dough forms. Turn out onto a lightly floured surface and knead until smooth. Wrap in clingfilm and chill in the refrigerator for 1 hour.

2. Preheat the oven to 180°C/350°F/Gas Mark 4. Grease a 26-cm/10½-inch round, fluted tart tin. Roll out the dough on a lightly floured surface and ease it into the prepared tin. Line with baking paper, fill with baking beans and bake in the preheated oven for 12 minutes. Take out of the oven, remove the paper and beans and return to the oven for a further 10 minutes. Remove from the oven and leave to cool.

3. Meanwhile, place the rice in a saucepan of boiling water and cook for 10–12 minutes until soft. Drain and set aside, covered, and keep warm. Put the sugar and water into a saucepan and heat until a syrup forms. Pour into a baking tray and stir in the coconut milk and salt. Add the hot rice to the coconut mixture – this will cause the mixture to become quite liquid. Leave in the tray for about 3 hours to absorb the coconut milk. Pour the rice mixture into the pastry case and spread evenly. Arrange the sliced mangos decoratively on top of the tart and chill in the refrigerator until ready to serve.

#333 Lemon & white chocolate creams

Makes 12

Ingredients

300 g/10½ oz white chocolate, roughly chopped

2 tbsp double cream

finely grated rind of 1 lemon

2 tbsp limoncello

55 g/2 oz butter, softened and diced

25 g/1 oz pistachio nuts, finely chopped

1. Put 100 g/3½ oz chocolate and all of the cream in a heatproof bowl set over a saucepan of gently simmering water and heat until melted. Remove from the heat, add the lemon rind, limoncello and butter, and whisk for 3–4 minutes, or until thickened. Transfer to an airtight container and chill in the refrigerator for 6–8 hours, or until firm.

2. Line a baking tray with baking paper. Scoop teaspoons of the mixture and roll them into truffle-sized balls with the palms of your hands Place the balls on the prepared tray, cover with clingfilm and freeze for 6–8 hours.

3. Put the remaining chocolate in a heatproof bowl set over a saucepan of gently simmering water and heat until melted. Using two forks, dip each truffle into the chocolate to coat evenly. Return to the tray, sprinkle over the nuts and chill in the refrigerator for 1–2 hours, or until firm.

#334 S'mores doughnuts

Makes 12

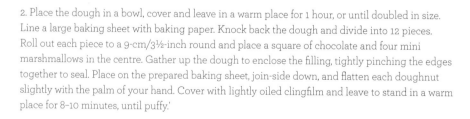

Ingredients

150 ml/5 fl oz milk

25 g/1 oz white vegetable fat

300 g/10½ oz strong white flour, plus extra for dusting and kneading

¼ tsp salt

1½ tsp easy-blend dried yeast

2 tbsp caster sugar

1 large egg, beaten

12 small squares plain chocolate

48 mini white marshmallows

oil, for deep-frying and oiling

55 g/2 oz icing sugar, sifted

2 tbsp water

biscuit crumbs, to decorate

1. Put the milk and vegetable fat into a small saucepan over a low heat and heat until the fat has melted. Leave to cool for 5 minutes. Sift the flour into a large bowl and stir in the salt, yeast and sugar. Pour in the milk mixture and the egg, and mix to a soft dough. Turn out the dough onto a floured surface and knead for 5–6 minutes until smooth and elastic, adding a little more flour if needed.

2. Place the dough in a bowl, cover and leave in a warm place for 1 hour, or until doubled in size. Line a large baking sheet with baking paper. Knock back the dough and divide into 12 pieces. Roll out each piece to a 9-cm/3½-inch round and place a square of chocolate and four mini marshmallows in the centre. Gather up the dough to enclose the filling, tightly pinching the edges together to seal. Place on the prepared baking sheet, join-side down, and flatten each doughnut slightly with the palm of your hand. Cover with lightly oiled clingfilm and leave to stand in a warm place for 8–10 minutes, until puffy.'

3. Heat enough oil for deep-frying in a large saucepan or deep-fryer to 180–190°C/350–375°F, or until a cube of bread browns in 30 seconds. Add the doughnuts, three at a time, and fry for 1–2 minutes on each side until golden. Remove and drain on kitchen paper.

4. Put the icing sugar and water into a bowl and beat together until smooth. Dip the top of each warm doughnut in the mixture to glaze. Sprinkle over the biscuit crumbs and leave to set.

335 Choc berry rockets

Ingredients

400 g/14 oz raspberries

2 tbsp lemon juice

250 ml/9 fl oz sugar syrup

250 g/9 oz plain chocolate, roughly chopped

100 g/3½ oz hundreds and thousands

8 ice pop moulds

8 ice pop sticks

1. Put the raspberries, lemon juice and sugar syrup in a blender and process until puréed. Pass through a fine metal sieve. Pour into 8 x 100-ml/3½-fl oz ice pop moulds. Insert the ice pop sticks and freeze for 3–4 hours, or until firm.

2. When the raspberry mixture is frozen, line a baking sheet with baking paper. To unmould the ice pops, dip the frozen moulds in warm water for a few seconds and gently release the pops while holding the sticks. Place them on the prepared baking sheet and return to the freezer for 1–2 hours.

3. Put the chocolate in a heatproof bowl set over a saucepan of gently simmering water and heat until melted. Remove from the heat and leave to cool slightly.

4. Tip the hundreds and thousands onto baking paper. Dip each ice pop into the melted chocolate so it is covered to about halfway up, then roll it in the hundreds and thousands. Return to the prepared baking sheet and freeze for 10–20 minutes, or until ready to serve.

336 Cupcake shooters

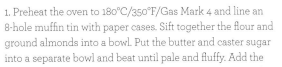

Ingredients

150 g/5½ oz self-raising flour

55 g/2 oz ground almonds

175 g/6 oz butter, softened

175 g/6 oz caster sugar

1 tsp vanilla extract

3 eggs, lightly beaten

Frosting

115 g/4 oz butter, softened

175 g/6 oz icing sugar, plus extra if needed

1 tbsp double cream

1. Preheat the oven to 180°C/350°F/Gas Mark 4 and line an 8-hole muffin tin with paper cases. Sift together the flour and ground almonds into a bowl. Put the butter and caster sugar into a separate bowl and beat until pale and fluffy. Add the vanilla extract, then add the eggs, one at a time, beating after each addition. Add half the flour mixture and beat until incorporated. Add the remaining flour mixture and mix. Spoon the mixture into the paper cases and bake in the preheated oven for 20 minutes until risen and golden. Leave to cool in the tin for 1–2 minutes, then transfer to a wire rack to cool completely.

2. To make the frosting, put all the ingredients into a bowl and beat until well combined. Add more icing sugar, if necessary, to achieve a piping consistency. Transfer the frosting to a piping bag fitted with a small star-shaped nozzle.

3. Crumble the cooled cupcakes into a bowl. Transfer to 16 clear shot glasses, filling each glass three-quarters full. Pipe the frosting onto the cake crumbs and serve.

#337 Mango sorbet

Serves
4–6

Ingredients

2 large, ripe mangoes, peeled, stoned and chopped, juice reserved, plus extra slices to decorate

juice of 1 lemon

pinch of salt

115 g/4 oz caster sugar

3 tbsp water

1. Put the mango flesh into a food processor or blender. Add the mango juice, lemon juice and salt and process until smooth. Pass through a nylon sieve into a bowl.

2. Put the sugar and water in a heavy-based saucepan and gently heat, stirring, until the sugar has dissolved. Bring to the boil, then boil without stirring, for 10 minutes to form a syrup. Do not allow it to brown. Remove from the heat and leave to cool slightly. Stir the purée into the syrup. Chill in the refrigerator for 2 hours, or until cold.

3. Freeze in a freezerproof container, uncovered, for 3–4 hours, or until mushy. Turn the mixture into a bowl and stir with a fork until smooth. Return to the container and freeze for a further 3–4 hours, or until firm. To store, cover the container with a suitable lid. Transfer to the refrigerator for 15–20 minutes before serving. Serve decorated with the mango slices.

#338 Vanilla cake pops

Makes
24

Ingredients

450 g/1 lb ready-made vanilla sponge cake

85 g/3 oz mascarpone cheese

70 g/2½ oz icing sugar

½ tsp vanilla extract

Decoration

225 g/8 oz milk chocolate, roughly chopped

150 g/5½ oz fondant icing sugar

pink food colouring

4 tsp cold water

24 sugar-coated chocolate drops

sugar sprinkles

24 lollipop sticks

1. Line a baking sheet with baking paper. Crumble the cake into a mixing bowl. Add the mascarpone cheese, icing sugar and vanilla extract, and mix to a thick paste.

2. Roll a 25 g/1 oz piece of the paste into a ball. Push into a mini paper case, pressing it down so that when it is removed from the case you have a mini cupcake shape. Shape the remaining 23 cake pops in the same way. Place on the baking sheet and chill for 1–2 hours to firm up.

3. Put the chocolate in a heatproof bowl set over a saucepan of gently simmering water and heat until melted. Remove from the heat. Push a lollipop stick into each cake pop. Dip each cake pop into the chocolate, turning to coat. Lift it from the bowl, allowing the excess to drip back into the bowl, then place it in a cup or tumbler. Repeat with the remaining cake pops. Chill or leave in a cool place until the chocolate has set.

4. Put the fondant icing sugar in a mixing bowl and beat in a dash of pink food colouring and the water until smooth. The icing should almost hold its shape. Spoon a little onto a cake pop, easing it slightly down the sides with a teaspoon. If the icing is too firm you might need to add a dash more water. Before the icing sets, place a sugar-coated chocolate drop in the centre of each cake pop and scatter with sugar sprinkles.

#339 Orange panna cotta in a jar

Makes 6

Ingredients

3 tbsp freshly squeezed orange juice

2¼ tsp powdered gelatine

1 litre/1¾ pints milk

100 g/3½ oz caster sugar

1 tsp vanilla extract

2 tsp grated orange rind

Compote

225 g/8 oz fresh or frozen blackberries

4 tbsp water

50 g/1¾ oz caster sugar

2 tbsp lemon juice

6 x 225 ml/8-fl oz wide-mouthed preserving jars, sterilized

1. Put the orange juice into a small bowl and sprinkle over the gelatine. Set aside until the gelatine has absorbed the liquid.

2. Put the milk, sugar and vanilla extract into a saucepan over a medium–high heat and bring to a simmer, stirring to incorporate the sugar. Remove from the heat and stir in the orange rind and the gelatine mixture. Whisk until the gelatine is fully dissolved. Divide the mixture between the jars. Leave to cool to room temperature, then seal the jars with their lids and refrigerate for at least 4 hours, until set.

3. To make the compote, put the ingredients into a saucepan over a medium-high heat and stir to combine. Bring to the boil, then reduce the heat to medium–low and simmer until the sugar is dissolved, the liquid is beginning to thicken and the fruit is beginning to break down. Remove from the heat and leave to cool to room temperature.

4. Remove the lids from the jars of panna cotta, spoon the blackberry compote over the tops and serve immediately.

#340 Real hot chocolate

Serves 2

Ingredients

40 g/1½ oz plain chocolate, broken into pieces

300 ml/10 fl oz milk

chocolate curls, to decorate

1. Place the chocolate in a large, heatproof jug. Place the milk in a heavy-based saucepan and bring to the boil. Pour about one quarter of the milk onto the chocolate and leave until the chocolate is soft.

2. Whisk the milk and chocolate mixture until smooth. Return the remaining milk to the heat and bring back to the boil, then pour onto the chocolate, whisking constantly.

3. Pour into warmed mugs or cups and decorate with chocolate curls. Serve immediately.

Popcorn marshmallow bars with cranberries

Ingredients

70 g/2½ oz soft light brown sugar

50 g/1¾ oz butter

25 g/1 oz golden syrup

50 g/1¾ oz sweet and salty or plain popcorn

50 g/1¾ oz dried cranberries

50 g/1¾ oz mini marshmallows

1. Line a 20-cm/8-inch square cake tin with baking paper.

2. Place the sugar, butter and golden syrup in a medium-sized saucepan and gently heat until the contents have melted. Remove from the heat.

3. Stir in the remaining ingredients and mix well. Tip into the prepared tin and firmly press down with the back of a spoon.

4. Leave to set in the refrigerator or in a cool place for about 1 hour.

5. Cut into 10 equal-sized bars and serve.

#342 Spiced plum pops

Ingredients

400 g/14 oz ripe plums, peeled, halved, stoned and sliced

1 tsp ground cinnamon

pinch of ground cloves

pinch of ground star anise

75 g/2¾ oz caster sugar

100 ml/3½ fl oz water

juice of 1 orange

8 cinnamon sticks

8 ice pop moulds

1. Put the plums, ground cinnamon, cloves, star anise, sugar and water in a saucepan. Place over a medium–high heat, stirring, for 6–8 minutes, or until the sugar has dissolved. Increase the heat to high until the mixture comes to the boil, then reduce the heat to medium and simmer for 4–5 minutes, stirring occasionally.

2. Transfer the mixture to a blender, add the orange juice, then process until puréed. Leave to cool completely, then pour into 8 x 50-ml/2-fl oz ice pop moulds. Insert the cinnamon sticks and freeze for 5 hours, or until firm.

3. To unmould the ice pops, dip the frozen moulds in warm water for a few seconds and gently release the pops while holding the cinnamon sticks.

#343 Mint chocolate bark

Ingredients

oil, for greasing

350 g/12 oz plain chocolate, broken into pieces

300 g/10½ oz white chocolate, broken into pieces

1½ tsp peppermint extract

1 tsp green food colouring

1. Lightly oil a 33 x 23-cm/13 x 9-inch Swiss roll tin and line the base and sides with baking paper. Put the plain chocolate in a heatproof bowl set over a saucepan of gently simmering water and heat until melted. Remove from the heat and stir until smooth. Set aside 4 tablespoons in a small, heatproof bowl.

2. Pour the remaining melted chocolate into the prepared tin and gently level the surface with a palette knife. Firmly tap the tin on a work surface to remove any air bubbles. Leave to stand for 15 minutes, or until cool, then chill in the refrigerator for 30–40 minutes, or until firmly set.

3. Put the white chocolate into a separate heatproof bowl set over a saucepan of gently simmering water and heat until melted. Remove from the heat, leave to cool for 5–10 minutes, then beat in the peppermint extract and food colouring. The chocolate will start to thicken, but continue beating for 1–2 minutes, until it becomes a smooth and spreadable consistency.

4. Spoon the mint-flavoured chocolate over the set chocolate and spread quickly with a palette knife. If necessary, re-melt the reserved plain chocolate by placing the bowl over a saucepan of gently simmering water. Drizzle it over the mint chocolate layer and lightly drag a fork through the chocolate to create a swirled effect. Chill in the refrigerator for a further 40–50 minutes, or until the bark is firmly set. Remove from the tin, peel off the paper and break into chunks to serve.

#344 Cola cupcakes

Makes 12

Ingredients

190 g/6¾ oz plain flour
1½ tsp baking powder
¼ tsp salt
115 g/4 oz butter, softened
150 g/5½ oz caster sugar
100 g/3½ oz soft dark brown sugar
1 tsp vanilla extract
2 large eggs
125 ml/4 fl oz cola syrup
4 tbsp soured cream

Frosting

115 g/4 oz butter
200 g/7 oz soft dark brown sugar
6 tbsp double cream
½ tsp salt
190 g/6¾ oz icing sugar, plus extra if needed

1. Preheat the oven to 180°C/350°F/Gas Mark 4 and line a 12-hole muffin tin with paper cases.

2. Sift together the flour, baking powder and salt in a bowl. Put the butter, caster sugar and brown sugar into a separate bowl and beat until pale and fluffy. Add the vanilla extract, then add the eggs, one at a time, beating after each addition. Add half of the flour mixture, the cola syrup and soured cream, and beat until well combined. Add the remaining flour mixture and mix to combine.

3. Spoon the mixture into the paper cases and bake in the preheated oven for 20 minutes, until risen and a cocktail stick inserted in the centre of a cupcake comes out clean. Leave to cool in the tin for 1–2 minutes, then transfer to a wire rack to cool completely.

4. To make the frosting, put the butter into a small saucepan over a medium heat and heat until melted. Add the brown sugar, cream and salt and cook, stirring constantly, for 4 minutes, or until the sugar has dissolved completely. Remove from the heat and set aside to cool for 30 minutes.

5. Transfer the caramel sauce to a bowl and beat in the icing sugar. Add more icing sugar, if necessary, to achieve a piping consistency. Transfer to a piping bag fitted with a star-shaped nozzle and pipe onto the cupcakes.

#345 Banana puddings

Serves 4

Ingredients

40 g/1½ oz butter, softened, plus extra for greasing
40 g/1½ oz caster sugar
1 egg white, lightly beaten
40 g/1½ oz self-raising flour, sifted
450 ml/15 fl oz double cream
1 tsp vanilla extract
150 ml/5 fl oz fresh custard
2 bananas
2 tsp lemon juice
2 tbsp demerara sugar

1. Preheat the oven to 220°C/425°F/Gas Mark 7. Grease two large baking sheets. Put the butter and caster sugar into a bowl and beat until pale and creamy. Gradually beat in the egg white, then fold in the flour. Drop about 30 tiny spoonfuls of the mixture onto the prepared baking sheets, spaced well apart. Bake in the preheated oven for 4–5 minutes, or until deep golden brown around the edges. Loosen the biscuits from the baking sheets with a palette knife, transfer to a wire rack and leave to cool completely.

2. Put the cream into a bowl with the vanilla extract and whip until it holds firm peaks. Fold in the custard. Thinly slice the bananas and toss them in the lemon juice.

3. To assemble the puddings, layer almost all the biscuits with the vanilla cream and bananas in four individual serving glasses. Crush the remaining biscuits, mix with the demerara sugar and sprinkle over the top of the puddings. Chill for 1 hour before serving.

#346 Layered nectarine creams

Serves 4

Ingredients

4 nectarines, peeled, stoned and sliced

2 tbsp amaretto liqueur

175 g/6 oz curd cheese

300 g/10½ oz peach-flavoured yogurt

1. Reserve a few nectarine slices for decoration. Put the remainder in a bowl, add the liqueur and gently toss, then set aside.

2. Beat together the cheese and yogurt in a separate bowl until thoroughly combined. Spoon half the mixture into four tall glasses. Divide the nectarine and liqueur mixture between them and top with the remaining cheese and yogurt mixture.

3. Decorate with the reserved nectarine slices and leave to chill in the refrigerator for at least 30 minutes before serving.

#347 Chocolate & peanut butter balls

Makes 36

Ingredients

250 g/9 oz smooth peanut butter

55 g/2 oz butter

20 g/¾ oz puffed rice cereal

200 g/7 oz icing sugar

200 g/7 oz plain chocolate, roughly chopped

1. Line two baking trays with baking paper. Put the peanut butter and butter in a heavy-based saucepan and heat until melted.

2. Put the rice cereal and icing sugar into a large mixing bowl. Pour in the melted butter mixture, then stir. When cool enough to handle, roll the mixture into 2.5-cm/1-inch balls with the palms of your hands, then put them on the prepared baking trays and chill in the refrigerator for 3–4 hours, or until firm.

3. Put the chocolate in a heatproof bowl set over a saucepan of gently simmering water and heat until melted.

4. Use a teaspoon to dip the balls in the chocolate, one at a time, making sure they are covered completely, then lift them out and return them to the trays. Chill in the refrigerator for 1–2 hours, or until set. Serve or store in an airtight container in the refrigerator for up to 5 days.

Fortune cookies

Makes
20

Ingredients

2 egg whites

½ tsp vanilla extract or 1 vanilla pod, scraped

½ tsp almond extract

3 tbsp vegetable oil

125 g/4½ oz plain flour

1½ tsp cornflour

pinch of salt

125 g/4½ oz caster sugar

3 tsp water

1. Write down fortunes or sayings on small strips of paper. Preheat the oven to 180°C/350°F/Gas Mark 4 and line a large baking tray with baking paper.

2. Mix all the ingredients together in a large bowl. Using a wooden spoon, drop 20 mounds of mixture onto the prepared baking tray, spaced well apart. Bake in the preheated oven for 10–15 minutes.

3. As soon as you remove the cookies from the oven, place a paper strip in the centre of each one, then fold the cookie over the handle of a wooden spoon. Place each folded cookie on the rim of a bowl and press the edges together on either side of the bowl to make the traditional fortune cookie fold. Transfer to a wire rack and leave to cool completely.

349 Hot pecan brownie cupcakes

Makes
6

Ingredients

115 g/4 oz butter, plus extra for greasing

115 g/4 oz plain chocolate, broken into pieces

2 eggs

115 g/4 oz soft light brown sugar

3 tbsp maple syrup

115 g/4 oz plain flour, sifted

55 g/2 oz pecan nuts, chopped

crème fraîche, to serve

1. Preheat the oven to 180°C/350°F/Gas Mark 4. Grease 6 x 150-ml/5-fl oz ovenproof teacups or ramekins.

2. Put the chocolate and butter into a heatproof bowl set over a saucepan of gently simmering water and heat until melted. Leave to cool for 5 minutes.

3. Put the eggs, sugar and maple syrup in a bowl and whisk together until well blended. Whisk in the chocolate mixture, then fold in the flour and two thirds of the nuts. Pour the mixture into the cups and scatter over the remaining nuts.

4. Put the cups on a baking sheet and bake in the preheated oven for 25–30 minutes, or until the cupcakes are risen and crisp on top but still feel slightly wobbly if lightly pressed. Serve hot, topped with a spoonful of crème fraîche.

#350 Choc chip cookie sundae push pops

Makes
10

Ingredients

85 g/3 oz butter, softened, plus extra
for greasing

70 g/2½ oz caster sugar

1 egg yolk

115 g/4 oz plain flour, plus extra for dusting

1 tbsp cocoa powder

2 tbsp chocolate chips

400 ml/14 fl oz double cream

1 tbsp chocolate sugar strands

10 fresh cherries, stalks on

Sauce

85 g/3 oz plain chocolate, broken
into pieces

25 g/1 oz butter

1 tbsp golden syrup

10 push pop containers

1. Put the butter and sugar into a large bowl and beat together until pale and creamy. Beat in the egg yolk, then sift in the flour and cocoa powder and mix to a rough dough. Gather together with your hands and knead lightly on a floured surface until smooth. Divide the dough into two pieces and roll each piece into a 14-cm/5½-inch long log. Wrap each log in clingfilm and chill in the refrigerator for 45 minutes.

2. Preheat the oven to 180°C/350°F/Gas Mark 4. Lightly grease two baking sheets. Slice each log into 20 rounds and place on the prepared baking sheets. Top each cookie with 2-3 chocolate chips. Bake in the preheated oven for 12-14 minutes until just set. Transfer to a wire rack and leave to cool completely.

3. To make the sauce, put the chocolate, butter and golden syrup into a heatproof bowl set over a saucepan of gently simmering water and heat until melted. Remove from the heat and stir until smooth. Leave to cool and thicken for 30 minutes, stirring occasionally.

4. To assemble the push pops, whip the cream in a bowl until it holds stiff peaks, then spoon into a large piping bag fitted with a large star-shaped nozzle. Place a cookie in the base of each push pop. Top with a swirl of cream and a drizzle of fudge sauce. Repeat to make three more layers, finishing with a larger swirl of cream. Sprinkle with chocolate sugar strands.

5. Repeat with the remaining cookies, cream and sauce to make 10 push pops in total. Top each push pop with a cherry and serve immediately or chill in the refrigerator for up to 1 day.

351 Strawberry & mint ice cream cones

Ingredients

55 g/2 oz butter

2 egg whites

225 g/8 oz caster sugar

a few drops of vanilla extract

55 g/2 oz plain flour

6 tbsp water

2 sprigs of mint

450 g/1 lb strawberries, hulled and sliced

3 tsp powdered gelatine

150 ml/5 fl oz double cream

1. Preheat the oven to 180°C/350°F/Gas Mark 4. Line three baking trays with baking paper. Melt the butter in a saucepan. Lightly whisk the egg whites until frothy but still translucent. Whisk in half of the caster sugar, then the butter and the vanilla extract. Sift in the flour, folding it in until smooth. Drop 8 x ½-teaspoons of the mixture on each of the prepared trays and spread each into a 6-cm/2½-inch round. Bake in the preheated oven, one tray at a time, for 3–5 minutes. Leave to harden for a few moments, then quickly shape into small cones using cone moulds. Leave to set for 1–2 minutes, then remove the moulds. Leave to cool.

2. Put the remaining sugar, 2 tablespoons of the water and the mint into a saucepan and heat until the sugar has dissolved. Add the strawberries, increase the heat and cook for 3 minutes. Discard the mint. Purée the mixture in a blender until smooth. Press through a sieve into a metal loaf tin. Sprinkle the gelatine over the remaining water in a small heatproof bowl, then set aside for 5 minutes. Set the bowl of gelatine over a saucepan of gently simmering water and heat for about 5 minutes. Stir into the purée, leave to cool, then freeze for 20 minutes. Whip the cream until it holds soft peaks. Transfer the strawberry mixture to a large bowl and whisk for a few minutes. Fold in the cream. Pipe the ice cream into the cones and freeze for 6 hours or overnight.

352 Chocolate mint cake pops

Ingredients

300 g/10½ oz plain chocolate, roughly chopped

25 g/1 oz butter, softened

50 g/1¾ oz hard-boiled mint sweets

450 g/1 lb milk chocolate

50 g/1¾ oz mini marshmallows, roughly chopped

chocolate sugar strands, to decorate

28 lollipop sticks

1. Line a baking tray with baking paper. Put the plain chocolate in a heatproof bowl set over a saucepan of gently simmering water and heat until melted. Stir in the butter. Leave to cool until the mixture is cool but not beginning to set.

2. Put the mint sweets in a polythene bag and tap firmly with a rolling pin until they are broken into tiny pieces. Finely chop 150 g/5½ oz of the milk chocolate, then stir it into the melted plain chocolate with the mints and marshmallows until thoroughly mixed. As soon as the mixture is firm enough to hold its shape, roll 20 g/¾ oz of it into a ball. Shape the remaining cake pops in the same way. Place them on the prepared tray and chill for 30–60 minutes, until firm but not brittle. Push a lollipop stick into each cake pop, then chill for 10 minutes.

3. Roughly chop the remaining milk chocolate, put into a heatproof bowl set over a saucepan of gently simmering water and heat until melted. Dip a cake pop into the chocolate, turning to coat. Lift it from the bowl, letting the excess drip back into the bowl, and place it in a cup or tumbler. Sprinkle with chocolate sugar strands. Repeat with the remaining cake pops. Chill or leave in a cool place to set.

#353 Peppermint creams

Makes
25

Ingredients

1 large egg white

325 g/11½ oz icing sugar, sifted, plus extra for dipping if needed

a few drops of peppermint extract

a few drops of green food colouring

100 g/3½ oz plain chocolate, roughly chopped

1. Line a baking tray with baking paper. Lightly whisk the egg white in a large, clean mixing bowl until frothy but still translucent.

2. Add the sifted icing sugar to the egg white and stir with a wooden spoon until it is stiff. Knead in the peppermint extract and food colouring. Using the palms of your hands, roll the mixture into walnut-sized balls and place them on the prepared tray. Use a fork dipped in icing sugar to flatten them. Transfer to the refrigerator to set for 24 hours.

3. Put the chocolate in a heatproof bowl set over a saucepan of gently simmering water and heat until melted. Dip the creams halfway in the chocolate and return to the baking tray for 1 hour, or until set.

#354 Shaker lemon pies

Makes
24

Ingredients

24 lemon slices

250 g/9 oz caster sugar, plus extra for sprinkling

4 tbsp water

grated rind and juice of 1½ lemons

60 g/2¼ oz butter, plus extra for greasing

3 eggs, beaten

450 g/1 lb ready-made sweet shortcrust pastry, chilled

plain flour, for dusting

egg white, to glaze

1. Lightly grease 2 x 12-hole mini muffin tins. Put the lemon slices in a saucepan with 100 g/3½ oz of the sugar and the water and stir. Cook over a low heat, stirring occasionally, for 30 minutes. Scoop them out of the pan, draining off the syrup, transfer to a plate and set aside.

2. Preheat the oven to 180°C/350°F/Gas Mark 4. Add the lemon rind and juice to the syrup with the butter and remaining sugar and heat gently until the butter is just melted. Remove from the heat and strain the eggs through a sieve into the mixture, stirring well. Return to the heat and cook very gently for 10 minutes, stirring frequently, or until the mixture has thickened and is jam-like. Increase the heat if needed but keep a watchful eye; too hot and the eggs will curdle. Leave to cool.

3. Thinly roll out half the pastry on a lightly floured surface. Using a 6-cm/2½-inch fluted cutter, stamp out 24 rounds and press gently into the prepared tins. Brush the top edges with a little egg white, then spoon in the filling. Top each with a prepared lemon slice.

4. Thinly roll out the remaining pastry on a lightly floured surface. Stamp out 24 x 5-cm/2-inch rounds and press onto the pie tops, pressing the edges together well. Make four small cuts in the top of each pie, brush the pies with egg white and sprinkle with sugar. Bake in the preheated oven for 15 minutes, or until golden. Leave to cool in the tins for 10 minutes, then loosen with a round-bladed knife and transfer to a wire rack. Serve warm or cold.

355 Tremendous truffles

Makes
4

Ingredients

400 g/14 oz plain chocolate, broken into pieces
100 g/3½ oz butter
300 ml/10 fl oz double cream
2 tbsp brandy (optional)
1 tbsp icing sugar
1 tbsp cocoa powder

1. Put the chocolate and butter into a large heatproof bowl set over a saucepan of barely simmering water and heat until melted, stirring occasionally. Remove from the heat and stir until smooth.

2. Gradually stir in the cream and brandy, if using. Leave to cool for 10 minutes, then beat for 3-4 minutes, until thickened. Cover and chill in the refrigerator for 3-4 hours until very firm.

3. Divide the mixture into four pieces and, with cold hands, quickly roll each piece into a ball. Sprinkle the sugar on a plate and sprinkle the cocoa powder on a separate plate. Roll two truffles in the sugar and roll the remaining two in the cocoa powder.

4. Place the truffles in paper muffin cases and chill in the refrigerator for up to 1 week. Remove from the refrigerator about 1 hour before serving to soften slightly.

356 Honeycomb ice cream

Serves
6-8

Ingredients

melted butter, for greasing
85 g/3 oz granulated sugar
2 tbsp golden syrup
1 tsp bicarbonate of soda
400 ml/14 fl oz whipping cream
400 g/14 oz canned condensed milk

1. Grease a baking sheet. Put the sugar and golden syrup in a heavy-based saucepan and heat gently, stirring, until the sugar has dissolved. Boil for 1-2 minutes, or until beginning to caramelize. Stir in the bicarbonate of soda and immediately pour the mixture onto the baking sheet, but do not spread. Leave to cool for about 10 minutes, or until cold and hard. Transfer to a strong polythene bag and crush into small pieces with a rolling pin.

2. Whip the cream until it holds its shape, then whisk in the condensed milk. Freeze in a freezerproof container, uncovered, for 1-2 hours, or until it begins to set around the edges. Turn the mixture into a bowl and stir with a fork until smooth. Add the crushed honeycomb, reserving a little for decoration. Return to the container and freeze for a further 2-3 hours, or until completely frozen.

3. To store, cover the container with a suitable lid. Transfer to the refrigerator 15-20 minutes before serving. Serve with the reserved honeycomb.

#357 Carrot & orange cupcakes

Makes
12

Ingredients

115 g/4 oz butter, softened

115 g/4 oz soft light brown sugar

finely grated rind of 2 large oranges

2 large eggs, lightly beaten

175 g/6 oz carrots, grated

25 g/1 oz walnut pieces, chopped

juice of 1 small orange

125 g/4½ oz plain flour

1 tsp ground mixed spice

1½ tsp baking powder

280 g/10 oz mascarpone cheese

4 tbsp icing sugar

1. Preheat the oven to 180°C/350°F/Gas Mark 4. Put 12 paper muffin cases in a 12-hole muffin tin.

2. Place the butter, sugar and half the orange rind in a bowl and beat together until light and fluffy, then gradually beat in the eggs. Squeeze any excess liquid from the carrots and add to the mixture with the walnuts and orange juice. Stir until well mixed. Sift in the flour, mixed spice and baking powder and fold in. Spoon the mixture into the paper cases and bake in the preheated oven for 25 minutes, or until well risen and springy to the touch. Transfer to a wire rack to cool completely.

3. Place the mascarpone cheese, icing sugar and remaining orange rind in a large bowl and beat together until they are well mixed. Spread the frosting on top of each cupcake, swirling it with a round-bladed knife.

#358 Vanilla soufflé omelettes

Makes
4

Ingredients

8 egg whites

2 tbsp honey, plus extra for drizzling

1½ tsp cornflour

2 tsp vanilla extract

225 g/8 oz ricotta cheese

sunflower oil, for brushing

200 g/7 oz raspberries

1. Whisk the egg whites in a large, grease-free bowl until they form soft peaks.

2. Add the honey, cornflour and vanilla and whisk to mix evenly. Beat the ricotta in a small bowl until smooth, then fold lightly into the egg white mixture.

3. Brush a large, heavy-based frying pan with oil and put over a medium heat. Spoon one quarter of the egg white mixture into the pan and spread evenly with a palette knife.

4. Cook for 3–4 minutes, or until a golden colour underneath. Turn the omelette over and cook for 2–3 minutes on the other side, then sprinkle with one quarter of the raspberries. Gently lift one side with the palette knife and fold the omelette in half to enclose.

5. Cook for a further few seconds, then flip over onto a serving plate. Keep warm and repeat with the remaining mixture to make a total of four omelettes. Serve immediately, drizzled with honey to taste.

359 Mini macaroons

Makes 20

Ingredients

125 g/4½ oz icing sugar, sifted

125 g/4½ oz ground almonds

2 large egg whites

110 g/3¾ oz caster sugar

3 tbsp water

a few drops of pink food colouring

Filling

140 g/5 oz butter, softened

280 g/10 oz icing sugar, sifted

1 tbsp milk

a few drops of vanilla extract

1. Preheat the oven to 150°C/300°F/Gas Mark 2. Line three large baking trays with baking paper. Put the sifted icing sugar, almonds and 40 g/2½ oz of the egg whites into a large mixing bowl and mix to a paste using a wooden spoon.

2. Put the caster sugar and water into a heavy-based saucepan. Heat gently for 5 minutes, until the sugar has dissolved, tilting the pan to mix the ingredients. Increase the heat and boil rapidly for 12–15 minutes, or until the mixture reaches 115°C/240°F on a sugar thermometer, goes syrupy and thickens. Whisk the remaining egg white until it holds stiff peaks, then gradually whisk in the hot syrup. Spoon into the almond paste and stir gently until stiff and shiny. Add the food colouring, then mix well. Spoon into a piping bag fitted with a 1-cm/½-inch nozzle and pipe 40 x 2-cm/¾-inch rounds onto the prepared trays, about 2 cm/¾ inches apart. Leave to stand for 30 minutes, or until a skin forms. Bake in the preheated oven for 12–15 minutes, with the door slightly ajar, until firm.

3. To make the filling, put the butter in a large mixing bowl and beat until soft. Add half the icing sugar and beat until smooth. Add the remaining icing sugar, milk and the vanilla extract and beat until creamy. Spoon the mixture into a piping bag fitted with a large star-shaped nozzle. Transfer the macaroons to wire racks. Leave to cool for 1–2 hours, then peel off the paper. Pipe a swirl of buttercream on 20 macaroons and top each with another macaroon.

360 Chocolate samosas

Makes 16

Ingredients

250 ml/9 fl oz whipping cream

250 g/9 oz plain chocolate chips

250 g/9 oz plain flour

100 ml/3½ fl oz ghee

oil, for deep-frying

1. Put the cream into a small saucepan and bring to the boil over a medium heat. Put the chocolate chips into a bowl, pour over the boiling cream and stir until melted. Chill in the refrigerator for 1 hour.

2. Sift the flour into a mixing bowl, add the ghee and rub in. If the dough is too stiff, gradually add a little cold water. Keep covered with a damp cloth. Divide the dough into 16 equal-sized pieces and roll each piece into a long rectangle. Put 1 teaspoon of the cream mixture on one end of the rectangle and repeatedly fold over the dough to make a triangle shape.

3. Heat enough oil for deep-frying in a large saucepan to 180–190°C/350–375°F, or until a cube of bread browns in 30 seconds. Add the samosas in batches and cook over a medium heat until crisp and golden. Do not overcrowd the pan. Transfer to kitchen paper to drain and leave to cool for 5 minutes. Serve warm.

361 Chevron cake

Serves
10

Ingredients

6 eggs, beaten

350 g/12 oz self-raising flour

350 g/12 oz caster sugar

350 g/12 oz butter, plus extra
for greasing

2 tsp baking powder

1 tsp vanilla extract

Filling

200 g/7 oz butter, softened

200 g/7 oz icing sugar, sifted

300 g/10½ oz raspberry or
strawberry jam

Decoration

500 g/1 lb 2 oz white ready-to-roll
fondant icing

100 g/3½ oz black ready-to-roll
fondant icing

icing sugar, for dusting

boiled water, cooled

black ribbon

1. Make a chevron template by printing off a generic chevron pattern online or cutting out a paper chevron about 1 cm/½ inch wide then tracing onto baking paper. Cut out and use the baking paper template to make the chevrons. Grease 2 x 20-cm/8-inch sandwich tins and line with baking paper. Preheat the oven to 180°C/350°F/Gas Mark 4.

2. Place the eggs, flour, caster sugar, butter, baking powder and vanilla extract in a mixing bowl and beat well for 2–3 minutes until pale, smooth and creamy. Divide the mixture between the prepared tins, smooth lightly with a palette knife and bake in the preheated oven for 30–35 minutes, until golden and risen and the tops spring back easily when lightly pressed. Leave to cool in the tins for 5 minutes, then turn out onto a wire rack to cool completely.

3. To make the buttercream filling, beat the butter until soft and creamy. Add the icing sugar and beat for a further 1–2 minutes, until smooth and creamy.

4. When the cakes are cool, place one on a cake board or serving platter and spread evenly with the jam. Top with two thirds of the buttercream. Place the remaining sponge on top. Use a palette knife to lightly coat the top and sides of the cake with the remaining buttercream.

5. Knead the white fondant on a work surface lightly dusted with icing sugar until soft. Roll out to a large round, then use the rolling pin to drape it over the cake. Use the palm of your hand to smooth it over the top and the sides. Trim off any excess fondant.

6. Roll out the black icing (not too thinly or it will be hard to handle) and cut out 2–3 lines of the chevron pattern and about 10 x 1-cm/½-inch rounds.

7. Paint a little boiled cooled water onto the cake where you want to position the chevrons and carefully lift into position. Use the same technique to stick the rounds on the sides, leaving room to pin the ribbon around the circumference of the cake at its base.

#362 Strawberry margarita pops

Makes
8

Ingredients

500 g/1 lb 2 oz strawberries, hulled and chopped

100 ml/3½ fl oz sugar syrup

finely grated rind and juice of 1 lime

2 tbsp tequila

1 tbsp triple sec

pinch of salt

150 ml/5 fl oz water

25 g/1 oz caster sugar, to serve

8 ice pop moulds

8 ice pop sticks

1. Put all the ingredients except the caster sugar in a blender and process until smooth.

2. Pour the mixture into 8 x 75-ml/2½-fl oz ice pop moulds. Insert the ice pop sticks and freeze for 6–8 hours, or until firm.

3. To unmould the ice pops, dip the frozen moulds in warm water for a few seconds and gently release the pops while holding the sticks.

4. To serve the ice pops, tip the caster sugar onto a plate and dip the ice pops in the sugar.

#363 Choc-coated doughnut holes

Makes
28

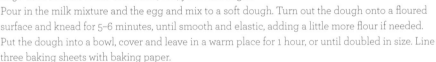

Ingredients

175 ml/6 fl oz milk

40 g/1½ oz butter

300 g/10½ oz strong white flour, plus extra for dusting and kneading

1 tbsp cocoa powder

2 tsp ground cinnamon

¼ tsp salt

1½ tsp easy-blend dried yeast

2 tbsp caster sugar

1 large egg, beaten

oil, for deep-frying and greasing

140 g/5 oz plain chocolate, broken into pieces

140 g/5 oz white chocolate, broken into pieces

chocolate sugar strands and hundreds and thousands, to decorate

1. Put the milk and butter into a small saucepan over a low heat and heat until the butter has melted. Leave to cool for 5 minutes. Sift together the flour and cocoa powder into a large bowl and stir in the cinnamon, salt, yeast and sugar. Pour in the milk mixture and the egg and mix to a soft dough. Turn out the dough onto a floured surface and knead for 5–6 minutes, until smooth and elastic, adding a little more flour if needed. Put the dough into a bowl, cover and leave in a warm place for 1 hour, or until doubled in size. Line three baking sheets with baking paper.

2. Knock back the dough. Roll out on a lightly floured surface to a thickness of 15 mm/⅝ inch. Use a 2.5-cm/1-inch cutter to stamp out 28 rounds. Place the rounds on two of the prepared baking sheets and cover with lightly oiled clingfilm. Leave to stand in a warm place for 5–10 minutes, until puffy.

3. Heat enough oil for deep-frying in a large saucepan or deep-fryer to 180–190°C/350–375°F, or until a cube of bread browns in 30 seconds. Add the rounds, 6–8 at a time, and fry for 2–3 minutes until golden, turning constantly. Remove and drain on kitchen paper. Leave to cool.

4. Put the plain chocolate and white chocolate into two separate heatproof bowls set over two saucepans of simmering water and heat until melted. Leave to cool for 5 minutes. Dip half the rounds in plain chocolate to completely coat and dip the remaining holes in white chocolate. Top with chocolate sugar strands. Transfer to the remaining baking sheet and leave to set.

364 Cashew nut brittle

Ingredients

150 g/5½ oz roasted, salted cashew nuts

350 g/12 oz caster sugar

¼ tsp cream of tartar

175 ml/6 fl oz water

15 g/½ oz butter

1. Line a 20-cm/8-inch square baking tin with baking paper.

2. Spread the cashew nuts over the baking tin in a thin, even layer.

3. Put the sugar, cream of tartar and water into a heavy-based saucepan. Bring to a gentle boil over a medium heat, stirring constantly.

4. Reduce the heat to low and simmer for 20–25 minutes, without stirring, until the mixture reaches 143°C/290°F on a sugar thermometer. Stir in the butter, then carefully drizzle the caramel over the nuts. Leave to cool completely.

5. Break the brittle into shards to serve.

365 Apple pies in a jar

Ingredients

400 g/14 oz ready-made shortcrust pastry

375 g/13 oz peeled and cored Bramley apples, diced

1 tbsp lemon juice

65 g/2¾ oz granulated sugar

2 tbsp soft light brown sugar

2 tbsp plain flour, plus extra for dusting

½ tsp ground cinnamon

⅛ tsp ground nutmeg

6 x 225-ml/8-fl oz wide-mouthed preserving jars, sterilized

1. Preheat the oven to 220°C/425°F/Gas Mark 7. Divide the pastry into two pieces, roll out one piece on a lightly floured work surface and cut out 6 x 7.5-cm/3-inch rounds. Place one round in the base of each jar. Press the pastry into the base and up the sides a little. Put the apples and lemon juice into a large bowl and mix together, then add the granulated sugar, brown sugar, flour, cinnamon and nutmeg, and toss to coat. Divide the mixture between the jars, packing it in tightly.

2. Roll out the remaining dough on a floured work surface and cut out 6 x 7.5-cm/3-inch rounds. Use a fork to pierce several small holes in each round, then place a round on top of the filling in each jar, tucking the edges inside the rims of the jars. Use the tines of a fork to create a decorative edge on the pastry. Place the jars on a Swiss roll tin and bake in the preheated oven for about 15 minutes, then reduce the heat to 190°C/375°F/Gas Mark 5 and bake for a further 30–35 minutes, until the filling is bubbling and the pastry is golden brown and crisp. Remove from the oven and leave to cool for 10–15 minutes. Serve warm.

366 Ginger refrigerator cakes

Makes
6

Ingredients

475 ml/16 fl oz double cream

50 g/1¾ oz sugar

grated rind and juice of 1 lemon

36 gingersnaps, 12 broken in half

40 g/1½ oz chopped crystallized ginger, to decorate

6 x 225-ml/8-fl oz wide-mouthed preserving jars, sterilized

1. Put the cream into a large bowl and whip until it holds stiff peaks. Add the sugar and the lemon rind and juice, and beat until combined.

2. Spoon about 2 tablespoons of the mixture into the base of each of the jars. Top each cream layer with 1½ biscuits in a single layer. Spoon another 2 tablespoons of the cream mixture on top of the ginger biscuits and top with another 1½ biscuits. Repeat until there are four layers of biscuits.

3. Finish with a layer of cream. Wipe the rims of the jars clean and seal the jars with their lids. Chill in the refrigerator for at least 4 hours. Just before serving, remove the lids and sprinkle the crystallized ginger over the top of the cakes.

367 Muesli muffins

Makes
12

Ingredients

140 g/5 oz plain flour

1 tbsp baking powder

280 g/10 oz unsweetened muesli

115 g/4 oz soft light brown sugar

2 eggs

250 ml/9 fl oz buttermilk

6 tbsp sunflower oil

1. Preheat the oven to 200°C/400°F/Gas Mark 6. Place 12 paper cases in a muffin tin.

2. Sift together the flour and baking powder into a large bowl. Stir in the muesli and sugar.

3. Place the eggs in a large jug or bowl and beat lightly, then beat in the buttermilk and oil. Make a well in the centre of the dry ingredients and pour in the beaten liquid ingredients. Stir gently until just combined; do not over-mix. Spoon the mixture into the paper cases.

4. Bake in the preheated oven for about 20 minutes, or until well risen, golden brown and firm to the touch. Leave to cool in the tin for 5 minutes, then serve warm or transfer to a wire rack to cool.

#368 Orange & hazelnut refrigerator cookies

Makes 32

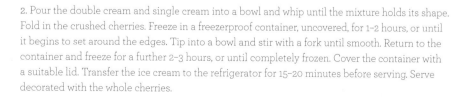

Ingredients

100 g/3½ oz butter, softened, plus extra for greasing
140 g/5 oz caster sugar
1 tsp finely grated orange rind
1 egg, beaten
225 g/8 oz plain flour, sifted
40 g/1½ oz chopped roasted hazelnuts
115 g/4 oz icing sugar, sifted
5 tsp fresh orange juice

1. Put the butter, caster sugar and orange rind into a bowl and beat together until creamy, then gradually beat in the egg. Stir in half the flour and mix to a soft paste, then add the remaining flour and the nuts, and mix to a smooth dough.

2. Shape the dough into a 25-cm/10-inch roll and wrap in clingfilm. Chill for 3–4 hours, occasionally rolling the wrapped dough on a flat surface to ensure a good round shape. Preheat the oven to 190°C/375°F/Gas Mark 5. Grease two large baking sheets with butter.

3. Slice the dough into 32 rounds and place on the prepared baking sheets, spaced well apart. Bake in the preheated oven for 10–15 minutes, until golden around the edges. Leave the cookies to cool on the baking sheets for a few minutes, then transfer to wire racks to cool completely.

4. Beat together the icing sugar and orange juice in a bowl until smooth. Spoon into a paper piping bag, snip off the end and pipe zig-zag lines of icing over each cookie. Leave to set.

#369 Crushed cherry ice cream

Serves 6

Ingredients

115 g/4 oz caster sugar
150 ml/5 fl oz water
225 g/8 oz fresh cherries, stoned, plus extra whole cherries to decorate
2 tbsp freshly squeezed orange juice
300 ml/10 fl oz double cream
150 ml/5 fl oz single cream

1. Put the sugar and water in a heavy-based saucepan and gently heat, stirring, until the sugar has dissolved. Bring to the boil, then boil for 3 minutes. Reduce the heat, add the cherries and simmer gently for about 10 minutes, or until soft. Leave to cool, then transfer the cherries and syrup to a food processor. Add the orange juice and process until the cherries are just roughly chopped.

2. Pour the double cream and single cream into a bowl and whip until the mixture holds its shape. Fold in the crushed cherries. Freeze in a freezerproof container, uncovered, for 1–2 hours, or until it begins to set around the edges. Tip into a bowl and stir with a fork until smooth. Return to the container and freeze for a further 2–3 hours, or until completely frozen. Cover the container with a suitable lid. Transfer the ice cream to the refrigerator for 15–20 minutes before serving. Serve decorated with the whole cherries.

#370 Hamburger cupcakes

Makes 12

Ingredients

250 g/9 oz plain flour

50 g/1¾ oz cocoa powder

1¾ tsp baking powder

175 g/6 oz butter, plus extra for greasing

350 g/12 oz caster sugar

3 tsp vanilla extract

3 large eggs

125 ml/4 fl oz milk

salt

Frosting

115 g/4 oz butter, softened

250 g/9 oz icing sugar, plus extra if needed

1 tbsp milk

1 tsp vanilla extract

red and yellow food colouring

Decoration

green food colouring

75 g/2¾ oz desiccated coconut

clear honey

sesame seeds

1. Preheat the oven to 180°C/350°F/Gas Mark 4 and grease two 12-hole cupcake tins. Sift together 60 g/2¼ oz of the flour, the cocoa powder, ⅛ teaspoon of the baking powder and ⅛ teaspoon of salt in a bowl. Put 60 g/2¼ oz of the butter and 150 g/5½ oz of the caster sugar into a separate bowl and beat until pale and fluffy. Add 1 teaspoon of the vanilla extract, then beat in one egg. Gradually add the flour mixture, beating until well combined. Spoon the batter into the cases in one of the prepared tins. Bake in the preheated oven for 20 minutes, or until a cocktail stick inserted into the centre of a brownie comes out clean. Leave to cool in the tin for 5 minutes, then carefully transfer to a wire rack to cool completely. Do not switch off the oven. Trim each brownie into a perfect round using a 5-cm/2-inch round cutter.

2. Sift together the remaining flour and baking powder and ¼ teaspoon of salt into a bowl. Put the remaining butter and caster sugar into a separate bowl and beat until pale and fluffy. Add the remaining vanilla extract, then add the remaining eggs, one at a time, beating after each addition. Add half of the flour mixture and the milk, and beat until incorporated. Add the remaining flour mixture and mix. Spoon the batter into the remaining prepared tin and bake for 20 minutes, until risen and a cocktail stick inserted in the centre of a cupcake comes out clean. Leave to cool in the tin for 1–2 minutes, then transfer to a wire rack to cool completely.

3. Put all the frosting ingredients except the food colouring into a bowl and beat to combine. Divide between two bowls. Add a little red colouring to one bowl and a little yellow colouring to the second and beat well. Transfer to two piping bags, each fitted with a small round nozzle.

4. To decorate, add a couple of drops of green food colouring to the coconut and toss. Slice the cupcakes in half horizontally and place a brownie burger on top of half of each cupcake. Pipe the red and yellow frostings onto the burgers to resemble sauce, top with coconut lettuce and the remaining cupcake halves. Brush the tops with honey, scatter over some sesame seeds and serve.

#371 Nutty peppermint bark

Ingredients

200 g/7 oz red and white striped peppermint candy canes, broken into pieces

500 g/1 lb 2 oz white chocolate, roughly chopped

100 g/3½ oz chopped mixed nuts

1. Line a 30 x 20-cm/12 x 8-inch baking tin with baking paper.

2. Put the broken canes into a large polythene food bag and seal tightly. Using a rolling pin, bash the bag until the canes are crushed into small pieces.

3. Put the chocolate in a heatproof bowl set over a saucepan of gently simmering water and heat until melted. Remove from the heat and stir in three quarters of the crushed canes.

4. Pour the mixture into the prepared tin, smooth the surface with a spatula and sprinkle over the chopped nuts and remaining crushed canes. Press down very slightly to ensure they stick. Cover with clingfilm and chill in the refrigerator for 30 minutes, or until firm. Break into small, uneven pieces.

#372 Snickerdoodle ice cream sandwiches

Ingredients

200 ml/7 fl oz canned condensed milk

300 ml/10 fl oz double cream

1½ tsp vanilla extract

3 tsp ground cinnamon

200 g/7 oz canned pumpkin purée

115 g/4 oz butter, softened

115 g/4 oz caster sugar

1 egg, beaten

200 g/7 oz plain flour

1½ tsp baking powder

1 tbsp granulated sugar

1. Put the condensed milk, cream and 1 teaspoon of the vanilla extract into a large bowl. Whip until it holds firm peaks. Fold in 1 teaspoon cinnamon and pumpkin purée. Spoon into a shallow freezerproof container. Cover and freeze overnight.

2. Preheat the oven to 180°C/350°F/Gas Mark 4. Line two large baking sheets with baking paper. Put the butter and caster sugar into a large bowl and beat together until pale and creamy. Gradually beat in the egg and remaining vanilla extract. Sift together the flour and baking powder into the bowl and stir to make a fairly stiff dough Mix together the granulated sugar and the remaining cinnamon on a flat plate. Divide the dough into 16 pieces and shape each piece into a ball, roll in the cinnamon sugar, then place on the prepared baking sheet. Use your fingertips to flatten each ball to a 6-cm/2½-inch round. Sprinkle over any remaining cinnamon sugar. Bake in the preheated oven for 12–14 minutes. Leave to cool on the baking sheets for 5 minutes, then transfer to a wire rack to cool completely.

3. Remove the ice cream from the freezer 30 minutes before serving. Sandwich pairs of cookies together with a large scoop of the ice cream and serve immediately.

#373 Sea-salted pecan candies

Ingredients

55 g/2 oz pecan nuts

300 g/10½ oz caster sugar

175 ml/6 fl oz water

2 tsp sea salt

1. Preheat the grill to medium. Put the nuts in a baking tray and toast them under the grill for 3–4 minutes, or until golden, shaking them halfway through. Divide the nuts between the sections of a 12-hole silicone mini muffin tin.

2. Put the sugar and water into a heavy-based saucepan. Heat gently until the sugar has dissolved, tilting the pan to mix the ingredients together, until the mixture is an even light brown colour. Cook until it is a slightly deeper brown, watching carefully so it doesn't burn. Scatter in the sea salt.

3. Transfer the mixture to a jug and quickly pour it into the holes of the muffin tin. Leave to cool for 10 minutes, until the sweets set and harden.

#374 Berry cobblers in a jar

Ingredients

575 g/1 lb 4½ oz mixed berries (blackberries, raspberries, blueberries and strawberries), thawed and drained, if frozen

100 g/3½ oz sugar

1 tbsp lemon juice

2 tbsp cornflour

Topping

125 g/4½ oz plain flour

25 g/1 oz granulated sugar

½ tsp ground cinnamon

pinch of salt

60 g/2¼ oz butter

4 tbsp double cream

1 large egg

4 tsp soft dark brown sugar

8 x 225-ml/8-fl oz wide-mouthed preserving jars, sterilized

1. Preheat the oven to 180°C/350°F/Gas Mark 4.

2. Put the berries, sugar, lemon juice and cornflour into a medium-sized bowl and mix to combine. Divide the mixture between the jars.

3. To make the topping, put the flour, sugar, cinnamon and salt into a food processor and pulse to combine. Add the butter and pulse until the mixture resembles coarse crumbs. Add the cream and egg and process until the mixture comes together into a loose, sticky ball.

4. Spoon the topping onto the berry mixture, dividing it between the jars. Sprinkle the brown sugar over the tops and bake in the preheated oven for about 35 minutes, until the topping is golden brown and cooked through. Serve warm.

375 Moon cakes

Makes
15–20

Ingredients

650 g/1 lb 7 oz plain flour, plus extra
for dusting

60 g/2¼ oz powdered milk

1 tbsp baking powder

1 tsp salt

4 eggs

250 g/9 oz caster sugar

1 tsp vanilla extract or 1 vanilla pod,
scraped

125 g/4½ oz butter, melted

2 tbsp water, for glazing

Filling

200 g/7 oz apricot jam

100 g/3½ oz dried dates, chopped

55 g/2 oz desiccated coconut

70 g/2½ oz raisins

1. Mix together the flour, powdered milk, baking powder and salt in a bowl. Put three of the eggs, the sugar, vanilla extract and melted butter into a separate bowl and beat for about 5 minutes until creamy. Stir in the dry ingredients and knead until a smooth dough forms. Wrap in clingfilm and chill in the refrigerator overnight.

2. To make the filling, mix together the jam, dates, coconut and raisins. Preheat the oven to 190°C/375°F/Gas Mark 5. Line two baking trays with baking paper. Dust a 5-cm/2-inch moon cake press or round cutter with flour. Remove the dough from the refrigerator and divide into 15–20 pieces. Shape each piece into a round and place 1 tablespoon of the filling in the centre of each round. Fold the edges over the filling and press together.

3. Take the filled balls of dough and, one at a time, press them in the prepared press, then remove. Alternatively, use the cutter to cut out rounds.

4. Lightly whisk the remaining egg with the water and brush over the moon cakes, then place on the prepared trays. Bake in the preheated oven for 30 minutes, or until the cakes are golden brown.

376 Spiced strawberry meringue soufflé

Serves
6

Ingredients

650 g/1 lb 7 oz fresh strawberries, diced

70 g/2½ oz caster sugar

4 tbsp water

1 tbsp cornflour

1 tsp vanilla extract

½ tsp pepper

Topping

3 egg whites

100 g/3½ oz caster sugar

¼ tsp cream of tartar

1. Preheat the oven to 200°C/400°F/Gas Mark 6. Put the strawberries, sugar and water in a saucepan and bring to a simmer over a medium heat, stirring frequently. In a small bowl, combine the cornflour with 1 tablespoon of water and stir. Add the cornflour mixture to the simmering strawberry mixture and cook, stirring, for about 1 minute, or until thickened. Stir in the vanilla extract and pepper, and remove from the heat. Set aside to cool.

2. In a large bowl, whisk the egg whites with an electric hand-held mixer on a medium–high speed until they form soft peaks. Gradually add the sugar and the cream of tartar, and continue to whisk until stiff, glossy peaks form. Scoop about 5 tablespoons of the strawberry mixture from the saucepan and, using a spoon, swirl it into the meringue in just a few stirs.

3. Spoon the remaining strawberry mixture into 6 x 175 ml/6 fl oz ramekins and set the ramekins on a baking tray. Top with the meringue mixture, swirling it up into peaks. Place the baking tray in the preheated oven and bake for 5–6 minutes, or until the peaks begin to turn a golden colour. Serve warm.

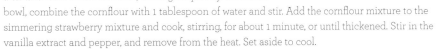

239

#377 Mega muffin

Ingredients

450 g/1 lb plain flour

5 tsp baking powder

1 tsp bicarbonate of soda

200 g/7 oz caster sugar

150 g/5½ oz butter, chilled

2 large eggs

300 ml/10 fl oz milk

175 g/6 oz fresh blueberries

1 giant muffin mould

1. Preheat the oven to 200°C/400°F/Gas Mark 6. Place the giant muffin mould on a baking sheet. Ease a large round of baking paper into the mould, pleating it smoothly against the sides.

2. Sift the flour, baking powder and bicarbonate of soda into a large bowl. Stir in the sugar. Coarsely grate in the butter. Stir with a fork to coat the butter in the flour mixture. Make a well in the centre. Beat together the eggs and milk and pour into the well. Lightly mix with a fork until just combined. Gently fold in 145 g/5¼ oz of the blueberries.

3. Spoon the mixture into the prepared mould. Sprinkle in the remaining blueberries. Bake in the preheated oven for 50 minutes, then reduce the oven temperature to 180°C/350°F/Gas Mark 4. Bake for a further 25-35 minutes, until risen and a cocktail stick inserted in the centre comes out clean. Leave to cool in the mould, then serve.

#378 White chocolate truffles

Ingredients

25 g/1 oz butter

5 tbsp double cream

350 g/12 oz white chocolate, broken into pieces

1 tbsp orange liqueur (optional)

1. Line a Swiss roll tin with baking paper. Place the butter and cream in a small saucepan and bring slowly to the boil, stirring constantly. Boil for 1 minute, then remove from the heat.

2. Add 225 g/8 oz of the chocolate to the cream. Stir until melted, then beat in the liqueur, if using. Pour into the prepared tin and chill for about 2 hours, until firm.

3. Break off pieces of the mixture and roll them into balls. Chill for a further 30 minutes.

4. To finish, put the remaining chocolate in a heatproof bowl set over a saucepan of gently simmering water until melted. Dip the balls into the chocolate, allowing the excess to drip back into the bowl. Place on baking paper, swirl the chocolate with the tines of a fork and leave to cool and harden.

Mexican corn cake

Serves
8–10

Ingredients

60 g/2¼ oz butter,
plus extra for greasing

2 tbsp white vegetable fat

50 g/1¾ oz polenta

5 tbsp cold water, plus extra if needed

280 g/10 oz fresh sweetcorn kernels

3 tbsp whipping cream

3 tbsp cornflour

50 g/1¾ oz caster sugar

¼ tsp baking powder

¼ tsp salt

1. Preheat the oven to 180°C/350°F/Gas Mark 4. Grease a 35-cm/14-inch loaf tin. Cream the butter with the vegetable fat until light and fluffy. Fold in the polenta. Add the water, a little at a time, mixing after each addition until a firm but pliable dough forms. Add the sweetcorn and mix well.

2. Mix together the cream, cornflour, sugar, baking powder and salt in a large bowl. Add the corn and butter mixture, and mix together until combined.

3. Transfer the mixture to the prepared tin and bake in the preheated oven for 40 minutes. If the cake is browning too quickly, cover it with foil. Remove from the oven and leave to cool in the tin for 1–2 minutes, then remove from the tin and transfer to a wire rack to cool completely. Cut into slices and serve.

380 Cosmopolitan pops

Makes
8

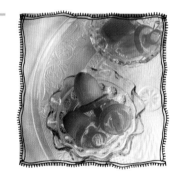

Ingredients

275 ml/9 fl oz sugar syrup

500 ml/17 fl oz cranberry juice

2 tbsp vodka

1 tbsp orange liqueur

juice of 1 lime

finely grated rind of 1 clementine

8 ice pop moulds

1. Put all the ingredients into a measuring jug and stir well.

2. Pour the mixture into 8 x 100-ml/3½-fl oz ice pop moulds. Insert the ice pop handles and freeze for 8–10 hours, or until firm.

3. To unmould the ice pops, dip the frozen moulds into warm water for a few seconds and gently release the pops while holding the sticks.

Chocolate & hazelnut cake balls

Ingredients

2 eggs

50 g/1¾ oz soft light brown sugar

50 g/1¾ oz caster sugar

100 g/3½ oz plain flour, sifted, plus extra for dusting

100 g/3½ oz butter, melted

1 tsp baking powder

2 tbsp cocoa powder, sifted

1 tsp vanilla extract

350 g/12 oz chocolate hazelnut spread

Decoration

350 g/12 oz plain chocolate, broken into pieces

70 g/2½ oz skinned whole hazelnuts

20 lollipop sticks or wooden skewers

1. Preheat the oven to 200°C/400°F/Gas Mark 6. Line an 18-cm/7-inch round cake tin and a baking tray with baking paper.

2. Place the eggs, brown sugar and caster sugar in a bowl and beat well until light and frothy.

3. Lightly fold in the flour, butter, baking powder, cocoa powder and vanilla extract. Leave to stand for 20 minutes. Pour into the prepared cake tin and bake in the preheated oven for 15–20 minutes, or until a skewer inserted in the middle of the cake comes out clean. Leave to cool in the tin for 10 minutes, then transfer to a wire rack to cool completely.

4. Use your fingertips to crumble the cooled cake into a mixing bowl. Stir in the chocolate hazelnut spread and mix together with a fork. Use an ice-cream scoop to remove a golf ball-sized piece of the mixture, then use your hands to form it into a ball. Place on the prepared tray. Repeat with the remaining mixture to make 20 balls, then transfer to the refrigerator to chill for at least 30 minutes.

5. Place the chocolate in a heatproof bowl set over a saucepan of gently simmering water and heat until melted.

6. Place the hazelnuts in a dry frying pan and heat for 2–3 minutes, stirring constantly to prevent burning. Tip the toasted nuts onto a chopping board and roughly chop.

7. When ready to decorate the cake balls, insert a lollipop stick into each one and dip the cakes in the melted chocolate, using a teaspoon to help you coat them completely. Return to the tray and sprinkle the top of each cake with hazelnuts. Transfer to a stand and leave to set.

Party-sized popcorn ball

Ingredients

1 tbsp sunflower oil

55 g/2 oz popping corn

225 g/8 oz sugar

2 tbsp golden syrup

150 ml/5 fl oz water

1. Line a baking sheet with baking paper and set aside. Heat the oil in a large, deep saucepan with a lid. Add the corn, cover the pan and cook over a high heat, shaking the pan frequently, until all the corn has popped. Transfer to a large, heatproof bowl, discarding any unpopped corn.

2. Put the sugar, syrup and water into a large, heavy-based saucepan and heat gently, stirring constantly, until the sugar has dissolved. Increase the heat and boil the mixture for 5-6 minutes, without stirring, until a golden caramel has formed.

3. Quickly pour the caramel over the popcorn and mix well. When just cool enough to handle, use buttered hands to shape into a large ball. Place on the prepared baking sheet and leave to cool.

383 Banana split pops

Ingredients

4 bananas

6 tbsp icing sugar

2 tbsp coconut cream

100 ml/3½ fl oz vanilla yogurt

400 g/14 oz plain chocolate, roughly chopped

100 g/3½ oz sweetened desiccated coconut, to decorate

8 ice pop moulds

8 ice pop sticks

1. Peel the bananas. Put them in a blender with the icing sugar, coconut cream and yogurt, and process until smooth. Pour the mixture into 8 x 60-ml/2-fl oz ice pop moulds. Insert the ice pop sticks and freeze for 4 hours, or until firm.

2. When the banana mixture is frozen, line a baking sheet with baking paper. To unmould the ice pops, dip the frozen moulds in warm water for a few seconds and gently release the pops while holding the sticks. Place them on the prepared baking sheet and return to the freezer for 1-2 hours.

3. Put the chocolate in a heatproof bowl set over a saucepan of gently simmering water and heat until melted. Remove from the heat and leave to cool slightly.

4. Dip each ice pop into the melted chocolate, then sprinkle over the desiccated coconut. Return to the prepared baking sheet and freeze for 10-20 minutes, or until ready to serve.

#384 Chocolate & saffron brioches

Makes 12

Ingredients

pinch of saffron threads

3 tbsp boiling water

55 g/2 oz butter, melted

350 g/12 oz plain flour

pinch of salt

1 tbsp caster sugar

2½ tsp easy-blend dried yeast

2 eggs, beaten

30 g/1 oz plain chocolate, broken into 12 pieces

milk, for glazing

1. Add the saffron to the boiling water and leave to cool completely. Lightly brush 12 individual brioche tins or fluted cake tins with some of the butter.

2. Sift together the flour, salt and sugar and stir in the yeast. Add the saffron liquid, eggs and remaining butter to make a soft dough. Knead until smooth, then cover and leave to stand in a warm place for 1–1½ hours, until doubled in size. Knead briefly, then shape three quarters of the dough into 12 balls.

3. Place a ball in every tin and press a piece of chocolate firmly into each. Shape the remaining dough into small balls with pointed ends. Brush with milk and press the balls into each brioche, sealing well.

4. Cover with oiled clingfilm and leave to stand in a warm place for 1½ hours, or until doubled in size. Meanwhile, preheat the oven to 200°C/400°F/Gas Mark 6. Brush the brioches with milk and bake in the preheated oven for 12–15 minutes, until firm and golden. Turn out and serve warm.

#385 Chocolate cherries

Makes 24

Ingredients

12 glacé cherries

2 tbsp dark rum or brandy

250 g/9 oz marzipan

125 g/4½ oz plain chocolate, broken into pieces

milk, plain or white chocolate, to decorate

1. Line a baking sheet with baking paper. Cut the cherries in half and place in a small bowl. Add the rum and stir to coat. Leave the cherries to soak for at least 1 hour, stirring occasionally. Divide the marzipan into 24 pieces and roll each piece into a ball. Press half a cherry into the top of each marzipan ball.

2. Put the chocolate in a heatproof bowl set over a saucepan of gently simmering water and heat until melted. Dip each marzipan ball into the melted chocolate using a cocktail stick, allowing the excess to drip back into the bowl. Place the coated cherries on the prepared baking sheet and chill until set.

3. To decorate, melt a little extra milk, plain or white chocolate and drizzle it over the top of the coated cherries. Leave to set.

#386 Frozen hot chocolate with hazelnut liqueur

Serves
4

Ingredients

85 g/3 oz plain chocolate, chopped

2 tbsp caster sugar

1 tbsp cocoa powder

350 ml/12 fl oz skimmed milk

900 g/2 lb ice cubes

1 banana

4 tbsp hazelnut liqueur

1. Put the chocolate into a heatproof bowl set over a saucepan of gently simmering water and heat, stirring frequently, until melted.

2. Add the sugar and cocoa powder and heat, stirring constantly, until the sugar has completely dissolved. Remove from the heat and slowly add the milk, stirring until combined. Leave to cool to room temperature.

3. Transfer the chocolate mixture to a blender and add the ice, banana and hazelnut liqueur. Blend until well combined and frothy. Pour into four glasses and serve immediately.

#387 Toffee ice cream

Serves
6

Ingredients

300 ml/10 fl oz milk

3 egg yolks

85 g/3 oz soft light brown sugar

450 g/1 lb jar dulce de leche

300 ml/10 fl oz whipping cream

1. Pour the milk into a heavy-based saucepan and place over a low heat. Slowly bring to a simmer, then remove from the heat. Put the egg yolks and sugar in a bowl and whisk together until pale and the mixture leaves a trail when the whisk is lifted. Add the milk and whisk thoroughly. Return the mixture to the rinsed-out saucepan and cook over a low heat for a further 10–15 minutes, stirring all the time, until the mixture thickens enough to coat the back of the wooden spoon. Do not allow the mixture to boil.

2. Remove from the heat, add the dulce de leche and whisk together until smooth. Submerge the base of the pan in a bowl of ice-cold water to stop the cooking process. Leave to cool for at least 1 hour, stirring from time to time to prevent a skin forming. Meanwhile, whip the cream until it holds its shape. Keep in the refrigerator until ready to use.

3. Fold the whipped cream into the caramel mixture and freeze in a freezerproof container, uncovered, for 1–2 hours, or until it begins to set around the edges. Tip the mixture into a bowl and stir with a fork until smooth. Return to the container and freeze for a further 2–3 hours, or until completely frozen.

4. Cover the container with a suitable lid to store in the freezer. Transfer to the refrigerator 15–20 minutes before serving.

388 Plentiful peanut butter cup

Serves 8–10

Ingredients

225 g/8 oz smooth peanut butter

115 g/4 oz soft light brown sugar

1 tsp vanilla extract

85 g/3 oz butter

115 g/4 oz icing sugar

350 g/12 oz milk chocolate, broken into pieces

350 g/12 oz plain chocolate, broken into pieces

1. Put the peanut butter, brown sugar, vanilla extract and half the butter into a saucepan and gently heat, stirring constantly, until the butter and sugar have dissolved. Simmer for 2–3 minutes, then remove from the heat and gradually beat in the icing sugar. Transfer to a bowl and leave to cool.

2. Line a 23-cm/9-inch fixed-base tart tin with 2 x 20-cm/8-inch cake liners. Put the milk chocolate, plain chocolate and remaining butter into a large, heatproof bowl set over a saucepan of barely simmering water and heat until melted. Remove from the heat and stir. Pour one third of the chocolate mixture into the base of the liner. Transfer to the refrigerator and leave for 20–30 minutes, until just set.

3. Shape the peanut butter mixture into an 18-cm/7-inch round and gently place it on top of the set chocolate. Pour the remaining chocolate over the peanut butter filling to cover it completely, then gently level the surface. Chill in the refrigerator until set. To serve, remove the peanut butter cup from the paper lining. Place on a serving plate and leave to stand at room temperature for about 1 hour before slicing into wedges.

389 Almond sticks

Makes 25–30

Ingredients

225 g/8 oz butter, softened

100 g/3½ oz caster sugar, plus extra for sprinkling

4 eggs

1 tsp almond extract

375 g/13 oz plain flour, plus extra for dusting

¼ tsp salt

200 g/7 oz almonds, chopped

1. Preheat the oven to 180 °C/350 °F/Gas Mark 4. Line a large baking tray with baking paper. Put the butter and sugar into a bowl and whisk until pale and fluffy. Add two eggs and the almond extract, and stir to combine. Sift together the flour and salt into a separate bowl, add to the butter and sugar mixture, and knead until smooth.

2. Turn out the dough onto a lightly floured work surface and roll out to a thickness of 2 cm/¾ inch. Using a sharp knife, cut out 25-30 strips, each measuring 2 x 5 cm/1 x 2 inches.

3. Beat the remaining eggs in a shallow bowl. Put the almonds into a separate bowl. Dip the dough strips into the beaten eggs, then into the chopped almonds. Generously sprinkle with sugar and place on the prepared baking tray. Bake in the preheated oven for 8-10 minutes, then remove from the oven and transfer to wire racks to cool.

390 S'mores cakes in a jar

Makes
8

Ingredients

Base

115 g/4 oz digestive biscuits, broken into pieces

75 g/2¾ oz caster sugar

115 g/4 oz butter, melted, plus extra for greasing

Cakes

125 g/4½ oz plain flour

60 g/2¼ oz cocoa powder

1½ tsp baking powder

¼ tsp salt

115 g/4 oz butter, at room temperature

200 g/7 oz caster sugar

2 tsp vanilla extract

2 large eggs

125 ml/4 fl oz double cream

40 g/1½ oz mini plain chocolate chips or chopped plain chocolate

32 large marshmallows

8 x 225-ml/8-fl oz wide-mouthed preserving jars, sterilized

1. Preheat the oven to 180°C/350°F/Gas Mark 4. Grease the jars and place them on a Swiss roll tin.

2. To make the base, pulse the biscuits in a food processor to coarse crumbs. Add the sugar and butter and pulse until just combined. Spoon about 2 tablespoons of the mixture into each of the prepared jars, using your thumb to flatten it into the base and up the sides. Bake in the preheated oven for about 12 minutes, until beginning to turn golden brown.

3. To make the cakes, sift the flour, cocoa powder, baking powder and salt into a medium-sized bowl. Put the butter and sugar into a large bowl and cream together. Add the vanilla extract, then add the eggs, one at a time, beating after each addition, until incorporated. Add half the flour mixture and beat until incorporated. Add the cream and beat until incorporated. Add the remaining flour mixture and beat until incorporated. Stir in the chocolate chips.

4. Scoop the mixture into the prepared jars and bake in the preheated oven for about 30 minutes, or until a cocktail stick inserted in the centre of a cake comes out almost clean.

5. Increase the oven temperature to 240°C/475°F/Gas Mark 9 and press four marshmallows into the top of each jar. Return the cakes to the oven and bake for a further 5–7 minutes, until the marshmallows are soft and lightly browned. Remove from the oven and leave to cool for a few minutes before serving warm.

Strawberry ripple marshmallows

Ingredients

oil, for greasing

cornflour, for dusting

icing sugar, sifted, for dusting

11 sheets of leaf gelatine
(about 20 g/¾ oz)

340 ml/11½ fl oz water

1 tbsp liquid glucose

450 g/1 lb caster sugar

3 egg whites

1 tsp strawberry extract

2 tsp pink food colouring

1. Lightly brush a 30 x 20-cm/12 x 8-inch baking tray with oil, then lightly dust it with cornflour and icing sugar. Put the gelatine into a small bowl and add 140 ml/4½ fl oz of the water, making sure the gelatine is absorbed. Set aside for 10 minutes.

2. Put the glucose, sugar and remaining water into a heavy-based saucepan. Bring to the boil, reduce the heat and simmer for 15 minutes, or until it reaches 127°C/260°F on a sugar thermometer. Remove from the heat. Stir the gelatine mixture, then carefully spoon into the pan. Pour into a jug and stir.

3. Whisk the egg whites until they hold stiff peaks, then gradually whisk in the hot syrup. The mixture will become shiny and start to thicken. Add the strawberry extract and whisk for 5–10 minutes, until the mixture holds its shape on the whisk. Spoon into the prepared tray and smooth with a wet palette knife. Sprinkle over the food colouring and use a small skewer to marble it through the mixture. Leave to set for 1 hour.

4. Loosen the marshmallow around the sides of the tray. Turn out onto a board. Cut into 32 squares, then lightly dust with cornflour and icing sugar. Place on a wire rack to dry, then serve.

Chocolate pretzel fudge squares

Ingredients

oil, for greasing

175 g/6 oz mini pretzels

25 g/1 oz butter, diced

300 g/10½ oz milk chocolate chips

400 ml/14 fl oz canned sweetened condensed milk

1 tsp vanilla extract

1. Lightly brush a 24-cm/9½-inch square baking tin with oil. Line it with baking paper, snipping diagonally into the corners, then pressing the paper into the tin so that the base and sides are lined and there is a 5-cm/2-inch overhang on all sides.

2. Roughly chop 55 g/2 oz of the pretzels. Put the butter, chocolate chips, condensed milk and vanilla extract into a heatproof bowl set over a saucepan of gently simmering water and heat until the chocolate has just melted and the mixture is smooth and warm but not hot. Remove from the heat and stir in the chopped pretzels.

3. Pour the mixture into the prepared tin, smooth the surface and push in the whole pretzels. Leave to cool for 1 hour. Cover with cling film, then chill in the fridge for 1–2 hours, until firm.

4. Lift the fudge out of the tin, peel off the paper and cut it into 16 squares.

#393 Polvorones biscuits

Ingredients

225 g/8 oz butter, plus extra for greasing

225 g/8 oz granulated sugar

40 g/1½ oz icing sugar

2 eggs

1 tsp vanilla extract

550 g/1 lb 4 oz plain flour, sifted, plus extra for dusting

1 tsp baking powder

½ tsp salt

100 g/3½ oz cinnamon sugar

1. Preheat the oven to 190°C/375°F/Gas Mark 5. Line a baking tray with greased baking paper. Put the butter, granulated sugar and icing sugar into a large bowl and beat until light and fluffy. Add the eggs, one at a time, gently stirring after each addition, then stir in the vanilla extract. Add the flour, baking powder and salt, and stir to combine.

2. Turn out the dough onto a lightly floured work surface and roll out to a thickness of 5 mm/¼ inch. Use a 5-cm/2-inch round fluted cutter to cut out 20–25 biscuits, re-rolling the trimmings if necessary. Place on the prepared tray and bake in the preheated oven for about 8–10 minutes until golden brown.

3. Remove the polvorones from the oven and sprinkle over the cinnamon sugar while they are still hot. Transfer to a wire rack to cool completely.

#394 Chocolate amaretto truffles

Ingredients

50 ml/2 fl oz amaretto liqueur

55 g/2 oz sultanas

100 g/3½ oz plain chocolate, roughly chopped

2 tbsp double cream

70 g/2½ oz ready-made chocolate cake or brownie, crumbled

100 g/3½ oz hazelnuts

55 g/2 oz chocolate sugar strands, to decorate

1. Put the amaretto and sultanas into a small mixing bowl, cover and leave to soak for 6-8 hours. Line a baking tray with baking paper.

2. Transfer the amaretto mixture to a food processor and process until puréed.

3. Put the chocolate and cream in a heatproof bowl set over a saucepan of gently simmering water and heat until melted. Remove from the heat, add the amaretto purée and cake, and stir well.

4. When cool enough to handle, use the palms of your hands to roll the mixture into truffle-sized balls and place on the prepared tray.

5. Preheat the grill to medium. Put the hazelnuts on a separate baking tray and toast them under the grill for 2-3 minutes, or until brown, shaking them halfway through, then chop finely.

6. Spread the chocolate sugar strands on one plate and the hazelnuts on another. Roll half the truffles in the chocolate and half in the hazelnuts. Return to the baking tray, cover with baking paper and chill in the fridge for 1-2 hours, or until firm.

Red wine sorbet

Ingredients

1 orange
1 lemon
600 ml/1 pint fruity red wine
140 g/5 oz soft light brown sugar
300 ml/10 fl oz water, chilled
2 egg whites, lightly beaten
fresh fruit, to serve

1. Peel the zest from the orange and lemon in strips, using a vegetable peeler, taking care not to remove any of the bitter white pith underneath. Place in a saucepan with the red wine and sugar. Heat gently, stirring until the sugar dissolves, then bring to the boil and simmer for 5 minutes. Remove from the heat and stir in the water.

2. Squeeze the juice from the fruit. Stir into the wine mixture. Cover and leave to sit until completely cool, then sieve into a freezerproof container. Cover and freeze for 7–8 hours, or until firm.

3. Working quickly, break the sorbet into chunks and transfer to a food processor. Blend for a few seconds to break down the chunks, then, leaving the processor running, gradually pour the egg whites through the feed tube. The mixture will become paler. Continue blending until smooth.

4. Freeze for a further 3–4 hours or until firm. Scoop into six chilled dishes or glasses and serve immediately with the fresh fruit.

396 Blackberry & orange bursts

Ingredients

500 ml/17 fl oz blood orange juice
100 ml/3½ fl oz sugar syrup
300 g/10½ oz blackberries

8 ice pop moulds
8 ice pop sticks

1. Put the blood orange juice and sugar syrup into a measuring jug and stir together well.

2. Drop the blackberries into 8 x 100-ml/3½-fl oz ice pop moulds, ensuring you have an even number of berries in each one.

3. Pour the blood orange juice mixture over the blackberries, insert an ice pop stick in each one and freeze for 4–5 hours, or until firm.

4. To unmould the ice pops, dip the frozen moulds in warm water for a few seconds and gently release the pops while holding the sticks.

#397 Citrus marzipan thins

Ingredients

200 g/7 oz ground almonds

200 g/7 oz caster sugar

1 large egg

a few drops of citrus extract

finely grated rind of ½ orange

icing sugar, for dusting

Icing

200 g/7 oz icing sugar, sifted

juice of 1 lemon

1. Line a 20-cm/8-inch square baking tin with baking paper, snipping diagonally into the corners, then pressing the paper into the tin so that the base and sides are lined.

2. Put the almonds and caster sugar into a mixing bowl and stir. Add the egg, citrus extract and orange rind, and mix to a stiff paste with your hands. Knead the marzipan briefly on a surface dusted with icing sugar, then press it into the base of the prepared tin using the back of a spoon, until even and smooth. Leave to set for 1 hour.

3. To make the icing, put the icing sugar and lemon juice into a bowl and stir until smooth, then spread evenly over the marzipan. Cover and leave in a cool place to dry overnight. Cut into bite-sized shapes using a fondant or cookie cutter.

#398 Mammoth mint cream

Ingredients

1 large egg white

a few drops of lemon juice

1–2 tsp peppermint extract

450 g/1 lb icing sugar, plus extra if needed and for dusting

200 g/7 oz plain chocolate, broken into pieces

1. Line a board with a sheet of baking paper. Put the egg white, lemon juice and peppermint extract into a large bowl and whisk with a fork until frothy. Gradually beat in the icing sugar until a stiff paste forms. Lightly knead until smooth, adding more icing sugar if the paste is too sticky.

2. Shape into a flat disc on a surface dusted with icing sugar, then roll out to a 20-cm/8-inch round. Place on the prepared board. Loosely cover with clingfilm and leave in a cool, dry place overnight, turning once, until firm and dry.

3. Place the chocolate in a heatproof bowl set over a saucepan of gently simmering water and heat until melted. Leave to cool for 10 minutes. Spread a thin layer of the melted chocolate over the top and sides of the peppermint cream. Chill in the refrigerator for 20 minutes, until just set. Spread the remaining chocolate over the peppermint cream and leave in a cool place for 1–2 hours, until set. Carefully remove the peppermint cream from the baking paper and place on a serving plate.

399 Popcorn cupcakes

Makes
12

Ingredients

125 ml/4 fl oz milk

50 g/1½ oz air-popped plain popcorn

190 g/6¾ oz plain flour

1½ tsp baking powder

175 g/6 oz butter, softened

500 g/1 lb 2 oz caster sugar

100 g/3½ oz soft light brown sugar

4 tsp vanilla extract

2 large eggs

55 g/2 oz golden syrup

¼ tsp cream of tartar

125 ml/4 fl oz water

225 ml/8 fl oz double cream

2 tsp vanilla extract

salt

1. Preheat the oven to 180°C/350°F/Gas Mark 4 and line a 12-hole muffin tin with paper cases. Put the milk into a small saucepan and heat until simmering. Add 10 g/¼ oz of the popcorn, remove from the heat and set aside for 10 minutes, then transfer to a food processor and purée. Set aside to cool.

2. Sift together the flour, baking powder and ¼ teaspoon of salt into a bowl. Beat together 115 g/4 oz of the butter, 100 g/3½ oz of the caster sugar and the brown sugar until pale and fluffy. Add half the vanilla extract, then beat in the eggs, one at a time. Add half the flour mixture and the popcorn purée, and beat to incorporate. Mix in the remaining flour mixture. Spoon into the cases and bake in the preheated oven for 20 minutes. Leave to cool in the tin for 1–2 minutes, then transfer to a wire rack to cool completely.

3. Put the remaining caster sugar, golden syrup, cream of tartar and water into a saucepan and heat over a medium heat, stirring constantly, until the sugar has dissolved. Increase the heat to medium–high, bring to the boil and cook, without stirring, for 8–10 minutes. Remove from the heat and stir in the remaining butter, then whisk in the cream. Stir in the remaining vanilla extract and ½ teaspoon of salt. Leave to cool for 5 minutes. Spread a spoonful of caramel over the top of each cupcake. Mix the remaining caramel with the remaining popcorn, stirring to coat. Top each cupcake with a scoop of the caramel-coated popcorn and leave to cool completely.

400 Sally Lunn bun

Serves
10

Ingredients

175 g/6 oz butter, plus extra for greasing

4 eggs

225 ml/8 fl oz milk

40 g/1½ oz fresh yeast

500 g/1 lb 2 oz plain flour, plus extra for dusting

50 g/1¾ oz caster sugar

2 tsp salt

1 egg yolk, beaten, for brushing

1. Melt the butter in a small saucepan. Whisk the eggs in a large bowl, then gradually add the butter, whisking constantly.

2. Heat the milk in a small saucepan, then remove from the heat and crumble in the yeast. Sift together the flour, sugar and salt into a separate bowl, then whisk in the egg and butter mixture. Add the yeast mixture and mix to a smooth dough. Put the dough into a bowl, cover with clingfilm and leave to rise in a warm place for about 90 minutes, until doubled in size.

3. Grease a 20-cm/8-inch round springform cake tin and dust with flour, shaking off any excess. Knock back the dough, knead for 1–2 minutes, then place in the prepared tin. Cover with a damp tea towel and leave to rise for 30 minutes. Preheat the oven to 190°C/375°F/Gas Mark 5. Brush the top of the dough with the egg yolk. Bake in the preheated oven for 15–20 minutes, until golden brown. Leave to cool slightly, then remove from the tin, slice and serve.

Celebrate

#401 Birthday party cupcakes

Makes 24

Ingredients

225 g/8 oz soft margarine

225 g/8 oz caster sugar

4 eggs

225 g/8 oz self-raising flour, sifted

175 g/6 oz butter, softened

350 g/12 oz icing sugar

Decoration

small sweets and chocolates, dried fruit, edible sugar flower shapes and hundreds and thousands

candles and candleholders (optional)

1. Preheat the oven to 180°C/350°F/Gas Mark 4. Line 2 x 12-hole muffin tins with paper cases.

2. Put the margarine, sugar, eggs and flour in a large bowl and beat together until just smooth. Spoon the mixture into the paper cases. Bake in the preheated oven for 15–20 minutes, or until well risen, golden and firm to the touch. Transfer to wire racks and leave to cool completely.

3. Put the butter in a bowl and beat until fluffy. Sift in the icing sugar and beat until smooth and creamy. Spoon the frosting into a piping bag fitted with a large star-shaped nozzle. When the cupcakes are cold, pipe circles of frosting on top of each cupcake, then decorate. If desired, place a candle in the top of each.

#402 Birthday cookies

Makes 24

Ingredients

115 g/4 oz butter, softened, plus extra for greasing

140 g/5 oz caster sugar

1 egg, beaten

½ tsp vanilla extract

250 g/9 oz plain flour

2 tbsp beaten egg white

175 g/6 oz icing sugar, sifted, plus extra for dusting

water or lemon juice, if needed

85 g/3 oz each pink, blue and yellow ready-to-roll fondant icing and some red writing icing, to decorate

1. Put the butter and sugar into a bowl and beat until creamy. Gradually beat in the egg and vanilla extract. Sift in the flour and blend with a wooden spoon to form a rough dough. Lightly knead until smooth. Shape into a square 20-cm/8-inch log and wrap in clingfilm. Chill in the refrigerator for 3–4 hours, re-shaping after 1 hour. Grease two baking sheets with butter. Preheat the oven to 180°C/350°F/Gas Mark 4.

2. Slice the dough into 24 squares and place on the prepared baking sheets, spaced well apart. Bake in the preheated oven for 12–15 minutes, until pale golden in colour. Leave to cool on the baking sheets for a few minutes, then transfer to wire racks to cool completely.

3. Meanwhile, place the egg white in a bowl and add a little of the icing sugar. Beat until smooth. Gradually beat in the remaining icing sugar to make a smooth, thick icing that holds soft peaks. Beat in a few drops of water to get a spooning consistency.

4. Spread the icing on the cookies. Thinly roll out the ready-to-roll icing on a work surface lightly dusted with icing sugar and cut out parcels, cupcakes and balloons. Place the shapes on the cookies and pipe ribbons, cherries and string with the writing icing. Leave to set before serving.

#403 Dotty chocolate chip cake

Ingredients

oil, for greasing

175 g/6 oz soft margarine

175 g/6 oz caster sugar

3 eggs, beaten

175 g/6 oz plain flour

1 tsp baking powder

2 tbsp cocoa powder

55 g/2 oz white chocolate chips

40 g/1½ oz small coloured sweets, to decorate

Icing

175 g/6 oz milk chocolate or plain chocolate, broken into pieces

100 g/3½ oz butter or margarine

1 tbsp golden syrup

1. Preheat the oven to 160°C/325°F/Gas Mark 3. Grease a 20-cm/8-inch round cake tin and line the base with baking paper.

2. Place the margarine, sugar, eggs, flour, baking powder and cocoa powder in a bowl and beat until just smooth. Stir in the chocolate chips, mixing evenly.

3. Spoon the mixture into the prepared tin and smooth level. Bake in the preheated oven for 40–45 minutes, until risen and firm to the touch. Leave to cool in the tin for 5 minutes, then turn out onto a wire rack to cool completely.

4. To make the icing, place the chocolate, butter and golden syrup in a saucepan over a low heat and stir until just melted and smooth. Remove from the heat and leave to cool until it begins to thicken enough to leave a trail when the spoon is lifted.

5. Pour the icing over the top of the cake, allowing it to drizzle down the sides. Arrange the sweets over the top of the cake.

#404 Chocolate squares

Makes
25

Ingredients

115 g/4 oz butter, softened, plus extra for greasing

175 g/6 oz caster sugar

1 large egg, beaten

225 g/8 oz plain flour

25 g/1 oz cocoa powder

½ tsp baking powder

Icing

70 g/2½ oz icing sugar

2 tbsp cocoa powder

5–6 tsp milk

1 tbsp white chocolate sugar strands

1 tbsp hundreds and thousands

1. Put the butter and sugar into a bowl and beat together until creamy, then gradually beat in the egg. Sift in the flour, cocoa powder and baking powder, and blend together with a wooden spoon to form a dough. Lightly knead until smooth. Shape into a square 20-cm/8-inch log and wrap in clingfilm. Chill in the refrigerator for 3–4 hours, re-shaping after 1 hour. Grease two baking sheets with butter. Preheat the oven to 180°C/350°F/Gas Mark 4.

2. Slice the dough into 25 squares and place on the prepared baking sheets, spaced well apart. Bake in the preheated oven for 12–15 minutes, until set. Leave to cool on the baking sheets for a few minutes, then transfer to wire racks to cool completely.

3. To make the icing, sift the sugar and cocoa powder into a bowl and stir in the milk to make a smooth, thick icing. Use a small palette knife to spread the icing over the cookies, then top with the white chocolate sugar strands and the hundreds and thousands. Leave to set.

#405 Piñata cupcakes

Makes
12

Ingredients

125 g/4½ oz plain flour

60 g/2¼ oz cocoa powder

1½ tsp baking powder

230 g/8¼ oz butter, softened

200 g/7 oz caster sugar

3 tsp vanilla extract

2 large eggs

125 ml/4 fl oz double cream

salt

250 g/9 oz icing sugar, plus extra if needed

2 tbsp milk

Decoration

350 g/12 oz plain chocolate-flavoured cake covering, broken into pieces

4½ tsp vegetable oil

450 g/1 lb mixed sweets

piping gel

hundreds and thousands

1. Preheat the oven to 180°C/350°F/Gas Mark 4 and line a 12-hole muffin tin with paper cases. Sift together the flour, cocoa powder, baking powder and ¼ teaspoon of salt in a bowl. Put half of the butter into a separate bowl with the caster sugar and beat until pale and fluffy. Add 2 teaspoons of the vanilla extract, then add the eggs, one at a time, beating after each addition. Add half of the flour mixture and the cream, and beat until incorporated. Add the remaining flour mixture and mix. Spoon into the paper cases and bake in the preheated oven for 20 minutes, until risen and a cocktail stick inserted into the centre of a cupcake comes out clean. Leave to cool in the tin for 1–2 minutes, then transfer to a wire rack to cool completely.

2. To make the frosting, put the remaining butter into a bowl and beat with an electric mixer until creamy. Add the icing sugar, milk, the remaining vanilla extract and a pinch of salt and beat until well combined. Add more icing sugar, if necessary, to achieve a piping consistency. Spread the frosting evenly on the cupcakes with a palette knife, making sure it goes all the way to the edges of the paper cases.

3. To decorate, put the cake covering and oil into a heatproof bowl set over a saucepan of gently simmering water and stir until melted. Spoon about 1 tablespoon of chocolate into a 7.5-cm/3-inch dome-shaped mould. Turn the mould slowly and use the back of a spoon to spread the chocolate in a thin layer, coating the entire cavity of the mould. Chill in the freezer for 5–10 minutes, or until the chocolate is set. Carefully unmould the chocolate dome and store in the refrigerator until required. Repeat to make 12 chocolate domes. Stand a dome upside-down on the work surface and fill it with a large spoonful of sweets. Place a frosted cupcake upside-down on top of the dome so that the frosting is pressed into the edge of the chocolate. Turn the cupcake right-side up and set aside. Repeat until you have assembled all 12 cupcakes. Brush the top of each dome with piping gel. Sprinkle with hundreds and thousands and leave to set.

#406 Chocolate moustaches

Makes 6

Ingredients

250 g/9 oz plain chocolate, roughly chopped

6 lollipop sticks

1. Put the chocolate in a heatproof bowl set over a saucepan of gently simmering water and heat until melted. Leave to cool for a few minutes.

2. Pour the melted chocolate into 6 x 100-ml/3½-fl oz moustache moulds.

3. Push a lollipop stick firmly into each moustache. Chill in the fridge for 1 hour, or until set. Gently turn out.

#407 Birthday balloons

Makes 24

Ingredients

400-g/14-oz packet ready-made vanilla sponge mix

200 g/7 oz butter, softened

300 g/10½ oz icing sugar

1 tsp vanilla extract

1 tbsp hot water

350 g/12 oz chewy sweets in 3 flavours, softened

100 g/3½ oz small red, green and yellow sugar-coated chocolate drops

24 lollipop sticks

1. Preheat the oven to 180°C/350°F/Gas Mark 4. Line 2 x 12-hole mini muffin tins with paper cases. Make up the sponge mix according to the packet directions and spoon into the paper cases. Bake in the preheated oven for 18–20 minutes. Leave to cool in the tin for 5 minutes, then transfer to a wire rack to cool completely.

2. Put the butter in a large bowl and beat until soft. Add the icing sugar and vanilla extract and beat until smooth and creamy. Pour in the hot water and beat until very soft and fluffy. Using a palette knife, spread a thin layer over the cakes.

3. Mould two sweets into a ball. Push each balloon shape onto the end of a lollipop stick. Pinch around the stick to create a knotted end. Repeat until you have 24 balloons, pushing each one into a cake.

4. For the streamers, soften the remaining sweets and roll them out thinly. Cut them into 5-cm/2-inch x 5-mm/¼-inch pieces and curl each one around a lollipop stick. Twist the sweets off the sticks. Scatter the cakes with the candy-coated sweets and the sweet twists to finish.

#408 Raspberry jellies

Ingredients

1 x 135-g/4¾-oz pack raspberry jelly, cut into small pieces

150 g/5½ oz fresh raspberries (reserve a few to decorate)

200 ml/7 fl oz double cream

2 egg yolks

1 tsp cornflour

1 tsp caster sugar

2 drops vanilla extract

hundreds and thousands, to decorate

1. Follow the packet instructions to make 600 ml/1 pint of jelly. Divide the raspberries between 6 x 250 ml/8½ fl oz small glass dishes. Pour the liquid jelly onto the raspberries, making sure there is the same amount in each dish. Place in the refrigerator for 1–2 hours to set.

2. Place the cream in a small saucepan and gradually bring to a boil. Put the egg yolks, cornflour, sugar and vanilla extract in a large, heatproof bowl and whisk with a fork until smooth. Pour the hot cream onto the egg and sugar mixture, whisking constantly with a balloon whisk. Pour the mixture back into the pan and continue whisking over a very gentle heat until it just starts to thicken. Remove from the heat and leave to cool.

3. Pour the custard onto the set jellies, decorate with hundreds and thousands and the reserved raspberries, and serve.

#409 Birthday number cake

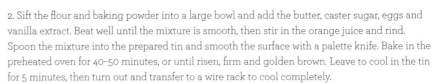
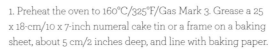
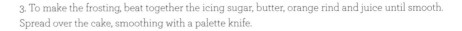

Ingredients

oil, for greasing

175 g/6 oz plain flour

1 tbsp baking powder

175 g/6 oz butter, softened

175 g/6 oz caster sugar

3 eggs, beaten

1 tsp vanilla extract

2 tbsp orange juice

finely grated rind of ½ orange

sugar orange slices and birthday candles, to decorate

Frosting

350 g/12 oz icing sugar, sifted

175 g/6 oz butter, softened

finely grated rind of ½ orange

1 tbsp orange juice

1. Preheat the oven to 160°C/325°F/Gas Mark 3. Grease a 25 x 18-cm/10 x 7-inch numeral cake tin or a frame on a baking sheet, about 5 cm/2 inches deep, and line with baking paper.

2. Sift the flour and baking powder into a large bowl and add the butter, caster sugar, eggs and vanilla extract. Beat well until the mixture is smooth, then stir in the orange juice and rind. Spoon the mixture into the prepared tin and smooth the surface with a palette knife. Bake in the preheated oven for 40–50 minutes, or until risen, firm and golden brown. Leave to cool in the tin for 5 minutes, then turn out and transfer to a wire rack to cool completely.

3. To make the frosting, beat together the icing sugar, butter, orange rind and juice until smooth. Spread over the cake, smoothing with a palette knife.

4. Arrange the orange slices on top of the cake, then add the birthday candles and serve.

#410 Chocolate whoopie pie cake

Ingredients

175 g/6 oz plain flour

1½ tsp bicarbonate of soda

40 g/1½ oz cocoa powder

large pinch of salt

85 g/3 oz butter, softened, plus extra for greasing

85 g/3 oz white vegetable fat

150 g/5½ oz soft dark brown sugar

1 large egg, beaten

1 tsp vanilla extract

150 ml/5 fl oz milk

175 g/6 oz white marshmallows

3 tbsp milk

200 ml/7 fl oz double cream

6 tbsp strawberry jam

icing sugar, to dust

birthday candles, to decorate

1. Preheat the oven to 180°C/350°F/Gas Mark 4. Grease 2 x 20-cm/8-inch round sandwich tins and line the bases with baking paper. Sift together the plain flour, bicarbonate of soda, cocoa powder and salt.

2. Place the butter, vegetable fat and sugar in a large bowl and beat until pale and fluffy. Beat in the egg and vanilla extract, followed by half the flour mixture and the milk. Stir in the remaining flour mixture and mix until thoroughly incorporated. Divide the mixture evenly between the prepared tins and gently level the surfaces. Bake in the preheated oven for 20–25 minutes until risen and just firm to the touch. Cool in the tins for 10 minutes then remove from the tins and transfer to a wire rack to cool completely.

3. Place the marshmallows and milk in a heatproof bowl set over a saucepan of gently simmering water and heat until melted, stirring occasionally. Remove from the heat and leave to cool.

4. Whip the cream in a separate bowl until it holds firm peaks. Fold the cream into the marshmallow mixture. Cover and chill in the refrigerator for 30 minutes. Sandwich the cakes together with the jam and marshmallow cream. Dust the top of the cake with icing sugar and add birthday candles to decorate.

#411 Baby shower cupcakes

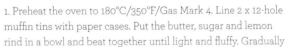

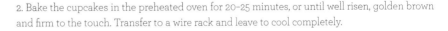

Ingredients

225 g/8 oz butter, softened

225 g/8 oz caster sugar

finely grated rind of 2 lemons

4 eggs, lightly beaten

225 g/8 oz self-raising flour, sifted

24 sugared almonds

Icing

350 g/12 oz icing sugar

6–8 tsp hot water

red or blue liquid or paste food colouring

1. Preheat the oven to 180°C/350°F/Gas Mark 4. Line 2 x 12-hole muffin tins with paper cases. Put the butter, sugar and lemon rind in a bowl and beat together until light and fluffy. Gradually add the eggs, beating well after each addition. Add the flour and, using a large metal spoon, fold into the mixture. Spoon the mixture into the paper cases to half fill them.

2. Bake the cupcakes in the preheated oven for 20–25 minutes, or until well risen, golden brown and firm to the touch. Transfer to a wire rack and leave to cool completely.

3. When the cakes are cold, make the icing. Sift the icing sugar into a bowl. Add the water and stir until the mixture is smooth and thick enough to coat the back of a wooden spoon. Dip a skewer into the food colouring, then stir it into the icing until it is evenly coloured pink or pale blue. Spoon some icing on top of each cupcake. Top each with a sugared almond and leave the cupcakes to set for 30 minutes.

Cheeky monkey cupcakes

Makes
12

Ingredients

115 g/4 oz butter, softened

85 g/3 oz soft light brown sugar

1 tbsp honey

2 eggs, lightly beaten

100 g/3½ oz self-raising flour

2 tbsp cocoa powder

350 g/12 oz ivory ready-to-roll
fondant icing

brown food colouring

icing sugar, for dusting

2 tbsp chocolate spread

24 large chocolate buttons

tubes of white and black writing icing

12 brown sugar-coated chocolate drops

1. Preheat the oven to 180°C/350°F/Gas Mark 4. Line a 12-hole muffin tin with paper cases. Place the butter, brown sugar and honey in a large bowl and beat together until light and fluffy. Gradually beat in the eggs. Sift in the flour and cocoa powder and fold in gently. Spoon the mixture into the paper cases. Bake in the preheated oven for 15–20 minutes, until risen and firm to the touch. Transfer to a wire rack and leave to cool.

2. Colour two thirds of the ivory fondant pale brown with a little brown food colouring. Roll out the brown fondant icing to a thickness of 5 mm/¼ inch on a surface dusted with icing sugar. Using a 7-cm/2¾-inch round cutter, stamp out 12 rounds. Roll out the remaining ivory fondant and, using the end of a large piping nozzle, cut out 24 small rounds. Re-roll the icing and cut out 12 ovals.

3. Spread the cupcakes with a layer of chocolate spread and top with the rounds of brown icing. Attach two ivory rounds and one oval on top of each cupcake with a little water for the face. Attach two chocolate buttons on the side of each cupcake with writing icing. Use the white and black writing icing to pipe eyes and a mouth, and attach a chocolate drop for a nose.

Makes
12

Ingredients

115 g/4 oz self-raising flour

¼ tsp baking powder

115 g/4 oz butter, softened

115 g/4 oz caster sugar

2 eggs, lightly beaten

1 tbsp milk

1 tsp vanilla extract

Decoration

150 g/5½ oz white ready-to-roll fondant icing

150 g/5½ oz pale blue or pink ready-to-roll fondant icing

icing sugar, for dusting

1 tbsp apricot jam, warmed and strained

tube of white writing icing

1. Preheat the oven to 180°C/350°F/Gas Mark 4. Line a 12-hole muffin tin with paper cases. Sift the flour and baking powder into a large bowl. Add the butter, caster sugar, eggs, milk and vanilla extract and beat until smooth. Spoon into the paper cases. Bake in the preheated oven for 15–20 minutes, then transfer to a wire rack to cool completely.

2. Roll out the white fondant icing to a thickness of 5 mm/¼ inch on a surface lightly dusted with icing sugar. Using a 6-cm/2½-inch cutter, stamp out six rounds. Repeat with the blue or pink fondant icing. Lightly brush each cupcake with a little jam and gently press an icing round on top.

3. Re-roll the blue or pink icing trimmings. Use a small teddy bear cutter to stamp out two teddy bears. Use a tiny flower cutter to stamp out four flowers. Re-roll the white icing trimmings. Use a small flower cutter to stamp out two small flowers. Use a 4-cm/1½-inch fluted cutter to stamp out two rounds, then cut away a small oval from each round to resemble a baby's bib. Use a 2.5-cm/1-inch cutter to stamp out two rounds. Mark with the end of a paintbrush to resemble buttons. Shape four booties and two ducks from the remaining trimmings. Attach the decorations to the top of the cupcakes with a little water. Use the writing icing to add bows on the booties.

#414 Anniversary cupcakes

Makes
24

Ingredients

225 g/8 oz butter, softened

225 g/8 oz caster sugar

1 tsp vanilla extract

4 large eggs, lightly beaten

225 g/8 oz self-raising flour, sifted

5 tbsp milk

Frosting

175 g/6 oz unsalted butter, softened

350 g/12 oz icing sugar

25 g/1 oz silver or gold dragées

1. Preheat the oven to 180°C/350°F/Gas Mark 4. Line 2 x 12-hole muffin tins with paper cases.

2. Put the butter, sugar and vanilla extract in a bowl and beat together until light and fluffy. Gradually add the eggs, beating well after each addition. Add the flour and, using a large metal spoon, fold into the mixture with the milk. Spoon the mixture into the paper cases.

3. Bake the cupcakes in the preheated oven for 15–20 minutes, or until well risen and firm to the touch. Transfer to wire racks and leave to cool completely.

4. To make the frosting, put the butter in a bowl and beat until fluffy. Sift in the icing sugar and beat well. Put the frosting in a piping bag fitted with a star-shaped nozzle.

5. When the cupcakes are cold, pipe circles of frosting on top of each cupcake to cover the tops. Sprinkle over the dragées just before serving.

#415 Mother's day breakfast muffins

Makes 12

Ingredients

280 g/10 oz plain flour

1 tbsp baking powder

pinch of salt

115 g/4 oz caster sugar

2 eggs

250 ml/9 fl oz milk

85 g/3 oz butter, melted and cooled

1 tsp orange extract

icing sugar, for dusting

fresh strawberries and fruit juice, to serve

1. Preheat the oven to 200°C/400°F/Gas Mark 6. Line a 12-hole muffin tin with paper cases. Sift together the flour, baking powder and salt into a large bowl. Stir in the caster sugar.

2. Lightly beat the eggs in a large jug, then beat in the milk, butter and orange extract. Make a well in the centre of the dry ingredients and pour in the beaten liquid ingredients. Gently stir until just combined; do not over-mix. Spoon the mixture into the paper cases. Bake in the preheated oven for about 20 minutes, until well risen, golden and firm to the touch.

3. Leave the muffins to cool in the tin for 5 minutes. Meanwhile, arrange the strawberries in a bowl and pour the juice into a glass. Dust the muffins with icing sugar. Serve warm with the strawberries and juice.

#416 Father's day chocolate rum pots

Makes 6

Ingredients

225 g/8 oz plain chocolate, broken into pieces

4 eggs, separated

6 tbsp caster sugar

4 tbsp dark rum

4 tbsp double cream

whipped cream and marbled chocolate shapes, to decorate

1. Put the chocolate into a heatproof bowl set over a saucepan of gently simmering water and heat until melted. Leave to cool slightly.

2. Whisk the egg yolks with the caster sugar in a clean bowl until very pale and fluffy.

3. Drizzle the melted chocolate into the mixture and fold in with the rum and double cream.

4. Whisk the egg whites in a clean bowl until they hold soft peaks. Fold the egg whites into the chocolate mixture in two batches. Divide the mixture between six serving dishes and chill in the refrigerator for at least 2 hours.

5. To serve, decorate with a little whipped cream and top with marbled chocolate shapes.

Strawberry & butter biscuit stack

Ingredients

175 g/6 oz self-raising flour

100 g/3½ oz unsalted butter, diced and chilled, plus extra for greasing

75 g/2¾ oz caster sugar

1 egg yolk

1 tbsp rosewater

600 ml/1 pint whipping cream, lightly whipped

225 g/8 oz strawberries, hulled and quartered, plus a few whole strawberries to decorate

icing sugar, for dusting

1. Preheat the oven to 190°C/375°F/Gas Mark 5. Grease two baking sheets and line with baking paper.

2. To make the shortcakes, sift the flour into a bowl. Rub in the butter with your fingers until the mixture resembles breadcrumbs. Stir in the caster sugar, then add the egg yolk and rosewater and mix to form a soft dough.

3. Divide the dough in half. Roll out each piece into a 19-cm/7½-inch round and transfer each one to a prepared baking sheet. Crimp the edges of the dough and prick all over with a fork.

4. Bake in the preheated oven for 15 minutes, until lightly golden. Transfer the shortcakes to a wire rack to cool.

5. Mix the cream with the strawberry quarters and spoon on top of one of the shortcakes. Cut the remaining shortcake round into wedges, then place on top of the cream. Dust with icing sugar and decorate with whole strawberries.

Valentine waffles

Ingredients

150 g/5½ oz plain flour

1½ tsp baking powder

pinch of salt

250 ml/9 fl oz milk

1 large egg

2 tbsp sunflower oil, plus extra for greasing

200 g/7 oz raspberries, to serve

Sauce

100 g/3½ oz plain chocolate, broken into pieces

4 tbsp single cream

1 tbsp dark rum or brandy

1 x waffle maker

1. To make the sauce, put the chocolate, cream and rum into a bowl set over a saucepan of gently simmering water and heat until the chocolate is melted. Stir until smooth, remove from the heat and keep warm. Sift the flour, baking powder and salt into a bowl. Add the milk, egg and oil, and whisk to a smooth batter. Leave to stand for 5 minutes.

2. Lightly grease a waffle maker and heat until hot. Pour the batter into the waffle maker and cook until golden brown. Repeat, using the remaining batter, while keeping the cooked waffles warm.

3. Using a 7-cm/2¾-inch heart-shaped cutter, stamp out a heart from the centre of each waffle. Serve the waffles on individual plates, with the raspberries in the centre and the chocolate sauce piped around in heart shapes.

419 Doodle birthday cake

Ingredients

4 eggs, beaten

225 g/8 oz self-raising flour

225 g/8 oz caster sugar

225 g/8 oz butter, plus extra
for greasing

1½ tsp baking powder

1 tsp vanilla extract

Filling

150 g/5½ oz butter, softened

150 g/5½ oz icing sugar, sifted

200 g/7 oz lemon curd

Decoration

400 g/14 oz white ready-to-roll
fondant icing

icing sugar, for dusting

selection of coloured icing tubes or pens

1. Grease two 18-cm/7-inch sandwich tins and line the bases with baking paper. Preheat the oven to 180°C/350°F/Gas Mark 4.

2. Place the eggs, flour, caster sugar, butter, baking powder and vanilla extract in a bowl and beat well, for 2–3 minutes, until pale, smooth and creamy. Divide the mixture between the two tins, smooth lightly with a palette knife and bake in the preheated oven for 25–30 minutes, until golden and risen and the tops spring back easily when lightly pressed with a fingertip. Leave to cool in the tins for 5 minutes, then turn out onto a wire rack to cool completely.

3. To make the buttercream filling, put the butter into a bowl and beat until soft and creamy. Add the sugar and beat for a further 1–2 minutes until smooth and creamy.

4. When the cakes are cool, place one on a cake board or serving platter and spread evenly with the lemon curd. Top with two thirds of the buttercream. Place the remaining cake on top.

5. Use a palette knife to lightly coat the top and sides of the cake with the remaining buttercream and smooth evenly all over.

6. Knead the white fondant icing on a work surface lightly dusted with icing sugar until soft. Roll out to a large round and use the rolling pin to drape it over the cake. Use the palm of your hand to smooth it over the top and the sides. Trim off any excess fondant.

7. Let the children have fun doodling on the cake with the coloured icing tubes.

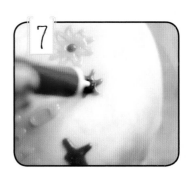

#420 Summer pudding

Ingredients

675 g/1 lb 8 oz mixed soft fruit, such as redcurrants, blackcurrants, raspberries and blackberries

140 g/5 oz caster sugar

2 tbsp crème de framboise liqueur (optional)

6–8 slices of day-old white bread, crusts removed

double cream, to serve

1. Place the fruit in a large saucepan with the sugar. Very slowly bring to the boil over a low heat, stirring carefully to ensure that the sugar has dissolved. Cook for 2–3 minutes, or until the juices run but the fruit still holds its shape. Add the liqueur, if using.

2. Line an 900-ml/1½-pint pudding basin with some of the slices of bread (cut them to shape so that the bread fits well). Spoon in the cooked fruit and juices, reserving a little juice. Cover the surface of the fruit with the remaining bread. Place a saucer on top of the pudding and weight it for at least 8 hours or overnight in the refrigerator.

3. Turn out the pudding onto a plate and pour over the reserved juices to colour any white bits of bread that may be showing. Serve immediately with the double cream.

#421 Valentine whoopie pies

Ingredients

250 g/9 oz plain flour

1 tsp bicarbonate of soda

large pinch of salt

265 g/9¼ oz butter, softened

150 g/5½ oz caster sugar

1 large egg, beaten

2 tsp vanilla extract

150 ml/5 fl oz buttermilk

¼ tsp red liquid food colouring

4 tbsp double cream

280 g/10 oz icing sugar, sifted

2 tbsp pink heart-shaped sugar sprinkles, to decorate

Icing

150 g/5½ oz icing sugar

1–2 tbsp warm water

a few drops of red liquid food colouring

1. Preheat the oven to 180°C/350°F/Gas Mark 4. Line three large baking sheets with baking paper. Sift together the plain flour, bicarbonate of soda and salt.

2. Place 115 g/4 oz of the butter in a large bowl with the caster sugar and beat until pale and fluffy. Beat in the egg and half the vanilla extract followed by half the flour mixture, the buttermilk and food colouring. Stir in the remaining flour mixture and mix well.

3. Pipe or spoon 28 mounds of the mixture onto the prepared baking sheets, spaced well apart. Bake in the preheated oven, one sheet at a time, for 9–11 minutes until risen and just firm to the touch. Leave to cool for 5 minutes, then transfer to wire racks and leave to cool completely.

4. Place the remaining butter and vanilla extract in a bowl and beat until pale and creamy. Beat in the cream, then gradually beat in the icing sugar and continue beating for a further 2–3 minutes.

5. To make the icing, sift the icing sugar into a bowl and stir in enough water to make a smooth icing that is thick enough to coat the back of a wooden spoon. Beat in a few drops of food colouring to colour the icing pale pink.

6. Spread or pipe the filling on the flat side of 14 cakes. Top with the remaining cakes. Spoon the icing over the whoopie pies and decorate with sugar sprinkles. Leave to set.

#422 Berry love pies

Ingredients

butter, for greasing

350 g/12 oz strawberries, roughly chopped

2 tsp cornflour

2 tbsp strawberry jam

grated rind of 4 limes

450 g/1 lb ready-made sweet shortcrust pastry, chilled

plain flour, for dusting

1 egg yolk mixed with 1 tbsp water, for glazing

caster sugar, for sprinkling

225 ml/8 fl oz double cream

2 tbsp icing sugar

1. Preheat the oven to 180°C/350°F/Gas Mark 4. Lightly grease 2 x 12-hole mini muffin tins. Put the strawberries in a bowl and stir in the cornflour, jam and half the lime rind.

2. Thinly roll out half the pastry on a lightly floured surface. Using a fluted cutter, stamp out 24 x 6-cm/2½-inch rounds and gently press into the prepared tins. Brush the top edges with the egg glaze, then spoon in the filling. Roll out the remaining pastry and stamp out 24 x 5-cm/2-inch rounds. Use a heart-shaped shaped cookie cutter to cut hearts from each round and use the hearts as lids, pressing the edges together. Brush egg glaze over the pastry and sprinkle with caster sugar.

3. Bake in the preheated oven for 15 minutes, or until golden. Leave to cool in the tins for 10 minutes, then transfer to a wire rack to cool. Whip the cream until it holds soft peaks, then fold in half the remaining lime rind and the icing sugar. Sprinkle with the remaining lime rind. Serve spoonfuls of the cream with the pies.

#423 Sweetheart macaroons

Ingredients

75 g/2¾ oz ground almonds

115 g/4 oz icing sugar

2 large egg whites

50 g/1¾ oz caster sugar

pink food colouring paste or liquid

115 g/4 oz white chocolate, finely chopped

300 ml/10 fl oz double cream

1. Place the ground almonds and icing sugar in a food processor and process for 15 seconds. Sift into a bowl. Line two baking sheets with baking paper and use a 7-cm/2¾-inch heart-shaped cutter to mark 12 heart shapes on the underside. Place the egg whites in a large bowl and whisk until they hold soft peaks. Gradually whisk in the caster sugar to make a firm, glossy meringue. Whisk in enough food colouring to give a pink colour. Fold the almond mixture into the meringue one third at a time, cutting and folding the mixture until it forms a shiny batter with a thick, ribbon-like consistency.

2. Pour into a piping bag fitted with a 1-cm/½-inch plain nozzle. Pipe heart shapes onto the prepared baking sheets. Tap the sheets firmly on a work surface to remove air bubbles. Leave at room temperature for 30 minutes. Preheat the oven to 160°C/325°F/Gas Mark 3. Bake in the preheated oven for 15–20 minutes. Leave to cool for 10 minutes, then peel the macaroons off the paper. Leave to cool completely.

3. Place the chocolate in a heatproof bowl. Heat half the cream in a saucepan until boiling, then pour over the chocolate and stir. Leave until cold. Whip the remaining cream until it holds soft peaks. Fold into the chocolate mixture. Use to sandwich pairs of macaroons together.

#424 Valentine heart cookies

Makes 14

Ingredients

100 g/3½ oz butter, softened, plus extra for greasing

55 g/2 oz caster sugar

1 tsp finely grated lemon rind

1 egg yolk

200 g/7 oz plain flour, for dusting

2 tsp beaten egg white

175 g/6 oz icing sugar, sifted

tube of white writing icing, to decorate

1. Put the butter and sugar into a bowl and beat together until pale and creamy. Beat in the lemon rind and egg yolk. Sift in the flour and mix to a firm dough. Lightly knead until smooth, then wrap in clingfilm and chill in the refrigerator for 30 minutes.

2. Preheat the oven to 180°C/350°F/Gas Mark 4. Grease two baking sheets. Roll out the dough on a lightly floured surface to a thickness of 5 mm/¼ inch. Using a 7-cm/2¾-inch heart-shaped cutter, stamp out 14 hearts. Place on the prepared baking sheets. Bake in the preheated oven for 12–15 minutes, until golden. Leave to cool on the baking sheets.

3. Beat the egg white with a little of the icing sugar until smooth. Beat in the remaining icing sugar to make a firm icing. Spoon 3 tablespoons into a piping bag fitted with a fine nozzle and pipe an outline around each cookie. Add a little water to the remaining icing and spoon onto the cookies to flood. Pipe white polka dots onto the cookies with white writing icing.

#425 Chocolate heart cupcakes

Makes 6

Ingredients

85 g/3 oz butter, softened

85 g/3 oz caster sugar

½ tsp vanilla extract

2 eggs, lightly beaten

70 g/2½ oz plain flour

1 tbsp cocoa powder

1 tsp baking powder

6 pink edible sugar flowers, to decorate

Marzipan hearts

icing sugar, for dusting

35 g/1¼ oz marzipan

red liquid or paste food colouring

Frosting

55 g/2 oz butter, softened

115 g/4 oz icing sugar

25 g/1 oz plain chocolate, melted

1. Line a baking tray with baking paper and dust with icing sugar. To make the hearts, knead the marzipan until pliable, then add a few drops of red colouring and knead until evenly coloured. Roll out the marzipan to a thickness of 5 mm/¼ inch on a surface dusted with icing sugar. Using a small heart-shaped cutter, cut out six hearts. Place these on the prepared tray and leave to dry for 3–4 hours.

2. To make the cupcakes, preheat the oven to 180°C/350°F/Gas Mark 4. Line a 6-hole muffin tin with paper cases.

3. Put the butter, sugar and vanilla extract in a bowl and beat together until light and fluffy. Gradually add the eggs, beating well after each addition. Sift in the flour, cocoa powder and baking powder and, using a large metal spoon, fold into the mixture. Spoon the mixture into the paper cases. Bake the cupcakes in the preheated oven for 20–25 minutes, or until well risen and firm to the touch. Transfer to a wire rack and leave to cool completely.

4. To make the frosting, put the butter in a large bowl and beat until fluffy. Sift in the icing sugar and beat until smooth. Add the melted chocolate and beat until well mixed. When the cupcakes are cold, spread some of the frosting on top of each cupcake and decorate with a marzipan heart and sugar flower.

#426 Chocolate fudge bites

Makes
20

Ingredients

200 g/7 oz lightly salted butter, cut into pieces, plus extra for greasing

200 g/7 oz plain chocolate, roughly chopped

100 ml/3½ fl oz double cream

3 eggs

150 g/5½ oz light muscovado sugar

100 g/3½ oz self-raising flour

Icing

200 g/7 oz plain chocolate

3 tbsp golden syrup

55 g/2 oz unsalted butter, cut into pieces

70 g/2½ oz icing sugar, sifted

1. Preheat the oven to 160°C/325°F/Gas Mark 3. Grease a 20-cm/8-inch square cake tin and line with baking paper. Grease the paper.

2. Put the butter, chocolate and cream in a heatproof bowl over a saucepan of gently simmering water and heat until melted. Leave to cool slightly. Put the eggs and muscovado sugar in a mixing bowl and beat until the mixture begins to turn frothy. Stir in the cooled chocolate mixture. Sift in the flour and stir it in gently. Tip the mixture into the tin and level the surface. Bake in the preheated oven for 35 minutes, or until risen and just firm to the touch. Leave in the tin for 10 minutes, then transfer to a wire rack to cool completely.

3. To make the icing, put 175 g/6 oz of the chocolate in a small, heavy-based saucepan with the golden syrup and butter. Heat gently, stirring frequently, until smooth and glossy. Transfer to a bowl and beat in the icing sugar. Leave until the icing has thickened enough to just hold its shape.

4. Split the cake in half horizontally and spread half the icing on the cut side of the bottom piece. Place the other piece on top, cut-side down, and spread the remaining icing on top of the cake. Using a sharp knife, carefully cut thin shards from the remaining chocolate. Trim off the edges of the cake to neaten it, then cut it into 20 rectangles. Scatter the shards on top.

#427 Apple & blackberry waffles

Serves
4

Ingredients

150 g/5½ oz plain flour

1½ tsp baking powder

pinch of salt

250 ml/9 fl oz milk

1 large egg

2 tbsp sunflower oil, plus extra for brushing

2 crisp eating apples, grated

200 g/7 oz blackberries

maple syrup, for drizzling

1 x waffle maker

1. Preheat a waffle maker to high. Sift together the flour, baking powder and salt into a mixing bowl. Make a well in the centre.

2. Add the milk and egg, then whisk to a smooth, bubbly batter. Add the oil and apple and beat well to mix.

3. Brush the waffle maker with a little oil, add a ladleful of batter and cook until puffed and golden. You will need to do this in batches, keeping the cooked waffles warm while you cook the remaining batter.

4. Serve the waffles hot in stacks of two, topped with blackberries and a drizzle of maple syrup.

#428 Wedding day fancy favours

Ingredients

115 g/4 oz butter, softened

100 g/3½ oz caster sugar

2 eggs, lightly beaten

140 g/5 oz self-raising flour, sifted

½ tsp vanilla extract

1–2 tbsp milk

icing sugar, for dusting

225 g/8 oz white ready-to-roll
fondant icing

3 tbsp runny honey, warmed

2–3 drops pink food colouring

tube of green writing icing

1. Preheat the oven to 200°C/400°F/Gas Mark 6. Line a 12-hole muffin tin with paper cases. Place the butter and caster sugar in a bowl and beat until pale and creamy. Gradually beat in the eggs. Fold in the flour using a metal spoon. Stir in the vanilla extract and milk.

2. Spoon the mixture into the paper cases. Bake in the preheated oven for 15–20 minutes, or until well risen and firm to the touch. Transfer to a wire rack and leave to cool.

3. Dust a surface with icing sugar. Roll out all but one eighth of the fondant icing to a 20 x 28-cm/8 x 11-inch rectangle. Use a 6-cm/2¼-inch biscuit cutter to stamp out 12 rounds. Brush the cake tops with honey and stick on the rounds.

4. To make rosebuds, knead the remaining icing with the pink food colouring. Roll out 12 strips of icing to 1 x 6 cm/½ x 2½ inches. Roll up and stick on top with honey. Draw on a stalk with the green writing icing. Leave to set.

Raspberry & white chocolate brûlées

Ingredients

200 g/7 oz white chocolate, broken into pieces

200 ml/7 fl oz single cream

500 g/1 lb 2 oz Greek-style yogurt

225 g/8 oz raspberries

85 g/3 oz caster sugar

3 tbsp water

1. Place the chocolate and cream in a heatproof bowl set over a saucepan of simmering water and heat, stirring occasionally, until melted and smooth. Remove from the heat and leave to cool slightly.

2. Stir the chocolate mixture into the yogurt, then fold in the raspberries. Divide between 6 x 150-ml/5-fl oz ramekin dishes and level the surfaces with the back of a teaspoon. Chill in the refrigerator for at least 30 minutes.

3. Place the sugar and water in a small, heavy-based saucepan. Heat gently until the sugar dissolves, then increase the heat and boil rapidly for about 4 minutes, without stirring, until the sugar turns a rich caramel colour.

4. Remove from the heat and allow the bubbles to subside, then quickly spoon some caramel over the top of each ramekin. The topping will set almost instantly. Serve immediately or chill and serve within 3 hours while the caramel is still crisp.

Chocolate heart cake

Ingredients

175 g/6 oz self-raising flour

2 tsp baking powder

55 g/2 oz cocoa powder

3 eggs

140 g/5 oz light muscovado sugar

150 ml/5 fl oz sunflower oil, plus extra for greasing

150 ml/5 fl oz single cream

225 g/8 oz plain chocolate, broken into pieces

250 ml/9 fl oz double cream

3 tbsp seedless raspberry jam

200 g/7 oz fresh or frozen raspberries

fresh mint sprigs, to decorate

1. Preheat the oven to 180°C/350°F/Gas Mark 4. Grease a 20-cm/8-inch heart-shaped cake tin and line the base with baking paper. Sift the flour, baking powder and cocoa powder into a large bowl. Beat the eggs with the sugar, oil and single cream. Make a well in the dry ingredients and add the egg mixture, then stir to mix thoroughly, beating to a smooth batter. Pour into the prepared tin and bake in the preheated oven for 25–30 minutes, or until risen and firm to the touch. Leave to cool in the tin for 10 minutes, then turn out onto a wire rack and leave to cool completely.

2. Put the chocolate and double cream in a heatproof bowl set over a saucepan of gently simmering water and heat until melted. Remove from the heat and stir until the mixture cools slightly and begins to thicken.

3. Use a sharp knife to cut the cake in half horizontally. Spread the cut surface of each half with jam, then top with about 3 tablespoons of the chocolate mixture. Scatter half the raspberries over the base and replace the top, pressing lightly. Spread the remaining chocolate mixture over the top and sides of the cake, swirling with a palette knife. Top with the remaining raspberries and decorate with mint sprigs.

#431 Rose wedding muffins

Makes
12

Ingredients

280 g/10 oz plain flour

1 tbsp baking powder

pinch of salt

115 g/4 oz caster sugar

2 eggs

250 ml/9 fl oz milk

85 g/3 oz butter, melted and cooled

1 tsp vanilla extract

175 g/6 oz icing sugar

3–4 tsp hot water

12 ready-made sugar roses, to decorate

1. Preheat the oven to 200°C/400°F/Gas Mark 6. Line a 12-hole muffin tin with paper cases. Sift together the flour, baking powder and salt into a bowl. Stir in the caster sugar.

2. Lightly beat the eggs in a large jug, then beat in the milk, butter and vanilla extract. Make a well in the centre of the dry ingredients and pour in the beaten liquid ingredients. Stir gently until just combined; do not over-mix. Spoon the mixture into the paper cases. Bake in the preheated oven for about 20 minutes, until well risen, golden brown and firm to the touch. Leave to cool in the tin for 5 minutes, then transfer to a wire rack and leave to cool completely.

3. Sift the icing sugar into a bowl. Add the water and stir until the mixture is smooth and thick enough to coat the back of a wooden spoon. Spoon over the tops of the muffins, then decorate with the sugar roses.

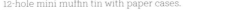

#432 Red velvet heart cupcakes

Makes
12

Ingredients

1 small raw beetroot, finely grated

1 egg

2 tbsp buttermilk or soured cream

1 tsp vinegar

55 g/2 oz lightly salted butter, softened

25 g/1 oz light muscovado sugar

55 g/2 oz self-raising flour

2 tsp cocoa powder

100 g/3½ oz unsalted butter

150 g/5½ oz icing sugar, plus extra for dusting

1 tsp vanilla extract

1 tbsp hot water

70 g/2½ oz white ready-to-roll fondant icing

deep red food colouring

1. Preheat the oven to 180°C/350°F/Gas Mark 4. Line a 12-hole mini muffin tin with paper cases.

2. Put the beetroot, egg, buttermilk and vinegar in a mixing bowl and stir together until well combined. Put the salted butter and muscovado sugar in a separate mixing bowl and beat together with an electric hand-held mixer until pale and fluffy. Sift half the flour and half the cocoa powder into the butter mixture and tip in the beetroot mixture. Stir gently until evenly combined. Sift in the remaining flour and cocoa, and stir again to mix. Spoon the mixture into the paper cases. Bake in the preheated oven for 15 minutes, or until risen and just firm to the touch. Leave in the tin for 5 minutes, then transfer to a wire rack to cool completely.

3. Put the butter in a large bowl and beat until soft. Add the icing sugar and vanilla extract and beat until smooth and creamy. Pour in the hot water and beat until very soft and fluffy. Spread over the cakes using a palette knife.

4. Colour the ready-to-roll icing deep red. Roll a 5-g/⅛-oz piece of icing into a thin rope 12 cm/4½ inches long. Flatten it with a rolling pin on a surface lightly dusted with icing sugar, keeping it no more than 1 cm/½ inch wide. Cut it in half lengthways, then cut across into 2.5-cm/1-inch pieces. Roll up each little piece between your thumb and finger to resemble a tiny rose. Use the roses to build heart shapes on top of all the cakes by gently pressing them down into the buttercream.

274

433 Wedding cupcakes

Makes
30

Ingredients

350 g/12 oz self-raising flour

1 tsp baking powder

225 g/8 oz butter, softened,
or soft margarine

225 g/8 oz caster sugar

finely grated rind of 1 large lemon

4 large eggs, lightly beaten

2 tbsp milk

650 g/1 lb 7 oz white ready-to-roll
fondant icing

3 tbsp apricot jam, warmed and sieved

15 white fondant roses, dipped in edible
silver glitter

2 tbsp egg white, lightly beaten

150 g/5½ oz icing sugar, sifted, plus extra
for dusting

1. Preheat the oven to 160°C/325°F/Gas Mark 3. Line 3 x 10-hole muffin tins with paper cases. Sift the flour and baking powder into a large bowl. Add the butter, caster sugar, lemon rind, eggs and milk, and beat until smooth.

2. Spoon the mixture into the paper cases. Bake in the preheated oven for 20–25 minutes, until risen, golden and firm to the touch. Transfer to wire racks and leave to cool completely.

3. Roll out the white fondant icing to a thickness of 5 mm/¼ inch on a surface lightly dusted with icing sugar. Use a 6-cm/2½-inch cutter to stamp out 30 rounds, re-rolling the icing as necessary. Lightly brush each cupcake with a little jam and gently press an icing round on top. Gently press a fondant rose into the centre of half the iced cupcakes.

4. Place the egg white in a bowl and gradually beat in the icing sugar to make a smooth icing. Spoon the icing into a small piping bag fitted with a fine writing nozzle. Starting at an edge, pipe a random meandering line of icing all over the surface of each plain cupcake. Try not to let the lines touch or cross and keep an even pressure on the piping bag so that the lines are of the same thickness. Leave to set.

434 Dark & white florentines

Makes
20

Ingredients

25 g/1 oz butter, plus extra for greasing

70 g/2½ oz unrefined caster sugar

15 g/½ oz plain flour, plus extra
for dusting

4 tbsp double cream

50 g/1¾ oz whole blanched almonds,
roughly chopped

50 g/1¾ oz flaked almonds, toasted

50 g/1¾ oz mixed peel, chopped

50 g/1¾ oz glacé cherries, chopped

50 g/1¾ oz preserved stem ginger,
drained and chopped

70 g/2½ oz plain chocolate, minimum
70% cocoa solids, broken into pieces

70 g/2½ oz white chocolate, broken
into pieces

1. Preheat the oven to 190°C/375°F/Gas Mark 5. Lightly grease two baking sheets and dust with flour. Put the butter, sugar and flour in a small saucepan and gently heat, stirring well, until the mixture has melted. Gradually add the cream, stirring constantly, then add all the remaining ingredients, except the chocolate, and stir thoroughly. Remove from the heat and leave to cool.

2. Drop 5 teaspoons of the mixture onto each of the prepared sheets, spaced well apart, then flatten with the back of a spoon. Bake in the preheated oven for 12–15 minutes. Leave to cool on the sheets for 2–3 minutes, then transfer to a wire rack to cool completely. Repeat with the remaining mixture.

3. Put the plain chocolate in a heatproof bowl set over a saucepan of gently simmering water and heat until melted. Using a teaspoon, spread the base of 10 of the biscuits with the melted chocolate and place, chocolate side-up, on a wire rack to set. Repeat with the white chocolate and the remaining 10 biscuits.

435 Marzipan-stuffed dates

Serves
6-8

Ingredients

500 g/1 lb 2 oz fresh dates

275 g/9½ oz marzipan

1. Using a small, sharp knife, cut lengthways along the side of each date and carefully remove and discard the stone. Divide the marzipan into the same number of pieces as there are dates and roll each piece into a long oval. Insert a marzipan oval into each date and press the sides of the dates lightly together.

2. Place the stuffed dates in petit-four cases and store in an airtight container in the refrigerator until about 30 minutes before they are required. Bring to room temperature before serving.

436 Festive holly cupcakes

Makes
16

Ingredients

125 g/4½ oz butter, softened

200 g/7 oz caster sugar

4 eggs, lightly beaten

a few drops of almond extract

150 g/5½ oz self-raising flour

175 g/6 oz ground almonds

450 g/1 lb white ready-to-roll fondant icing

55 g/2 oz green ready-to-roll fondant icing

icing sugar, for dusting

25 g/1 oz red ready-to-roll fondant icing

1. Preheat the oven to 180°C/350°F/Gas Mark 4. Line 2 x 8-hole muffin tins with paper cases.

2. Place the butter and caster sugar in a large bowl and beat together until light and fluffy. Gradually beat in the eggs and almond extract. Sift in the flour and, using a metal spoon, fold into the mixture with the ground almonds.

3. Spoon the mixture into the paper cases. Bake in the preheated oven for 20 minutes, or until risen, golden and firm to the touch. Transfer to a wire rack and leave to cool completely.

4. Roll out the white fondant icing to a thickness of 5 mm/¼ inch on a surface lightly dusted with icing sugar. Using a 7-cm/2¾-inch plain cutter, stamp out 16 rounds, re-rolling the icing as necessary. Place an icing round on top of each cupcake.

5. Roll out the green fondant icing to the same thickness. Using a holly cutter, cut out 32 leaves, re-rolling the icing as necessary. Brush each leaf with a little water and place two leaves on top of each cupcake. Roll the red fondant icing to form 48 small berries and place on the leaves.

Lebkuchen

Makes
60

Ingredients

3 eggs

200 g/7 oz golden caster sugar

55 g/2 oz plain flour

2 tsp cocoa powder

1 tsp ground cinnamon

½ tsp ground cardamom

¼ tsp ground cloves

¼ tsp ground nutmeg

175 g/6 oz ground almonds

55 g/2 oz chopped mixed peel

115 g/4 oz plain chocolate, broken into pieces

115 g/4 oz white chocolate, broken into pieces

sugar crystals, to decorate

1. Preheat the oven to 180°C/350°F/Gas Mark 4. Line several baking trays with baking paper.

2. Put the eggs and sugar in a heatproof bowl set over a saucepan of gently simmering water. Whisk until thick and foamy. Remove the bowl from the saucepan and continue to whisk for 2 minutes.

3. Sift the flour, cocoa powder, cinnamon, cardamom, cloves and nutmeg into the bowl and stir in with the ground almonds and mixed peel. Drop heaped teaspoonfuls of the mixture onto the prepared baking trays, spreading them gently into smooth mounds.

4. Bake in the preheated oven for 15–20 minutes, until light brown and slightly soft to the touch. Leave to cool on the baking trays for 10 minutes, then transfer to wire racks to cool completely.

5. Put the plain chocolate and white chocolate in two separate heatproof bowls set over two saucepans of gently simmering water and heat until melted. Dip half the biscuits in the melted plain chocolate and half in the white chocolate. Sprinkle with sugar crystals and leave to set.

438 Snowflake gingerbread

Makes
30

Ingredients

350 g/12 oz plain flour, plus extra for dusting

1 tbsp ground ginger

1 tsp bicarbonate of soda

100 g/3½ oz butter, softened, plus extra for greasing

175 g/6 oz soft light brown sugar

1 egg, beaten

4 tbsp golden syrup

115 g/4 oz icing sugar

2 tbsp lemon juice

1. Preheat the oven to 180°C/350°F/Gas Mark 4. Grease three baking sheets. Sift the flour, ginger and bicarbonate of soda into a bowl. Add the butter and rub into the flour until the mixture resembles fine breadcrumbs, then stir in the brown sugar.

2. In a separate bowl, beat together the egg and golden syrup with a fork. Pour into the flour mixture and mix to a smooth dough, kneading lightly with your hands. Roll out the dough on a lightly floured work surface to a thickness of 5 mm/¼ inch and cut into shapes using a star-shaped cutter. Transfer to the prepared baking sheets.

3. Bake in the preheated oven for 10 minutes, or until golden brown. Leave to cool on the sheets for 5 minutes, then transfer to wire racks to cool completely.

4. Mix the icing sugar and lemon juice together until smooth and put in a piping bag fitted with a very small nozzle. Pipe snowflake shapes onto each biscuit. Leave to set for a few hours.

#439 Mexican wedding cookies

Makes
35

Ingredients

225 g/9 oz butter, softened

1 tsp vanilla extract

50 g/1¾ oz icing sugar, sifted, plus extra
for dusting

280 g/10 oz plain flour, sifted

100 g/3½ oz pecan nuts or walnuts,
finely chopped

1. Preheat the oven to 190°C/375°F/Gas Mark 5. Line two baking trays with baking paper.

2. Place the butter and vanilla extract in a mixing bowl and beat until pale and creamy. Beat in the icing sugar until fully combined.

3. Gradually beat in the flour and the chopped nuts until just combined, taking care not to overwork the dough.

4. Use a teaspoon to remove 35 x 10-g/¼-oz pieces of dough, then roll each piece into a small sausage shape, tapering the ends slightly. Shape each one into a crescent and place on the prepared trays, flattening gently with the palm of your hand. Bake in the preheated oven for 20-25 minutes, until just starting to turn golden and crisp at the edges. Watch them carefully to ensure they don't burn.

5. Remove from the oven and leave to cool on the trays for 1–2 minutes, then transfer to a wire rack to cool completely. Generously dust with icing sugar and serve.

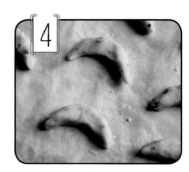

#440 Christmas tree cookies

Makes
16

Ingredients

225 g/8 oz plain flour, plus extra for dusting

2 tsp ground ginger

½ tsp bicarbonate of soda

55 g/2 oz butter, plus extra for greasing

3 tbsp golden syrup

70 g/2½ oz soft light brown sugar

1 large egg yolk

2 tbsp beaten egg white

175 g/6 oz icing sugar, sifted

green liquid food colouring

tubes of red and yellow writing icing

1. Preheat the oven to 180°C/350°F/Gas Mark 4. Grease two baking sheets. Sift the flour, ginger and bicarbonate of soda into a bowl and mix. Put the butter, golden syrup and sugar into a saucepan and gently heat until syrupy. Add to the flour mixture with the egg yolk and mix to a firm dough. Lightly knead until smooth. Roll out on a lightly floured surface to a thickness of 5 mm/¼ inch. Using a 10-cm/4-inch Christmas tree-shaped cutter, cut out 16 trees. Place on the prepared sheets, spaced well apart, and bake in the preheated oven for 10–15 minutes, until golden. Leave to cool on the baking sheets for a few minutes, then transfer to a wire rack to cool completely.

2. Put the egg white in a bowl with a little icing sugar and beat until smooth. Gradually beat in the remaining icing sugar until smooth, thick and holding soft peaks. Beat in a little water, add a little green food colouring, mix thoroughly, then gently spread on the cookies. Pipe decorations on the cookies with the writing icing. Leave to set.

#441 Dark chocolate Yule log

Serves
8

Ingredients

butter, for greasing

150 g/5½ oz caster sugar, plus extra for sprinkling

115 g/4 oz self-raising flour, plus extra for dusting

4 eggs, separated

1 tsp almond extract

280 g/10 oz plain chocolate, broken into squares

225 ml/8 fl oz double cream

2 tbsp rum

holly, to decorate

icing sugar, for dusting

1. Preheat the oven to 190°C/375°F/Gas Mark 5. Grease a 40 x 28-cm/16 x 11-inch Swiss roll tin, line with baking paper, then dust with flour. Sprinkle a sheet of greaseproof paper with caster sugar.

2. Reserving 2 tablespoons, put the caster sugar into a bowl with the egg yolks and whisk until thick and pale. Stir in the almond extract. Whisk the egg whites in a separate bowl until they hold soft peaks. Gradually whisk in the reserved sugar until stiff and glossy. Sift half the flour into the egg yolk mixture and fold in, then fold in one quarter of the egg white. Sift and fold in the remaining flour, followed by the remaining egg whites. Spoon the mixture into the tin, spreading it evenly with a palette knife. Bake in the preheated oven for 15 minutes, until lightly golden. Turn out onto the prepared paper, then roll up and leave to cool.

3. Place the chocolate in a heatproof bowl. Bring the cream to boiling point in a small saucepan, then pour it over the chocolate and stir until the chocolate has melted. Beat until smooth and thick. Reserve about one third of the chocolate mixture and stir the rum into the remainder. Unroll the cake and spread with the chocolate and rum mixture. Re-roll and place on a plate or silver board. Evenly spread the reserved chocolate mixture over the top and sides. Mark with a fork so that the surface resembles tree bark. Just before serving, decorate with holly and a sprinkling of icing sugar to resemble snow.

442 Snowman cake pops

Ingredients

200 g/7 oz ready-made angel food cake

300 g/10½ oz icing sugar

4 tbsp double cream

2 tsp peppermint extract

300 g/10½ oz fondant icing sugar, plus extra for piping

3 tbsp cold water

black, orange, red and yellow food colourings

100 g/3½ oz marzipan

20 lollipop sticks

1. Line a baking tray with baking paper. Crumble the cake into a mixing bowl. Add the icing sugar, cream and peppermint extract and mix together until you have a thick paste, adding a dash more cream if the mixture feels too dry.

2. Roll 20 x 20-g/¾-oz pieces of the paste into balls. Roll 20 x 5-g/⅓-oz pieces into balls. Press the small balls onto the larger ones to make snowmen. Place on the baking tray and chill in the refrigerator for 1–2 hours.

3. Put the fondant icing sugar in a mixing bowl and beat in the water to make a paste that coats the back of a spoon in a thin layer. Push a lollipop stick through each snowman so it goes halfway into the smaller ball. Dip a snowman in the icing, turning to coat. Lift it out, allowing the excess to drip back into the bowl, then place it in a cup. Repeat with the remaining snowmen, reserving some icing.

4. Beat a dash of black food colouring and a little icing sugar into the icing left in the bowl until the mixture holds its shape. Put the icing in a small paper piping bag and snip off the tip. Colour a cherry-sized ball of marzipan orange, then half the remaining marzipan red and half yellow. Use the red and yellow marzipan to shape tiny hats and scarves, pressing them into the fondant icing to secure. Shape and secure pointed noses in orange marzipan. Pipe eyes, mouths and buttons with black icing.

443 Christmas cranberry & orange pies

Ingredients

butter, for greasing

175 g/6 oz frozen cranberries

1 tbsp cornflour

3 tbsp freshly squeezed orange juice

2 star anise

55 g/2 oz caster sugar, plus extra for sprinkling

225 g/8 oz ready-made sweet shortcrust pastry, chilled

plain flour, for dusting

milk, for glazing

caster sugar, for sprinkling

1. Preheat the oven to 180°C/350°F/Gas Mark 4. Lightly grease a 12-hole mini muffin tin. Put the cranberries in a saucepan with the cornflour and orange juice. Add the star anise and cook over a low heat, stirring occasionally, for 5 minutes, or until the cranberries are soft. Add the sugar and cook for a further 5 minutes, then leave to cool.

2. Thinly roll out the pastry on a lightly floured surface. Using a fluted cookie cutter, stamp out 12 x 6-cm/2½-inch rounds and gently press into the prepared tin. Reserve the trimmings. Brush the top edges of the pie cases with a little milk. Discard the star anise, then spoon in the filling.

3. Thinly roll out the pastry trimmings. Using a fluted pastry wheel, cut thin strips of pastry. Arrange these over each pie, brush with milk and sprinkle with sugar. Bake in the preheated oven for 20 minutes. Leave to cool in the tin for 10 minutes, then transfer to a wire rack. Serve warm or cold.

#444 Mince pies

Makes
16

Ingredients

100 g/3½ oz butter, plus extra
for greasing

200 g/7 oz plain flour, plus extra
for dusting

25 g/1 oz icing sugar, plus extra
for dusting

1 egg yolk

300 g/10½ oz mincemeat

2–3 tbsp milk, plus extra for glazing

1. Preheat the oven to 180°C/350°F/Gas Mark 4. Grease a 16-hole tartlet tin with butter. Sift the flour into a bowl. Rub in the butter with your fingertips until the mixture resembles fine breadcrumbs.

2. Stir in the sugar and egg yolk. Stir in enough milk to make a soft dough, turn out onto a lightly floured surface and lightly knead until smooth. Shape the dough into a ball and roll out to a thickness of 5 mm/¼ inch. Use fluted cutters to cut out 16 x 7-cm/2¾-inch rounds and use to line the holes in the tartlet tin. Reserve the trimmings.

3. Half-fill each pie with mincemeat. Cut out 16 star shapes from the trimmings, brush with milk and place on top of each pie. Glaze with milk and bake in the preheated oven for 15 minutes. Transfer to a wire rack to cool. Dust with icing sugar before serving.

#445 Christmas ginger cake

Serves
6–8

Ingredients

175 g/6 oz butter, softened, plus extra
for greasing

175 g/6 oz unrefined caster sugar

3 large eggs, beaten

1 tbsp black treacle

2 tbsp ginger syrup

225 g/8 oz self-raising flour

1 tsp ground ginger

1 tsp mixed spice

1 tbsp ground almonds

2 tbsp milk

70 g/2½ oz stem ginger, chopped

edible gold leaf or silver leaf,
to decorate

Icing

225 g/8 oz icing sugar

1 tsp ginger syrup

1. Preheat the oven to 160°C/325°F/Gas Mark 3. Grease a 15 x 25-cm/6 x 10-inch square cake tin and line the base and sides with baking paper.

2. Cream the butter and caster sugar in a large bowl until pale and fluffy. Put the eggs and treacle into a jug with the ginger syrup and whisk together. Sift the flour and spices onto a plate. Alternately add a little of the egg mixture and then a spoonful of the flour mixture to the butter and sugar mixture until you have used up both. Add the almonds and milk and mix together until smooth. Fold in the stem ginger.

3. Spoon the mixture into the prepared tin, smooth the surface with a palette knife and bake in the preheated oven for 45–50 minutes, until well risen and firm to the touch. Leave to cool in the tin for 10 minutes, then turn out onto a wire rack to cool completely.

4. To make the icing, put the icing sugar in a large bowl. Beat in the ginger syrup and just enough cold water to make a thick icing. Remove the cake from the tin and spread the icing over the top, allowing it to run down the sides. Decorate with gold or silver leaf.

#446 Iced stars

Ingredients

225 g/8 oz butter, softened
140 g/5 oz caster sugar
1 egg yolk, lightly beaten
½ tsp vanilla extract
280 g/10 oz plain flour
salt

Decoration

200 g/7 oz icing sugar
1–2 tbsp lukewarm water
edible food colourings
silver and gold dragées
hundreds and thousands
desiccated coconut (optional)

1. Put the butter and sugar into a bowl and mix well, then beat in the egg yolk and vanilla extract. Sift the flour and a pinch of salt into the mixture and stir until thoroughly combined. Halve the dough, shape into balls, wrap in clingfilm and chill in the refrigerator for 30–60 minutes.

2. Preheat the oven to 190°C/375°F/Gas Mark 5. Line two baking sheets with baking paper. Roll out the dough between two sheets of baking paper to a thickness of about 3 mm/⅛ inch. Stamp out cookies with a star-shaped cutter and put them on the prepared baking sheets, spaced well apart. Bake in the preheated oven for 10–15 minutes, until light golden brown. Leave to cool on the baking sheets for 5–10 minutes, then carefully transfer to wire racks and leave to cool completely.

3. Sift the icing sugar into a bowl and stir in the water until the mixture has the consistency of thick cream. Divide between several bowls and add a few drops of your chosen food colourings to each. Spread the icing on the cookies right to the edges. Arrange dragées on top and sprinkle with hundreds and thousands. If you like, colour desiccated coconut with edible food colouring in a contrasting colour, sprinkle over the cookies and leave to set.

#447 Chocolate chestnut roulade

Ingredients

6 large eggs, separated
150 g/5½ oz unrefined caster sugar
½ tsp vanilla extract or
chocolate extract
50 g/1¾ oz cocoa powder
icing sugar, for dusting
250 ml/9 fl oz double cream
250 g/9 oz sweetened chestnut purée
2 tbsp brandy
70 g/2½ oz cooked, peeled chestnuts, chopped

1. Preheat the oven to 180°C/350°F/Gas Mark 4. Line a 23 x 45-cm/9 x 17¾-inch Swiss roll tin with baking paper.

2. Beat the egg yolks, caster sugar and vanilla extract together in a bowl for 10 minutes, or until doubled in volume and pale and fluffy. Whisk the egg whites in a separate bowl until they hold soft peaks. Fold a tablespoonful of egg white into the egg yolk mixture, then gently fold in the remaining egg white and the cocoa powder. Spoon into the prepared tin and smooth the surface with a palette knife. Bake in the preheated oven for 20 minutes, until risen. Leave to cool in the tin.

3. Put a large piece of baking paper on a clean tea towel and dust with icing sugar. Invert the cake onto the paper and carefully peel away the lining paper. Whip the cream until it holds stiff peaks, then stir in the chestnut purée and brandy. Spread over the sponge, leaving a 2.5-cm/1-inch margin around the edges, and scatter over the chestnuts. Using one end of the tea towel, carefully roll up the roulade. Dust with more icing sugar to serve.

#448 Christmas macaroons

Ingredients

75 g/2¾ oz ground almonds
115 g/4 oz icing sugar
1 tsp ground mixed spice
2 large egg whites
50 g/1¾ golden caster sugar
½ tsp freshly grated nutmeg
1 tsp gold dragées

Filling

55 g/2 oz butter, softened
finely grated rind and juice of ½ orange
1 tsp ground mixed spice
115 g/4 oz icing sugar, sifted
25 g/1 oz glacé cherries, finely chopped

1. Place the ground almonds, icing sugar and mixed spice in a food processor and process for 15 seconds. Sift into a bowl. Line two baking sheets with baking paper.

2. Place the egg whites in a large bowl and whisk until they hold soft peaks. Gradually whisk in the caster sugar to make a firm, glossy meringue. Using a spatula, fold the almond mixture into the meringue one third at a time, cutting and folding the mixture until it forms a shiny batter with a thick, ribbon-like consistency. Pour into a piping bag fitted with a 1-cm/½-inch plain nozzle. Pipe 32 small rounds onto the prepared baking sheets. Tap the baking sheets firmly on a work surface to remove air bubbles. Sprinkle half the macaroons with the grated nutmeg and gold dragées. Leave at room temperature for 30 minutes. Meanwhile, preheat the oven to 160°C/325°F/Gas Mark 3.

3. Bake in the preheated oven for 10–15 minutes. Leave to cool for 10 minutes, then carefully peel the macaroons off the baking paper and leave to cool completely.

4. Beat together the butter and orange juice and rind until fluffy. Gradually beat in the mixed spice and icing sugar until smooth and creamy. Fold in the glacé cherries. Use to sandwich the macaroons together.

449 Chocolate truffles

Ingredients

225 g/8 oz plain chocolate, minimum
70% cocoa solids

175 ml/6 fl oz whipping cream

cocoa powder, icing sugar or chopped
toasted almonds, for coating

1. Chop the chocolate and put in a large, heatproof bowl.

2. Put the cream in a saucepan and bring to boiling point. Pour
it over the chocolate and whisk until smooth. Leave to cool at
room temperature for 1½–2 hours.

3. Line two baking sheets with clingfilm or baking paper. Using a teaspoon, take bite-sized
scoops of the chocolate mixture and roll into balls, then coat in the cocoa powder, icing sugar or
chopped nuts. Place on the prepared baking sheets and chill in the refrigerator until set.

450 Cherry cream pies

Ingredients

a little butter, for greasing

300 g/10½ oz mascarpone cheese

2 tsp plain flour, plus extra for dusting

85 g/3 oz caster sugar, plus extra
for sprinkling

2 eggs

6 tbsp natural yogurt

1 tsp vanilla extract

450 g/1 lb ready-made sweet shortcrust
pastry, chilled

a little milk, to glaze

36 fresh or canned cherries, stoned and
drained well

1. Lightly grease a 12-hole muffin tin. Preheat the oven to
180°C/350°F/Gas Mark 4.

2. Spoon the mascarpone cheese into a mixing bowl and add the flour, sugar, eggs, yogurt and
vanilla. Beat with a wooden spoon or electric hand-held mixer until just combined.

3. Roll the pastry out thinly on a lightly floured surface. Using a plain cookie cutter, stamp out 12
circles each 10 cm/4 inches in diameter. Press these gently into the prepared tin, re-rolling the
trimmings as needed and reserving any remaining pastry. Brush the top edges of the pie cases
with a little of the milk glaze and spoon in the filling. Add three cherries to each pie.

4. Roll the reserved pastry out thinly on a lightly floured surface. Cut strips about 1-cm/½-inch
wide. Arrange four strips over each pie to make a lattice, pressing the edges together well to seal,
then brush milk over the pastry and sprinkle with a little sugar.

5. Bake in the preheated oven for 25–30 minutes, or until the lattice is golden and the filling is just
set. Leave to cool in the tin for 10 minutes, then loosen with a round-bladed knife and transfer to a
wire rack to cool. Serve at room temperature.

Blueberry fools

Ingredients

25 g/1 oz custard powder

300 ml/10 fl oz skimmed or
semi-skimmed milk

2 tbsp caster sugar

150 g/5½ oz fresh or frozen blueberries,
thawed if frozen

200 g/7 oz low-fat natural fromage frais

1. Blend the custard powder with 50 ml/2 fl oz of the milk in a heatproof bowl. Bring the remaining milk to the boil in a small saucepan and pour over the custard mixture, mixing well. Return the custard to the saucepan and bring to the boil over a medium-low heat, stirring constantly, until thickened. Pour the custard into the bowl and sprinkle the sugar over the top of the custard to prevent a skin forming. Cover and leave to cool completely.

2. Reserve 12 blueberries for decoration. Put the remaining blueberries and the cold custard into a blender and blend until smooth.

3. Spoon the fromage frais and the blueberry mixture in alternate layers into four tall glasses. Decorate with the reserved blueberries and serve immediately.

Reindeer cookies

Ingredients

10 cardamom pods

100 g/3½ oz butter, softened, plus extra
for greasing

55 g/2 oz caster sugar

1 egg, beaten

finely grated rind of ½ orange

225 g/8 oz plain flour,
plus extra for dusting

25 g/1 oz cornflour

½ tsp baking powder

Decoration

90 g/3¼ oz icing sugar

4 tsp lemon juice

red food colouring

25 silver dragées

1. Lightly crush the cardamom pods and discard the shells. Grind the seeds to a powder. Beat together the butter and caster sugar until creamy, then gradually beat in the egg, orange rind and cardamom powder.

2. Sift in the flour, cornflour and baking powder, and stir with a wooden spoon to form a soft dough. Wrap in clingfilm and chill in the refrigerator for 30 minutes.

3. Preheat the oven to 180°C/350°F/Gas Mark 4. Grease three baking sheets. Roll out the chilled dough on a lightly floured surface to a thickness of 3 mm/⅛ inch. Cut out shapes using a reindeer-shaped cutter and place on the prepared baking sheets. Re-knead and re-roll trimmings and cut out more shapes until all the dough is used up.

4. Bake in the preheated oven for 15 minutes, until just golden. Leave to cool on the baking sheets for 5 minutes, then transfer to wire racks to cool completely.

5. Mix together the icing sugar and lemon juice until smooth. Spoon 2 tablespoons of the mixture into a separate bowl and colour it with the red food colouring. Spoon the remaining icing into a piping bag fitted with a fine nozzle and pipe antlers, hooves, tails, collars and a saddle on the cookies. Pipe a nose using the red icing. For the eye, fix a dragée in place using a blob of icing.

453 Golden Christmas cake

Serves
16–18

Ingredients

175 g/6 oz dried apricots, chopped
85 g/3 oz dried mango, chopped
85 g/3 oz dried pineapple, chopped
175 g/6 oz sultanas
55 g/2 oz chopped stem ginger
55 g/2 oz chopped mixed peel
finely grated rind and juice of 1 orange
4 tbsp brandy
175 g/6 oz butter, plus extra for greasing
100 g/3½ oz light muscovado sugar
4 eggs, beaten
2 tbsp clear honey
175 g/6 oz self-raising flour
2 tsp ground allspice
85 g/3 oz pecan nuts, chopped
800 g/1 lb 12 oz marzipan
900 g/2 lb white ready-to-roll fondant icing
silver dragées, to decorate

1. Place the chopped apricots, mango and pineapple in a bowl with the sultanas, ginger and peel. Stir in the orange rind and juice and brandy. Cover the bowl and leave to soak overnight.

2. Preheat the oven to 160°C/325°F/Gas Mark 3. Grease a 23-cm/9-inch round springform cake tin and line with baking paper.

3. Cream together the butter and sugar until the mixture is pale and fluffy. Add the eggs to the mixture, beating well between each addition. Stir in the honey. Sift the flour with the allspice and fold into the mixture using a metal spoon. Add the soaked fruit and pecan nuts, mixing thoroughly. Spoon the mixture into the prepared tin, spreading evenly, then make a slight dip in the centre.

4. Place in the centre of the preheated oven and bake for 1½–2 hours, or until golden brown and firm to the touch and a skewer inserted into the centre comes out clean. Leave to cool in the tin.

5. Turn out the cake, remove the paper and wrap in clean baking paper and foil. Store in a cool place for at least 1 month before use. If desired, cover the cake with marzipan and white ready-to-roll icing, following the pack instructions, then decorate with icing stars and silver dragées.

454 Snowflake Christmas whoopie pies

Makes
14

Ingredients

200 g/7 oz plain flour
2 tsp baking powder
large pinch of salt
55 g/2 oz ground almonds
260 g/9½ oz butter, softened
150 g/5½ oz caster sugar
1 large egg, beaten
1 tsp almond extract
100 ml/3½ fl oz milk
8 tbsp double cream
400 g/14 oz icing sugar, sifted
1–2 tbsp warm water
1 tbsp silver dragées

1. Preheat the oven to 180°C/350°F/Gas Mark 4. Line three large baking sheets with baking paper. Sift together the plain flour, baking powder and salt. Stir in the ground almonds.

2. Place 115 g/4 oz butter and the caster sugar in a large bowl and beat until pale and fluffy. Beat in the egg and almond extract, followed by half the flour mixture, then the milk. Stir in the remaining flour mixture and beat well. Pipe or spoon 28 mounds of the mixture onto the prepared baking sheets, spaced well apart. Bake in the preheated oven, one sheet at a time, for 10–12 minutes until risen. Leave to cool for 5 minutes, then transfer to a wire rack to cool completely.

3. To make the filling, place the remaining butter in a bowl and beat for 2–3 minutes, until pale and creamy. Beat in the cream, then gradually beat in 280 g/10 oz icing sugar and continue beating until very light and fluffy. To make the icing, sift the remaining icing sugar into a bowl and stir in enough water to make a smooth icing. Spread the filling on the flat side of 14 cakes. Top with the remaining cakes. Spoon the icing into a piping bag and pipe snowflakes on the top of the pies. Decorate with dragées and leave to set.

#455 Chocolate orange rind

Makes
36

Ingredients

rind of 3 large navel oranges, cut into
36 6 x 1-cm/2½ x ½-inch strips
200 g/7 oz granulated sugar
200 ml/7 fl oz water
200 g/7 oz plain chocolate,
roughly chopped

1. Bring a small saucepan of water to the boil, add the orange rind and simmer for 10 minutes. Drain, then rinse under cold running water. Pour more water into the pan and bring to the boil, then return the rind to the pan and simmer for 10 minutes. Repeat one more time.

2. Put the sugar and water into a heavy-based saucepan. Bring to the boil and simmer, stirring, for 5 minutes, or until the sugar has dissolved and the mixture has reduced a little. Add the rind and simmer for 15 minutes. Transfer to a wire rack with a slotted spoon and leave to cool for 1–2 hours. Line a baking tray with baking paper.

3. Put the chocolate in a heatproof bowl set over a saucepan of gently simmering water and heat until melted. Dip a third of the length of each orange strip in the chocolate and place on the prepared tray. Leave to cool for 1–2 hours, or until set.

#456 Santa sugar cookies

Makes
40

Ingredients

350 g/12 oz plain flour, plus extra
for dusting
1 tsp baking powder
¼ tsp salt
115 g/4 oz butter, softened, plus extra
for greasing
175 g/6 oz caster sugar
1 egg, beaten
2½ tsp vanilla extract
1 tbsp milk

Decoration

225 g/8 oz icing sugar
1 egg white
½ tsp glycerine
red and black food colouring

1. Grease four baking sheets. Sift together the flour, baking powder and salt in a bowl. Cream the butter and the caster sugar together until light and fluffy. Beat in the egg, 2 teaspoons of the vanilla extract and the milk until smooth, then add the flour mixture and mix to a soft dough. Cover with clingfilm and chill in the refrigerator for 30 minutes.

2. Preheat the oven to 180°C/350°F/Gas Mark 4. Roll out the dough on a lightly floured surface to a thickness of 5 mm/¼ inch. Use a Santa-shaped cutter to cut out shapes. Transfer to the prepared baking sheets and bake in the preheated oven for 10 minutes, until golden brown. Leave to cool on the sheets for 5 minutes, then transfer to a wire rack and leave to cool completely.

3. Whisk together the icing sugar, egg white, the remaining vanilla extract and the glycerine for 5 minutes until stiff and glossy. Colour one third of the mixture red and colour 2 tablespoons of the mixture black. Apply the red icing evenly with a small palette knife to create Santa's hat and pipe eyes in black icing using a piping bag fitted with a fine nozzle.

4. Place some of the remaining white icing in a piping bag fitted with a small star-shaped nozzle to create the fur cuffs, eyebrows, moustache and bobble on Santa's hat. Apply the remaining white icing with a small palette knife, using a swirling action to create his beard. Leave to set for a few hours.

457 Christmas spiced loaf

Ingredients

450 g/1 lb strong white flour, plus extra for dusting

pinch of salt

2 tsp mixed spice

115 g/4 oz butter, chilled and diced

1 sachet easy-blend dried yeast

115 g/4 oz unrefined caster sugar

115 g/4 oz currants

115 g/4 oz raisins

50 g/1¾ oz mixed peel, chopped

finely grated rind of 1 orange

1 egg, beaten

150 ml/5 fl oz milk, warmed

oil, for greasing

1. Sift the flour, salt and mixed spice into a bowl and rub in the butter until the mixture resembles breadcrumbs.

2. Stir in the yeast, sugar, dried fruit, mixed peel and orange rind, then add the egg and the milk and bring together to form a soft dough. Knead briefly on a floured work surface. Dust a clean bowl with flour and add the dough. Cover and leave to rise in a warm place for 2 hours.

3. Preheat the oven to 180°C/350°F/Gas Mark 4 and grease a 900-g/2-lb loaf tin. Knead the dough briefly, then place it in the tin, cover and leave to rise for 20 minutes. Bake in the preheated oven for 1 hour 10 minutes – the loaf should be golden and well risen. Leave to cool in the tin.

458 Holiday eggnog

Ingredients

6 large eggs

100 g/3½ oz caster sugar, plus 2 tbsp extra

500 ml/18 fl oz single cream

500 ml/18 fl oz milk

125 ml/4 fl oz brandy

4 tbsp light rum

1 tsp vanilla extract

500 ml/18 fl oz double cream

freshly grated nutmeg

1. Whisk the eggs with an electric hand-held mixer on medium speed until thick and a lemon colour, then gradually add the 100 g/3½ oz sugar, whisking well.

2. Put the single cream and milk into a large saucepan over a medium–low heat and heat until thoroughly hot but not boiling. Gradually add the hot milk mixture to the egg mixture, stirring with a balloon whisk. Transfer the mixture back to the large saucepan and cook over a medium–low heat, stirring continuously with a balloon whisk until hot but not boiling. Remove from the heat and leave to cool. Stir in the brandy, rum and vanilla extract with a balloon whisk. Cover and refrigerate until thoroughly chilled.

3. Just before serving, whisk the double cream and the remaining 2 tablespoons of sugar in a large bowl until soft peaks form. Pour the chilled eggnog mixture into a large punch bowl. Gently fold the whipped cream into the eggnog mixture just until combined. Decorate each serving with freshly grated nutmeg.

459 Popping candy toffee apples

Makes
4

Ingredients

4 crisp sweet apples
225 g/8 oz caster sugar
½ tsp malt vinegar
125 ml/4 fl oz water
1–2 drops red food colouring
1–2 tsp popping candy, to decorate
1 tbsp hundreds and thousands,
to decorate

4 wooden skewers or lollipop sticks

1. Line a baking tray with baking paper. Place the apples in a heatproof bowl and pour over boiling water to cover. This will help the toffee layer to adhere to the apple skin. Remove the stalks and push a skewer or stick into each apple. Place the apples on the prepared tray.

2. Place the sugar, vinegar and water in a heavy-based saucepan. Bring to the boil and boil for 20–25 minutes until it reaches a temperature of 140°C/275°F on a sugar thermometer. If you don't have a sugar thermometer, test by dropping a little of the toffee into a bowl of cold water. It should harden immediately. If it remains soft, it needs further boiling. Once it has reached the correct temperature, stir in the food colouring.

3. When the toffee is ready, quickly dip each apple in the toffee to coat and immediately scatter the tops with the popping candy and hundreds and thousands. Leave to harden on the baking tray. The apples can be prepared in advance and will keep for several days in a cool, dry place.

#460 Double choc mint sponge

Serves 10

Ingredients

oil, for greasing

150 g/5½ oz plain flour

2 tbsp cocoa powder

1 tbsp baking powder

175 g/6 oz butter, softened

175 g/6 oz caster sugar

3 eggs, beaten

1 tbsp milk

40 g/1½ oz chocolate mint sticks, chopped, plus extra sticks to decorate

140 g/5 oz chocolate spread, plus extra for drizzling

1. Preheat the oven to 180°C/350°F/Gas Mark 4. Grease 2 x 20-cm/8-inch round sandwich cake tins and line with baking paper.

2. Sift the flour, cocoa and baking powder into a bowl and beat in the butter, sugar and eggs, mixing until smooth. Stir in the milk and chopped chocolate mint sticks.

3. Spread the mixture into the prepared tins. Bake in the preheated oven for 25–30 minutes, until risen and firm. Leave to cool in the tin for 2 minutes, then turn out onto a wire rack to cool completely.

4. Sandwich the cakes together with chocolate spread and decorate with chocolate mint sticks. Drizzle chocolate spread over the top.

#461 Pecan pie

Serves 8–10

Ingredients

Pastry

200 g/7 oz plain flour, plus extra for dusting

115 g/4 oz butter

2 tbsp caster sugar

Filling

70 g/2½ oz butter

100 g/3½ oz light muscovado sugar

140 g/5 oz golden syrup

2 large eggs, beaten

1 tsp vanilla extract

115 g/4 oz pecan nuts

1. To make the pastry, place the flour in a bowl and rub in the butter with your fingertips until it resembles fine breadcrumbs. Stir in the sugar and add enough cold water to mix to a firm dough. Wrap in clingfilm and chill for 15 minutes, until firm enough to roll out.

2. Preheat the oven to 200°C/400°F/Gas Mark 6. Roll out the pastry on a lightly floured surface and use to line a 23-cm/9-inch loose-based round tart tin. Prick the base with a fork. Chill in the refrigerator for 15 minutes.

3. Place the tart tin on a baking sheet and line with a sheet of baking paper and baking beans. Bake in the preheated oven for 10 minutes. Remove the beans and paper and bake for a further 5 minutes. Reduce the oven temperature to 180°C/350°F/Gas Mark 4.

4. To make the filling, place the butter, sugar and golden syrup in a saucepan and gently heat until melted. Remove from the heat and quickly beat in the eggs and vanilla extract.

5. Roughly chop the nuts and stir into the mixture. Pour into the pastry case and bake for 35–40 minutes, until the filling is just set. Serve warm or cold.

#462 Mini Thanksgiving apple pies

Makes
24

Ingredients

450 g/1 lb cooking apples, peeled, quartered, cored and diced

25 g/1 oz butter, plus extra for greasing

55 g/2 oz caster sugar, plus extra for sprinkling

55 g/2 oz sultanas or raisins

grated rind of 1 lemon

3 tbsp whisky or brandy

650 g/1 lb 7 oz ready-made sweet shortcrust pastry, chilled

plain flour, for dusting

milk, for glazing

whipped cream, to serve

1. Preheat the oven to 180°C/350°F/Gas Mark 4. Lightly grease 2 x 12-hole mini muffin tins.

2. Put the apples in a saucepan with the butter, sugar, sultanas and lemon rind, and cook over a low heat, stirring occasionally, for 8–10 minutes, or until the apples are soft but still hold their shape. Add the whisky and cook until just bubbling. Keeping it over the heat, flame with a long match, stand well back and cook for 1 minute, until the flame subsides. Leave to cool.

3. Thinly roll out the pastry on a lightly floured surface. Using a fluted cookie cutter, stamp out 48 6-cm/2½-inch rounds and gently press 24 into the prepared tins. Reserve the trimmings. Brush the top edges of the pie cases with milk, then spoon in the filling, doming it up high in the centre. Arrange the remaining pastry rounds on top of the pies, pressing the edges together well to seal. Brush with a little milk.

4. Shape tiny ropes from the pastry trimmings into the initials of your dinner guests or family. Press these onto the pie tops, brush with a little milk and sprinkle with sugar. Bake in the preheated oven for 15 minutes, or until golden. Leave to cool in the tins for 10 minutes, then transfer to wire racks to cool completely. Serve warm or cold, sprinkled with caster sugar, with spoonfuls of whipped cream.

#463 Halloween pumpkin cookies

Makes
30

Ingredients

100 g/3½ oz butter, softened, plus extra for greasing

55 g/2 oz caster sugar

1 egg, beaten

225 g/8 oz plain flour

25 g/1 oz cornflour

1½ tsp mixed spice

Decoration

350 g/12 oz orange ready-to-roll fondant icing

icing sugar, for dusting

tube of green writing icing

1. Put the butter and sugar into a bowl and beat until creamy, then gradually beat in the egg. Sift in the flour, cornflour and mixed spice and beat together to form a rough dough. Gather together with your hands and lightly knead until smooth. Shape the dough into a 15-cm/6-inch log and wrap in clingfilm. Chill in the refrigerator for 3–4 hours, occasionally rolling on a flat surface to ensure a good round shape.

2. Preheat the oven to 180°C/350°F/Gas Mark 4. Grease two large baking sheets with butter. Thinly slice the dough into 30 rounds and place on the prepared baking sheets, spaced well apart. Bake in the preheated oven for 15 minutes, until golden brown. Leave to cool on the baking sheets for a few minutes, then transfer to wire racks to cool completely.

3. Thinly roll out the icing on a surface lightly dusted with icing sugar. Use a pumpkin-shaped cutter to stamp out 30 shapes. Use the writing icing to attach the pumpkins to each cookie and to pipe on stalks and leaves. Use the tip of a sharp knife to score vertical curved lines in the orange icing. Leave to set.

Squished witch cupcakes

Makes
12

Ingredients

190 g/6¾ oz plain flour
1½ tsp baking powder
¼ tsp salt
115 g/4 oz butter, softened
200 g/7 oz caster sugar
2 tsp vanilla extract
2 large eggs
125 ml/4 fl oz milk
finely grated rind and juice of 1 lime
green food colouring
250 g/9 oz lime curd

Decoration

280 g/10 oz white ready-made gum paste
cornflour, for dusting
black food colouring
red edible-ink marker

1. To make the witch legs for decoration, knead the gum paste on a board dusted with cornflour until it is a workable texture. Break off a 2.5-cm/1-inch piece and roll into a cylinder about 5 mm/¼ inch in diameter and about 13 cm/5 inches long. Cut in half to make two legs. Repeat until you have 24 legs. Add several drops of black food colouring to the remaining gum paste and knead until the colour is evenly incorporated. Break off 1-cm/½-inch pieces and form them into boots with chunky heels and pointed toes. Attach one boot to the end of each leg by pressing the pieces together. Repeat until all of the legs have boots. Set aside to dry.

2. Preheat the oven to 180°C/350°F/Gas Mark 4 and line a 12-hole muffin tin with paper cases.

3. Sift together the flour, baking powder and salt in a bowl. Put the butter and caster sugar into a separate bowl and beat until pale and fluffy. Add the vanilla extract, then add the eggs, one at a time, beating after each addition. Add half of the flour mixture and the milk and beat until incorporated. Add the remaining flour mixture and the lime rind and juice and mix.

4. Spoon the mixture into the paper cases and bake in the preheated oven for 20 minutes, until risen and golden. Leave to cool in the tin for 1–2 minutes, then transfer to a wire rack to cool completely.

5. Stir a few drops of green food colouring into the lime curd and then spoon onto serving plates. Use the red edible-ink marker to draw stripes on the legs, then position over the lime curd. Top each pair of legs with an overturned cupcake so that the cupcake conceals the top parts of the legs. Serve.

465 Pumpkin pie

Ingredients

350 g/12 oz ready-made shortcrust
pastry, thawed, if frozen

plain flour, for dusting

400 ml/14 fl oz pumpkin purée

2 eggs, lightly beaten

150 g/5½ oz sugar

1 tsp ground cinnamon

½ tsp ground ginger

¼ tsp ground cloves

350 ml/12 fl oz evaporated milk

350 ml/12 fl oz double cream

55 g/2 oz icing sugar

1 tbsp brandy, or to taste

1 tbsp light or dark rum, or to taste

freshly grated nutmeg, to serve

1. Preheat the oven to 200°C/400°F/Gas Mark 6. Roll out the dough on a lightly floured surface into a 30-cm/12-inch round and use to line a 23-cm/9-inch deep pie dish. Line with baking paper and fill with baking beans. Bake in the preheated oven for 10 minutes. Remove from the oven and take out the paper and beans. Reduce the oven temperature to 180°C/350°F/Gas Mark 4.

2. Meanwhile, put the pumpkin purée, eggs, sugar, cinnamon, ginger, and cloves in a bowl and beat together, then beat in the evaporated milk. Pour the mixture into the pastry case, return to the oven and bake for 40–50 minutes, until the filling is set and a knife inserted in the centre comes out clean. Transfer the pie dish to a wire rack and set aside to cool completely.

3. Put the cream in a bowl and beat until it thickens. Just as it starts to stiffen, sift in the icing sugar and continue beating until it holds stiff peaks. Add the brandy and rum and beat – be careful not to over-beat or the mixture will separate. Cover and chill until required. Serve with a dollop of whipped cream and a light grating of nutmeg.

466 Toffee apple cupcakes

Ingredients

2 eating apples

1 tbsp lemon juice

250 g/9 oz plain flour

2 tsp baking powder

1½ tsp ground cinnamon

70 g/2½ oz light muscovado sugar

55 g/2 oz butter, melted,
plus extra for greasing

100 ml/3½ fl oz milk

100 ml/3½ fl oz apple juice

1 egg, lightly beaten

Sauce

2 tbsp double cream

40 g/1½ oz light muscovado sugar

15 g/½ oz butter

1. Preheat the oven to 200°C/400°F/Gas Mark 6. Grease 2 x 8-hole muffin tins.

2. Roughly grate one of the apples. Cut the remaining apple into 5-mm/¼-inch thick slices and toss in the lemon juice. Sift the flour, baking powder and cinnamon into a large bowl, then stir in the sugar and grated apple.

3. Combine the butter with the milk, apple juice and egg. Stir the liquid ingredients into the dry ingredients, mixing lightly until just combined.

4. Spoon the mixture into the prepared tin and arrange two of the apple slices on top of each cupcake. Bake in the preheated oven for 15–20 minutes, or until risen, golden and firm to the touch. Transfer to a wire rack and leave to cool.

5. To make the sauce, place all the ingredients in a small saucepan and heat, stirring, until the sugar is dissolved. Increase the heat and boil rapidly for 2 minutes, or until slightly thickened and syrupy. Leave to cool slightly, then drizzle over the cupcakes and leave to set.

#467 Halloween spider cupcakes

Ingredients

115 g/4 oz self-raising flour
115 g/4 oz butter, softened
115 g/4 oz caster sugar
2 eggs, lightly beaten

Decoration

200 g/7 oz orange ready-to-roll
fondant icing
icing sugar, for dusting
55 g/2 oz black ready-to-roll
fondant icing
tubes of black and yellow writing icing

1. Preheat the oven to 180°C/350°F/Gas Mark 4. Line a 12-hole muffin tin with paper cases. Sift the flour into a large bowl. Add the butter, caster sugar and eggs, and beat until smooth.

2. Spoon the mixture into the paper cases. Bake in the preheated oven for 15–20 minutes, or until risen, golden and firm to the touch. Transfer to a wire rack and leave to cool.

3. Roll out the orange fondant icing to a thickness of 5 mm/¼ inch on a surface lightly dusted with icing sugar. Using a 5.5-cm/2¼-inch plain cutter, stamp out 12 rounds, re-rolling the icing as necessary. Place an icing round on top of each cupcake. Roll out the black fondant icing to the same thickness. Using a 3-cm/1¼-inch plain cutter, cut out 12 rounds and place one on the centre of each cupcake. Using black writing icing, pipe eight legs onto each spider and, using yellow writing icing, pipe two eyes and a mouth.

#468 Pumpkin cupcakes

Ingredients

190 g/6¾ oz plain flour
1½ tsp baking powder
1¾ tsp ground cinnamon
¾ tsp ground ginger
⅛ tsp ground nutmeg
⅛ tsp ground allspice
230 g/8¼ oz butter, softened
100 g/3½ oz caster sugar
100 g/3½ oz soft light brown sugar
2 tsp vanilla extract
2 large eggs
175 g/6 oz canned pumpkin purée
salt
250 g/9 oz icing sugar
1 tbsp milk
red and yellow food colouring
orange sugar crystals
55 g/2 oz green ready-to-roll fondant icing

1. Preheat the oven to 180°C/350°F/Gas Mark 4 and line a 12-hole muffin tin with paper cases. Sift together the flour, baking powder, ¾ teaspoon of the cinnamon, the ginger, ¼ teaspoon of salt, the nutmeg and allspice into a bowl. Put half the butter, the caster sugar and brown sugar into a separate bowl and beat until pale and fluffy. Add half the vanilla extract, then add the eggs, one at a time, beating after each addition. Add half the flour mixture and the pumpkin purée, and beat until incorporated. Add the remaining flour mixture and mix. Spoon the mixture into the paper cases and bake in the preheated oven for 20 minutes, until risen and golden. Leave to cool in the tin for 1–2 minutes, then transfer to a wire rack.

2. To make the frosting, put the remaining butter, the icing sugar, milk, remaining vanilla extract, the cinnamon and a pinch of salt into a bowl and beat until well combined. Add more icing sugar, if necessary, to achieve a piping consistency. Add a few drops of red and yellow food colouring and beat until evenly incorporated. Add more of either or both colours until the desired shade of orange is achieved. Place a generous tablespoon of orange frosting on top of each cupcake. Use a palette knife to spread around, building a rounded dome on top. Make a small indent into the top of the frosting.

3. Place the sugar crystals in a shallow bowl and press the top of each cupcake into the crystals to coat. Pinch off a small piece of the green fondant and shape it into a 2.5-cm/1-inch stem. Repeat to make 12 stems in total. To serve, insert the stems into the indents in the frosting.

#469 Halloween mud pie

Ingredients

85 g/3 oz plain chocolate, chopped
85 g/3 oz butter
85 g/3 oz light muscovado sugar
2 eggs, beaten
100 ml/3½ fl oz single cream
1 tsp vanilla extract

Pastry

175 g/6 oz plain flour, plus extra for dusting
25 g/1 oz cocoa powder
40 g/1½ oz light muscovado sugar
85 g/3 oz butter
2–3 tbsp cold water

Topping

250 ml/9 fl oz whipping cream
85 g/3 oz plain chocolate, chopped

1. Preheat the oven to 200°C/400°F/Gas Mark 6. To make the pastry, sift the flour and cocoa powder into a bowl and stir in the sugar. Rub in the butter with your fingertips until the mixture resembles fine breadcrumbs. Add water to bind to a dough.

2. Roll out the dough on a lightly floured work surface to a round large enough to line a 20 x 3-cm/8 x 1¼-inch deep flan tin. Use the pastry to line the tin. Prick the base with a fork, cover with a piece of greaseproof paper and fill with baking beans, then bake in the preheated oven for 10 minutes. Remove from the oven and take out the paper and beans. Reduce the oven temperature to 180°C/350°F/Gas Mark 4.

3. Put the chocolate and butter into a saucepan and heat over a low heat, stirring, until melted. Put the sugar and eggs into a bowl and whisk together until smooth, then stir in the chocolate mixture, cream and vanilla extract. Pour the chocolate mixture into the pastry case and bake in the oven for 20–25 minutes, or until just set. Leave to cool.

4. To make the topping, whip the cream until it just holds its shape, then spread over the pie. Place the chocolate in a bowl set over a saucepan of gently simmering water and heat until melted, then spoon into a piping bag and pipe decorations over the cream. Serve cold.

#470 Trick-or-treat vanilla fudge

Ingredients

oil, for greasing
450 g/1 lb caster sugar
85 g/3 oz butter
150 ml/5 fl oz full-fat milk
150 ml/5 fl oz evaporated milk
2 tsp vanilla extract

1. Lightly grease a 20-cm/8-inch square baking tin. Line it with baking paper, snipping diagonally into the corners, then pressing the paper into the tin so that the base and sides are lined.

2. Put the sugar, butter, milk and evaporated milk into a heavy-based saucepan and gently heat, stirring, until the sugar has dissolved. Increase the heat and boil for 12–15 minutes, or until the mixture reaches 116°C/240°F on a sugar thermometer (if you don't have a sugar thermometer, spoon a little of the syrup into some iced water; it will form a soft ball when it is ready). As the temperature rises, stir the fudge occasionally so the sugar doesn't stick and burn.

3. Remove the pan from the heat, add the vanilla and beat using a wooden spoon until thickened. Pour the mixture into the prepared tin and smooth the surface using a spatula. Leave to cool for 1 hour, or until set. Lift the fudge out of the tin, peel off the paper and cut into small squares.

#471 Ghost cupcakes

Makes 6

Ingredients

140 g/5 oz plain flour

2 tsp ground mixed spice

¾ tsp bicarbonate of soda

85 g/3 oz butter, softened

85 g/3 oz dark muscovado sugar

1 tbsp black treacle

2 large eggs

Frosting

85 g/3 oz butter, softened

1 tbsp dulce de leche

175 g/6 oz icing sugar, plus extra if needed

Decoration

350 g/12 oz white ready-to-roll fondant icing

icing sugar, for dusting

black writing icing

1. Preheat the oven to 180°C/350°F/Gas Mark 4. Line a 12-hole muffin tin with paper cases and line a 6-hole mini muffin tin with paper cases. Sift together the flour, mixed spice and bicarbonate of soda into a bowl. Put the butter, sugar and treacle into a separate bowl and beat until fluffy. Add the eggs, one at a time, beating after each addition. Add half of the flour mixture and beat until incorporated. Add the remaining flour mixture and mix.

2. Spoon the batter into the paper cases. Bake the mini cupcakes in the preheated oven for 10 minutes and the standard cupcakes for 20 minutes, until risen and golden. Leave to cool in the tin for 1–2 minutes, then transfer to a wire rack to cool completely.

3. To make the frosting, put the butter, dulce de leche and icing sugar into a bowl and beat until well combined. Add more icing sugar, if necessary, to achieve a piping consistency.

4. To assemble and decorate, remove the paper cases from six of the standard cupcakes and all of the mini cupcakes. Spread a layer of frosting over the top of the remaining cupcakes. Top each with an upturned standard cupcake, and then an upturned mini cupcake. Spread frosting over the stacked cakes, then transfer to the refrigerator to chill for 30 minutes.

5. Take 50 g/1¾ oz of white fondant icing and roll into six small balls. Place one on top of each of the cakes. Divide the remaining fondant into six pieces and roll out each piece on a surface dusted with icing sugar to a 14-cm/5½-inch round. Drape over the cupcakes, then use the black writing icing to pipe eyes onto the cakes. Serve.

#472 Irish cream cheesecake

Ingredients

oil, for greasing
175 g/6 oz chocolate chip cookies
55 g/2 oz butter
crème fraîche and fresh strawberries, to serve

Filling

225 g/8 oz plain chocolate, broken into pieces
225 g/8 oz milk chocolate, broken into pieces
55 g/2 oz golden caster sugar
350 g/12 oz cream cheese
425 ml/15 fl oz double cream, lightly whipped
3 tbsp Irish cream liqueur

1. Line the base of a 20-cm/8-inch round springform cake tin with baking paper and brush the sides with oil. Place the cookies in a polythene bag and crush with a rolling pin. Put the butter in a saucepan and gently heat until melted. Stir in the crushed cookies. Press into the base of the prepared tin and chill in the refrigerator for 1 hour.

2. Put the plain chocolate and milk chocolate into a heatproof bowl set over a saucepan of gently simmering water and heat until melted. Leave to cool. Put the sugar and cream cheese in a bowl and beat together until smooth, then fold in the cream. Fold the melted chocolate into the cream cheese mixture, then stir in the liqueur.

3. Spoon the mixture into the tin and smooth the surface. Chill in the refrigerator for 2 hours, or until quite firm. Transfer to a serving plate and cut into slices. Serve with crème fraîche and strawberries.

#473 Chocolate & stout cupcakes

Makes 12

Ingredients

125 g/4½ oz plain flour
60 g/2¼ oz cocoa powder
1½ tsp baking powder
¼ tsp salt
275 g/9¾ oz butter, softened
200 g/7 oz caster sugar
2½ tsp vanilla extract
2 large eggs
125 ml/4 fl oz stout
3 large egg whites
160 g/5¾ oz soft light brown sugar

Decoration

55 g/2 oz green ready-to-roll fondant icing
icing sugar, for dusting
yellow sugar crystals

1. Preheat the oven to 180°C/350°F/Gas Mark 4 and line a 12-hole muffin tin with paper cases. Sift together the flour, cocoa powder, baking powder and salt in a bowl. Put 115 g/4 oz of the butter and the caster sugar into a separate bowl and beat until pale and fluffy. Add 1 teaspoon of the vanilla extract, then beat in the eggs, one at a time. Add half the flour mixture and the stout, and beat until incorporated. Add the remaining flour mixture and mix. Spoon the mixture into the paper cases and bake in the preheated oven for 20 minutes, until risen and a cocktail stick inserted in the centre of a cupcake comes out clean. Leave to cool in the tin for 1–2 minutes, then transfer to a wire rack to cool completely.

2. Put the egg whites and brown sugar in a heatproof bowl set over a saucepan of gently simmering water and whisk until the sugar has completely dissolved. Remove from the heat and whisk for 4–5 minutes. Add the remaining butter, 2 tablespoons at a time, and continue to whisk until it holds stiff peaks. Add the remaining vanilla extract and beat until just combined. Spoon the frosting into a piping bag fitted with a star-shaped nozzle and pipe it onto the cupcakes. To make the clover decorations, roll out the green fondant icing on a surface lightly dusted with icing sugar to a thickness of 5 mm/¼ inch. Cut out 12 clover shapes and set aside to dry. Place a clover leaf on top of each cupcake and sprinkle with yellow sugar crystals.

#474 Traditional Easter biscuits

Makes
30

Ingredients

225 g/8 oz butter, softened

140 g/5 oz caster sugar, plus extra
for sprinkling

1 egg yolk, lightly beaten

280 g/10 oz plain flour

1 tsp mixed spice

pinch of salt

1 tbsp chopped mixed peel

55 g/2 oz currants

1 egg white, lightly beaten

1. Place the butter and sugar in a large bowl and beat until light and fluffy, then beat in the egg yolk. Sift the flour, mixed spice and salt into the mixture, add the mixed peel and currants and stir until thoroughly combined. Halve the dough, shape into balls, wrap in clingfilm and chill in the refrigerator for 30–60 minutes.

2. Preheat the oven to 190°C/375°F/Gas Mark 5. Line three large baking sheets with baking paper.

3. Unwrap the dough and roll out between two sheets of baking paper. Cut out rounds with a 6-cm/2½-inch fluted cutter and place them on the baking sheets, spaced well apart. Bake in the preheated oven for 7 minutes, then brush with the egg white and sprinkle with the sugar. Bake for a further 5–8 minutes, or until light golden brown. Leave to cool on the baking sheets for 5–10 minutes, then transfer to wire racks to cool completely.

#475 Easter marzipan fruit cake

Serves
16

Ingredients

oil, for greasing

175 g/6 oz butter, softened

175 g/6 oz light muscovado sugar

3 eggs, beaten

225 g/8 oz plain flour

½ tsp baking powder

2 tsp ground mixed spice

finely grated rind of 1 small lemon

100 g/3½ oz currants

100 g/3½ oz sultanas

55 g/2 oz chopped mixed peel

700 g/1 lb 9 oz marzipan

3 tbsp apricot jam

1. Preheat the oven to 150°C/300°F/Gas Mark 2. Grease and line a 20-cm/8-inch deep round cake tin with baking paper.

2. Place the butter and sugar in a bowl and cream together until pale, light and fluffy. Gradually beat in the eggs, beating well after each addition. Sift together the flour, baking powder and mixed spice. Use a large metal spoon to fold into the creamed mixture. Stir in the lemon rind, currants, sultanas and mixed peel, mixing evenly. Spoon half the mixture into the prepared tin and smooth level.

3. Roll out 250 g/9 oz of the marzipan to a 20-cm/8-inch round and place over the mixture in the tin. Add the remaining cake mixture and smooth level. Bake the cake in the preheated oven for 2¼–2¾ hours, or until firm and golden, and the sides are beginning to shrink away from the tin. Leave to cool in the tin for 30 minutes, then turn out onto a wire rack to cool completely.

4. Brush the top of the cake with jam. Roll out two thirds of the remaining marzipan to a round to cover the top of the cake. Use a knife to mark a lattice design in the surface and pinch the edges to decorate.

5. Roll the remaining marzipan into 11 small balls and arrange around the edge of the cake. Place under a hot grill for 30–40 seconds to brown slightly. Leave to cool completely before storing.

#476 Easter egg cupcakes

Makes
12

Ingredients

115 g/4 oz butter, softened
115 g/4 oz caster sugar
2 eggs, lightly beaten
85 g/3 oz self-raising flour
25 g/1 oz cocoa powder
260 g/9½ oz mini sugar-coated
chocolate eggs

Frosting

85 g/3 oz butter, softened
175 g/6 oz icing sugar
1 tbsp milk
2–3 drops of vanilla extract

1. Preheat the oven to 180°C/350°F/Gas Mark 4. Line a
12-hole muffin tin with paper cases.

2. Put the butter and sugar in a bowl and beat until light and
fluffy. Gradually add the eggs, beating well after each addition. Sift in the flour and cocoa powder
and, using a large metal spoon, fold into the mixture. Spoon the mixture into the paper cases.

3. Bake the cupcakes in the preheated oven for 15–20 minutes, or until well risen and firm to the
touch. Transfer to a wire rack and leave to cool.

4. To make the frosting, put the butter in a bowl and beat until fluffy. Sift in the icing sugar and
beat until well mixed, adding the milk and vanilla extract. Put the frosting in a piping bag fitted
with a large star-shaped nozzle. When the cupcakes are cold, pipe circles of frosting on top of the
cupcakes to form nests. Decorate with chocolate eggs.

#477 Chocolate orange ring cake

Serves
8–10

Ingredients

2 small oranges
85 g/3 oz plain chocolate
250 g/9 oz self-raising flour
1½ tsp baking powder
175 g/6 oz butter, softened, plus extra
for greasing
200 g/7 oz caster sugar
3 eggs, beaten

Topping

175 g/6 oz icing sugar
2 tbsp orange juice
55 g/2 oz plain chocolate, broken
into pieces

1. Preheat the oven to 160°C/325°F/Gas Mark 3. Grease an
900-ml/1½-pint ring tin. Grate the rind from one of the oranges.
Pare the rind from the other orange. Cut the oranges into
segments by cutting down between the membranes with a sharp
knife. Chop into small pieces, reserving as much juice as possible. Coarsely grate the chocolate.

2. Sift the flour and baking powder into a bowl. Add the butter, caster sugar, eggs, grated orange rind
and any reserved juice and beat until smooth. Fold in the chopped oranges and grated chocolate.
Spoon into the prepared tin and bake in the preheated oven for 40 minutes, or until well risen and
golden brown. Leave to cool in the tin for 5 minutes, then turn out onto a wire rack to cool completely.

3. Sift the icing sugar into a bowl and stir in enough orange juice to make a coating consistency.
Drizzle it over the cake. Put the chocolate in a heatproof bowl set over a saucepan of gently
simmering water and heat until melted. Drizzle the melted chocolate over the cake. Cut the
reserved pared orange rind into thin strips and scatter over the cake.

#478 Meringue party nests

Ingredients

4 egg whites
250 g/9 oz caster sugar
2 tsp pink food colouring
300 ml/10 fl oz double cream
1 vanilla pod
1 tbsp icing sugar, sifted
assorted mini sweets, to decorate

1. Preheat the oven to 150°C/300°F/Gas Mark 2. Line two baking trays with baking paper.

2. Place the egg whites in a clean, grease-free bowl and whisk until they hold stiff peaks. Gradually add the caster sugar, a spoonful at a time, whisking well between each addition, until all the sugar has been incorporated and the mixture is thick and glossy. Whisk in the pink food colouring.

3. Place the meringue mixture in a piping bag fitted with a plain nozzle and pipe 15 x 8-cm/3-inch nests, starting in the centre of the base and working in a spiral to form the base, then upwards to create the sides.

4. Bake in the preheated oven for 1½ hours, or until completely dried out. Remove from the oven and leave to cool.

5. Whip the cream until just thick. Cut the vanilla pod in half lengthways and remove the seeds with a teaspoon. Fold into the cream with the icing sugar. To serve, spoon a little cream into each nest and top with sweets.

#479 Toffee bananas

Serves 4

Ingredients

70 g/2½ oz self-raising flour

1 egg, beaten

9 tbsp iced water, plus extra for setting

4 large, ripe bananas

3 tbsp lemon juice

2 tbsp rice flour

oil, for deep-frying

115 g/4 oz caster sugar

2 tbsp sesame seeds

1. Sift the flour into a bowl. Make a well in the centre, add the egg and 4 tablespoons of the water. Beat until smooth. Peel the bananas and cut into 5-cm/2-inch pieces. Gently shape into balls with your hands. Brush with lemon juice, then roll them in rice flour until coated.

2. Pour the oil into a saucepan to a depth of 6 cm/2½ inches and heat to 180–190°C/350–375°F, or until a cube of bread browns in 30 seconds. Coat the balls in the batter and cook in batches in the hot oil for about 2 minutes each, until golden. Lift them out and drain on kitchen paper.

3. Put the sugar into a small saucepan over a low heat. Add the remaining water and heat, stirring, until the sugar dissolves. Simmer for 5 minutes, then remove from the heat and stir in the sesame seeds. Toss the banana balls in the toffee, scoop them out and drop into the bowl of iced water to set. Divide between individual serving bowls to serve.

#480 Mango & ginger roulade

Serves 6

Ingredients

oil, for greasing

150 g/5½ oz plain white flour

1½ tsp baking powder

175 g/6 oz butter, softened

175 g/6 oz golden caster sugar, plus extra for sprinkling

3 eggs, beaten

1 tsp vanilla extract

2 tbsp orange juice

1 large ripe mango

3 tbsp chopped glacé ginger

5 tbsp crème fraîche

1. Preheat the oven to 180°C/350°F/Gas Mark 4. Grease and line a 23 x 33-cm/9 x 13-inch Swiss roll tin with baking paper 1 cm/½ inch above the rim. Lay a sheet of baking paper on the work surface and sprinkle with caster sugar.

2. Sift the flour and baking powder into a large bowl and add the butter, sugar, eggs and vanilla extract. Beat well until smooth, then beat in the orange juice. Spoon the mixture into the prepared tin and smooth into the corners with a palette knife. Bake in the preheated oven for 15–20 minutes, or until risen, firm and golden brown.

3. Meanwhile, peel and stone the mango. Reserve a few pieces for decoration and finely chop the remainder. Transfer to a small bowl and stir in 2 tablespoons of the glacé ginger.

4. Turn out the sponge onto the prepared paper and spread with the mango mixture. Firmly roll up the sponge from one short side to enclose the filling, keeping the paper around the outside to hold it in place. Lift onto a wire rack to cool, removing the paper when firm.

5. When cold, top with spoonfuls of crème fraîche and decorate with the reserved mango and the remaining glacé ginger.

#481 Chocolate liqueurs

Makes 40

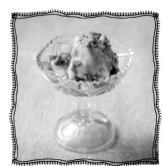

Ingredients

100 g/3½ oz plain chocolate, broken into pieces

20 glacé cherries

20 hazelnuts or macadamia nuts

150 ml/5 fl oz double cream

2 tbsp icing sugar

4 tbsp liqueur

Decoration

50 g/1¾ oz plain chocolate, melted

marbled chocolate caraque

1. Line a baking tray with a sheet of baking paper. Put the chocolate in a heatproof bowl set over a saucepan of gently simmering water and heat until melted. Spoon the chocolate into 40 paper sweet cases, spreading up the sides with a spoon or brush. Place upside down on the prepared tray and leave to set.

2. Carefully peel away the paper cases. Place a cherry or nut in each cup.

3. To make the filling, place the cream in a mixing bowl and sift the icing sugar on top. Whisk the cream until it just holds its shape, then whisk in the liqueur.

4. Place the cream in a piping bag fitted with a 1-cm/½-inch plain nozzle and pipe a little into each chocolate case. Leave to chill for 20 minutes.

5. To decorate, spoon the plain chocolate over the cream to cover it. Add the caraque and leave it to harden.

#482 Butterscotch sundae

Serves 4

Ingredients

100 g/3½ oz light muscovado sugar

100 g/3½ oz golden syrup

55 g/2 oz butter

100 ml/3½ fl oz double cream

½ tsp vanilla extract

1 large, ripe mango

115 g/4 oz ginger biscuits

1 litre/1¾ pints vanilla ice cream

2 tbsp roughly chopped almonds, toasted

1. Melt the sugar, golden syrup and butter in a small saucepan, then simmer for 3 minutes, stirring, until smooth.

2. Stir in the cream and vanilla extract, then remove from the heat. Peel and stone the mango and cut into 1-cm/½-inch cubes. Place the ginger biscuits in a polythene bag and lightly crush with a rolling pin.

3. Place half the mango in four sundae glasses and top each with a scoop of the ice cream. Spoon over a little sauce and sprinkle with crushed biscuits. Repeat with the remaining mango, ice cream, sauce and biscuits.

4. Sprinkle the almonds over the top of each sundae and serve immediately.

#483 Chikki brittle pops

Makes 12

Ingredients

250 g/9 oz caster sugar

¼ tsp cream of tartar

150 ml/5 fl oz water

2 tbsp pistachio nuts, finely chopped

1 tbsp ready-to-eat dried apricots, finely chopped

1 tbsp dried rose petals (optional)

large pinch of ground cardamom seeds

12 lollipop sticks

1. Line a large baking tray with baking paper. Put 12 lollipop sticks on the prepared tray, spaced well apart.

2. Put the sugar, cream of tartar and water into a heavy-based saucepan. Bring to a gentle boil over a medium heat, stirring all the time. Reduce the heat to low and simmer for 20–25 minutes without stirring, until the mixture reaches 143°C/290°F on a sugar thermometer.

3. Remove the pan from the heat and stir in the pistachios, apricots, rose petals (if using) and ground cardamom. Working quickly, spoon a large teaspoonful of the syrup onto one end of each lollipop stick. Leave to set for 5 minutes, until hard.

#484 Raspberry almond ring

Serves 8–10

Ingredients

oil, for greasing

175 g/6 oz plain white flour

1 tbsp baking powder

175 g/6 oz butter, softened

175 g/6 oz caster sugar

3 eggs, beaten

1 tsp almond extract

70 g/2½ oz ground almonds

225 g/8 oz fresh raspberries

1 large egg white

140 g/5 oz icing sugar

1 tbsp golden syrup

¼ tsp cream of tartar

toasted flaked almonds, to decorate

1. Preheat the oven to 160°C/325°F/Gas Mark 3. Grease a 1.5-litre/2¾-pint ring cake tin, preferably non-stick.

2. Sift the flour and baking powder into a large bowl and add the butter, caster sugar, eggs and almond extract. Beat well until the mixture is smooth, then stir in the ground almonds. Mash half the raspberries with a fork and stir into the mixture.

3. Spoon the mixture into the prepared tin and smooth the surface with a palette knife. Bake in the preheated oven for 40–45 minutes, or until risen, firm and golden brown. Leave to cool in the tin for 10 minutes, then carefully turn out onto a wire rack to cool completely.

4. Place the egg white, icing sugar, golden syrup and cream of tartar in a heatproof bowl over a saucepan of hot water and whisk vigorously with an electric hand-held mixer until thick enough to hold its shape. Swirl the frosting over the top of the cake. Decorate with the remaining raspberries and the flaked almonds.

485 Steamed syrup puddings

Serves
10

Ingredients

2 tbsp golden syrup, plus extra to serve

115 g/4 oz butter, plus extra for greasing

115 g/4 oz caster sugar

2 eggs, lightly beaten

175 g/6 oz self-raising flour

2 tbsp milk

grated rind of 1 lemon

1. Grease two 600-ml/1-pint pudding basins and divide the syrup evenly between the bases of each.

2. Beat the butter and sugar until soft and creamy, then beat in the eggs, a little at a time.

3. Fold in the flour and stir in the milk to make a soft dropping consistency. Add the lemon rind. Divide the mixture evenly between the pudding basins.

4. Cover the surfaces with rounds of baking paper and top with a pleated sheet of foil. Secure with some string or crimp the edges of the foil to ensure a tight fit around the basins.

5. Place the puddings in large saucepans filled with enough simmering water to reach halfway up the sides of the basins. Steam for 1½ hours, or until risen and firm. Keep checking the water level and top up with boiling water as necessary.

6. Remove the pans from the heat and lift out the basins. Remove the covers and loosen the puddings from the sides of the basins using a knife. Turn out into a warmed dish and heat a little more syrup to serve with the puddings.

486 Crème brûlée

Serves
6

Ingredients

225–300 g/8–10½ oz mixed soft fruits, such as blueberries and stoned fresh cherries

1½–2 tbsp orange liqueur or orange flower water

250 g/9 oz mascarpone cheese

200 ml/7 fl oz crème fraîche

2–3 tbsp dark muscovado sugar

1. Place the fruit in the bases of 6 x 150-ml/5 fl oz ramekins. Sprinkle with the liqueur.

2. Cream the mascarpone cheese in a bowl until soft, then gradually beat in the crème fraîche.

3. Spoon the cheese mixture over the fruit, smoothing the surface and ensuring that the tops are level. Chill in the refrigerator for at least 2 hours.

4. Sprinkle the tops with the sugar. Using a cook's blowtorch, grill the tops for 2–3 minutes until caramelized. Alternatively, cook under a preheated grill, turning the dishes, for 3–4 minutes, or until the tops are lightly caramelized all over.

5. Serve immediately or chill in the refrigerator for 15–20 minutes before serving.

#487 Peach melba meringue

Serves 8

Ingredients

sunflower oil, for brushing
600 g/1 lb 5 oz fresh raspberries
115 g/4 oz icing sugar
2 tsp cornflour
300 g/10½ oz caster sugar
5 large egg whites
1 tsp cider vinegar

Filling

3 peaches, peeled, stoned and chopped
200 ml/7 fl oz crème fraîche
150 ml/5 fl oz double cream

1. Preheat the oven to 150 °C/300 °F/Gas Mark 2. Grease a 35 x 25-cm/14 x 10-inch Swiss roll tin and line with greaseproof paper.

2. To make the raspberry coulis, process 350 g/12 oz raspberries and the icing sugar to a purée. Press through a sieve into a bowl and reserve.

3. To make the meringue, sift the cornflour into a bowl and stir in the caster sugar. In a separate, grease-free bowl, whisk the egg whites until they hold stiff peaks, then whisk in the vinegar. Gradually whisk in the cornflour and sugar mixture until stiff and glossy. Spread the mixture evenly in the prepared tin, leaving a 1-cm/½-inch border. Bake in the centre of the preheated oven for 20 minutes, then reduce the heat to 110 °C/225 °F/Gas Mark ¼ and cook for a further 25–30 minutes, or until puffed up. Remove from the oven. Leave to cool for 15 minutes. Turn out onto a sheet of baking paper and carefully remove the baking paper from the meringue.

4. To make the filling, place the peaches in a bowl with the remaining raspberries. Add 2 tablespoons of the coulis and mix. In a separate bowl, whisk together the crème fraîche and cream until thick. Spread over the meringue. Scatter the fruit over the cream, leaving a small border at one short edge. Using the baking paper, roll the meringue, starting at the short edge without the border and finishing with the join underneath. Transfer to a plate and serve with the coulis.

#488 Fresh black cherry pies

Makes
8

Ingredients

225 g/8 oz plain flour,
plus extra for dusting

115 g/4 oz butter, diced

2 tbsp icing sugar

1 tsp vanilla extract

1 egg yolk

2–3 tbsp cold water

250 g/9 oz mascarpone cheese

55 g/2 oz icing sugar

2 eggs

150 ml/5 fl oz double cream

250 g/9 oz black cherries, stoned
and halved

3 tbsp black cherry or
blackcurrant jam

1 tbsp water

1. Place the flour in a large bowl. Add the butter to the flour and rub it in with your fingertips until the mixture resembles fine breadcrumbs. Add the icing sugar, vanilla extract, egg yolk and enough water to form a soft dough. Cover with clingfilm and chill in the refrigerator for 15 minutes. Roll out the pastry on a floured surface and use to line eight tartlet tins. Chill for 30 minutes.

2. Preheat the oven to 200°C/400°F/Gas Mark 6. Prick the bases of the cases, then line with baking paper and fill with baking beans. Bake in the preheated oven for 10 minutes, then remove the paper and beans and bake for a further 5–10 minutes, or until crisp and golden. Transfer the tins to a wire rack. Reduce the oven temperature to 180°C/350°F/Gas Mark 4.

3. Whisk together the mascarpone cheese, icing sugar and eggs, then stir in the cream. Remove the cases from the tins and place on a baking sheet. Fill each case with the mascarpone mixture and bake for 10 minutes, or until starting to set. Leave to cool, then chill for 2 hours. Arrange the cherries on the tarts. Melt the jam with the water in a saucepan, then drizzle over.

#489 Orange cheesecake gateau

Serves
10

Ingredients

oil, for greasing

175 g/6 oz plain flour

1 tbsp baking powder

175 g/6 oz butter, softened

175 g/6 oz golden caster sugar

3 eggs, beaten

2 tsp orange flower water

6 tbsp orange juice

600 g/1 lb 5 oz mascarpone cheese

finely grated rind of 1 orange

55 g/2 oz icing sugar

1 orange, peeled and sliced

maple syrup, for brushing

1. Preheat the oven to 180°C/350°F/Gas Mark 4. Grease and line two 23-cm/9-inch sandwich cake tins.

2. Sift the flour and baking powder into a large bowl and add the butter, caster sugar, eggs and 1 teaspoon of the orange flower water. Beat well until smooth, then stir in 2 tablespoons of the orange juice. Spoon the mixture into the prepared tins and smooth the surfaces with a palette knife. Bake in the preheated oven for 25–30 minutes, or until risen and golden brown. Leave to cool in the tins for 5 minutes, then turn out onto a wire rack to cool completely.

3. Beat together the mascarpone cheese, orange rind, icing sugar and the remaining orange juice and orange flower water until smooth, then spread about a third over one cake. Spoon the remainder into a piping bag fitted with a large, star-shaped nozzle and pipe swirls around the edge of the cake.

4. Place the second cake on top. Pipe the remaining frosting around the top edge. Fill the centre with the orange slices and brush with maple syrup.

#490 Apricot & almond clusters

Makes
24–28

Ingredients

115 g/4 oz plain chocolate, broken into pieces

2 tbsp clear honey

115 g/4 oz ready-to-eat dried apricots, chopped

55 g/2 oz blanched almonds, chopped

1. Put the chocolate and honey in a heatproof bowl set over a saucepan of gently simmering water and heat until melted and smooth.

2. Stir in the apricots and almonds.

3. Drop teaspoonfuls of the mixture into paper sweet cases. Leave to set.

#491 Gold star cupcakes

Makes
12

Ingredients

85 g/3 oz butter, softened

85 g/3 oz soft light brown sugar

1 large egg, beaten

85 g/3 oz self-raising flour

½ tsp ground cinnamon

1 tbsp milk

85 g/3 oz yellow ready-to-roll fondant icing

icing sugar, for dusting

edible gold dusting powder (optional)

Icing

85 g/3 oz icing sugar

2–3 tsp lemon juice

1. Preheat the oven to 180°C/350°F/Gas Mark 4. Line a 12-hole muffin tin with paper cases.

2. Beat together the butter and sugar until light and fluffy. Gradually beat in the egg. Sift in the flour and cinnamon and, using a metal spoon, fold them into the mixture with the milk. Spoon the mixture into the paper cases.

3. Bake the cupcakes in the preheated oven for 20 minutes, or until golden brown and firm to the touch. Transfer to a wire rack and leave to cool completely.

4. Roll out the yellow fondant icing on a surface lightly dusted with icing sugar and, using a small star cutter, stamp out 12 stars. Brush each star with a little gold dusting powder, if using. Set aside on a sheet of baking paper.

5. To make the icing, sift the icing sugar into a bowl and stir in enough lemon juice to make a smooth and thick icing.

6. Spoon the icing on top of the cupcakes and top each with a gold star. Leave to set.

#492 Banana & coconut ice cream balls

Serves 6

Ingredients

3 ripe bananas

4 tbsp evaporated milk

75 g/2¾ oz plain chocolate, cut into small pieces

1 tbsp rapeseed oil

3 tbsp desiccated coconut

1. Peel the bananas and cut into small pieces. Put into a freezerproof container and freeze for at least 2 hours. Transfer to a food processor or blender and add the evaporated milk. Process until smooth and creamy. Scrape the mixture into a freezerproof container, cover and freeze for about 1 hour, until firm.

2. Put the chocolate and oil in a heatproof bowl set over a saucepan of gently simmering water and heat, stirring frequently, until melted. Place the coconut in a bowl.

3. Line a baking tray with baking paper. Use a small scoop to make 5-cm/2-inch balls of the banana mixture and set them on the prepared tray. If the balls begin to soften, place them in the freezer for 15 minutes, or until firm. Working quickly, spear an ice cream ball with a cocktail stick and dunk it into the melted chocolate, twirling to coat completely. Allow the excess chocolate to drip off, then transfer the ball to the bowl of desiccated coconut and turn to coat lightly.

4. Place the balls on the tray and continue until all of the balls are coated in chocolate and coconut. Place the tray in the freezer for a few minutes, chill until firm and serve immediately.

#493 Fruit jelly squares

Makes 30

Ingredients

450 ml/16 fl oz clear apple juice

3 tbsp powdered gelatine

400 g/14 oz caster sugar

500 g/1 lb 2 oz apricot jam

1. Put half the apple juice into a mixing bowl, then sprinkle the gelatine over the surface, making sure the powder is absorbed. Set aside for 10 minutes.

2. Meanwhile, put the remaining apple juice and half the sugar into a heavy-based saucepan. Boil, stirring, for 5–6 minutes, or until the sugar has dissolved. Whisk in the jam, then return to the boil and cook for 3–4 minutes, until the mixture is thick and syrupy. Whisk the gelatine into the syrup until it dissolves. Pour the mixture through a fine-mesh sieve into a bowl. Transfer it to a 25 x 18-cm/10 x 7-inch non-stick rectangular cake tin. Chill in the refrigerator for 3–4 hours, or until set.

3. Spread the remaining sugar over a large baking tray. Cut the fruit jelly into 30 squares and remove from the tin with a palette knife. Toss in the sugar to coat just before serving.

Chilli & cardamom chocolate thins

Makes
40

Ingredients

Plain chocolate thins

200 g/7 oz plain chocolate,
roughly chopped

large pinch of hot chilli powder

edible glitter, to decorate

White chocolate thins

200 g/7 oz white chocolate,
roughly chopped

½ tsp cardamom seeds, crushed

25 g/1 oz pistachio nuts, finely chopped,
plus extra to decorate

edible glitter, to decorate

1. Line four baking trays with baking paper.

2. For the chilli plain chocolate thins, put the plain chocolate in a heatproof bowl set over a saucepan of gently simmering water and heat until melted. Remove from the heat and stir in the chilli powder.

3. Drop teaspoonfuls of the chocolate mixture onto two of the prepared trays. Scatter over a little glitter before the chocolate sets. Leave to set in a cool place, but not in the refrigerator, for 1-2 hours.

4. For the cardamom white chocolate thins, put the white chocolate in a heatproof bowl set over a saucepan of gently simmering water and heat until melted. Remove from the heat and stir in the cardamom and pistachio nuts.

5. Drop teaspoonfuls of the white chocolate mixture onto the remaining two prepared trays. Scatter over the remaining chopped pistachio nuts and a little glitter before the chocolate sets. Leave to set in a cool place, but not in the refrigerator, for 1-2 hours.

#495 Dark choc & nut cookies

Ingredients

200 g/7 oz plain flour, plus extra for dusting

½ tsp bicarbonate of soda

115 g/4 oz butter, chilled and diced, plus extra for greasing

85 g/3 oz soft light brown sugar

2 tbsp golden syrup

1 egg, beaten

55 g/2 oz blanched hazelnuts, chopped

55 g/2 oz pecan nuts, chopped

140 g/5 oz plain chocolate, broken into pieces

1. Preheat the oven to 190°C/375°F/Gas Mark 5. Lightly grease two large baking sheets. Sift the flour and bicarbonate of soda into a large bowl. Add the butter and rub it in with your fingertips until the mixture resembles fine breadcrumbs. Stir in the sugar, golden syrup, egg and two thirds of the hazelnuts and pecan nuts, and mix thoroughly.

2. Drop dessertspoons of the mixture onto the prepared baking sheets, spaced well apart. Flatten slightly with the back of the spoon and top with the remaining nuts. Bake in the preheated oven for 7–9 minutes, or until golden brown. Leave to cool on the baking sheets for 5 minutes, then transfer to a wire rack to cool completely.

3. Put the chocolate in a heatproof bowl set over a saucepan of gently simmering water and heat until melted. Dip the top of each cooled cookie in the chocolate, then leave on a wire rack in a cool place until the chocolate has set.

#496 Crème caramel

Ingredients

butter, for greasing

200 g/7 oz caster sugar

4 tbsp water

½ lemon

500 ml/17 fl oz milk

1 vanilla pod

2 large eggs

2 large egg yolks

fresh mint leaves, to decorate

1. Preheat the oven to 160°C/325°F/Gas Mark 3. Lightly grease 2 x 600-ml/1-pint soufflé dishes. Place 75 g/2¾ oz of the sugar in a saucepan with the water and cook over a medium–high heat, stirring, until the sugar dissolves. Boil until deep golden brown. Remove from the heat and squeeze in a few drops of lemon juice. Divide evenly between the soufflé dishes and swirl around. Set aside.

2. Pour the milk into a saucepan. Slit the vanilla pod lengthways and add it to the milk. Bring to the boil, remove from the heat and stir in the remaining sugar, stirring until it dissolves. Set aside.

3. Beat the eggs and egg yolks together. Pour in the milk mixture, whisking. Remove the vanilla pod. Strain the egg mixture into a bowl, then divide evenly between the soufflé dishes. Place the dishes in a roasting tin with enough boiling water to come two thirds of the way up the sides. Bake in the preheated oven for 1–1¼ hours, or until a knife inserted in the centre comes out clean. Leave to cool completely. Cover with clingfilm and chill for at least 24 hours, then run a round-bladed knife around the edges of each dish. Place an upturned serving plate with a rim on top of each dish, then invert the plate and dish, giving a sharp shake when halfway over. Lift off the soufflé dishes and serve, decorated with fresh mint leaves.

313

#497 Peach popovers

Makes
12

Ingredients

1 tsp sunflower oil, plus extra
for greasing

100 g/3½ oz plain flour

1 large egg white

275 ml/9 fl oz semi-skimmed milk

1 tsp vanilla extract

3 peaches, sliced

maple syrup, to serve

1. Preheat the oven to 200°C/400°F/Gas Mark 6. Grease a 12-hole muffin tin. Put the oil, flour, egg white, milk and vanilla extract in a large bowl. Beat until smooth and bubbly.

2. Put the prepared tin in the preheated oven for 5 minutes. Remove from the oven and quickly divide the peach slices between the holes, then pour the mixture evenly into each hole. Bake for 15–20 minutes, or until well risen, crisp and a golden colour.

3. Carefully remove the popovers from the tin with a small palette knife. Serve immediately with maple syrup.

#498 Strawberry mousse cake

Serves
10

Ingredients

oil, for greasing

175 g/6 oz plain flour

1 tbsp baking powder

175 g/6 oz butter, softened

175 g/6 oz golden caster sugar

3 eggs, beaten

1 tsp vanilla extract

2 tbsp milk

Filling

4 tsp powdered gelatine

3 tbsp orange juice

550 g/1 lb 4 oz fresh strawberries

3 tbsp golden caster sugar

400 ml/14 fl oz double cream

100 g/3½ oz redcurrant jelly, warmed

1. Preheat the oven to 160°C/325°F/Gas Mark 3. Grease a 23 cm/9-inch round springform cake tin and line with baking paper.

2. Sift the flour and baking powder into a large bowl and add the butter, sugar, eggs and vanilla extract. Beat well until the mixture is smooth, then stir in the milk. Spoon the mixture into the prepared tin and smooth the surface with a palette knife. Bake in the preheated oven for 45–55 minutes, or until risen, firm and golden brown.

3. Leave to cool in the tin for 5 minutes, then turn out onto a wire rack and leave to cool completely. Cut the sponge in half horizontally and place one half back in the tin.

4. To make the filling, dissolve the gelatine in the orange juice in a small bowl placed in a saucepan of hot water. Put 400 g/14 oz of the strawberries and the sugar into a food processor and process to a purée. Whip the cream until it holds its shape. Quickly stir the gelatine mixture into the strawberry mixture, then fold in the cream.

5. Pour the mixture into the tin and place the second half of the cake on top. Chill in the refrigerator until set. Turn out the cake and spread the top with the warmed redcurrant jelly. Decorate with the remaining strawberries.

Rum & chocolate cups

Ingredients

55 g/2 oz plain chocolate, broken into pieces

12 toasted hazelnuts

Filling

115 g/4 oz plain chocolate, broken into pieces

1 tbsp dark rum

4 tbsp mascarpone cheese

1. Place the chocolate in a heatproof bowl set over a saucepan of gently simmering water and heat until melted but not too runny, then remove from the heat. Spoon about ½ teaspoon of melted chocolate into a foil sweet case, brushing it over the base and up the sides. Coat 11 more foil cases in the same way and leave to set for 30 minutes. Chill in the refrigerator for 15 minutes. If necessary, reheat the chocolate to melt it again, then coat the foil cases with a second, thinner layer. Chill in the refrigerator for an additional 30 minutes.

2. Meanwhile, make the filling. Place the chocolate in a heatproof bowl set over a saucepan of gently simmering water and heat until melted. Leave to cool slightly, then stir in the rum and beat in the mascarpone cheese until smooth. Leave to cool completely, stirring occasionally.

3. Spoon the filling into a piping bag fitted with a 1-cm/½-inch star-shaped nozzle. If preferred, carefully peel away the foil cases from the chocolate cups. Pipe the filling into the cups and top each one with a toasted hazelnut.

500 Baked pears with honey, cinnamon & saffron

Ingredients

3 tbsp clear honey

100 ml/3½ fl oz dessert wine, such as vin santo or muscat

4 tbsp water

2 cinnamon sticks

3 cloves

2 cracked allspice berries

1 tsp saffron threads

4 ripe pears

1. Preheat the oven to 200°C/400°F/Gas Mark 6. To make the syrup, combine the honey and wine with the water in a saucepan. Add the spices, simmer for 4 minutes until slightly reduced, then leave to cool.

2. Peel, halve and core the pears. Lay them out in a roasting tin and pour over the syrup. Bake in the preheated oven for 8–10 minutes.

3. To serve, arrange the pears on plates and pour over the syrup.

Index